Red on Silver

Naxalites in Cinema

Red on Silver

Naxalites in Cinema

Edited by
Pradip Basu

Setu Prakashani

Red on Silver

Naxalites in Cinema

First Edition
March 2012

Cover Designed by
Dilip Ghosh

ISBN No. 978-93-80677-22-4(Pb)
978-93-80677-23-1(Hb)

Published by
Archana Das and Subrata Das
on behalf of Setu Prakashani
12A, Shankar Ghosh Lane, Kolkata-700 006 (India)
Phone : +91 33 2219 0704, +91 94330 74548
Delhi Branch Office :
A-43, Mahendru Enclave, Galli No. 3,
G. T. Karnal Road, Post Office : Azadpur, Delhi-110 033

Price
Rupees Four hundred eighty (Pb)
Rupees Six hundred fifty (Hb)

Printed by
Imprinta
243/2B, A. P. C. Roy Road, Kolkata - 700 006

Typesetting and make-up by
Unique Phototype
49, Guru Prosad Chowdhury Lane, Kolkata - 700 006

To

Sri Dulal Chandra Saha

Smt. Shila Saha

Smt. Dola Saha

Acknowledgements

Mrinal Sen, Sandip Ray and Gautam Ghosh (filmmakers); Darshana Sreedhar. M, JNU; Binayak Bhattacharya and Dibyakusum Ray, EFLU; Samrat Sengupta, Kharagpur College & CSSSC; Shoma A. Chatterji, ICSSR; Partha Chatterjee, Columbia University & CSSSC; Werner Menski, SOAS; Joanna Goldsworthy, writer & editor; Ben Baer, Princeton University; Sjahari Pullam, University of California; Manasi Guha, Scottish Church College Library; Subrata Das & Archana Das & Srijani Banerjee, Setu Prakashani; my brother Partha Basu; wife Mala Saha Basu, Naba Ballygunge College, son Samyo, daughter Ritama.

Pradip Basu

Scottish Church College
(University of Calcutta), Kolkata
Email : pradipbasu1@gmail.com
20 February 2012

Contents

Prologue 1

Overview

Naxalite Movement and Indian Cinema :
A Political Analysis
Kanchan Sarkar 23

Thematic

The Rebellious Politics and Film Spectatorship :
A Note on Bengali Popular Films Now
Binayak Bhattacharya 45

The Ideological and the Existential :
Naxalite Ideology in 'Hazaaron Khwaishein Aisi' and 'Herbert'
Dibyakusum Ray 61

The Subject-in-Process :
Female Characters in Transition in
'Hazaar Chaurasi ki Ma' and 'Kaalbela'
Indranil Mitra and Sananda Sen 76

The Other Side of Spectacle in 'Herbert' :
Return of Naxalbari or the Haunting of an Inescapable Past?
Saikat Maitra & Samrat Sengupta 91

Naxalism in Cinema :
The Absent Community
M. K. Raghavendra 106

Reading 'Red Alert - The War Within' :
A Convenient Reality
Amitava Nag 120

Narrative Coping with Naxal Violence :
'Red Alert - The War Within' and Mainstream Hindi
Cinema's Story Strategies
Bernd Zywietz 134

Running Away… The Buddhadeb Dasgupta Trilogy
Shoma A. Chatterji 151

Representing a Fragmented Society :
'Hazaar Chaurasi ki Maa'
Sukanta Acharya 166

Intersection of 'Middle Class Bhadralok'
and Naxalite Movement : A Montage of Selected Movies
Monalisa Basu 182

Historical

Reappearance of the 'Uncanny' :
Naxalite Memory in Malayalam Cinema
Darshana Sreedhar. M 199

'Thalappavu' :
When the Ghost Haunts the Conscience
Arya Aiyappan 217

Naxalite Movement :
As Captured by Films
Indrani Bhattacharya 233

The Naxalite Movement :
In Reality, Reel and People's Perception
Manoj Kumar 251

Filming the Young Brigade
Praskanva Sinharay 266

Particularistic

Rehashing Narrative Archetypes in Retrospect :
In Khwaja Ahmad Abbas' 'The Naxalites' (1980)
Torsa Ghosal 283

'Red Alert':
Dialectics of Engagement and Ambivalence
Ketaki Dwivedi 299

Film and Naxalism :
A Case Study of 'Hazaaron Khwaishein Aisi'
Radhakanta Barik 314

The End is not Really the End : 'Sesh Sanghat' and the Media Obsession with Armed Resistance
Samata Biswas 328

'Hazaar Chaurasi ki Maa'
Shatarupa Sengupta 342

Celluloid Narrative of Power-Plunder-Protest Syndrome :
An Avant-garde Study of Ray's 'Hirak Rajar Deshe'
Debasis Poddar 356

Comparative

'Hazaar Chaurasi ki Maa' :
A Faithful Document of the Turbulent Times on the Silver Screen
Ketaki Datta 375

Films and Naxalism : The in-between
Sumana Sanyal 389

On Cinematic Reconstruction of Blazing and Bleeding Hearts :
A Naxalbari Follower's Appreciation of Two Bengali Films - 'Path' and 'Atmaja'
Saumen Guha 407

From 'Hazaar Chaurasi ki Maa' to 'Hazaaron Khwaishen Aisi'-- A Million Dreams :
A Study of Naxalism in Hindi Cinema
Devapriya Sanyal 423

The Naxalite Movement, the Trilogy of Satyajit Ray and Beyond
Ananda Das Gupta 437

Editor and Contributors 452

A Still from 'Kalbela'

Courtesy - Gautam Ghose

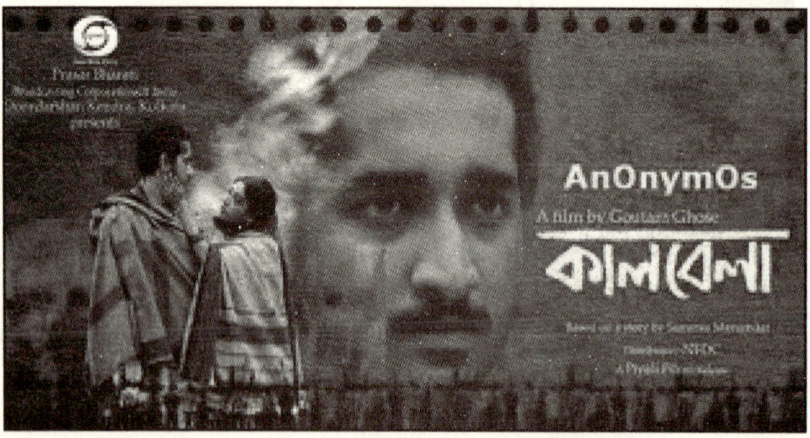

A Poster of 'Kalbela'

Courtesy - Gautam Ghosh

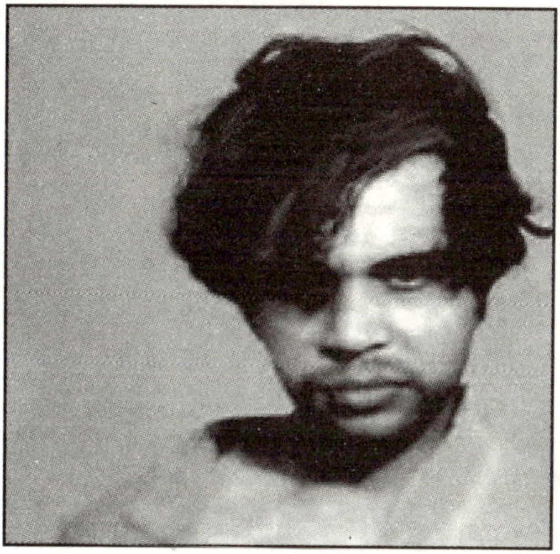

A Still from 'Pratidwandwi'

Courtesy - Ray Family

A Still from 'Chorus'

Courtesy - Mrinal Sen

Prologue :

What is a film? According to Jean-Louis Comolli and Jean Narboni, a film is, on the one hand, a particular product, manufactured within given economic relations, and involving labour to produce. This is a condition to which even 'independent' filmmakers and the 'new cinema' are subject, assembling a number of workers. On the other hand, as a material product of the system, it is also an ideological product of the system. No filmmaker can, by individual efforts, change the economic relations governing the manufacture and distribution of her/his films. "Because every film is part of economic system it is also a part of the ideological system, for 'cinema' and 'art' are branches of ideology. None can escape : somewhere, like pieces in the jigsaw, all have their own allotted place. The system is blind to its own nature, but in spite of that, indeed because of that, when all the pieces are fitted together they give a very clear picture. But this does not mean that every film-maker plays a similar role. Reactions differ. It is the job of criticism to see where they differ, and slowly, patiently, not expecting any magical transformations to take place at the wave of a slogan, to help change the ideology which conditions them"[1]. No doubt that this rather highly ideological evaluation is equally true in case of the films which depict the Naxalites directly or indirectly, the films which feature in this book.

But what was the Naxalite movement? In this context, it would be pertinent to look at the perceptions of Mrinal Sen, the eminent art/political film director of India, about the Naxalite movement : "The struggle! On the political front, the struggle of the extremist faction had already assumed immense proportions. Starting with a peasant uprising in 1967, at Naxalbari, an area in North Bengal, it soon spread like a firestorm in several pockets of the country, all restricted to peasant-belts. A quote from Mao Tse-tung, 'a single spark can start a prairie fire' (1930), became popular among the extremists, known all over as *Naxalites*. Strangely, the quote invaded the city walls and the suburbs in no time. Rightly or wrongly, the movement eventually turned out to be an urban phenomenon. The students erupted not totally in my city (Kolkata) but also, to an extent, elsewhere too - in Andhra Pradesh, in Kerala, in Punjab, in Orissa and Bihar. Simultaneously, or, before or after, the movement surfaced in various parts of the world. The most telling was the Latin American scene, where, to combat the so-called *peace* of the neo-colonial system, the people learned to *hate*. In his feature-length explosive documentary, 'The Hour of the Furnaces', Fernando Solanas of Argentina said it unabashedly, "We fear peace more than war".

"That was a decade of violent protest. As a contrast, the European scene was short-lived and largely romantic. One that got wide publicity was at Frankfurt and then, on a comparatively bigger scale, at Sorbonne. But, one that immediately got worldwide attention was the scene in West Bengal. Protests and violence went on. Police atrocities went unabated in mad fury. The big city (Kolkata), and most particularly, a large section of the Bengali youth, were caught in the maelstrom. The most advanced and, naturally, the most dedicated among them were the university and college students. Kunal (Mrinal Sen's son), still in school, brought a secret pamphlet one day and kept it in hiding. In his absence, I pulled it out, read it and gently put it where it was. I felt a little disturbed. Being more practical, Gita (Sen's wife) asked me not to create a scene. Amidst the *Naxalite* maelstrom, yet another spark, another slogan rent the air. New posters flooding the city. Outside the border, suburbs, and further interior, the countryside. The new slogan - *sattor'r dashak mukti'r dashak!* "(the decade of the '70s is the decade of liberation!)"[2].

To this, I would like to add : the Naxalite Movement registered a revolutionary critique against the election-centric Parliamentary Left of India whose sole aim had been to capture the governmental power within the existing reactionary framework. It exposed the naked opportunism of the social elite and statesmen, their sheer lack of moral values, all-pervading corruption and degeneration. In contrast, it created exemplary self-sacrifice and idealism. It further drew our attention to the peasants' revolutionary struggle, respectfully projected the peasant viewpoint, and underscored the need to judge history, especially the so-called Indian Renaissance, on the basis of the peasant standard, which later academically inspired the Subaltern Studies etc. But, at the same time, it made major mistakes on the questions of tactical line : such as–left adventurism, stunt actions such as beheading of statues of established national leaders, rash attacks on educational institutions; oversimplification of the sense of history; '*khatam*' (killing) of individuals such as other party cadres, police constables, *jotedars*; pointless valorization of violence, inter-party killings; uncritical repudiation of distinguished personalities; hasty actions for short-cut to revolution, boycott of all kinds of mass movements, mass organizations, elections etc[3].

This is a well-known fact that India is the largest film producing country in the world and a huge number of Indians regularly frequent to the cinema halls. Curiously enough, there is a perceptible trend among the Indian viewers that they are inclined to resist the influence of the Hollywood films. As Ashish Rajadhyakshya, a noted film expert, pointed out, "Pick up any amount of the Indian cinema and you usually face a phrase about it being the 'world's largest filmmaking nation', usually presented as a self-explanatory matter of national pride ...it is of course true that the terrain that cinema spans in India can be of astonishing dimensions : an approximate 23 million people, over 2% of our total national population (and possibly half the population of many established film making nations), go to the cinema every day. It is also the case that this audience has been, over the broad part of this century, remarkably resistant to the cultural invasion of Hollywood"[4]. Elsewhere, Hollywood established its hegemony not only economically but transformed cinema into a means to disseminate American values. In my consideration, therefore, in the context of the recent postcolonial awareness, this, is a positive trend almost unique to India, but unfortunately enough, the mainstream Indian cinema and its countless spectators have not demonstrated any significant amount of interest in the screening of social movements, people's revolts, peasant uprisings, etc. such as the Naxalite movement, even though these have had visible impact on Indian society and culture. The reasons might be a deserving field of inquiry for competent researchers.

Ideological currents have, however, always been discernible in Indian cinema and after the explorations by the French structuralist Marxist philosopher Althusser and the Italian Marxist thinker Gramsci, we have reasons to believe that the depiction of reality in Indian films has been intervened, enabled and mediated by ideological hegemony, even if often imperceptibly. "Many oppressed groups have used 'progressive realism' to unmask and combat hegemonic images. Women and third world filmmakers have attempted to counterpose the objectifying discourse of patriarchy and colonialism with a vision of themselves and their reality as seen 'from within'. But this laudable intention is not always unproblematic. 'Reality' is not self-evidently given and 'truth' cannot be immediately captured by the camera"[5]. Prominent filmmakers post Independence were ideationally connected with Nehruvian nationalism. In the late 1950s, the 'good' Indian film, or the 'art' film began to appear, funded by the state-owned Film Finance Corporation. By the 1970s, the realist film was modulated into what Madhava Prasad described as the 'developmentalist aesthetic' of the films by Shyam Benegal and others. These served the crucial function of distancing for their urban audience the feudal set up which is now realistically 'othered' as the rural, the folk, etc. "While on the one hand, the 1970s are marked by the rise of the new realist Indian cinema, the period also sees, on the other hand, the emergence of the avant-garde filmmakers like Kumar Shahani or Mani Kaul who innovate in terms of film-form. The two currents appear to converge in a director like Mani Ratnam in the 1990s, who combines them with the idiom of commercial cinema"[6]. But at the same time it must be noted that Indian commercial mainstream cinema has never represented any left revolutionary movements such as the Tebhaga, the Telangana or the Naxalite movement which were able to register only a remarkably small influence on the parallel stream of art film. But then, could these movements leave any lasting impact on film theory and film studies?

Film theory is a recently developed academic discipline, that aims to examine and explore the essence of the cinema and provide adequate conceptual frameworks for understanding film's relationship to reality, particularly social reality, the other arts, individual viewers, and larger community or society. Film theory, however, is not to be confused with general film criticism. At the end of the 19th century the French idealist philosopher Bergson in his book, *Matter and Memory* (1896), anticipated the development of film theory during the birth of cinema. Bergson underscored the need for new ways of thinking about movement, and coined the terms 'the movement-image' and 'the time-image'. However, ten years later, in 1906, he discarded film as an exemplification of his ideas. Notwithstanding that, decades later, the French post-structuralist thinker Gilles Deleuze in *Cinema I and Cinema II* (1983-1985), considered *Matter and Memory* as the basis of his own philosophy of cinema and conducted a re-examination of Bergson's notion, combining them with the semiotics of Peirce. In the 1960s and 1970s, film theory imported concepts from social sciences and humanities especially from anthropology, literary theory, semiotics, psychoanalysis, gender studies, and linguistics. Humanistic, auteur theory predominated which concentrated on the practical elements of film writing, production, editing and criticism. Film theory gradually witnessed an enhanced importance. Since the 1970s, film studies were largely based on the ideas of structuralist linguist Ferdinand Saussure, post-structuralist psychoanalyst thinker Lacan, structuralist Marxist Louis Althusser, and structuralist and later post-structuralist Rolland Barthes. According to Chidananda Das Gupta,the veteran film specialist, "If there is a case for freeing art from the grip of social and ethical theory in order to establish its autonomy and subjectivity, there is a doubly valid one for freeing film criticism from the same constraints. Recognition of the subjectivity of Art also opens the door for subjectivity in criticism. Invalidation of the cry for 'scientific criticism' becomes inevitable. Not that this would make the discussion of social issues in criticism unacceptable. Only it would admit subjectivities of many kinds and propensities, freely using different methods. For decades critics have connected films to events and trends in society using Marxist methods, deconstructed their elements, analyzed their structures, gone into psychoanalytic explanations, sometimes all within the same article, without ballyhoo, without signing structuralist, post-structuralist or deconstructionist manifestoes and getting straitjacketed into a theory bearing a label. Indeed, free criticism represents a revolt against the tyranny of the academic labelling industry which has of late been working overtime. Very often the grand announcement of a new label means no more than old wine in new bottles"[7]. In late 1980s or early 1990s, the established mode of emphasis began to get shifted. During the 1990s, the digital revolution in image technologies left an indelible imprint on film theory. There occurred a refocus onto celluloid film's capacity to capture an 'indexical' image of a moment in time by theorists conversant with psychoanalysis. From a psychoanalytical perspective, after the post-structuralist Lacanian notion of 'the Real', the Slovenian philosopher Slavoj Zizek projected new aspects of 'the gaze' widely employed in current film study. At the same time academic film theorists have often been criticized as insistently Marxist. Film studies gradually look into the broader issues of social and political ideology which are refracted through the characteristic concerns with genre and stylistic analysis, in the wider perspective on the place of film within changing cultural and political arrangements. The cultural and gender studies workshops were organized by the Center for Studies in Social Sciences, Calcutta; the Madras Institute of Development Studies, Chennai, and the Central Institute for English and Foreign Languages, Hyderabad, between 1995 and 1998. "Here the theoretical objects were re-framed through the cultural categories of self, subjectivity, and the imaginary. Literary material was inducted to understand the formation of ideas about public life, community, nationhood, and citizenship"[8]. This emerged as an influential framework toward the study of films as well. It has become necessary to understand the various meetings of the different disciplines and research agenda. In this book, different researchers have tried to understand the representation of the Naxalites in the films, the depiction of the diverse aspects of the Naxalite movement, using different theoretical tools. Keeping the contemporary perspectives in mind, this book undertakes an academic probe into the varied responses of political cinema to social phenomena such as the Naxalite movement.

Political cinema depicts the current or historical social conditions in a partisan way with a deliberate motive to inform the spectator/audience and may exist in different forms such as documentaries, feature films, TV movies, short films etc. Movies which penetrate the complex issues of the Naxalites obviously belong to the category of 'political cinema'. The concept of 'the political' in films and film analysis has, however, been a subject of controversy for many film critics as well as film theoreticians. Political cinema refers to political films which do not conceal their political stance. Nevertheless, they are not necessarily pure propaganda. The political film is alternatively called 'confrontation cinema', 'social problem film' and 'ideological film'. Jean-Louis Comolli and Jean Narboni correctly observed, "...*every film is political,* inasmuch as it is determined by the ideology which produces it (or within which it is produced, which stems from the same thing). The cinema is all the more thoroughly and completely determined because unlike other arts or ideological systems its very manufacture mobilizes powerful economic forces in a way that the production of literature (which becomes the commodity 'books') does not - though once we reach the level of the distribution, publicity and sale, the two are in rather the same position"[9]. Some theorists pay attention to the audience-dependent, communicative aspect of the political. In the recent period, many of them obtain the required theoretical support for their academic sustenance from the poststructuralist conception of comparing cinematic structure with a linguistic system. Some, however, derive their theoretical legitimacy still from the Marxist view of language as a social phenomenon. But if we are now aware of the French post-structuralist philosopher Jacques Derrida's *deconstruction,* we may meaningfully look beyond the binarypolitical and non-political films as well as the binary of the Marxist and non-Marxist film studies. Obviously, the hierarchy around the meaning of the political film gets dismantled. One would also notice that what was political seventy years back is no longer adjudicated political today even though the concerns remain contending as well. Such a film invokes current evaluations founded upon new criteria, which may shift the designation towards a historical cinema which is marked by the representation of power structures, authoritative institutions, engaging contestations and ideological apparatuses frozen in a specific time and space. So the film's interpretation concerns the process of re-interpreting or finding inferences and possible explications of the discourse from the past. The interpretational method for politicized silver screen contemplates and deliberates on the function of the pictures in a particular period as an agent of transmission of political memorandum, as an ideologised and discursive vehicle of a political message. In case of most pictures related to the Naxalites this is true.

Other films are not, however, different, as they are non-political. After the French post-structuralist philosopher Michel Foucault's brilliant and devastating exposition on power, knowledge and discourse, it is widely accepted that 'non-political' itself indicates a hidden politics. No film can remain above discourse, power, politics, institutions of society, language. Political films are generally designated so because of their overt political positions, not necessarily any party-political one. Even apparently apolitical escapist films with a distinct overtone of withdrawal or resignation from politics, which pledge to provide 'mere entertainment' as a flight from the conflicts of everyday's lived experience, however, fulfill a political function. The authorities in Nazi Germany organized a large production of deliberately escapist movies while Nazi propagandist films were anti-Semite. In other entertainment movies, for example 'westerns', the ideological bias is evident in the distortion of historical reality. A 'classical' western would rarely portray black cowboys, although there were many. Hollywood Cinema, or Dominant Cinema, was often accused of misrepresenting black, women, gays and working class people. A film's aesthetic impact may, however, obscure the ideological effects. Not only is the content of individual films political but also the institution of cinema. People congregate not to act together or to talk to each other but, to sit silently, to be spectators separated from each other. Guy Debord, a critic of the society of the spectacle, for whom separation is the marker of the spectacle, was opposed to Cinema, though he made movies portraying his ideas. During the Weimar Republic, many films about Frederick II of Prussia had a conservative nationalistic agenda and the Communists like Willi Münzenberg saw the Russian cinema as a model of political cinema. Soviet films by Sergei Eisenstein, Dziga Vertov and others combined a partisan view of the Bolshevist regime with artistic innovation which appealed to western audiences. Forty years ago, Fernando Solanas and Octavio Getino remarked, "Filmmaking is increasingly within the reach of larger social layers ... this has opened up unheard- of- prospects for the cinema; above all, a new conception of filmmaking and the significance of art in our times. Imperialism and capitalism, whether in the consumer society or in the neo-colonialized country, veil everything behind a screen of images and appearances. *The image of reality* is more important than reality itself. It is a world peopled with fantasies and phantoms in which what is hideous is clothed in beauty, while beauty is disguised as the hideous"[10]. Cinematic Form has always been a concern for political filmmakers. Some argued that radical films, in order to liberate the imagination of the spectator, have to break not only with the content but also with the form of Dominant cinema. The falsely reassuring clichés and stereotypes of conventional narrative filmmaking should go. Other directors preferred to work within mainstream cinema to reach a wider audience. The subversive tradition dates back to the French avant-garde of the 1920s. Even in his more conventional films Luis Buñuel stuck to the spirit of outright revolt. The bourgeoisie had to be expropriated and its values destroyed, the surrealists believed. Especially in the last decades of the twentieth century, many filmmakers considered focusing on remembrance of and reflection upon collective crimes such as The

Holocaust, slavery and disasters such as the Chernobyl disaster to be their political and moral duty. One must note that the political cinema of the twenty-first century seems to focus on globalization, AIDS, environment, world energy resources, consumption and climate change, terrorism, war, peace, religious and related forms of intolerance, and civil and political rights and other human rights.

Beside the predominant mainstream commercial cinema, India has an important parallel stream of serious/ realist/ art films also. The Indian People's Theatre Association (IPTA), an art movement with a communist inclination, began to take shape through the 1940s and the 1950s. A number of realistic IPTA plays prepared the ground for the solidification of realism in Indian cinema. But one has to ponder over the apparently unproblematic notion of realism in cinema. The cinema reproduces reality. This is what a camera and film stock are for - so says the ideology. But the tools and techniques of filmmaking themselves are a part of reality. Moreover, reality is an expression of the prevailing ideology. Thus, the classical theory of cinema that the camera is an unprejudiced instrument which grasps the world in its concrete reality is reactionary. "What the camera in fact registers is the vague, unformulated; untheorised, unthought-out world of the dominant ideology. Cinema is one of the languages through which the world communicates itself to itself. They constitute its ideology for they reproduce the world as it is experienced when filtered through the ideology"[11]. Naxalite movement refers to a social reality but when we watch the different movies related to this movement, we perceive how diversely this reality has been experienced as mediated through a variety of ideologies. Indeed, while Indian mainstream commercial cinema was thriving, the same age saw the emergence of a new Parallel Cinema movement. Early examples of films in this movement which were laying the foundations for Indian neorealism and New Wave, include Chetan Anand's social realist film 'Neecha Nagar' (1946), Ritwik Ghatak's 'Nagarik' (1952), and Bimal Roy's 'Do Bigha Jamin' (1953). The last one was both a commercial and a critical success. It may be noted that the Parallel Cinema movement began in the Bengali film industry in the

1950s. According to a veteran scholar, for more than fifty years, Marxism has been the overriding ideology in Bengal. It has, however, been so tinted by the humanism of Tagore as to acquire a local form suggestive of what was previously christened as Eurocommunism in Parisian leftist circles. "The Bengali's innate love of literature and his preoccupation with culture in general provided the soil on which the seeds of Marxism were sown, giving a very middle-class orientation to the mix of the two. Both strands promoted, among other things, an internationality of outlook to which the cinema, a West-born medium, eminently lent itself"[12]. Parallel Cinema, Art Cinema or New Wave, is a specific movement in Indian cinema, marked by realism and naturalism, concerned with the social-political climate. This movement is distinct from mainstream Bollywood[13] cinema and began around the same time as the French New Wave and Japanese New Wave. The neo-realist filmmakers were Satyajit Ray, Ritwik Ghatak, Mrinal Sen, Shyam Benegal, Adoor Gopalakrishnan, K. Viswanath and Girish Kasaravalli. Ray's films include The Apu Trilogy, consisting of 'Pather Panchali' (1955), 'Aparajito' (1956) and 'Apur Sansar' (1959). Parallel Cinema was influenced by a combination of theatre (e.g. Sanskrit drama) and literature (e.g. Bengali literature), and by European cinema (e.g. Italian neorealism, French poetic realism) rather than Hollywood. The Apu Trilogy led to the Parallel Cinema movement being established in India.

Chidananda Das Gupta further opined that moreover, the film society movement, mostly induced by the British instance, grasped the European creative innovations and South American revolutionary zeal. Ray's leadership of the film society movement helped to accommodate a variety of tendencies. Hollywood narrative techniques, Italian Neorealism, German expressionism, and a Sovietique glorification of The People in the abstract, became grounded in Tagore's world view. "This mix has its ambiguities and caused subterranean conflicts between individual creativity in cinema with an agit-prop restatement of the Marxist class struggle formula. This continued till the early 1980s which saw the beginning of a reassertion of the worth of the individual who, until now, had been regarded by the dominant ideologues as a cog in the wheels of social engineering"[14]. In a number of movies somehow or other connected with the Naxalite politics these 'subterranean conflicts between individual creativity with an agit-prop restatement of the Marxist class struggle' can be detected. Today we can see that many films on the Naxalites, while refuting all inroads against the notion of class struggle invoked and endorsed by American liberalism, sought to evaluate the Naxalite movement in the 1960s in the perspectives of struggle against all kinds of war especially the Vietnam War, imperialism, feudalism, authoritarianism, racism, sexism and the like launched by students, blacks, browns and women. It reminds us what Frederic Jameson once remarked, "One of the most persistent leitmotivs in American liberalism's ideological arsenal, one of the most effective anti-Marxist arguments developed by the rhetoric of liberalism and anti-Communism, is the notion of the disappearance of class...On the left, meanwhile, the failure of a theory of class seemed less important practically and politically during the antiwar situation of the 1960s, in which attacks on authoritarianism, racism, and sexism had their own internal justification and logic, and were lent urgency by the existence of the Vietnam War, and content by the collective practice of social groups, in particular students, blacks, browns and women"[15].

Indeed, Realistic Parallel Cinema continued throughout the 1970s to be made by Adoor Gopalakrishnan, Shaji N. Karun, John Abraham and G. Aravindan in Malayalam cinema; Nirad Mohapatra in Oriya cinema; Mani Kaul, Kumar Shahani, Ketan Mehta, Govind Nihalani and Vijaya Mehta in Hindi cinema; and Satyajit Ray, Ritwik Ghatak, Mrinal Sen, Shyam Benegal, Buddhadeb Dasgupta and Gautam Ghose in Bengali cinema. There has been a radical political Bengali cinema tradition of the 1970s and 1980s. In the 1980s and 1990s Ray's neglected contemporaries, Ritwik Ghatak and Guru Dutt, received recognition and some other filmmakers joined the veterans such as, T. V. Chandran from the Malayalam industry. In the late 1990s, Parallel Cinema resurgence in Hindi cinema, largely due to the success of 'Satya' (1998), directed by Ram Gopal Varma, led to the emergence of a distinct genre known as Mumbai noir, which includes Madhur

Bhandarkar's 'Chandni Bar' (2001) and 'Traffic Signal' (2007), Ram Gopal Varma's 'Company' (2002) and its prequel 'D' (2005), Anurag Kashyap's 'Black Friday' (2004), Irfan Kamal's 'Thanks Maa' (2009), and Deva Katta's 'Prasthanam' (2010). Other art film directors active today include Santosh Sivan in Malayalam cinema; Mira Nair, Nagesh Kukunoor, Sudhir Mishra, Shekhar Kapur, and Nandita Das in Hindi cinema; Mani Ratnam in Tamil cinema; Deepa Mehta, Anant Balani, Homi Adajania, Vijay Singh and Sooni Taraporevala in Indian English cinema; and Sandip Ray, Aparna Sen and Rituparno Ghosh in Bengali cinema. Realistic cinema which dissects the ideological anatomy of the Naxalites, however, must not overindulge into 'objective scientism', 'technocentrism' and 'hyper-rationalism' of the European Enlightenment of eighteenth century which indicates the culmination of Western modernity which has been subjected to thorough critique by the postmodernists and post-structuralists, along with some streams of postcolonialism and feminism. A truly realist cinema that has undertaken a cerebral illumination of the Naxalite movement, in contrast to the beliefs of the Enlightenment, must take into account the instinct, creative urge, artistic drives, passions as well. "Outside the purely Marxist discourse in the West, the denial of the magic of creativity and of establishing 'political correctness' above all considerations of the autonomy of art may have its roots in consumerism. The call for 'scientific criticism' may have taken its birth in the very modernism the postmodernists so strenuously denigrate. Otherwise why should 'scientific criticism' be so unconcerned with emotional, visceral responses to art and so obsessed with the explicable as opposed to the ineffable?"[16].

Here we present a rather long excerpt from John W. Hood which provides a concise survey of a few significant films associated with Naxalism, "There have also been a number of films inspired to some extent by the Naxalite movement. Although the source and possibly the epicenter of Naxalism was in West Bengal, the movement was by no means confined to that state and, not long after of the initial uprising in Naxalbari, it spread in varying degrees throughout the country.

However, while there is some reference to its incidence in Kerala in Gopalakrishnan's 'Kathapurushan', it has been treated by the major filmmakers largely as a Bengali phenomenon. However, two non-Bengalis, Benegal and Nihalani, made films in a Naxalite context set in West Bengal. Benegal's 'Aarohan' is a rather didactic piece, concentrating on the issue of land reforms while trying to focus interest on the dramatic plight of an oppressed poor peasant. Nihalani's 'Hazar Chaurasi ki Maa' has an urban setting and is a more personal film; when it takes Naxalism as its essential basis it concentrates on the growth in self-awareness of its central character, the mother of a dead activist. Four Bengalis have also brought Naxalism into the cinema. Satyajit Ray has it unequivocally as background in 'Jana Aranya' and 'Pratidwandi', Ritwik Ghatak embraces it as part of a broader ideological notion in 'Jukti Takko ar Gappo', and Buddhadeb Dasgupta uses it as a vehicle to foreground the ethical implications on the notion of commitment in 'Duratwa', 'Grihayuddha' and 'Andhi Goli'. However, Naxalism is most substantially treated by Mrinal Sen. It appears briefly in the guise of social unrest in 'Calcutta 71', its political bases are subjected to some critical questioning in 'Padatik', while in 'Mahaprithibi' Sen tries to present a reassessment of the movement and its idealism in a broad historical perspective"[17].

The attitude of Ray towards his own filming of the Naxalites is explicit : "You can see my attitude in 'The Adversary' where you have two brothers. The younger brother is a Naxalite. There is no doubt that the elder brother admires the younger brother for his bravery and convictions, the film is not ambiguous about that. As a filmmaker, however, I was more interested in the elder brother because he is the vacillating character. As a psychological entity, as a human being with doubts, he is a more interesting character to me"[18]. John W. Hood is of the opinion that 'Pratidwandi' ('The Adversary', 1970), 'Seemabaddha' ('Company Limited'), 1971) and 'Jana Aranya' ('The Middle Man ', 1975), are of greater significance. In them, Calcutta is more than an incidental setting. The definition and resolution of the conflicts portrayed is largely determined by the city itself. "The three films, often loosely referred to as the Calcutta trilogy, could well have been sent in any big city where anonymity, alienation, impersonality, cynicism and callousness are intrinsic, except that Calcutta in the 70s was also characterized by the Naxalite agitation, a movement that was relevant to Ray's films of the time in that it represented the anger, mistrust and confusion held out by the younger generation, so many of whom were educated yet frustrated by unemployment. The social unrest brought about by the Naxalite movement was exacerbated by the Bangladesh War and its huge influx of refugees..."[19].

Regarding Mrinal Sen's films on Naxalites, Chidananda Das Gupta's investigations have been conventional. The early 1970s in West Bengal witnessed a grim if fleeting challenge to what the Naxalites considered as the Communist Party's capitulation to the ruling bourgeois-democratic forces. While it lasted, it let loose a Pol Pot-like terror regime in West Bengal, most visibly in Calcutta. It became impossible for a receptive filmmaker to take no notice of the events overtaking his surroundings. "It is in this context that one needs to see Mrinal Sen's political trilogy. No wonder the films of this middle period show a broad inclination towards the socialist idea. But (they are) unlike the Sovietique agit-prop films of Russia that had once set the pattern for officially blessed political films..."[20]. Das Gupta, however, admitted that Sen's response to the circumstances was unusual even though profoundly felt. Even the direct address by the protagonist of 'Interview' did not rob the film of its multipolarity. His independent thought and interest in cinematic innovation were too strong to allow such a simplistic course. His style, even in his most directly political films—'Interview', 'Calcutta 71' and 'Padatik' - was never altogether free from "a playful buoyancy laced with a contradictory neo-realism". Sen was more concerned with the human condition than with the particular political impulses. "Sen's films of the period do not paint the horrors of the present in order to replace them with the promised land... and this at a time when murder and mayhem were raging in Calcutta with extremists trying to overpower the ruling order through maximal, brazen violence on both sides"[21]. Das Gupta further elaborated the reasons why Sen had selected the particular topics for his films during the Naxalite movement. In retrospect, he explicated, one can see that Sen chose this time to speak of poverty in general. No difference could be detected in the rhetoric of right and left on this question. Nor did he concern himself with the inter-party slaughters carried on to impose one version of Marxism on the others and the people. "This enabled him to express anger without attracting either governmental censorship or the deadly wrath of the extremists. None of the powers that be could either claim him as theirs or reject him. The only way to make a political film at that point of time was to make it apolitically, by choosing the commonalities and ignoring the differences"[22]. Das Gupta quoted Sen : "I made 'Calcutta 71'when Calcutta was passing through a terrible time. People were getting killed everyday. The most militant faction of the Communist Party - the Naxalites - had rejected all forms of party politics. At the same time, they had a host of differences with the other two Communist factions. These in turn led to inter-party clashes and invariably ignored the main issue of mobilizing forces against the vested interests, the establishment. This was the time I felt I should spell out the basic ills of the country, the fundamental ills we were suffering from and the humiliations we had been subjected to. This was the time to speak of poverty - the most vital reality. I wanted to interpret the restlessness, the turbulence of the period that was 1971 and what it was due to"[23]. While commenting on the making of 'Padatik', Sen acknowledged that when making 'Interview', he never knew it would have a follow-up. It just happened to be like that - titled, 'Calcutta 71', where the protagonist of 'Interview' was charged with a criminal offense for breaking the show-window of a Metropolitan departmental store and for stripping a suited mannequin. The film was a kind of collage of apparently unrelated objects. Again, fact, fiction, fantasy - all mixed up, but not in the same manner or in the same order. "Then, on completion of 'Calcutta 71', it occurred to me that I must make yet another. Eventually, the third one was made, 'Padatik' (Guerrilla Fighter). Structurally, unlike the first two films, non-linear, 'Padatik' had a linear framework, a complete narrative in a pattern that suited the film"[24].

According to a few noted scholars, the list of films associated with the Naxalites and other left extremists, includes not only Ray's trilogy situated in a turbulent Kolkata, Ghatak's polemical self-portrait ('Jukti, Takko ar Gappo') or Sen's Brechtian narration of the prerequisites of a revolution ('Calcutta 71'), but also Benegal's 'Nishant' (1975), Nihalani's 'Aakrosh' (1980), 'Hazar Chaurasi ki Maa', Kumar Sahani's 'Tarang' (1984), Tapan Sinha's 'Apanjan' (1986), and the early works by B. Narasing Rao and Utpalendu Chakrabarty. Buddhadev Dasgupta's trilogy ('Dooratwa', 'Grihayuddha' and 'Andhi Gali') depicts the repercussions of a failed revolution and the traumatized psyche of a failed revolutionary. But they hardly feature the various nuances of the ideological struggle[25]. There are a few other films which directly or indirectly relate to the Naxalites : 'Ankur'; 'Anu' (1998) and 'Appayan' by Shatarupa Sanyal; 'Atmaj'; 'Calcutta' by Louis Molle; 'Hazaaron Khwaishein Aisi' (2005) by Sudhir Mishra; 'Herbert' (2006) by Suman Mukherjee; 'Kalbela' by Gautam Ghosh; 'Lal Salaam : Revolution is Always Written in Blood' (2002) by Gaganvihari Borate; 'Path'; 'Red Alert : The War Within' (2010) by Ananth Narayan Mahadevan; 'Red Tidings'; 'Sesh Sanghat' (2009); 'Sopan' (1994) by Ajay Banerjee; 'Sunya Theke Suru' (1993) by Asok Biswanathan; 'Tara' (2010) by Bratya Basu; 'The Naxalites' (1980) by Khwaja Ahmad Abbas; 'Mukhamukham' (1981) and 'Kathapurushan' (1995) by Adoor Gopalakrishnan; 'Amma Ariyan'; etc.

As I perceive, arguably thongh, while in this book the contributors probe into the ways the Naxalites have been represented in movies, we all are inevitably guided by the contradictory reasons prevailing in the community we inhabit. We find that our reason is ultimately nothing but the logically structured and condensed individual passion working in a particular community at a particular time which has capability of communication on social level. Reason and passion both go together into any such filmmaking. Finally, rational intellect and creative passion generate these Naxal-related films as an intellectual-cum- artistic product. In this book we are concerned with the fact that cinema seeks to represent on the silver screen a red political movement and our academic articulations analyze those political cinemas. Three drives are discernible in these films : creative passion, intellectual response and social objectivity (i.e., a sense of objectivity which is valid in a given social context). In this book, we have contributors of three kinds of expertise : film theory expertise, knowledge in social sciences and understanding of the Naxalite Movement. Understandably, some degree of overlap has been unavoidable. The book consists of twenty-seven research papers which are original, unpublished and fully referenced. We have arranged the different articles in five consecutive sections depending on the nature of the particular articles. Of course, there are overlaps here too which are unavoidable. The sections are as follows :

1. **Overview** : we have only one article in this section which provides a general survey of a large number of films related to the Naxalite Movement.
2. **Thematic** : there are ten articles in this section which are more or less theme-based.
3. **Historical** : in this group five articles have been accommodated which have largely related historical reality and cinema.
4. **Particularistic** : these articles, total six in number, mainly deal with particular films.
5. **Comparative** : we have included here five articles which are mostly comparative in nature.

Notes :

1. Jean-Louis Comolli and Jean Narboni, 'Cinema/Ideology/Criticism' in Bill Nichols (ed.), *Movies and Methods,* Volume I, Calcutta : Seagull Books Private Ltd., 1993, p. 24.
2. Mrinal Sen, *Always Being Born : A Memoir,* New Delhi : Stellar Publishers, 2004, pp. 98 - 99.
3. For details on Naxalite Movement, see

   i. Sumanta Banerjee, *In the Wake of Naxalbari,* Kolkata : Sahitya Samsad,

2008.

ii. Pradip Basu (ed,) *Discourses on Naxalite Movement, 1967 - 2009,* Kolkata : Setu Prakashani, 2010.

iii. Tarun Banerjee, *The Naxalite Movement : Currents and Cross-Currents,* Kolkata : Progressive Publishers, 2010.

4. Ashish Rajadhyakshya, 'Viewership and Democracy in the Cinema' in Ravi S. Vasudevan (Ed.), *Making Meaning in Indian Cinema,* New Delhi : Oxford University Press, first published 2000, Oxford India Paperbacks 2002, second impression 2009, p. 267.
5. Robert Stam and Louise Spence, 'Colonialism, Racism, and Representation : An Introduction' in Bill Nichols (Ed.), *Movies and Methods,* Volume 2, Calcutta : Seagull Books Private Ltd., 1993, p.639.
6. Vivek Dhareshwar and Tejaswini Niranjana, 'Kaadalan and the Politics of Re Signification : Fashion, Violence and the Body' in Ravi S. Vasudevan (Ed.), op.cit., p. 204.
7. Chidananda Das Gupta, *Seeing is Believing : Selected Writings on Cinema,* New Delhi : Penguin/ Viking, 2008, pp. 122-3.
8. 'Introduction' in Ravi S. Vasudevan (ed.), op. cit., pp. 2-3.
9. Jean-Louis Comolli and Jean Narboni, op. cit., pp. 24-- 25.
10. Fernando Solanas and Octavio Getino, 'Towards a Third Cinema' in Bill Nichols (ed.), op. cit., Volume I, pp.54.
11. Jean-Louis Comolli and Jean Narboni, op. cit., pp.25.
12. Chidananda Das Gupta, op. cit., pp. 256-7.
13. This term has recently been coined. I would rather like to avoid this term since in my opinion it expresses a kind of colonised mentality.
14. Chidananda Das Gupta, op. cit., p. 250.
15. Fredric Jameson, 'Class and Allegory in Contemporary Mass Culture : Dog Day Afternoon as a Political Film' in Bill Nichols (ed.), op. cit., volume 2, pp.717-718.
16. Chidananda Das Gupta, op. cit., pp. 122-3.
17. John W. Hood, *The Essential Mystery : Major Filmmakers of Indian Art Cinema,* New Delhi : Orient Longman, 2000, pp. 413-414.
18. 'Art Politics Cinema', *The Cineaste Interviews,* edited by Dan Georgakas

and Lenny Rubenstein cited in Proloy Shur, 'Satyajit Ray-er Kolkata' [Kolkata of 'Satyajit Ray] in Subrata Rudra (Ed.), *Satyajit : Jiban ar Shilpa* (Satyajit : Life and Arts), Kolkata : Protibhas, 1996, p. 799.

19. John W. Hood, op. cit., pp. 80-81.
20. Chidananda Das Gupta, op. cit., pp. 254.
21. Ibid, pp. 256-7.
22. Ibid.
23. Ibid.
24. Mrinal Sen, op. cit., pp. 109-110.
25. Ashis Rajadhyaksha and Paul Willemen (ed.), *Encyclopedia of Indian Cinema*, London and New Delhi : BFI and Oxford University Press, 1995 cited in Parichay Patra, 'The Exterminating Angels and their Cinematic Representatives : A Study of Naxalism in Malayalam Cinema' in Pradip Basu (ed.), op. cit., pp. 64 - 65.

Overview

Naxalite Movement and Indian Cinema : A Political Analysis

Kanchan Sarkar

Movements and movies often interact and it is one important facet of the greater interaction between life and art. In Cuba, Chile, Mexico, Russia - everywhere movements influenced movies and we also hear echoes of the Naxalite movement in the films of India. The time between the late 1960s and early 1970s was marked by massive social unrest. The winds of change were blowing hard from everywhere. The slogans of protest rent the air which was so much charged with the spirit of revolution that the peasant uprising in 1967 at Naxalbari sparked off the 'prairie fire' of the Naxalite movement that set ablaze the administration's peace. Mrinal Sen writes in his memoir, *Always Being Born,*

> ...one that immediately got worldwide attention was the scene in West Bengal. Protests and violence went on. Police atrocities went unabated in mad fury. The big city and most particularly, a large section of the Bengali youth was caught in the maelstrom.

At the beginning, there were two streams in this movement : the urban youth movement and the peasant uprising. In the process, the two streams merged in the dream of an armed revolution when cities will be surrounded by villages to end the feudalism and capitalist imperialism.

This paper is an analysis of the movies related to this Movement. My selection includes the movies which directly talk about this movement as well as those that depict the socio-economic and political situation of that time. I should mention few things in this prelude : first, the name of this article is a misnomer; Indian cinema means cinemas in all Indian languages, but I do not have knowledge of any other Indian languages except Bengali and Hindi; second, not all movies are available now in any form as most of them were made 30-40 years ago. So, this is not a comprehensive article on this boasted title. Besides, as regards the methodology of analysis, I do not expect to find Marx, Ray, and Tagore in one individual. I believe that Marx, Tagore could not make movies like Ray, on the other hand, Ray could not write *Communist Manifesto* or *Gitanjali.* It is not the task of any single movie to present the movement in its entirety. Ray's perspective may not match with Buddhadeb Dasgupta's, and the plurality of perspectives will enrich the range of interpretations and enable the spectators to cultivate original thinking.

The Movies :

My first inclusion is Tapan Sinha's 'Apanjan' (1968), which most of us so far have failed to recognize in this category. But Sinha is the first who depicts the unemployment, the social unrests, the anomie among the youth, and the unkindness of the 1960s in this movie. Sinha is never as critical as his contemporaries like Satyajit Ray, Ritwik Ghatak, or Mrinal Sen. In 'Apanjan' he shows the unemployed aimless youths and their culpability to be the prey of the bourgeois politics. This movie does not have much indication of the revolutionary movement in the coming years, but it shows the cloud in the sky. Sinha also exposes the mockery of parliamentary democracy, which reminds us that participation in parliamentary democracy was an important issue when CPI (ML) was formed out of CPI (M).

The three movies by Satyajit Ray which capture the milieu of the 1960s and 1970s, but in different ways, are : 'Pratidwandi' (1970), 'Seemabaddha' (1971), and 'Jana Aranya' (1975). While 'Pratidwandi' and 'Jana Aranya' are based on the struggle of middle class families, 'Seemabaddha' is a story of corporate ambition and culture with an allusion to revolutionary politics. Ray points out that unemployment is the prime cause of social unrest and this diagnosis ultimately forms the basis of the similarity of these three movies.

In 'Pratidwandi', the central character is Siddhartha, a middle class youth and a medical drop-out, looking for a job after his father's death. He finds no job as he is 'politically incorrect' in answering a question on 'the most significant event of the preceding decade;' his answer is : Vietnam. To the employers, the right answer is : landing on the moon. This prompts one board member asking him if he is a communist. Ray rightly portrays the time when a political (presumably left) leader tells Siddhartha : 'In the end, you will come to believe that you have no worth of anything.'

Siddhartha has one sister and one brother. Siddhartha is a moralist, once an active member of student union; sold two medical books to buy a book by Che Guevara. His sister is a survivor; makes adjustments with the middle class morality. His brother is an activist of the revolutionary politics. Three siblings : one of the three adjusts, another protests, and the third, namely Siddhartha, gets confused. Ray shows how changes in economy change the social relationship : the adorable relationships among the siblings are changing; sister defies Siddhartha for his impracticality, brother ignores him for his political inactivity. Siddhartha's confusion is shown in various ways : he wants to kill the boss of his sister who allegedly exploits her, but he can't. The sudden change of his reaction to a car accident when he sees the make of the car (Mercedes Benz) indicates his class hatred as well as helplessness. He protests in an interview when a candidate faints because of inadequate seats for 75 candidates with only one fan, and when suddenly the interview is called off during the lunch break. His frustration is clear. Finally, Siddhartha accepts a medical salesman job in a distant suburban city, finds his refuge in the love of his girlfriend. Many may think that when Siddhartha is an escapist, why his revolutionary brother Tunu is not made the central character of this movie? But I think Ray, through Siddhartha, successfully shows the contradictions among the middle class.

'Seemabaddha' is a story of upper-class people, their culture, and greed, but here also Ray cannot ignore unemployment and social problems. The central character is Shyamalendu Chaterjee, an ambitious corporate manager, adopting odious ways to move upward. Ray shows the penetration of westernized corporate culture in their family life, where even parents are not welcomed for dinner if they show up without notice. However, among all these negativities, Ray defends one character in this film who is Tutul, the sister-in-law of Shyamalendu, an honest and sensitive woman, whose boyfriend is an unemployed youth and a revolutionary.

'Jana Aranya' comes when the state with its organized goons have crushed the Naxalite Movement. The hope of 'converting the decade of 70s into a decade of liberation' is shattered : state atrocities, killing of youths, unemployment, and an unreliable examination system with mass-plagiarism. A humble, middle class youth, Somnath looks for a job with a poor result in graduation. The employer is despotic. Somnath is asked in an interview - how much is the weight of the moon? Finding no job, Somnath starts a business of order supply (middle man) and finally, uses his friend's sister as a call girl to get a large order. Does middle class degrade itself so much? Probably, not. But this shows the cruelty of that time. There are random mentionings of killings of revolutionaries by the state. Ray questions through the father of Somnath what the boys can do, if they do not get a job? Either they will take on the wrong path or go for revolution. He says that the revolutionaries who sacrifice their lives must have a strong ideology and courage. That is his comment on Naxalites.

I have selected three films by Mrinal Sen : 'Interview' (1970), 'Calcutta 71' (1972), and 'Padatik' (1973). 'Interview' starts with some interview questions on the title scene, followed by the removal of colonial statues in the opening scene. We gradually get into the connection between these two. Ranjit is the central character. His father expires when he is the only earning member of a family of three : his mother and a separated elder sister. He works as a compositor for a printing press, a low paying uncertain job. He looks for a better job in a mercantile company. He needs to be dressed in 'appropriate attire', i.e. in a western suit for the interview. Despite all intentions to be appropriately dressed, he finally attends the interview in a national dress, and does not get the job. On this attire issue, Ranjit later defies his father's friend - an insider of the company helping him to get the job. More than two decades have passed since independence, but the legacy of colonialism still continues. There is no direct input from Naxalite movement though the division of communist movement is mentioned and a procession with a banner imprinted with 'the history will take its own course' is shown. As we know, Naxalite movement is not only a movement of political protest but also of cultural protest, where traditional values, norms, rituals are also questioned. Ranjit's unwillingness to wear a coronet during marriage is one such example. This is the generation that later participates in the Naxalite Movement.

'Calcutta 71' goes back to '33', '43', '53' to trace the historicity of the 1970s and goes beyond Calcutta. The movie starts with a news bulletin which says that an unidentified body is found at maidan with bullet injuries. This was not uncommon in the then Kolkata. Naxalite youths were killed either in the name of encounters or were falsely released from the jail at isolated places and shot. Tracing back to '1933', Sen shows poverty, inhumanity and helplessness of the poor that culminated in the man-made famine in Bengal of 1943, which took 50 lakh lives; when a mom is forced to send her daughter for prostitution, asks her son to steal. The situation has not changed in 1953; young boys are killed by the police while smuggling rice to support their families. The outburst of the 70s is the continuation of this deprivation of people. But, there is one class, which always remains well-to-do. He shows more about this privileged class in the '1971' part of this movie : the affluence, the hypocrisy, and their indifference. Sen gives two messages : exploitation does not change only with the change in government, and the movement of 70s is not just an emotional or instantaneous outburst, but the eventuality of the long-drawn exploitation.

While 'Interview' and 'Calcutta 71' depict the objective condition of the Movement, Padatik raises some very important questions on revolutionary politics. It is probably the best movie by Sen in this category. Sen traces the origin of the Naxalite Movement to the so-called 'terrorist' appendage of Freedom Movement. Sumit is an absconding revolutionary youth who takes shelter at an upper-middle class apartment, possessed by Shila, a very sensitive woman. As mentioned above Sen brings up some key issues of revolutionary politics such as, who is a foe and who is a friend? However, the most important question he brings up here is on the party bureaucracy, where you can not question; if you question, you will be labelled as a 'reactionary' or a 'revisionist,' or at least a 'deviator.'

This question is important in present day left politics also. In this connection we can mention the trade union bureaucracy in tea plantation as shown in another movie, 'Sagina Mahato' by Tapan Sinha. However, Naxalites are getting shelter at an upper-middle class apartment indicates that even people from upper middle class could be an ally in revolution. Naxalite Movement had a tendency to reject everything traditional. Sumit's father is a freedom fighter and he questions his son's Naxalite ideology and violence. This generation was more or less ignored in Naxalite Movement. Despite old age, his father's continuation in politics, joining a procession and his uncompromising ideology, not yielding to the pressure of the management to give a bond not to join strike, prove that it is important also to consider these people as an ally.

Ritwik Ghatak's 'Jukti Takko ar Gappo' (1974) is a collage of the fragmented events towards a journey in search of 'Bengaliness.' Ritwik never accepted 'Partition.' It is to some extent his autobiographical story. At the end, while discussing with some Naxalites, he admits that the Naxalite youth reminds him of the revolutionaries of *agniyug*. He praises their courage and sacrifice but doubts that they suffer from leftwing infantile disorder. There was, however, more expectation from an acclaimed director like Ghatak, rather than tuning in with the commoners' analysis of this movement.

After the great trio, I would like to move to the next generation of film makers, for instance, Buddhadeb Dasgupta's three movies : 'Duratwa' (1978), 'Grihayuddha' (1982), and 'Andhi Gali' (1984). Dasgupta believes in the inner self. 'Duratwa' starts with a narration of the time : 'the time is apparently peaceful now, organized goons have killed those people who were responsible for earlier chaos...' indicating the post-Naxalite period. Mandar, currently a professor of political science, once was associated with the Naxalites. He is no longer active, though has contacts with old comrades. He teaches Morgan's *Ancient Society as well as Engels' Origin of the Family, Private Property, and the State* and explains how women's status in society changed in relation to private property. Mandar has every opportunity to be a revolutionary considering his political background as well as his profession. But he is not. That is the *Duratwa* or distance. Anjali is introduced to him by a common friend Amit, who is also a friend of Anjali's deceased elder brother. Amit and Anjali have a relationship and Anjali becomes pregnant. Amit avoids responsibility and suggests an abortion. Anjali opposes. At this juncture, Mandar and Anjali fall in love and get married. However, when Anjali confesses her pregnancy to Mandar, they end up in a divorce. This is the archetypal contradiction between individual consciousness and political ideology. Dasgupta raises this question also through Mandar's younger brother, Shaibal, who is a Naxalite : 'if theory is correct, does it matter if a few people make mistakes' - he asks. Shaibal accuses his parents that they have done injustice to Anjali. He maintains a good relation with Anjali. This is what is expected from a Marxist. Anjali is shown as non-interested in politics, but when situation demands, she has the courage to overcome feudalistic social stigma and the challenge of being a 'Kunti.' She denies an abortion, gives birth to her child, completes her study, secures a teaching job and takes responsibility of the child as a single parent. She wants individual freedom where a child can survive without father's identity. This is one of the aims of Marxist revolution, but only political affiliation cannot take us there.

'Grihayuddha' is made when the initial tides of Naxalbari movement have waned and the right-wing political anarchy has filled up the vacuum. This is a story of the nexus among corporation, media, police, and politics. An honest labour welfare officer, Gupta, who knows some company secrets, is killed by the management followed by another killing of an uncompromising trade union leader, Prabir. The killers have even come up to Prabir's house in search of Bijan, a comrade as well as a friend of Prabir. Not finding Bijan there, they ransack the house, admonish Prabir's parents, and physically abuse Prabir's sister Nirupama. After Prabir's murder, his family lodges a complaint with the police. No action is taken, instead one day they come to Prabir's house to find Bijan's whereabouts. This reflects the true situation in post-Naxalite period. Bijan and Nirupama have been in love. After Prabir's murder Bijan escapes to Mumbai and settles with a sales job in Nasik. When things settle down, Bijan returns to Kolkata. This is a disillusioned Bijan; he wants to forget his 'erroneous' past including Prabir. But Nirupama wants to live with those memories when Prabir and Bijan used to discuss politics sitting on the balcony. A silent listener, Nirupama has enjoyed the discussions and her love for Bijan has grown in the course of these conversations. Nirupama notices the changes in Bijan. Her love for Bijan is not without his ideology though she is never active in politics. Bijan is in a hurry to marry Nirupama. Nirupama is in a dilemma : on the one side, her conscience, memories of the bygone days; on the other, Bijan's degeneration. She feels that if she delays, she can't marry Bijan. So she requests Bijan to bring forward the date of marriage. Meanwhile, a committed journalist Sandipan investigates this case on behalf of a daily newspaper and finds some clues that the management is behind the murders. He finds the killer, Sekhar Das, an aspiring goalkeeper and a lumpen proletariat, appointed by the management in lieu of a promise for a job. Nirupama is in touch with Sandipan and wants justice for her brother's murder. When Sandipan wants to publish his findings, the editor refuses as the newspaper earns advertisement revenue from this company. The management of the firm is aware of Sandipan's investigative journalism. Sandipan was supposed to be one of the witnesses on behalf of Nirupama at this marriage. Coincidentally he is murdered in fake car accident on that day. To Bijan this is just a sad news. To Nirupama it is a death of an ideology. She decides not to marry Bijan. Dasgupta shows that ideology is not all about involvement in a party; it is about how the individual moulds herself into this ideology.

'Andhi Gali' is more directly related to the Naxalite Movement than the other movies by Dasgupta. Hemanta Ray, a Naxalite and a betrayer under police torture, escapes to Mumbai. There he accepts all means to earn money, forces his wife Jaya to take on modelling. He gives up revolutionary politics. In a new world he wants to forget his past. Once again Dasgupta says that politics is not merely an external affair, showing the changes in Hemanta.

Govind Nihalani's 'Aakrosh' (1980) is relevant for realizing the exploitation of the poor and the *dalits,* and the nexus among different institutions of state power, while in 'Hazar Chaurasi ki Maa' (1997), the significance lies in the state atrocities perpetrated on the Naxalites.

In 'Aakrosh' a tribal man Lahanya Bhiku faces a trial for allegedly killing his wife; though the truth is that his wife was raped and killed by the local forest contractor in collaboration with the local hospital doctor. Lahanya is represented by a young prosecutor Bhaskar Kulkarni. Initially Kulkarni thinks it is a simple case : Lahanya Bhiku was drunk and killed his wife. As he proceeds Kulkarni gets some hints from a local tabloid that the truth is different. He approaches the editor of the local newspaper, but the editor refuses him as he doubts that Kulkarni is an agent of the local power structure. Not only Lahanya, his father, his sister, and the neighbours too, maintain silence despite Kulkarni frequents visits to this village. A revolutionary young man (presumably Naxalite) organizes the *dalits* there who reveals the truth to Kulkarni who now investigates how Lahanya's wife was raped and killed. Helpless villagers do not speak up although they know it. The local power attacks on Kulkarni's life despite security provided by the court; they also attack the editor of the local tabloid. Even the defence lawyer, who belongs to the same ethnic group of the victim, yet a part of the system of the local power, is threatened by the forest contractor as he has given shelter to Kulkarni. Nihalani has shown often the local Officers' Club where the local MLA, forest contractor, police super, lawyers, and the doctor play cards - the nexus among the different institutions of state power. At the end, Lahanya is freed on parole to perform the last rites at his father's cremation. Suddenly, he snatches an axe from one villager and kills his sister as he knows that she is awaiting the same fate as his wife. Though Nihalani does not include much of Naxalite politics except the lone organizer, he portrays the feudal exploitation, which is still relevant considering the Maoist movement in India.

'Hazar Chaurasi ki Maa' is on the state's atrocities and political violence of that time. Bratin is a Naxalite. He and his four comrades are murdered by political goons, presumably of the ruling rightist party, in front of the parents of one. Police calls Bratin's mother to identify Bratin's body. In the morgue, a number is attached to each body, and not their names. Bratin's no. is 1084. Suddenly, a person is reduced to a number! There, Bratin's mother is treated with cruelty instead of sympathy, which a mother of a deceased always deserves. She is not even given the body of his son for funeral. After a state-arranged funeral, the police come to Bratin's house to search his room. The way the police handle Bratin's belongings, is a reflection of the state's brutality. The Police find Bratin's notebook of his poems. Bratin's mother requests the police to give it to her, but the police refuse. The police even do not spare Bratin's comrade and love Nandini, who loses partial vision of her eyes due to police torture. The Movement, however, does not die. Bratin's mother joins a human rights group, and Nandini starts working among the poorest Indians : the tribals. Though the movie is mostly on state atrocities, yet political debates among the Naxalites on annihilation of class-enemy including the poor constable are also discussed.

If 'Aakrosh' shows the objective situation of rural India and state atrocities, 'Hazar Chaurasi ki Maa' is more about state atrocities in urban India. In both, role of right-wing (presumably) state with its brutality, corruption and class character are of central importance.

Asok Biswanathan's 'Sunya Theke Suru' (1993) begins at the Naxalite Movement at early 1970s and then moves forward to early

1990s. In the beginning, Biswanathan shows debates on the annihilation of class enemies, role of intelligentsia in the leadership, and the cliché of party bureaucracy. Questioning the leadership is shown as a deviation though it is admitted that argument is the only way to reach the truth, which I believe, is the continuing legacy of communist organizations. From this, the movie takes us 20 years forward when Dr. Bhiswadev Sharma, a Naxalite activist, a former professor of Economics and an alumnus of Presidency College, is released from prison after two decades. He suddenly meets Dr. Sanat Gupta, his friend and senior in Presidency College who takes him to his residence. After torture for 20 years in prison, Sharma suffers from mental and physical breakdown. He undergoes treatment and recovers. But, he is confused as to what would be his political role now. He meets Pragya, the daughter of Gupta at their residence. Pragya is honest and sensitive, and an analytical writer. A kind of friendship grows between these two of unequal age out of their ideology and honesty. They discuss society, politics and economy. He also meets a new generation activist who believes that they need to move with the questions, and can reach the truth only by practice. Sharma also believes that one reaches the truth if one tries honestly, as he once says to Pragya. The two beliefs unite and start again from zero. Biswanathan raises some questions on party bureaucracy; at the same time, when many ex-Naxalites become confused and idle, seeing the apparent failure of their dream, he tells us that, they need to start from zero with unrevealed questions.

Gautam Ghosh's 'Kalbela' (2009) is the recent addition in this group. Kalbela is a portrait of the most tumultuous time (1967-1977) in post-independence West Bengal. The film begins with a collage of 'Calcutta 71', 'Interview', and 'Pratidwandi' as the backdrop for the names of the cast which scroll across the screen preparing us for the content of the film.

Animesh, a suburban boy of North Bengal suffers a stray bullet injury on his first day in Kolkata seeking higher education. The fiery political environment draws him into active politics. He joins BPSF, an undivided student wing of CPI and CPIM. While pursuing his studies and participating in politics, he meets Madhabilata, a fellow-student. From this moment onward, the movie intertwines Madhabilata's love and Animesh's politics and raises some complex questions on revolution.

This is a critical time for politics as CPIML is being born out of the CPIM. West Bengal, along with the entire country, is experiencing the labour pains of a revolutionary communist party. The Naxalbari (CPIML) movement is spreading like wildfire. The bourgeois state begins adopting all means, legal and illegal, to crush the movement.

Animesh is sent, presumably by the CPIM, to North Bengal to campaign for an upcoming assembly election. His experiences with the villagers and other comrades culminate into his joining the CPIML. Politics and love are evolving side by side. Animesh continues debating political questions with his comrades; Madhabilata continues to shower her love on Animesh. She acknowledges to Animesh that even though his politics may not be her path, her love will not be judgmental.

Animesh goes underground. That is the last time Madhabilata meets him before he is arrested a few years later. He is paralyzed by police torture as he refuses to disclose the whereabouts of a Naxalite leader. Meanwhile, Madhabilata leaves home after dispute with her father about her relationship with Animesh, takes a job, and starts living in a slum. She is pregnant.

The police bring in the expecting Madhabilata to persuade Animesh to disclose his leader's hideout. Animesh does not yield to pressure. The police then strip Madhabilata. Despite the debase manner in which they treat Madhabilata, she tells Animesh not to give up.

Madhabilata gives birth to a son and wants to name him 'Revolution'. Animesh jokes that it is risky to name their son 'Revolution' because he may become a counter-revolutionary when he is older. She also brings homemade desserts for Animesh because it is customary for the father of a newborn baby to enjoy sweets. This is indicative of Madhabilata's earthiness.

In 1977, political prisoners were released after the Left Front Government came into power in West Bengal. Now, Animesh's ex-comrades are in power. One of his closest friends becomes a minister in this government. He meets Animesh and promises that despite differences of paths, both of theirs dreams are same, so they should fight together.

Madhabilata brings Animesh to her slum-home and reminds him that at least one dream has come true. Animesh says that although they took a few wrong steps, at least they have moved forward. The next generation will be more judicious.

The questions raised in this movie can be divided into two groups : one on the path and time of revolution and the other on the consciousness of a seemingly non-political individual : Madhabilata.

While, the politics at that time raised questions such as whether an objective condition is mature enough for revolution; why did Lenin take part in a Duma election despite the presence of the revolutionary situation in Russia? Is political consciousness increasing with the surge in membership of left wing student organizations? The dependence of the proletarian party on the landlords; on the line of politics of killing class-enemies ultimately gives way to politics of annihilation; slogans like : Chinese Premier is Our Premier; People's Political Power Comes from the Barrel of a Gun etc. Not all the questions are answered, but the questions on objective condition, subjective awareness, and call for revolution are answered by the CPIML leadership quoting Mao : Can we gulp down a plate of rice at once? We have to have it in spoonfuls? Or if you do not drive into the water, how could you learn to swim? However, the same question is answered by CPIM leadership in a different way : Lenin does not like to rush; he prefers to take tactical steps such as one step forward, two steps back.

In the end, this movie shakes our common belief that political parties are the only hatching ground for revolutionaries and forces us to consider that even a so called commoner can raise some vital political questions, such as when Madhabilata asks : do the political parties think about the sufferings of common people during a strike; why doesn't the communist party consider a patriotic tagore-song appropriate as a mass-song? After all, you cannot fight barehanded against an army. Above all else, it is Madhabilata's tireless support and regard for Animesh's politics that is so prodigious (awe-inspiring) despite knowing the fate of joining a revolutionary communist party.

Animesh finally realizes the relevance of Madhabilata's questions while he is in prison and he proclaims : Madhabilata is the Other Name of Revolution. I would have probably named the movie : Madhabilata : The Eternal Revolutionary.

Finally I would like discuss four Hindi movies and four Bengali movies in this category.

The Hindi movies are : 'The Naxalites' (1980) by Khwaja Ahmad Abbas, 'Lal Salaam : Revolution is Always Written in Blood' (2002) by Gaganvihari Borate, 'Hazaaron Khwaishein Aisi' (2005) by Sudhir Mishra, 'Red Alert : the War Within' (2010) by Ananth Narayan Mahadevan.

'The Naxalite' is probably one of the first movies made directly on this movement. Although basically a 'commercial' movie, it follows the movement from its origin at Naxalbari over the land question, feudal relations and shows the participation of youths, students along with the peasantry, raises the question on the relation between the leadership and the members, as well as the regimentation of the organization, state atrocities etc. This movie does not deserve much discussion.

'Lal Salaam' is a more contemporary version of Naxalbari Movement on the issue of right to forest, exploitation of the tribal people, corruption, and feudalism. It is much better than the previous one, well-documented, delved realistically into the reasons why people join the movement, and shows how uneducated tribals become politically conscious through the active participation in movements. It also shows a parallel way to end this exploitation using the existing system, through organization building. Though there is no clear indication regarding the right path, the Naxalite resistances against the state atrocities are praiseworthy; the film shows the director's inclination towards armed resistance.

'Hazaaron Khwaishein Aisi' is a thought-provoking, complex and sensitive film that moves round three characters : Siddhartha, Geeta, and

Bikram, all classmates at St. Stephen's College, Delhi. Siddhartha is a son of a retired judge, Geeta is a London-returned South Indian girl, and Bikram is a son of a politician of the Gandhi-Nehru era. Siddhartha and Geeta love each other; and Bikram has a crush on Geeta. Three friends are ideologically different : Siddhartha is an ideologist; Bikram is a careerist, while Geeta, once associated with the radical student movement, is now reluctant. The movie is set on the radical student movements of the 60s and the 70s. Mishra details the recklessness of this time. These youths indulge in debates like whether the name of a party is able to justify its character, US imperialism, and so on. Siddhartha moves to Bhojpur to join the peasant struggle; Bikram, a power-broker, stays in Delhi. Geeta marries an IAS officer. Siddhartha writes to Geeta from the battlefield, about the real India : exploitation, poverty, violence of the upper class, and state atrocities. This prompts him to question why violence of the oppressed is wrong, while violence of the oppressor is right. In the course of the movement, a new face of Indian society is revealed to him : A landlord's son rapes a *dalit* woman. The landlord and his son are besieged by the *dalits* helped by the revolutionaries and demand justice. This is quite unusual in feudal India where the poor *dalits* daren't rise against the upper caste landlord. Suddenly, the landlord suffers a heart attack. The *dalits* turn into a saviour and bring a doctor. But since the doctor belongs to the lower caste, the son initially refuses his treatment. This incident raises an important question in Indian society which is mostly ignored by Indian Marxists : does caste supersede the class question? The question of democracy in party organisation is also discussed as well. Meanwhile, Geeta divorces her husband and joins Siddhartha in the battlefield. State terrorism continues. Geeta is arrested, along with Siddhartha and others, tortured and sexually assaulted. Her ex-husband frees her and she returns to Delhi. Because of torture and fear of being killed by the police, Siddhartha contacts his father. Requested by Geeta, Bikram also starts for Bihar to free Siddhartha, using his influence in New Delhi. On his way, he is injured in a car accident and taken to the same hospital where Siddhartha is admitted after torture. One night his fellow comrades rescue him from police custody. Police mistakenly assumes that Bikram is responsible for this. Bikram tries to flee, but fails. Police almost kills him but he is luckily saved by a political leader who knows Bikram. Bikram is paralysed due to torture. Finally, Siddhartha goes to London to study medicine and Geeta returns to the battlefield. Their relationship does not end, but does not remain the same. Geeta's love for Siddhartha is not without his ideology (remember the relation between Nirupama and Bijan in 'Grihayuddha'). Siddhartha writes to Geeta, sends books to his old comrades, wishes for the revolution from a safe distance. The movie ends up showing Geeta taking care of Bikram in paralysis. The movie has the perspective of the participant's class background, human relationship, and state's brutality. However, one question remains : why Mishra always shows the defeats of the revolutionaries under state terrorism? Why no resistance? The 'Lal Salaam' differs in that way.

The worst among these is the 'Red Alert : the War Within' by Mahadevan which deals with forced recruitment in the party, party bureaucracy, sexuality, and treachery in the movement. It finally shows that multinational development projects are the solution despite admitting that without armed struggle, government would not hear the poor.

The four Bengali movies are : 'Sopan' (1994) by Ajay Banerjee, 'Anu' (1998) by Satarupa Sanyal, 'Herbert' (2006) by Suman Mukherjee, and 'Tara' (2010) by Bratya Basu.

'Sopan' reminds the killing of Saroj Dutta at the *maidan* by the police. The movie shows the nexus among the media, police, and the celebrities. Despite choosing a significant episode from the 60s and 70s, the movie has failed to create any impact due to its directional and other weaknesses.

'Anu', a better film, explores the turbulence in the relationship among Sugata, an ex-Naxalite, released from jail, his love Ananya (Anu), and Sugata's former comrade Bharat. As a revolutionary, Sugata used to criticize the customs of women's wearing sankha, loha, sindur after marriage and the teenager girl Anu's usual passion for grooming her look. After Sugata's arrest and the murder of his comrade Anu's brother, Anu was raped and tortured by the local goons of presumably the rightist party in connivance with the police. Her fault is that she loves Sugata. Anu is refused by her own parents, who are scared of social stigma. She leaves her parental home, gets a teaching job at a suburban school, and waits for Sugata. Sugata is released after Left Front comes to power. Four years of lone struggle pass by and only Bharat keeps in touch with Anu. However, Sugata like many ex-Naxalites has changed. Now he agrees to put sindur on Anu's forehead to show that they are married. But the political ideology of Bharat does not die; he runs a press, organizes new generation to advance the revolution. He tries to bring Sugata back to this movement, but Sugata avoids. The most upsetting is that the scratches of torture on Anu's body deter him from physical relationship. He asks Anu : 'did not you protest?' Sugata fails in both the litmus tests, political as well as social. Anu, however, never joined the movement, but loved Sugata who was in this movement. Like Nirupama in 'Grihayuddha', Geeta in 'Hazaaron Khwaishein Aisi', Anu's love has loved a person with his ideology. Finally the changed Sugata is rejected by Anu.

'Herbert' is a story of an individual : Herbert Sarkar, an orphan, growing up in a joint family, running errands for the family members, ill-treated by cousins, and is a laughing stock in the neighbourhood. Thus, an unusual character, Herbert starts a business 'Dialogues with the Dead' and commits suicide when International Rationalistic Society declares him a fraud. The movie flashbacks into his childhood and adolescence and finds his relations with the underground activities of Naxalites. Despite commendable directorial techniques, there is not much about the Naxalite Movement.

'Tara' is made on the recent Maoist activities in Jungal Mahal area of West Bengal, its inner contradictions, and atrocities by a Leftist state on the Maoists. Contradictions among the Maoists on the annihilation of poor police constables are discussed. However, much discussion is on the individual relations and the party's mandate (Naxalite) and the CPI (M)'s role as a party and as a state. While the director fails to give any directive on the first issue, despite some truth his portrayal of the ruling Left is miserable. Surprisingly he is silent on the role of the rightist central government in the state atrocities. Overall, this movie suffers from directional weakness, excessive drama, and problematical facts.

Conclusion :

Almost all Bengali movies related to the Naxalite Movement describe the urban youth movement, rather than the peasantry; but some Hindi movies have shown the peasant struggle. Probably, the intensity of the movement in 60-70s in their vicinity, i.e. in urban areas, tempted the Bengali directors to be urban-centered. Moreover, there are differences also in the perspectives - when Ray emphasizes the socio-economic aspects, Sen highlights politics, Dasgupta stresses individual consciousness, Nihalani exposes the oppressive character of state.

The study of the 22 movies shows :

First, there were confusion and contradictions among the masses about the Naxalites. There were debates in the communist parties on armed struggle, and the call for revolution, but the masses probably were not ready for that. Naxalite movement spread like a forest fire before the masses were able to comprehend it. This confusion is shown in a number of movies like 'Pratidwandi', 'Jana Aranya', 'Padatik', 'Hazaaron Khwaishein Aisi' etc. In Sen's 'Padatik', detecting the friends and the foes is a prime point.

Gautam Ghosh's 'Kalbela' is a stand alone movie among all. Ghosh, besides showing discussion of some political questions among the left, has also shown left politics from a commoner's (Madhabilata) perspective and raises some apparently simple, but important questions, which are usually overlooked by the left parties. Those questions are questions from the soil, ignoring them may turn out to be costly. In addition, which takes this movie to a different level is again Madhabilata as an individual. She is neither Buddhadeb's Anjali, Nirupama, or Jaya, nor Satarupa's Anu. She loves Animesh, probably differs with his political view, but never tries to stop him despite knowing the uncertain future of their life; suffers humiliation of being striped by the police, yet strengthens Animesh not to give in. That is why Madhabilata is an internal revolutionary.

However, the three points on which most celluloid is spent are : the character of the so-called democratic states, party bureaucracy, and the internalization of ideology - which are relevant in the Indian communist movement.

These movies induce one to rethink the role of the so-called democratic state which fails to provide bare necessities, but when people protest, it launches atrocities on these people. Is representative democracy the last word towards a true democracy?

The second point, important to communist party, reminds us of Mao's document : 'Bombard the Headquarters : My First Big Character Poster' written during the cultural revolution of 1966, in which Mao criticised the party bureaucracy. Almost all the movies, which address party-politics, show the problem of questioning the party leadership due to lack of inner-party democracy.

Finally, the question of internalization of ideology : three movies of Buddhadeb Dasgupta and Satarupa Sanyal's 'Anu', show the problem of political hypocrisy. Politics is not merely some buzz words or revolutionary slogans or posters; it is about the merging of one's political-self and social-self. Until revolutionaries succeed in doing this, revolution is miles away. The movies further show how women internalize the progressive values of Marxism, even if none is a party activist, at most a silent listener/ observer. It reminds us of Mao's quotation : 'Women Hold up Half the Sky.'

References :

Sen Mrinal. 2004. *Always Being Born*. Steller Publishers. New Delhi. p.90.

Bandyopadhyay Samik. 2001. *Dekha Cinema : Cinema Dekha*. Anustup. Kolkata.

Bhowmik Someswar. 2008. *Behind the Glitz : Exploring an Enigma Called India Cinema*. Thema. Kolkta.

Chattopadhay Soumitra. 2002. *Manikdar Sangey*. Ajkal. Kolkata.

Dasgupta Buddhadeb. 2011.*Kibhabe Chabi Kori Kibhabe Chabi Hoi.* Parampara Prakashan. Kolkata.

Goopta Sharmistha. 2010. *Bengali Cinema - An Other Nation.* Roli Books. New Delhi.

Hood W. John. 2009. *The Essential Mystery of Indian Art Cinema.* Orient Blakswan. Hyderabad.

Raha Partha. 2000. *Cinemar Itibrittanta. Dey's Publishers.* Kolkata.

Ray Satyajit. 1976. *Bishoy Chalachchitra.* Ananda Publishers. Kolkata.

- : 2008. *Apur Panchali.* Ananda Publishers. Kolkata.

- : 2010. *Our Films, Their Films.* Orient BlackSwan. Hyderabad.

Thematic

The Rebellious Politics and Film Spectatorship : A Note on Bengali Popular Films Now

Binayak Bhattacharya

Introduction :

In the political history of West Bengal, recent years may be marked as significant as 1960s or 1970s. The point is, for the last 3-4 years, West Bengal has been enduring a series of events that made its socio-political scenario a site of enquiry. Through this period, interestingly the hitherto differently known symbols and rhetoric are now being re-acquainted within the newer context of popular politics[1]. Also, violence has visibly become the principal language of power after a period of a few decades. The sublimated form of violent resolution of contradictions arisen within the praxis of cultural enquiry, in my opinion, is taking the form of a silhouette. After the 1970s, there was no such proclaimed political force which had advocated the path of violence as an apparatus of its political achievement except within some infrequent occurrence of violent movements like in Gorkhaland, Kamtapur and Jharkhand. Hence it is conceivable that before the emergence of 'Maoism' of present day, the political scenario of West Bengal was dominated by a reconciled population of peace, non-violence and parliamentary leftist organizations. The most important difference between Maoist movement of present day and the Naxalite Movement of 1970s, accepted by most of the scholars of social sciences, is the approach of its politics. Now the activities of Maoists are not confined within a few pockets and urban centres, neither they rely nor do they make their force with a handful of middle class youths like 1970s. I argue, the effect of the new incarnation of Naxalite

Movement is not felt directly as it was in 1970s. Rather it has a sublimed existence in the domain of observables, particularly forming a new rhetorical function of violence as assertion of politically subjugated.

In this paper, I shall therefore try to identify these direct and mostly indirect effects of new age Naxalism of twenty-first century, popularly known as 'Maoism' within the domain of popular aesthetic productions. For my discussion I shall consider the case of recent popular mainstream commercial films. My purpose will be to identify these flutters within some sequences of a popular Bengali film to contextualize the symptoms of disturbances in the existing aesthetic paradigm. For my discussion I wish to take examples from a fairly recent film, the Mithun Chakrabarty starrer and Haranath Chakrabarty directed 'Tulkalaam' (The Tumult : 2007). The film is based on land eviction issue and offers a direct address towards the political problems. I would like to contextualize my theoretical arguments with these sections taken from the film within the specificity of the political space that has emerged through a period of turmoil in West Bengal. For me, to envisage the effects of violence of Maoist Movement, there is no other tool available except this indirect method of approach. To map it out we need to construct a theoretical model which will lead us to study the nature of traffic between Maoist politics of revolutionary violence and popular aesthetics. In that way, it would be possible to locate the role of the 'tactical use of violence' (in which Maoists play a catalytic role) behind the screen of projection.

'Tactical Use of Violence' and the Jeopardized Domain of 'Bhadralok':

To start with, I would like to refer to a debate initiated through an article by Partha Chatterjee titled 'Democracy and Economic Transformation in India' (DET). While focusing on peasant culture and political society, he mentioned that the notion of the classical peasantry of India is rapidly changing under the pressure of the market forces, and to cope with the change, new techniques of political activity are being resorted (Chatterjee 2008 53-62). And, for him, '...the frequently spectacular quality of actions in political society, including the resort of violence, is a sign of ability of relatively small groups of people to make their voices heard and to register their claims with governmental agencies' (61). Chatterjee argued that the significant change in the nature of the peasant politics in last two or three decades, may now be taken as the principal factor acting behind the scripts of the violent movement which is being driven by an almost utilitarian logic. Violence is being used to create the space of this assertion. Chatterjee called this as tactical use of violence. This is not to punish or terrorize anyone, but to present the existence in the public spaces. So, the enacted violence here 'serves the rhetorical function of converting populations into a people' (62). Satish Despande, in response to Chatterjee's propositions, has raised the question of 'very specific groups' that occupy 'a luminal zone framed by the tension between their formal illegality (in terms of civil society) and electoral importance (within political society). This luminal zone is dominated by non-corporate forms of capital (petty production in the service or unorganized sectors) but it is also able to create and sustain effective forms of political mobilizations through local associations and links to mainstream parties' (Despande 85). So, for him the so-called 'outside' zone of political society is restructured through the various forms of resistances. It helps to determine the shape of practical politics. In this way, it is possible to envisage the political unrest in the western districts of Bengal.

Historically, the series of armed conflicts in present day West Bengal were initiated in late 1990s, with the (in) famous Keshpur-Garhbeta incidents. It continued up to 2001, when the Left Front government bounced back to power with a two-third majority amidst the speculations of losing to new-born Trinamool Congress. Interestingly, this kind of armed reshuffling of power between the mainstream parliamentary parties didn't take place within the mainland 'developed' Bengal. Rather, it had found its ground within the mostly marginal populations of the most backward districts of the state (Bandopadhyay 2001 440-41). The legacy of violence continued thereafter and was gradually taken over by the Maoists. After the breaking out of Lalgarh

Movement in 2008-09, it was detectable that the impetus of the tribal and marginal angst was hardly addressed before. We may note the point that the primary demands of the Lalgarh Movement were not directed towards 'revolution'.[2] The demands presented by the tribal and non-tribal habitants of the region simply signify the mode of getting justice. And this in turn created a space for violent assertion. This is, in a way definite because "Lalgarh undermines conventional ideas about the relationship between 'peaceful' and 'violent' forms of struggle and inaugurates possibilities of resistance unfettered by given notions of political subjectivity or by subservience to the 'rule of law'" (Giri 2009). Point is, this form of resistance offered by the people subjugated within the present structure of political society not only enters through the events like Singur, Nandigram and Lalgarh, but through the numerous spectacular popular upsurges like the 'Ration Revolt' in 2007, the 'Rizwanur Incident' etc. Particularly the case of Nandigram first established the nature of subversive resistance of the day where mostly by the marginal (politically, like the subordinated mass by the ruling party; socially, like the Muslims and socially backwards and also from the margin of familial space. Women played a significant role almost in every movement from Singur) this politics of assertion emerged through the tactical use of violence. Nevertheless, the language of negotiation has become futile.

However, both the Central and at least a dozen state governments have taken several measures to undertake developmental activities and to tackle the growing menace of Maoist movement in a vast part of central, south and east India.[3] This process has got momentum especially after the Lalgarh uprising. Chatterjee in his rejoinder pointed out that these governmental measures like reforms and outcomes, need to be examined within the field of mass democracy where 'policy and politics mutually constitute each other' (Chatterjee 2008 92). The characters of democratic demands necessarily constitutes through verbalization of populist politics. He referred to Ernesto Laclau here, as the latter argued that the 'populism is the only morally legitimate form of democratic politics today' (92). In his book On *Populist*

Reasons, Laclau argued that populism is not a type of political movement; rather it should be comprehended as a political logic (Laclau 2005 16). This logic of populism becomes visible through the study of rhetoric. The function of rhetoric bears immense importance, because 'if through rhetorical operations they [populists] constitute broad popular identities which cut across many sectors of the population, they actually constitute subject, and there is no point in dismissing this as mere rhetoric' (12). According to this argument we can discuss the term 'Change'. It is the recent popular rhetoric of toppling down the existing political order in West Bengal.[4] In that way, I argue while taking references from our previous discussions that the violence of Jangal Mahal has served the function of the 'rhetoric of assertion' in a different plane.

Now we can move our discussion into the plane where politics shares space with aesthetics. Applying the theoretical scheme of Jaques Ranciere, we can argue that at the time of turmoil, the stable form of 'system of representation[5] is disturbed by the new elements of populism. Ranciere introduced the idea of 'The Distribution of the Sensible', where this distribution establishes the shared and common sensible parts of experiences that we perceive through our sensory organs. This allocation of parts and position is constructed on the basis of space, time and the form of activity. This combination determines the way through which the 'common' is placed into the domain of participation and maintains the manner which allows the individuals to take part in the distribution. Now, this perceived notion of distribution of the sensible establishes the idea of representation with set boundaries and modalities of what can be heard, watched, shown, spoken, learnt, thought etc. For Ranciere, the steady form of this representation is 'police'[6]. And intervention of politics in this domain actually redraws its boundary. It is important because, 'the question of relationship between aesthetics and politics be raised at this level, the level of the sensible delimitation of what is common to the community, the form of its visibility and of its organization' (Ranciere *et al.* 2004 12). From this perspective, it is possible to look into the frames of representation and the intervention of politics within the police.

How is it possible to identify this intervention? Rhetoric plays a crucial role in the domain of representation. It is important to read the films systematically and to sort out the segments which will permit us to explore the site of enquiry. However, the task here is not only to find out the meaning of a particular segment, but 'It is, moreover, chiefly through rhetoric that critics learn inferential processes and encounter exemplars, analogies, and schemata. Rhetoric also constructs a critical persona and an implied audience' (Bordwell 34). The function of rhetoric is to create a space where a particular style of language and politics is articulated. Here I shall try to observe critically the terrains of discourses where politics shares the ground with cultural production and where the act of resistance/violence (politics) enters the domain of senses (police) and plays a crucial role in forming the film rhetoric. In this way, it would also be possible to connect the acts of 'revolutionary violence' with the process of violent resolution of ambiguity developed within the terrain of mainstream popular films.

The Political Culture of Bengali Films :

Most of the Bengali mainstream commercial films apart from the art-cinema practice in 1980s and 1990s worked within the framework of family drama. Especially the middle class spectators always find a comfortable space within the aesthetic strategy of these films. In most of the Bengali films till the 1980s, there was an omnipresent existence of Calcutta as an imagery of space. That representation tends to reflect the position of a hierarchical domain where the ultimate resolution of narrative conflict takes place. This hierarchy played a distinct role in establishing the cultural landscape of Calcutta dominant over the rest of Bengal. It can also be shown that the hierarchy of 'Calcutta Culture' has become the primordial tendency of dominant cultural praxis of the state.[7] But from the late 1990s, though city remained as the central space for narrative elaboration, Calcutta gradually lost its significance as the principal site. This change can also be comprehended from another aspect- the change in the notion of spectatorship of Bengali Cinema.

The re-formation of spectator subject, especially in rural Bengal, acted as a principal factor behind the characterization of the changing landscape of Bengali cinema in this period. This involves the creation of a pattern of power structure that was not quite evident previously. Briefly it can be said that after the land reform and decentralization of power in West Bengal from 1970s, the land owners and the proprietors were almost ousted from their dominating social and political position. The new power institutions formed mostly in the rural Bengal constructed a new space of activity and participation (Chatterjee *The Coming Crisis* 2009 42-45). On one side, it facilitated the non-urban citizen-subject to occupy a position from which it is capable to counteract the prevalent notion of concentric power structure. On the other hand, it gradually untied the possibilities for the designing of a different territory that overruns the legitimate domain of democracy (44-45). After the successful installation of television and the entry of commodity market, the possibility to access and cultivate rural consumers boosted to a new degree. That created the objective necessity for a new viewership of Bengali cinema, space for changing the locus of desire.[8]

The story of the other sphere of aesthetic production has run parallel to this route. In 1970s, there was a triumph of politically motivated films with a relatively wide viewership. But by the 1990s, it became confined within a handful of urban sophisticated spectators. On one side, the films for rural Bengal, which run successfully in rural and sub-urban cinema halls and attract audience from mainly those localities, other side the art films, running in limited numbers of theatres and confined within a handful of spectators remain as the hegemonic emblem. The political objectivity of this kind of aesthetic productions is essentially linked with the creation of a broad based 'Bengali intellectual' section that through its activities in the domain of representation erected the idea of depoliticized aesthetic of social progress. Also, the conscious effort to maintain distance from down-market mould of mainstream commercials has fabricated the idea of an antiseptic interior.[9] Though the construction of the cultural entity called *Bengali Bhadralok* has its roots in colonial period, but it is almost considered that within the left front regime from 1977, a new variety of its culture is manufactured with stabilized cultural norms. This argument also gets ground in the course of the evidences like electoral success of the lefts, cultural mobilization like Film Festival, Drama Festival etc. Through various social agencies and a kind of political management in social units in almost every locality, these activities carried forward a valued combination of nationalist ethics with socialist politics (Biswas 2009 196-205). But after 1990s, especially after liberalization process gained momentum, we can see a regenerated form of cultural construction. That is the crisis in the domain of political, within the hitherto existing values.[10] I shall say, it would be hardly possible to locate the position of so-called 'political films' today. This is not because of the absence of any politically motivated director, but for the change in the plane of politics of aesthetic productions. Henceforth, it is necessary to trace the sublimated location of performing political reality to get a notion of resistance/violence apparently non-existent in the per-conceived cultural forms. The thrust created by the resistance movements therefore created a space of conflict within the popular aesthetic productions. In the previous sections, I have tried to show that the violence and resistance offered by a large number of (mostly marginal) people in West Bengal is asymptotically aligned in a coherent relation with the Naxalites/ Maoists movement, then it would also be discernible in aesthetic paradigm as the formal assemblage, as narrative break or as disturbance set in opposition of the dominant discourse of narrative resolution. Therefore, my purpose is to locate these ruptures within the popular films which in turn will situate the disturbances within the existing domain of aesthetics.

Identified Violence—Segregated Activity :

The scope of 'Tulkalam' (The Tumult) is primarily the land eviction issue and its intervention within the realm of aesthetics is somehow direct in approach. Mithun Chakrabarty acts here in lead as Tufan. From the very beginning, it continues to refer to the 'party' as a socially determining entity, which self-evidently establishes links with the erstwhile ruling party CPI (M). Interestingly, for a long time the word 'party' has become synonymous to CPI (M) in the state. The basis for this construction is a matter of political and sociological enquiry, which is beyond the scope of this paper.[11] Nevertheless, we can take this word in its pedagogical sense as it not only refers to CPI (M) as a party, but also as a distinct power structure.[12] The site of the film is similar to Singur, the locality in Hooghly district of West Bengal where the agitation started against the land eviction for proposed car factory by Tata Motors in 2006. The industrialist, represented as the industrial aggressor here, is easily identifiable with the investors of Indonesian Salim Group. The narrative stands on the question of eviction, corruption, hooliganism etc. There is an ambiguous reference that the origin or all sorts of ill-practice and messy politics has its root in the party-system. 'Tulkalam' has a track-record of being an interventionist film. *Hindustan Times* reports that the film was screened at Domkal (Murshidabad) and Cooper's Camp (Nadia) two days before the Panchayat Election in 2008. The promotional poster at a local hall in Domkal read "Singur thekey Nandigram, dikey dikey tulkalam" (Singur to Nandigram, tumult everywhere). CPI (M) supporters dismantled some of these posters and even stopped screening. But the general public rose in resistance, organized a rally and demonstrated in front of the party office. It ran successfully for more than 50 days in all the 54 theatres it was released in April 2008. The only competitor of 'Tulkalam' was 'Spiderman' 3 in Hindi and English versions. Evidently, it got big response in Calcutta also. The popular dialogue in the film 'Public-er maar, keoratola paar' (the public's hit takes to the cemetery's pit) became a popular rhetoric (even used in wall graffiti) when CPI (M) faced a landslide defeat in that election.

The opening sequence of 'Tulkalam' shows a two storied building- 'party office'- with a flag hoisted on the top in a low-angle shot. The camera then tilts down and shows that the office is named after a party leader. Subsequently, we see the local MLA Abinash coming by a convoy with red-light sirens. He gets down from the car and enters the office, accompanied by the youth leader Haripada. Their style of dressing in white kurta-pajama directly connects with the practical representation of the political party in power. The way the hierarchy of the establishment is shown; the spectator readily identifies her/himself with the unease of being governed. The space is designed according to the centrality of the image- the picture of the beloved leader hanging on wall and the present leaders talking about 'development'. As the camera zooms-out, we see the silent listeners sitting in rows. It is as if the spectators are recognizing themselves with the object of the speech- the villagers. The phrases like 'tin-fosola chasher jomi' (multi-cropped land where one can farm three times in a year), 'goriber party' (party of poor people), 'bideshi logni' (foreign investment), "na bujhte chaile 'bojhabe" (if they still don't understand, 'convince' them) just played the catalytic role to convey the message. The rhetorical style in which signs and symbols used, the arrangement of mise-en-scene actually invites a gaze to identify the subject here. Also, rhetoric plays its own role to unfold the objectivity of historical message.

The use of dialogue is important here as it bears the note of direct address. Mentioning this issue of rhetorical function of film dialogues, Moinak Biswas commented that 'most of it is the empty rhetoric of populism, and it is hard to locate its target. But a very large audience has come to receive the declamations according to logic of the cult, in discrete blocks both aligned to the plot and independent of it' (Biswas 2009 203). The central character Tufan is a rebel who comes from outside, and leads the movement against land acquisition. He intervenes in the domain of malfunctioned hospital; he punishes corrupted school authority denying mid-day meal to children. Gradually the audience gets to know that the former leader of the party, Parimal was actually killed by the present MLA Abinash and the local police officer because he denied latter's proposal to grab farmland for industrialization. The role of the local police and administration is also depicted as subordinate to the party. The narrative is not unfamiliar. But the point is how it is contextualized within the ongoing movements and debates regarding the land issue throughout the state.

I can cite another segment here as an example of rhetorical function and how it is enacted the visibility of populist politics and shifting paradigm of populism. An old fellow comrade of murdered leader Parimal comes to Tufan and expresses his solidarity. He is also the witness of the murder. On the very next day of alleged killing, Abinash came to his house and gave him a threat to life. He leaves home and takes refuge in another place. Having heard the story of struggle, he returns. After the brief interaction, he chants the slogan- "Laal Salaam". Tufan replies with same gesture raising his arms with the pose of Red Salute. We can take this segment as a notable site of enquiry, because it places the question of popular assertion of plunging into the traditional arena of leftism. I have discussed earlier how the traditional left bastion is on the verge of erosion and how the new politics of populism is taking its place by appropriating the rhetorical function on its own terms. On one side it is trying to resist and combat the hegemonic function of symbols by portrayal of reversed achievement; on the other hand developing its own logic of cult and fixing it in resolute action. Therefore there are ambiguous references regarding the real identity of Tufan. Within the film Tufan distanced himself from the traditional political parties. Even he refused the lucrative offers from both the sides. We see, all existing political parties are getting united to tackle him as he is continuously feeding the people's initiative. This signifier of identity leaves us in a plane where Tufan can either be a rebel/revolutionary or somebody employed by army/state bureaucracy. Finally we come to know that he is a CBI officer. Confirming the supremacy of nation and making the subject adherent to it, the articulation of narrative here offers the spectator a space where the declared rights of a citizen in operational democracy can be assured. But my point is, being a CBI officer he is resorting, rather inciting a violence which is unacceptable within the constitutional domain of India. Henceforth, the cognitive significance of this very act necessarily concedes with the illegal form of struggles, hitherto considered as threat to the domain of nation-state. Resistance, in the form of assertion is articulated in the narrative strategy while the inputs of populism play the main role in shaping the film rhetoric here.

Conclusion :

From the examples I have cited here, it is not signified that every corner of the industry is now engaged or affected with the same process. Rather we can take this as an approach through which the change of politics within the aesthetic strategy of films can be comprehended. I shall recommend considering these discrete segments only as symptoms of political anomaly. And to advance with it, one has to study it within the greater domain of politics. The changes in the aesthetic strategy in Bengali mainstream commercials are someway being directed towards negating the traditional values. Tradition of Bengali Culture, which strongly recommends about the 'purity' and 'aesthetic ability' of artistic productions, can be seen as jeopardized by the influential and incumbent factors of subversive assertions. Perhaps, it is moving towards a re-placement of existing binaries like good film/bad film (art/popular) or rural-urban in the realm of aesthetic production. Violence, hitherto rejected as a crude form of expression of down mould film aesthetics plays a important political role here. For me, it is nothing but the political violence of assertion that has ultimately come out through this phenomenon.

The political averment of Nandigram to Lalgarh, from the number of militant popular movements to Maoist/Naxalite revolutionary armed struggles is responsible for it. For now, it is only possible to anticipate about the forthcoming strategic developments. So we must need a frame of reference which will help us to get the sense of those proceedings. I have tried to construct a possible framework for this purpose. 2011 and its adjacent years bear certain importance, because the numerous events that have been taking place will be articulated within the domain of sensible and that process of articulation will definitely tend to re-shape the boundary of this domain. I think, one should carefully observe the process of this adjustment rather to look for the outcomes. Bengali popular films can be a significant ground feeding the cause of this exploration.

References :

Bandopadhyay, Raghab. 'Agrarian Backdrop of Bengal Violence', *Economic and Political Weekly,* 36. (3-10 February, 2001): p 440-41.

Biswas, Moinak. "Changing Scenes". *Fear : Sarai Reader* 08 (2010). 196-205. SARAI. Web. 16 Oct. 2010.

Bordwell, David. *Making Meaning : Inference and Rhetoric in the Interpretation of Cinema.* Cambridge, Massachusetts : Harvard University Press, 1991.

Chatterjee, Partha. 'Classes, Capital and Indian Democracy,' *Economic and Political Weekly.*46. (15 November, 2008): 89-93.

- 'Democracy and Economic Transformation in India.' *Economic and Political Weekly.*16. (19 April, 2008): 53-62.

- *Politics of the Governed : Reflections on Popular Politics in Most of the Worlds.* New Delhi : Oxford University Press, 1993.

- *The Present History of West Bengal.* New Delhi : Oxford University Press, 1993.

Deshpande, Satish and Mary E John. 'Theorising the Present : Problems and Possibilities.' *Economic and Political Weekly.*46. (15 November, 2008): 83-86.

Giri, Saroj. 'Lalgarh and the Radicalisation of Resistance : From 'Ordinary Civilians' to Political Subjects?' mrzine.monthlyreview.org. 9 July, 2009. Web. 14 July, 2011.

Kohli, Atul. *The State and Poverty in India : The Politics of Reform.* Cambridge : Cambridge University Press, 1987.

Laclau, Ernesto. *On Populist Reasons.* London : Verso, 2005.

- *Politics and Ideology in Marxist Theory : Capitalism-Fascism-Populism.* London : NLB, 1977.

Mallick, Ross. *Development Policy of a Communist Government : West Bengal since 1977.* Cambridge : Cambridge University Press, 2008.

Prasad, M Madhava. *Ideology of the Hindi Film : A Historical Construction.* New Delhi : Oxford University Press, 2008.

Ranciere, Jacques. *Aesthetics and Its Discontents.* Cambridge : Polity Press, 2009.

Ranciere, Jacques and Slavoj Zizek. *The Politics of Aesthetics.* London : Continuum, 2004.

Notes :

1. The leftist rhetoric is now widely being used by the so-called 'rightist' parties of West Bengal. TMC leader Mamata Banerjee herself continues to claim in public rallies that CPI(M) has 'lost its credibility to continue with the spirit of people'. After coming to power, for the first time she organized the official commemoration ceremony for the Food Movement martyrs of 1959. It has become often confusing to identify the 'lefts' and 'rights' through their statements and sayings.
2. Partho Sarathi Ray "Nov 13, 2008 : Background of the Movement". *Lalgarh Movement - Mass uprising of adivasis in West Bengal.* Sanhati. 13 November, 2008. Web. 12 July, 2011. <http://sanhati.com/front-page/1083/#1>
3. See the Report of An Expert Group to the Planning Commission, Government of India, New Delhi, April 2008. <http://planningcommission.nic.in/reports/publications/rep_dce.pdf>
4. This particular term has emerged in the eve of General Election in 2009 and in the post Singur-Nandigram-Lalgarh scenario. In its original essence, it reflects the idea of defeating the ruling Left Front in the election to be replaced by Trinamool Congress led centre-left coalition.
5. For further elaboration of the idea see Jacques Ranciere and Slavoj Zizek. *The Politics of Aesthetics.* London : Continuum, 2004. p 12-19.
6. Police, for Ranciere is not merely the tool of repression, rather a rule which operates within the realm of sensible. I am quoting here from the note given in the glossary about police- "As the general law that determines the parts and roles in the community as well as its forms of exclusion, the police is first and foremost an organization of "bodies" based on a communal distribution of the sensible, i.e a system of coordinates defining modes of being, doing, making and communicating that establishes the borders between visible and the invisible, the audible and the inaudible, the sayable and the unsayble. This term should not be confused with the la basse police or the low-level police force that the word commonly refers to in both French and English. *La basse police* is only one particular instantiation of an overall distribution of sensible that purports to provide a totalizing account of the population by

assigning everyone a little and a role within the social edifice. The essence of the police, therefore, is not repression but a certain distribution of the sensible that precludes the emergence of politics" (ibid. p 89).

7. For a more elaborate discussion on this area see Diksha Dhar. "Consuming City Spaces. Rituals of Commemoration : A Study of the Antorjatik Boi Mela in Calcutta." Unpublished MA Dissertation. The English and Foreign Languages University, Hyderabad. 2011.
8. From 1980s, there was a big leap in film viewership in West Bengal. Not only the cinema halls, but video halls were also set up even in the remote areas of the state. Also, the new social section that emerged through the decentralization of power and expansion of rural market and economy started investing their money in film market. This is peculiar in character, because they have only shared a part of the total cost, not the entire sum. So, it was their sole interest to expand the domain of film viewership.
9. Interior that is resistant to the external effects, specially the cultural insertions of 'down-mould' popular films.
10. A depoliticized narrative has started to gain its ground. It is capable to render the hitherto developed ethical ground into another plane. The orientation of middle class became more 'governmental' than the 'political'. See the chapter "Are Indian Cities Becoming Bourgeois At Last?" in Partha Chatterjee. *Politics of the Governed : Reflections on Popular Politics in Most of the Worlds.* New Delhi : Oxford University Press, 1993.
11. For more discussion in this regard see Partha Chatterjee. *The Present History of West Bengal.* New Delhi : Oxford University Press, 1993. Also see Dwaipayan Bhattacharyya. "Of Control and Factions : The Changing 'Party-Society' in Rural West Bengal". *Economic and Political Weekly.* XLIV.09. (28 February, 2009): 59-69; Rajarshi Dasgupta. "The CPI(M) 'Machinery' in West Bengal : Two Village Narratives from Kochbihar and Malda". *Economic and Political Weekly.* XLIV.09. (28 February, 2009): 70-81; Partha Chatterjee. "The Coming Crisis in West Bengal". *Economic and Political Weekly.* XLIV.09. (28 February, 2009): 42-45.
12. For further reference, see Atul Kohli. *The State and Poverty in India : The Politics of Reform.* Cambridge : Cambridge University Press, 1987.

The Ideological and the Existential : Naxalite Ideology in 'Hazaaron Khwaishein Aisi' and 'Herbert'

Dibyakusum Ray

The problem regarding the position of the subject in a context of ideology occupies an ambiguous niche in history. The cognitive totality of the subjective perception in a Kantian argument is challenged by the Nietzschean problematization of values and perspectives; the Marxist polemics of the functioning of the subject under the rubrics of economy is counterpoised by the existential ideology of Sartre. The present argument aspires to form an analysis of the ramifications of the Naxalite ideology in a similar dialectical context - exemplary idealist to some, the Naxalite indicates to others an expression of immature disaffection that has nothing constructive to offer. In either case, the Naxalite subject embodies the crisis of a soul at the battleground of morality, radicalism, determinism and unfixed signification. The crisis has been argued on through the analysis of two films concerning the depiction of a revolutionary subject in anomalous social milieu. 'Hazaron Khwaishein Aisi' (2005) and 'Herbert' (2005) depict the journey of a subject from a preordained ideological duality to the multiple fracture of convenient dialectical schema. This is a journey from external polarity to arguable internalization through a positional shift among supposedly conflicting social strata. Exposed in the consideration of Naxalite events in hindsight, a battery of similar problems may prove to be more significant pointers to the nature of their involvement with the events, their affiliated standpoints and prejudices, than the answers that they finally arrived at. The final aim of the argument is to keep alive such discursive spaces.

The dialectical nature of the subject's ideological position does not appear so long as we consider the 'I' to be a priori - Cartesian concept that amply influences the structure of an edenic Kantian subject who reaches the state of universal goodness successfully rationalizing problems of subjective appreciation. The 'interested' pleasure gives way to the disinterested appreciation of things that makes the subject aware of the universal harmony among natural elements. Kant, however, affirms that not to reach conceptualization does not need to be a frustrated judgment but rather the opposite. No matter how many conceptual understanding offers for that aesthetic unity, no concept ever suffices. Yet the attempts in finding an appropriate concept cannot be abandoned. This principally endless process of reconstruction and its frustration finds a new interpretation in the Marxist analysis that purports an instrumental understanding of ideology, signifying that all social/personal enterprises of the subject are but the ramifications of an economic superstructure. The supposed dialectics of Kantian polemics turns into a Sisyphean reproduction of static class position of a bourgeois economy. In this more comprehensive context, class position, far from being a context that described an empirical existence, emerges as an 'Ought' in two senses. First, it postulates that there is a particular way in which its saviour, the proletariat, ought to think; and second, it presents a moral or even categorical imperative for the revolutionary to replace the Hegelian idea by incorporating the functions of real living men. Ironically, he did so in a form in which ideas are bound by ties of interest to social groups - a tendency only intensified by the evolution of Leninism which related the whole realm of the ideological to a class interest and pave the way for a avowal of the class character of thought itself. The moment a signifier attempts to escape the stringent counter-position, the Marxist argument threatens to negate the existence of such a signifier. The revolutionary ideals of Marxism, though Nietzschean in its declaration of complete subversion and upsetting of socio-normative relations, cannot escape Nietzsche's fear of a repetition of the same hegemonic enterprises. The development of existentialism as a critical theory, however, devotes itself to the exploration of the existential world postulating a necessary connection between the theoretical ideological universe and the subjective and existential. Drawing inference from Kierkegaard, who declares himself to be unwilling to be cocooned in a system and who, against Hegel's intellectualism, asserts unrelentingly the irreducibility and the specificity of what is lived, Sartre concludes that the infinite distance between man and Ideal cannot be object of an instrumental knowledge; it is a subject of a subjective faith that with its strength and spontaneous affirmation, will never be reduced to a moment which can be surpassed and classified. Sartre speaks :

> In fact, the *subjective* life, just in so far as it is lived, can never be made the object of a knowledge. On principle it escapes knowing, and the relation of the believer in transcendence can only be conceived of in the form of a *going beyond*. This inwardness, which in its narrowness and its infinite depth claims to affirm itself against all his philosophy, this subjectivity rediscovered beyond language as the personal adventure of each man in the face of others and of God - this is what Kierkegaard called *existence* (Sartre : 1960, 8-9).

So what we face here is essentially a crisis of the 'I' and the 'Ideal' caught into a seemingly infinite paradox of the attempt and the frustration of such attempt to reach enlightenment. The very idea of revolution is sufficiently problematized at this juncture, as awareness of the original character of existential ideology raises indeed the question as to whether it can be shared at all. While it is quite possible to sidestep this crisis by denying the shared nature of existential ideology altogether by assuming that social subjects are but agents of a hermetic bourgeois machinery[1], the ideology's implication in a programme of social action in which one's experienced identity is pitted against what others perceive it to be, social and shared characters of both this ideology and its social signification cannot be avoided.

The Naxalite movement, ignited in May, 1967 at Naxalbari in

North Bengal, was susceptible to such crisis from its very initiation. Although, crushed by the police within a few months, the long suffering peasants appeared to have rediscovered their traditional militancy. From 1967 to 1972, an array of often violent conflicts, debates, retaliation and retribution formed the parameters of one of the bloodiest state feuds in Indian political history. The division of the Communist Party of India (Marxist) escalated the calamity, while the forerunners of the newly formed CPI (M-L) denounced participation in the electoral process and aimed to establish the rule of the vast majority of the nation, composed specifically of the peasantry, the proletariat, the petty-bourgeoisie and the national bourgeoisie, upsetting the rule of the landlords, the U.S. imperialists and the Soviet social-imperialists, who constituted a tiny minority.[2] The terminology through which the Marxist-Leninist-Maoist leaders like Charu Mazumdar addressed the semi-feudal, semi-colonial socio-economic reality of the country, offers an intensely ideological and holistic paradigm, one that cannot be addressed within any tradition other than the generic 'petty-bourgeois revolutionism' and 'armed struggle' - bringing a powerful critique, theoretical and practical, of revisionism. The Naxalites reacted against the interpretation of history by the revisionist which allows the subject to controvert his spirit, both in the context of its social realization and, more importantly for the revolutionary, in the context of his own personal life. Naxal revolution boldly dispensed with all revisionist subjective claims and expressed an impatience with scholarly undertakings, encouraging a Nietzschean violent rejection of heritage and iconography. Saroj Dutta, supporting the destruction of intellectual property by the students, spoke :

> Have they analyzed the records of the works of those whose statues they are destroying? No, they have not! But still, they are doing the right things. They have been born and brought up in the era of the victory of the revolution. They are not burdened with any revisionist past as is the case with their elders. They are not required to go through the agonizing process of making a

> break with the past ties like their elders (Saroj Dutta : 1970, "In Defence of Iconoclasm", *Deshbharati,* qtd. in Sumanta Banerjee : 2009, 203).

Yet, the very Nietzschean polemic of nihilism is inherently problematic. While the revolutionaries interpreted nihilism to be a subversion of the valueless bourgeois world by invoking a completely new system of signification, Nietzsche himself interpreted nihilism to be based on a fundamental shift in meaning, describing that the apathetic and radical outlook of a nihilist is generated from a great sense of personal worth. The deep sense of the valuelessness of the self is a projection of a psyche conscious of its own value. Arguably, the Naxals thus generated a new iron-bound paradigmatic interpretation of history while rejecting all paradigms. Sushital Ray Chowdhury wrote about the party high command's decision of mass annihilation, guerrilla methods and red terror :

> All these things where done in the name of the new national and the international situation, denying the uneven character of the revolutionary situation. Sentimental students were used to perform democratic and socialist revolution simultaneously. Such activities as burning educational institutions, libraries, laboratories and destroying the educational system were prescribed. It is enough to say that no discussions were held in the party Central Committee before these tasks were adapted (Sushital Ray Chowdhury, "Combat Left Adventurism", qtd in Sumanta Banerjee : 2009, p. 225).

After the debacle in the 1971 mid-term pole indicated a reversal of political trends among the West Bengal middle-class population, it was a time confusion and revaluation among the revolutionaries. Faced with the dwindling support of urban middle class and the brutal autocratic power of Central government, several comrades faced the same existential crisis that forms the core of our argument. While Charu Mazumdar from all these events were seeking to discover a qualitative change in the people and clinging to his theory that 'every corner of India was explosive', his critics were stressing a loss in quantity. Revolutionary student leader Ashim Chatterjee asked in despair :

> Sacrifice of lives in battles is inevitable. But why shouldn't we have the courage to seriously consider whether it was necessary to sacrifice all the lives of heroes in Calcutta (BBOBRC document, July, 1971, qtd. in Sumanta Banerjee : 2009, p. 226).

The existential fallout of a holistic paradigm due to its internalized elements of dialectics (one that Derrida talks about) is apparent here. Mazumdar's critics in Andhra Pradesh and Debra and Gopiballabhpur felt that because of the uneven development of political consciousness and preparedness among the peasantry, it was necessary to vary the tactics from area to area. Shourin Bose's visit to China as a CPI (M-L) emissary in 1970 brought bad tidings as well with Chou En-Lai and Kang Shěng criticizing the attempted replication of Chinese Marxist-Leninist class struggle on Indian soil. Taking exception to the slogan : "China's Chairman is our Chairman", Chou En-Lai stressed on sharing hardship with the masses as well as rejecting secret assassination of police and perceived class enemies[3]. Kang Sheng, on the other hand, advised the Indian party regarding corrections of old mistakes that the action of the revolutionary must never hurt the enthusiasm of the masses and should be based upon debates, discourse and consultation with the masses. Watching the entire state of affair in retrospect, one can grasp the contemporary dialectical nature of the ideological and the existential. The with-world that the revolutionary postulated in theory is the radical counter-position to the one he encountered in experience. The Utopia remains denied in life - in both the social life to which the revolutionary counter-poses himself and which he experienced in his own organization. The binary division between the self and the world thus gives way to an internalized retrospection where the revolutionary is forced to critique the enterprise of party directives, revolutionary ideals and personal choices. In the following discourse it is argued that the nature of this very crisis is transcendental and it relentlessly functions on a discursive plane, continuously challenging socio normative tendencies and revisionist attempts, yet never attaining conclusion.

Sudhir Mishra's 'Hazaaron Khwaishein Aisi' (2005) offers a fairly simplistic argument of the positional dialectics between the film's male protagonists - Siddharth Tyabji and Vikram Malhotra. The first chooses a Marxist-Leninist revolutionary's life thwarting his preordained bourgeois comforts as a bureaucrat's son. While the other escapes his ideological baggage of being a Gandhian former freedom fighter's son in favour of earning a life of privilege. Mishra is careful in keeping the positional dialectics alive between the two male protagonists by making exclusively separate scenes regarding them both. Siddharth's Marxist - Leninist zeal is typical of the Naxalite youth upsurge under the aegis of CPI (M-L) witnessed during the 1970s[4]. Siddharth and his group of compatriots attempt youth awareness of peasant uprising through extempore theatrical skits in Delhi University Campus in the middle of cultural events, deftly staged to nudge political conscience of the educated youth. His socialist activism also depicts the political agenda of the then ongoing demonstrations and iconoclastic disruptions of urban youth. Siddharth also plans to reach the grass root level in order to ingratiate himself with the peasant uprising,[5] from which many of his compatriots shirked away. His ideological soundness is reaffirmed in his relentless activities in the remotest corner of rural uprising where the landless peasants pick their scythes in hungry desperation and seething anger and in the next instant humbly tend their injured landlord out of a centuries-ingrained ideal of servile responsibility towards the privileged master. Siddarth's studied ideology faces an adaptive challenge as he moderates and gets moderated by the proletarian upsurges he experiences in real life situations[6].

Vikram, on the other hand, is an ambitious opportunist with few morals and hardly any ideology to stick to. He has no socialist communist background (unlike Siddharth, who with a Hindu-Muslim parentage was encouraged to follow a secular socialist ideology) and his

Gandhian Congressman father is a high-stickler to inflexible moral stances and decidedly anti-communist according to then Congress policies.[7] Vikram exploits his connection with the members of the Youth Congress and is tacitly contemptuous of Siddharth's Marxist-Leninist views. He is unashamedly a "fixer", who pimps for economic profit.

Sudhir Mishra maintains this supposed duality of the ideological positions of these two characters. Their lives are shown in separate shots, explaining their ideology and moral baggage - Siddharth with his socialist and Vikram with his existential struggle. However, there is an obvious plane of connection between these two positional dualities through Gita Rao. Gita with all her practical sensibilities is strangely attracted to Siddharth. Though, she refuses to help him as a committed compatriot initially and goes on to have her bright future and a well placed bureaucratic husband, she apparently cannot give him up. In a friendly level, Gita deals extremely well with Vikram who understands her compulsions and is openly obsessed with her. There is a time leap, in the plot narration which is covered by Siddharth's letters to Gita describing his changing ideological stance, as he experiences the real life peasant revolt unmatched with his studied ideals. Gita eventually leaves her husband and marries Siddharth and agrees to live in the rural poverty running a school and helping with Siddharth's revolutionary activities. Here, she observes the stringent repressive policies that the Congress Government undertakes against the Communist activists through state machinery like the police and the prejudiced bourgeois panchayat. Gita's letters to Vikram is starkly contrasted to his upward mobility and affluence. The emergency[8] follows with dire consequences for both Vikram, whose father is taken into custody with many of his political patrons, and Siddharth, who is captures and tortured, while Gita is brutally raped in the police station. This event marks the interchange of the ideal/existential positional dialectics between the two male characters. While Siddharth faces the apex of ideological and existential crisis as he watches Gita's rape and learns of the police plan to murder him in a staged encounter, Vikram plunges into the chaos to save them. Siddharth is ultimately rescued by his compatriots and returns to his privileged life. Vikram is tortured and loses his senses in clinical catatonia. As their position is reversed, Gita's love for them is also flipped. She leaves Siddharth and cares for Vikram as they return together in the roots of rural disquiet in search of a contrasting peace. It is as if, the ideological position defines the person and the general reaction towards him. This adoption and gradual adaptation of ideology is successfully depicted by Mishra as he portrays the gradual internalization and subsequent resolution of the ideological-existential dialectics through the three characters. The politics of 'Hazaaron Khwaishein Aisi' endows Gita's final choice an irrevocable validity by manipulating the audience's sympathy towards the catatonic Vikram and Gita ruminating in the remote country-side. Gita's values are that of the director and of the movie itself. 'Hazaaron Khwaishein Aisi' thus partially nullifies the open ended strain of dialectics despite its complex narrative of positional shift. The internalization of the existential finds a resolution here.

The surreal narrative of Suman Mukhopadhaya's 'Herbert' (2005), depicts the aftermath of the extensive internalization of existential crisis. There is no alternate paradigm in this movie. Relinquishing the traditional film-making morality and narrative technique, Suman Mukhopadhayay (aided by Nabarun Bhattacharya's cult postmodernist novel) makes 'Herbert' an open ended discursive plain where even the protagonist is denied of an instrumental, ideological grounding. Naxalite ideology is turned into an element of a melancholic past bereft of its defined positional surety, yet possessing a dormant radicalism that, through the unlikeliest medium, can upset not only the static and squalid bourgeois system, but even the state machinery as well. Herbert Sarkar belongs to the farthest position possible from a copybook Naxal revolutionary. Descended of a dwindled urban bourgeois family, Herbert from his very childhood belongs to a whimsical world of his own often comprising overblown images of past grandeur and a myriad of pop cultural pastiche[9] Bullied, coerced and partially forgotten, Herbert wants to establish a direct relationship with his idealized ancestry of which Naxalism - incorporated by the actions of Binu - forms a vital part. His revenge on the over rationalized, revisionist modern society comes in his nihilist rejection of the existential and adopting the role of a faux psychic.

The subversive value system of Suman Mukhopadhay's movie endows this quack a visionary quality of reliving the revolutionary ideal. In Herbert's character we witness a successful amalgamation of the Nietzschean ideals of nihilism[10] - the first active and revolutionist, the other passive, apathetic and reductive. In an utterly valueless world, Herbert himself is an agent of further devaluation, yet he envisions himself as a guerrilla fighter while remembering Binu's dying words and his brief brush with urban Naxalites. 'Herbert' makes us look not for an idealized binary division of good and evil, but for the protagonist in a subjective, liminal space of ideal/existential dialectics. We sympathize for Herbert who dreams of lost love, lazes away his time with the local lumpens and aspires to industrialize his quackery in a consumerist bourgeois fashion, while the purported elements of rationalism, namely the members of the "Juktibadi samity" are counter poised as derogatory and cruel. Herbert's suicide again invokes Nietzsche's philosophizing on the question of nihilism.

> What does nihilism mean? That the highest vales devalue themselves. The aim is lacking; 'why?' Finds no answer (Rabindra Ray : 1988, p.9).

An explicit awareness of nihilism entails the rhetorical question, deemed unanswerable on the ground of any idea - 'why leave?', in the face of a life which reduces such a question to absurdity. To interpret nihilism in terms of values and goals is to be unaware of the vital ground of the question, and to distance it to the decency of ideals. Herbert's suicide, while seemingly escapist, is a manifestation of his attacks on any justification of life, and he seeks in the act of suicide to create a definitive protest against the paradigm of valuelessness. While it is unclear whether Herbert knew about the bombs in his mattress, the very act of his suicide and subsequent explosion at the burning ghat validates the inspectors final catch phrase : "No one can foretell the time and place of a sudden eruption". His suicide note, comprising a seemingly nonsensical network of colloquial expletives and imagery, serves as a warning of the unpredictability of the ideological-existential dialectics, where an unprecedented and epoch making incident like the Naxalite revolution may resurface with its violent connotations.

Thus, it is attempted to display how the ideological and existential elements endemic to the Naxalite struggle forms the backbone of two contemporary cinematic arguments. From the bipolar demarcations of revolutionary ideology we have witnessed a gradual concurrence of fluidity between unfixable significations.

Notes :

[1] Obviously, "the artifactual objectivity of the literate ideology is by itself grounds for some kind of social identity" - as Rabindra Ray would put it. (Rabindra Ray : 1988, p. 47).

[2] The Political Resolution of CPI (M-L) supports this agenda :

> The increasing concentration of lands in the hands of a few landlords, the expropriation of almost the total surplus produced by the toiling peasantry in the form of rent, the complete landlessness of about forty percent of the rural population, the back-breaking usurious exploitation, the ever growing evictions of the poor peasantry coupled with the brutal social oppression - including lynching of 'harijans'... and the complete backwardness of the technique of production clearly demonstrate the semi-feudal characters of our society (Political Resolution of CPI (M-L), 1969).

[3] Chou En-Lai said : "To regard the leader of one country as the leader of another party is against the sentiment of the nation; it is difficult for the working class to accept it." About the CPI (M-L)'s insistence on the self-sacrifice for a socialist India, Chou En-Lai is reported to have said : "Shared

hardship with the masses, not isolated from them." He was against "sacrifice for adventurism", and also commented : "secret assassination of police is anarchist, is isolated from the masses, is short-lived" (qtd. in Sumanta Banerjeee : 2009, p.228, 229).

[4] Sumanta Banerjee in his 2009 book mentions the political resolutions of CPI (M-L) which has been faithfully followed by Mishra in his adaptation of Siddarth's character and activities :

> The CPI (M-L) urban movement had three aspects. There was first the cultural side, marked by organized effort to debunk the intellectual heritage of the Indian, particularly Bengali middle class. The second was an attempt to reproduce the annihilation campaign in the cities, the targets being the police personnel, informers and political rivals. The third was a preparatory move to build up the arsenal by mass scale snatching of arms (Sumanta Banerjee : 2009, p. 196).

[5] This coincides with the 1969 urban movements of the communist revolutionary students through demonstrations in and out of the urban sphere in defence of the peasant's armed struggle. This is undoubtedly a reference of the CPI (M-L) attempt to redirect the sporadic student outbursts towards selected targets by providing an ideological justification.

[6] This onscreen representation of ideological crisis and resolution is also explored by Rabindra Ray :

> In the rival materialist determinisms of academic American sociology (structural functionalism) and orthodox Marxism the concept of 'ideology' surfaces as the principle of cohesiveness of social groups, in the former as a 'value system', in the latter as 'class consciousness'. ... At a remove from fundamental structural determination it provides nevertheless the crucial, if unexplored (and unexplorable) locus of structural change. Within these parameters the very exploration of the meaning, content and integration of ideology is transformed into a

partisan enterprise that threatens the validity not only of the local premises that serve to underpin these parameters but the social premises as well (Rabindra Ray : 1988, p.10).

[7] The Congress Government was relentlessly following its anti-communist policies propounded by Sardar Patel in 1950s when he announced that he would not allow a single communist to be alive in Telengana. There were repression by the Indian military in Coastal Andhra and Telengana. CPI leader Ravi Narayan Reddy described the atrocities perpetrated by the Indian army with graphic details about the manner in which the army eliminated every suspect in countless villages. The communist revolutionaries were beaten up with bayonets and were publicly tortured and lynched in the design of the hammer and the sickle. Thousands were shot dead and families were brutally dealt with (Sumanta Banerjee : 2009, p. 26).

[8] Indira Gandhi's growing intolerance of dissent both within and outside her party argued that the obligation for accountability for every action (particularly when such actions departed from her expected support of 'democracy' and 'socialism') stopped her in taking drastic and pragmatic measures in the favour of her class and in the interest of herself. She declared emergency in June 26, 1975, concentrating all power in her hands and in that of a coterie of loyal henchmen. Hundreds of opposition leaders were imprisoned and anybody with any Marxist-Leninist tendency were hunted down followed by strict precensorship of news and suspension of fundamental rights.

Mishra also portrays one of the most debated events during the emergency - the forced emasculation of hundreds of villagers. The Naxalite refutation of this event is represented through the onscreen activities of Siddharth and Gita and the other members who get indoctrinated in the Marxist-Leninist ideals after facing this incident.

[9] Suman Mukhopadhyay's film craft is a play of image, pastiche and hyper-resemblance. Herbert's hallucinations of his forefathers filming, sympathizing, polemicizing are all fragments of an idealized past that acquire their bizarreness in the present existential milieu. Jaques Ranciere discusses this key

concept of modern film making :

> It is what emerges in the contemporary stress on distinguishing the genuine image from its simulacram on the basis of the precise mode of its material reproduction ... compared with pictoral artifices, it is now perceived as the very emanation of the body, as a skin detached from its surface, positively replacing the appearances of resemblance and defeating the efforts of the discourse that would have it expressed a meaning (Jaques Ranciere : 2007, p.9).

[10] *The Complete Works of Friedrich Nietzsche*, No. 2, p.9.

Rabindra Ray explains Nietzsche's nihilistic ideals in the following words :

> To interpret nihilism in terms of values or goals as he does is to be unaware of the vital grounds of the question, and to distract it to the decency of ideals. And why he should do so is as manifest as his attacks on any justification of life - he seeks in the act of destroying to create his own... This is the active nihilism he extols. It is ofcourse the 'higher men' ... who ask for an answer to 'why live?', an answer that will encompass their lives as whole. But life itself is prior and forms the necessary ground of the question (Rabindra Ray : 1988, p.219).

References :

Derek Sayer (1979), *Marx's Method : Ideology, Science and Critique in Capital*, Sussex : Harvester Press.

Friedrich Nietzsche (1911), *Complete Works of Friedrich Nietzsche*, London and Edinburgh : T.N. Foulis.

Haridwar Rai and K.M. Prasad (1972), 'Naxalism : A Challenge to the Proposition of Peaceful Tradition to Socialism?', *Indian Journal of Political Science*, xxxiii, 4 (October-December, 1972)

Jaques Ranciere (2010), *The Future of the Image*, New Delhi : Navayana.

Jean-Paul Sartre (1976), *Critique of Dialectical Reason,* London : New Left Books.

Karl Mannheim (1936), *Ideology and Utopia,* (trans.) Louis Wirth and Edward Shils. London : Routledge and Kegan Paul.

Rabindra Ray (1988), *The Naxalites and their Ideology,* Delhi : Oxford University Press.

Sumanta Banerjee (2009), *In the Wake of Naxalbari : Four Decades of Simmering Revolution,* Kolkata : Shishu Sahitya Samsad Pvt. Ltd.

The Subject-in-Process : Female Characters in Transition in 'Hazaar Chaurasi Ki Ma' and 'Kaalbela'

Indranil Mitra and Sananda Sen

What we propose to do in the course of this paper is to look at the position and role of women within the Naxalite movement in Bengal vis-à-vis the characters of Sujata (Brati's mother) and Nandini in Govind Nihalani's film 'Hazaar Chaurasi Ki Ma', and the character of Madhabilata in Goutam Ghose's film 'Kaalbela'. Whether directly or indirectly involved in the Naxalite movement during the 1960's and 70's, the role of women seems to have been relatively marginal. However, our paper will focus on the revolutionary consciousness that is stirred up in the characters of Sujata and Madhabilata in the two aforementioned films by their indirect or quasi-direct contact with the revolutionary spirit. But, before we come to that, it is imperative to comprehend the true nature of this revolutionary spirit.

Rabindra Ray, in *The Naxalites and their Ideology* (1988), speaks of a dualistic character of the Naxalite movement, comprising two ideologies - the literate and the existential. There are two approaches to the literate ideology of the Naxalite movement. One of them rests on the idea of poor and landless peasants fighting for political power. The other approach views the Naxal movement as a socio-economic one arising as a response to the exploitation and subjugation prevalent in the semi-feudal and semi-colonial socio-economic structure. Both are problematic because they necessitate the vision of an alternative and reformed political or socio-economic order, which the sporadic and decentralized Naxal movement was devoid of (Ray : 1988).

Ray asserts that the existential ideology of the Naxalites, underlying the misleading immediate aetiological bases, was fundamentally a nihilist one, which undertook to destroy the sham of values it had seen through, and concerned itself with the collapse of ontology, adopting a stand that can only be deemed 'anti-political' (Ray : 1988).

This fundamentally nihilistic anti-political existential ideology is what we, in our interpretation of the same, would describe as a violent revolution against the *name-of-the-father.* It is a revolt against what Lacan defined as the symbolic order, that phallogocentrically governed matrix of discursive socio-cultural structures which constitute and regulate human subjectivity and identity. Any political discourse is a direct manifestation of this alienating symbolic order. The Naxal rebellion is a revolution against the very notion of a political ideology itself, the political having become too technocratic, too totalitarian and conflated with the repressive and rigorous apparatuses of the symbolic order. It is this particular category of revolutionary spirit that imbues not only the Naxal rebellion, but also the lives of the women characters in the two films.

We have adapted from the feminist psychoanalytic theorization of Julia Kristeva the concepts of the semiotic and the symbolic - two ideas that we have found to be commensurate with our own theoretical speculations. For Kristeva, the 'symbolic' is the same as that described by Lacan. By 'semiotic', Kristeva speaks of the un-discursive signifying material comprising a disorganized prelinguistic flux of movements, gestures, sounds and rhythms centering on the mother, that the infant is subject to, and that acts as a precursor to and remains active beneath the mature linguistic and discursive matrix of the symbolic constituting the adult subject. The mastery of the symbolic over the semiotic remains challenged, as, every now and then, the subversive openness of the semiotic gushes out, disrupting society's closed, 'logical' and 'rational' symbolic order. This possibility of destabilizing authoritarian discourses coincides with Kristeva's view that the subject, in contradiction to western thought, is far from being unified and a stable blank awaiting its social or sexual role. Rather, the subject is 'in process', i.e. capable of being other than what it is, and hence capable of disrupting the normative and hegemonic structures believed to constitute human subjectivity. We would like to argue that, the Naxalite revolution is a manifestation of the semiotic's invasion of the symbolic, and the female characters in the two films, through being embroiled in the movement in whatever capacity, become subjects-in-process and enter into an irreconcilable conflict with the normative order.

Govind Nihalani's film, 'Hazaar Chaurasi Ki Ma' (1998), provides an exemplar of a woman who, through her vicarious involvement in the Naxal movement, evolves into a revolutionary subject-in-process. In fact, we are compelled to ask who is the actual protagonist of the story - Brati, the full-fledged Naxalite revolutionary, or his mother, Sujata? It is really Sujata who, through the course of the film, appears as the active agent partaking of the actions as they unfold before us, Brati remaining more of an absent-presence. Our first glimpse of Brati in the film is in the form of his mutilated corpse. He has, in a sense, completed the transition from the politico-symbolic through anarchico-semiotic Naxalitism into the nihilistic void. Brati's revolutionary activities are only seen in *flashback,* through the investigations and snatches of memory of Sujata, and from the recountings of Brati's friend Somu's mother and of Brati's girlfriend Nandini. Considering the film in its entirety convinces us that the story is really about Sujata's intellectual journey. It becomes, for her, not just a desire to know what Brati's life was all about, but, in essence, also the desire to become a subject other than and different from who she has been accustomed to being so far. It is a process of self-discovery set into motion by the posthumous discovery of who her son had evolved to become. Brati has already been the subject-in-process, unsettling the repressive and patriarchal symbolic order. Now, it is her turn to do so. The viewing of the Naxalite movement through Sujata's maternal gaze is not simply a narrative or cinematic technique, but a product of consummate craftsmanship illustrating a woman's journey to liberation from the blinding and claustrophobic hold of a closed symbolic order. The film is not so much about the revolutionary Brati, but as the title suggests, about the mother of 1084, that arbitrary sign, taken as a reified category, that the deceased Brati has been reduced to in the characteristic manner of the signifying process of the symbolic. He lives now only in his mother's memory. Lacan feels that the mother's desire appears as an enigma to the small child (not yet in the symbolic) and it struggles to name or understand that desire. Over here, that situation almost seems to be reversed. It is Brati's desire that initially appears as an enigma to his mother, and through the process of comprehending that desire, she assumes that desire as her own.

The first scene of the film opens in 1949. Sujata gets out of a taxi, carrying a suitcase in her hand, and enters a building, which bears the hoarding 'Mamta Maternity Clinic'. It makes sense to presume that she has come to be admitted to give birth to a child. It is not clear whether Brati is the child being given birth to (Sujata has two sons and two daughters). But even if we assume the child concerned to be Brati, what is really striking is that she is unaccompanied, her husband conspicuously missing from the scene. From there on, the film jumps forward by twenty-one years to 17 January 1970 (Brati's birthday). On that fateful night, the phone rings in the dead of night and Brati's family is summoned by the police to come down and identify a body - presumably Brati's, of course. There also, strangely enough, Brati's mother goes to identify Brati's body, accompanied only by her daughter Tuli. Her husband is once again missing. Even if we can explain away the absence of Brati's father at the time of his death on the ground that his father wanted to disown all responsibility vis-à-vis his son's murder in a 'political and anti-social' context (the film clearly reveals an emphatic ideological clash between father and son), perhaps his non-presence at the time of Brati's birth indicates a figurative prognostication of the antipathy towards the repressive name-of-the-father that would become the defining feature both of Brati's revolutionary sentiments and also Sujata's ultimate revolt against the patriarchal framework of her household. Above everything else, the representation is of the semiotic mould within which the protests of mother and child are united.

Brati, by virtue of becoming embroiled in the movement, has now no place within the symbolic realm represented by his father. Within a couple of days of Brati's death, his father and brother ensured that his name does not feature in any of the reports on the incident issued in the dailies of the city, and all traces and vestiges of his memories are removed from every corner of the house. He has been erased from the symbolic order, a fact that jars and pains Sujata. In the initial stages, Sujata blames herself for her utter state of oblivion about Brati's lifestyle and activities. It is almost as if she had internalized the patriarchal values that would insist on the mother's responsibility in driving her son along the 'right path' and shaping him up as a future responsible citizen and not as some kind of 'anti-social criminal'. In one of the scenes in flashback, Brati's father barks at his mother in his characteristic manner, blaming her for leading their son astray and even turning him against his father. Sujata continues to bear the brunt of these allegations even after Brati's death, when Inspector Saroj Pal, who has come to the Chatterjee residence to undertake a search of Brati's room, accuses her of not having brought up her son in a proper manner, which had resulted in his falling into anti-social ways. Sujata, for a long time, continues to put up with these indignities silently. She seems initially not to have a voice, reduced rather to a mere object, non-resistantly fulfilling all her patriarchal responsibilities and obligations as a wife, a mother and an earning member (she holds a job in a bank) of 'a dignified and cultured' Bengali family. Brati tells his girlfriend Nandini, 'my father literally uses my mother as a step'. Even in her occasional conversations with Brati where she asks him about his whereabouts, his activities, why he stays out late, and so on and so forth, and Brati tells her about his dreams of a classless, exploitation-less, poverty-less society, and his desire to 'paint the city red', Sujata is somehow unable to comprehend the import of what her son implies. It is not that she is unintelligent; rather, so deeply is her subjectivity enmeshed in the patriarchal symbolic order of values and beliefs, that her capability to question those values has become paralyzed.

It is the brutal murder of Brati by local goons of the ruling political party, and Sujata's subsequent investigative journey to discover the truth and motives of Brati's life, that proves to be, for Sujata, a movement from spiritual blindness to a fervent recognition of not only Brati's noble ideals, but that of the revolutionary potential lying dormant within herself. The rebelliousness had always been there, but had only expressed itself in small hints in Sujata's behaviour as a form of resistance against the arrogant, domineering and even unfaithful ways of Brati's father. Brati overhears an argument between his parents where his mother refuses to wear bright sarees and appear with his father in one of his client's parties (as if he wants to show her off as some kind of sex object to please his clients). Brati's father is involved in some sort of extra-marital affair, which results in his returning home late from work every day. On one such night, he tries to be physically intimate with Sujata, who balks his advances showing clear signs of repulsion towards him. On Brati's death anniversary, she enters their bedroom and finds her husband enjoying an oil massage on the bed. Once the massage is over, and he leaves the room, she throws the bed sheet and the pillow onto the floor in utter disgust.

But the final turning point in the transition of her subjectivity transpires during her intense meeting with her son's girlfriend Nandini Mitra. The day is 17 January 1972, which, apart from being Brati's birth and death anniversary, is also, ironically, the date of her daughter Tuli's engagement. Unlike Sujata, Nandini has been a Naxalite and an active agent in the goings-on in Brati's life. She tells Sujata about their comrade Anindya's betrayal that led to the murder of Brati and his comrades, about her two years in prison and the brutal torture that she had to endure, and also about whatever Brati had shared with her regarding his love for his mother. Nandini convinces Sujata about the true nature of their revolutionary ideals, and that they were far from being the misguided generation that people took them to be. She also breaks Sujata's misconception that things were calmer and better now, asserting that she had shunned the normative course of life (marriage, family, etc) to continue on her revolutionary path. What is interesting is that, in this scene Nandini assertively makes herself audible, in contrast to the scene of the secret Naxal meeting where she plays a very marginal role - her activities involve turning on the radio so that their words are not audible outside the room, and she mostly keeps quiet through the course of the meeting which is dominated by the voices of her male colleagues. But her subjectivity seems to have evolved and been completely revolutionized during the two years of pain and torture in prison. As she says herself, her mind and senses were sharpened and made more determined during her years in jail. Mallarika Sinha Roy, in her article 'Magic Moments of Struggle : Women's Memory of the Naxalbari Movement in West Bengal, India (1967-75)', states that, though the position of women directly involved in the Naxal movement was a peripheral one (as we certainly see in the case of Nandini before she goes to prison), the experiences of the women involved in the movement in whatever capacity were rendered more memorable as they got a platform 'where women shared certain grounds of self-identity as women as well as comrades-in-arms' (p.226) and also '... their particular context enriched their understanding and appreciation of each other rather than divide them during the struggle'(p.227). Sure enough, here too, Nandini and Sujata are confirmed as comrades-in-arms. The subjective transformation of Sujata is complete following the meeting, as is evident from the events that occur when she reaches home.

Back home, arrangements are well under way for her daughter's engagement party. For the first time in her life, she retaliates uninhibitedly to her husband's questioning regarding her whereabouts and the reason for her delay : 'I have always fulfilled my duties and obligations around the house. Why don't you do the same for a change? You and Neepa were there to oversee things? And, besides, how dare you ask me where I have been and why I am late? For the last thirty years, have I ever questioned you on why you return home late from work every evening? Have I for once asked you where you have been? Or why you happen to pay the house rent of that woman who works as a typist in your office? Just get out of this room right now! If you don't, I will get out of the house!' Stupefied by this outburst, her husband has no choice but to comply with her wishes. What follows is even more fantastic. After taking her bath, while she is dressing for the evening, she boldly eschews wearing *sindoor.* Sujata explains to her faithful maid servant, 'all my life, all that I have done is fulfill my responsibilities towards other people. I have kept the household in order and kept everybody happy. I have always ensured that everything is as it should be. But what have I got in return? Life has passed me by...I haven't been able to find myself. And, what's more, I have lost Brati forever.' Her refusal to apply the *sindoor* signifies her rejection of her patriarchal identity of 'wife' and 'mother' of the Chatterjee household. She is now her own person. During the party she is disturbed by the celebrations, music and dance. It's not just about all this occurring on Brati's death anniversary, but, also, the overarching notion of an entire generation of selfish, class-conscious, wealth-hungry, haughty people, blind and blissfully glib about the social inequities around them, that agues Sujata; it is a scene that would have been anathema to Brati, and is now anathema to Sujata, who has completed the departure from the repressive stranglehold of the symbolic and assumed the subversive openness of the semiotic, consequently seeing through the injustice and exploitation of a system that forces itself on our subjectivities. The bursting of Sujata's appendix, accompanied by her agonized scream and collapse, in the final scene of the party, presents a metaphor of the annihilation of Sujata's past life, and the spawning of a new revolutionary era, which is further bolstered by the following subliminal scene where she hallucinates that she has given birth to the revolutionary Brati all over again.

The film jumps forward by twenty-three years. Sujata is now retired from her service in the bank and is working for the Human Rights Documentation Center, where Brati's friend Neetu Paul comes to meet her. He is now a professor who is about to be sent to Patna on election duty. A terrible incident happens. Just outside Sujata's office, Neetu is shot and murdered by two goons possibly from an opposition political party. We are left speechless at the radical way in which Sujata apprehends one of the goons even as the other one manages to escape. Forgetting all her sophistication and reserve, she lunges at one of the goons and administers a vice-like grip on his leg, stopping him from getting away long enough for a crowd of people to gather around and overpower him. Sujata's transformation into a fearless revolutionary is indeed complete at this moment. That night, Sujata writes a kind of a posthumous letter to Brati (it seems like she has made a habit of writing these letters) where she tells her son about what transpired that day. Her conclusion is that she is no longer only Brati's mother, but his equal and comrade-in-arms in his nihilistic revolutionary ideals. It is only Brati's death that has made this possible. The death of one revolutionary has spawned another one. One subject-in-process has paved the way for another.

Goutam Ghose's film 'Kaalbela' provides another interesting study of a woman who becomes a subject-in-process against the backdrop of the Naxal revolution. The character concerned is Madhabilata, a young lady hailing from a cultured upper middle-class family of Kolkata, who becomes indirectly embroiled in the revolution through her romantic involvement with the young and impressionable Naxalite, Animesh Mitra, her classmate in the post-graduate Bengali course at Scottish Church College. Unlike Nandini in 'Hazaar Chaurasi ki Ma', Madhabilata is not an active Naxalite. Although she repeatedly tells Animesh that his political ideology is not her path, still, she seems to uncannily endorse it by encouraging and taking pride in his firm adherence to his ideology.

In a scene focusing on a romantic moment involving Animesh and Madahabilata on a boat ride on the Ganga, Madhabilata says to Animesh :

> I trust you Ani.
> Your political ideals are not mine…
> But I will not stand in your way.
> I love you a lot…
> Love has no ideology

Her initial non-concurrence with his political ideals is undebatable, considering the right-wing conservative ideological space she hails from (evident from her father's behaviour towards Animesh later in the film), that would make it quite sacrilegious for her to embrace Naxalism. However, it is her statement, 'Love has no ideology', that is problematic. Love is a fantasy of fulfillment that involves two subjects, and, by definition, a subject is always constituted by some ideological matrix. At a point in the film, Animesh's grandfather comments, 'No ideology is constant, but subject to changes'. That is precisely in keeping with the point about the subject-in-process that we have been trying to establish. If no ideology is constant, then those who are the subjects of those ideologies are bound to be in a state of flux also. But the fact remains that, at any given point in time, the subject always belongs somewhere, whether it be the field of the symbolic or the semiotic. And the interesting point is that, Madhabilata, through her romantic engagement with Animesh, also comes to love someone who is in the process of becoming a subject of the semiotic or the nihilistic existential ideology of Naxalism. In other words, she learns to silently love the ideological space (quite alien to her own) that Animesh comes to occupy. The question, then, is why.

What is interesting is that not only are the two lovers' familial origins discordant with one another, but the common ground of the Naxal revolution that unites them is also equally alien to their respective backgrounds. Animesh is a middle-class *moffusil* boy from North Bengal. His father is rather conservative, and views his plans to come to study in Scottish Church College in a politically volatile Kolkata with skepticism. The year that Animesh comes to Kolkata in is 1967 - a time when the political milieu of West Bengal is charged with radical left-wing.

Animesh's arrival at Kolkata is marked by a most inauspicious beginning as he is accidentally caught up in a crossfire and shot in the leg. The political crisis in West Bengal is at its peak, reflected through the hurling of bombs and the continual spate of agitations, processions and strikes. Animesh, too, inevitably undergoes an ideological induction into the fast emerging domain of left-wing student politics. During a

(BPSF) political meet, Animesh is called upon the dais, without any prior warning, to reveal the bullet wound on his leg, which serves as a convenient tool to provoke mass sentiments by claiming that 'the bullet has created a soldier for future battles'. From a balcony above, Madhabilata, not yet very well acquainted with Animesh, watches on in utter disdain and disapprobation of what is transpiring down below. Not realizing that Animesh's actions were forced on him, she castigates him, dismissing the act as a display of 'cheap sentiments'.

Prima facie, the worlds of Animesh and Madhabilata seem quite incapable of intersecting. We are presented with a scene where, in fact, there is a direct confrontation between Animesh and Madhabilata. Animesh encourages his batchmates to boycott classes and join a procession to visit the US Embassy to protest against the imperialist atrocities committed by America in Vietnam. Madhabilata angrily accosts Animesh, reminding him that they are there to study, and asks what would happen if they failed to pass their exams. She argues that Animesh and his political cohorts would be taken care of by the Party even if they failed to pass, but what would become of them. She further questions how boycotting classes in Kolkata could possibly impact what was happening in Vietnam, and, also, who had given Animesh the responsibility of protesting against all the violence in the world. Animesh is bewildered by what he feels to be the utter naïveté of Madhabilata's argument, and tries to drive home the relevance of international opinion. Shortly afterwards, once their rally has been dispersed by the police, Madhabilata and Animesh's dialogue on the same issue continues in the Coffee House. Madhabilata asks Animesh what exactly they were trying to achieve, and how the situation in the world outside could possibly change by burning trams and distressing people. She skeptically questions whether Animesh really considers himself a communist. Animesh speculates about his ideals about a classless, exploitation-free society. Madhabilata tries to bypass the matter by claiming that she is an ordinary human being and all these things are perhaps beyond her reach. Despite this, her growing interest in Animesh is quite obvious. This is reinforced by Animesh's question to

Madhabilata regarding why she chooses to hound him about these matters, and not other senior students better equipped to handle her questions. Nervously evading the question, she offers the excuse that he just happened to be within her reach and so she decided to catch hold of him and pose these questions. Why is she so interested in him, given that she repeatedly tells him that his political ideals are not hers?

In the initial stages, we are struck by the same political and ideological ignorance and naiveté in Madhabilata, which we noted in Sujata while Brati was still alive. Like Sujata, Madhabilata too is gradually drawn into the revolutionary realm of Naxalism through her growing attachment to another person more directly involved in that field. In a way, it is through the radical semiotic matrix of the Naxal revolution that both Animesh and Madhabilata find themselves and the true revolutionary potential of their beings.

We find Madhabilata gradually casting off of the shadow of the dependent and weak feminine figure defined by patriarchy, and beginning to assert her strength and independent identity. At times, she even takes the upper hand, showing herself to be the stronger between Animesh and herself. There is a refrain in Madhabilata's dialogues with Animesh that keeps recurring - 'Leave it to me'. In a scene in the Coffee House, where Animesh is embarrassed because he is not in a position to afford a snack, Madhabilata orders mutton afgani, toast and coffee for Animesh and sponsors the entire meal. Animesh starts to protest but is snubbed by Madhabilata. In another scene in another café, Animesh and Madhabilata are suddenly warned by the proprietor that a police spy is skirting the premises. Animesh is nonplussed into inaction, and Madhabilata promptly takes the reins, asking him to leave everything to her. She simulates a romantically intimate scene, where the spy, who has drawn the curtains of their cabin apart to take a sneak peek, is literally embarrassed away. We find a certain kind of bold, sexually assertive character beginning to emerge in Madhabilata's personality that is not entirely commensurate with her socio-cultural background. In yet another, more full-blown, love-making scene later in the film, once again we find Madhabilata taking the initiative. The episode transpires in one of their political sojourns in Shantiniketan with Subhashda. One afternoon, after lunch, Madhabilata suggests to Animesh that they rest for a bit. Animesh is shy to sleep in the same bed with her and prepares to sleep in a nearby couch. Madhabilata cajoles him into lying with her on the bed, and then, in her femininely alluring and quasi-diffident way, invites him to consummate their love. Pre-marital sex is somewhat unimaginable given the conservative family background to which she belongs. The fact of the matter is that, touched by the revolutionary consciousness of the Naxal rebellion with which she indirectly engages, she too has become a subject-in-process, breaking out of the suffocating familio-cultural realm of the name-of-the-father that has controlled her life so far.

The crowning moment of her revolutionary consciousness is perhaps defined by her display of strength of character in deciding to move out of her parents' house and live on her own terms, after the humiliating episode where her father insults Animesh. The high point of that episode is her father's curiosity regarding Animesh's awareness about what Madhabilata's 'market value' might be. Grooms earning a starting salary in the range of rupees one thousand five hundred to three thousand a month were all queued up to marry her (Animesh certainly doesn't belong to that category). He dismisses Animesh as 'a puny dwarf reaching out for the moon' and no better than a 'communist idiot'.

What is significant about this episode is that, more than being an insult to Animesh, it is an insult to Madhabilata's womanhood. In the asphyxiatingly patriarchal universe of Madhabilata's father, a woman's worth is only determined by the starting salaries of men who desire her. But, the anarchic, revolutionary, semiotic matrix, in which the lovers find themselves enmeshed, has now given each of them a new worldview. Madhabilata decides to assume an identity and a desire of her own. She walks out of her parents' house, relinquishing a life of luxury, moves into the college hostel, and takes up a job to support herself. In the scene that takes place in front of Job Charnock's tomb, Animesh confesses to Madhabilata his feeling of utter helplessness because of his inability to support her, and his complete financial dependence on his father. Madhabilata, as always, snubs him, asserting that he should leave everything to her. Animesh perplexedly wonders about what leads Madhabilata to take such rebellious decisions - is it her stubbornness or the depth of her love? Whatever it is, it happens to be a product of the ideological framework that defines her subjectivity. And the fact of the matter is, that she has passed over from the symbolic to the semiotic realm (very much in the manner of Sujata), and what drives her consciousness now is the fierce rebellion against the name-of-the-father. Her desiring potential is no longer governed by patriarchy. After Animesh is apprehended by the police, Madhabilata discovers that she is pregnant. Despite her friend Neela's advice to abort, she decides to go ahead and have the baby, being fully aware all the while of the social stigma that she would bring upon herself as an unmarried mother. In the scene, where she is humiliated and disrobed in front of Animesh at the police station, very much in the style of Draupadi, in an effort by the police to emotionally pressurize Animesh into disclosing the whereabouts of the Naxal leader Mahadeb Sen, Madhabilata, far from calling out to be rescued like Draupadi, incites Animesh not to say a single word no matter what they did to her.

Of course, the point of culmination of Madhabilata's assertion of her subjectivity comes at the end of the film. Freed from prison, a crippled Animesh is supported by Madhabilata all the way back to the scrawny little hovel where she has set up her home. It is, as Madhabilata tells Animesh, their 'new home'. Animesh is moved to see everything that Madhabilata has achieved on her own. She maintains a domestic establishment within that small shack, of course in keeping with her limited means, and has also single-handedly raised their sterling young son, who is now in school. Animesh tells Madhabilata that they had dreamt many dreams, most of which have collapsed. The Naxalite rebellion had failed, and their prominent leaders had died. But one dream had survived - that of the two lovers to be united. And Animesh rightly claims that Madhabilata had made it. The revolutionary dream of the Naxal revolution to subvert one order so as to give birth to a new one lives on in Madhabilata. It is not exactly a political victory (in any case, the existential ideology of Naxalitism is really anti-political), but rather a victory on the personal front, where Madhabilata has managed to completely annul the hold of the patriarchal symbolic, and assert herself as an autonomously desiring subject of the semiotic. Though not directly a Naxalite activist, the revolutionary spirit of the Naxal movement has breathed a new life into her being and helped her find herself.

References :

'Hazaar Chaurasi Ki Ma' (1998), dir. Govind Nihalani.

'Kaalbela' (2009), dir. Goutam Ghose.

McAfee, Noëlle (2004), *Julia Kristeva : Routledge Critical Thinkers,* Routledge : New York.

Mohanty, Manoranjan (1977), *Revolutionary Violence : A Study of the Maoist Movement in India,* Delhi : Sterling Publishers.

Ray, Rabindra (1988), *The Naxalites and their Ideology,* Delhi : Oxford University Press.

Roy, Mallarika Sinha (2009), 'Magic Moments of Struggle : Women's Memory of the Naxalbari Movement in West Bengal, India (1967-75)', *Indian Journal of Gender Studies,* Vol. 16, No. 2.

Sjöholm, Cecilia (2005), *Kristeva and the Political,* Routledge : New York.

The Other Side of Spectacle in 'Herbert' : Return of Naxalbari or the Haunting of an Inescapable Past?

Saikat Maitra & Samrat Sengupta

In a neoliberal political culture where life is infiltrated by power, where the subject becomes a mere effect of power - a desiring machine whose desire, however, is shaped by negotiations with structures of governance, how does the notion of revolution/resistance appear to us? Does it haunt us as an inalienable past or is it something we have gotten over? Resistances do still happen, as dystopic encounters of modernity. Indeed, the more universal and 'accommodating' the global order is becoming, the more violent and estranged resistance is becoming, although people living and enjoying the fruits of the universal world order fail to recognize the nature and purpose of such resistances and often think of them as aberrations to an otherwise normal life. This essay through a reading of the Bengali film 'Herbert', directed by Suman Mukhopadhyay and released in 2006, attempts to understand how and in what forms extremist resistances are still a part of our global millennia of perpetual peace, lying dormant within its fold and having the capacity of irrupting through the terror and excesses of violence.

The movie 'Herbert' revolves around two epochal periods. One, the rise of the radical leftist party C.P.I. (ML) in Bengal between 1967-75, marked by a belief in armed struggle and the annihilation of class enemies; the other, the present neo-liberal world order dominated by the logic of the market, where all moral considerations are subsumed under the demands of the market[1]. As we can infer, the first is a moment of ideological motivation and the dream of a radical break from the existing social order by means of violence. The second moment appears more rational on its surface, where individuals negotiate grids of power and try not to waste their energies in excess of revolution/resistance because "peace" is essential for the market to operate. "Perpetual peace", to quote a phrase from Kant becomes necessary not as a moral imperative but as a dictum of market rationality. This rationality enables individuals to act freely without hindering each other's growth and choices vis-à-vis the market guiding the operations of individual self-interests. 'Herbert' links up these two frames of historical reference and speaks of the complex and compelling ways in which the Naxalbari movement of the 1960s and early 70s continues to pervade ways of thinking about the category of the *political* in the quotidian life of Kolkata in the present moment of rapidly evolving neo-liberal economic and societal transformations.

The moment of Naxalite violence remains couched in a neo-liberal world of negotiation with difference, multiplicity and insecurity. In the summer of 2008, the vernacular media in Kolkata and especially the local cable news network channels were animated by images of a huge police contingent trying to arrest five women who had barricaded themselves in a one-room apartment in the Jadavpur-Garfa region of south Kolkata. The women, most of them university students in their early twenties, had apparently stockpiled posters, pamphlets, perhaps even weapons in order to start a violent anti-statist and Maoist uprising in the city, or so the rumor went. Indeed the role of rumor in the entire incident was of no little consequences, as the nervous system of the city went into an overdrive trying to speculate what possibly could be hidden in the apartment that had sparked the police raid. Once the standoff ended, the apartment in question was shown in detail to contain nothing but some torn posters containing mild and somewhat clichéd criticism of the economic policies of the West Bengal government. It was never revealed what might possibly have been the link between the group of women and the Ultra-leftist Maoist organizations that were seen to be on the verge of organizing a violent mass mobilization in the city. The consequences of the raid were however of lesser importance than the actual intensity of fear generated in the urban landscapes where several government spokesperson repeatedly warned the citizens of Kolkata about the impending crisis faced by the city from those who did not want the regime of development to continue but were keen to hark back to the violent days of the Naxalbari Movement.

One of the major anxieties that continue to haunt the apparent peace of this city is the coming back of what is seen as a moment of unmitigated horror, anarchy and series of killings by Naxalites, the various mainstream political parties and the state-machinery. In the introduction of a collection of essays on 1970's - the period of Naxalite movement in Kolkata - the editor Anil Acharya comments : " 'Don't bring back the 70's' is a slogan which is used nowadays regularly during elections."[2] The years 1968-1971 are repeatedly invoked to legitimize the police action in the present, for these years had been marked by an unprecedented level of violence in the city that had stalled all flow of capital into Kolkata, crippling its development and continuing its stereotypical representation as the underdeveloped city par excellence. Surely, just when the Government is coming up with promises of global finance and unfettered migration of capital to the city, the self-interests of the urban public would not reside in receding back to the days of 1968 or would it? If the perception and identification of threat is integral to the present form of bio-political governmentality[3] the maintenance of the backdrop of threat to contemporary Kolkata is legitimated by the constant invocation of the years of Naxalite movement, and what they stood for. This threat becomes the fundamental point of avoidance and exclusion on which present structure of neo-liberalism sustains and therefore, needs to be invoked ever so often with the purpose of negating it as the irrational and threatening *Other* of developmentalist discourses.

Furthermore, in contemporary Kolkata, as neo-liberal economic policies of the provincial government come increasingly under scrutiny and intense contestations, which often assume violent proportion between the state and those sections of the urban populations marginal to its economic interests, the years 1968-71 in general and the Maoist

Naxalbari Movement have also become an index to talk about resistance as well. Depending on which side of the political divide one is on, the Naxal movement, as it is known in the popular imaginary, may stand in for a regressive, reactionary phase of left-wing politics that had stymied the development of the state. In contradistinction, the image and the memory of the movement is also utilized to re-animate narratives of resistance that speaks out against the heightened forms of exploitation made possible in the city in the name of development and economic liberalization today. In either case what has happened is the incorporation of the memory of the Naxal movement within the ordinary life of the city. If the ordinary, as Kathleen Stewart[4] reminds us, is an assemblage of habits and practices that snap into place, the term Naxalbari facilitates the automatic, almost un-reflexive way of habitation in the city that constitutes the ordinary in contemporary Kolkata. The generative potential of the term allows a whole range of affective surges within the city, allowing for variegated ways of thinking and feeling the city, but always retaining the ability to experience the city as a shock, *to sense something in the city that properly feels like something.*[5]

However, the proximity between the events of the Naxalbari Movement of the late 1960s and the contemporary moment does not repose in linear contiguity or passive cultural memory that is transposed seamlessly across time. What we refer to as the contemporary really starts in the early 1990s, when the Indian state decided to adopt liberalization in order to revive a dormant economy, and the years in which the novel itself is based. 'Herbert', therefore, is conditioned by the manner in which the text creates, what we would call, a ruptured continuity, between the contemporary present of global capital and an earlier moment that, in and through the logic of the text, gets identified with the Naxalbari phase.

Who then is Herbert ?

Herbert is born in a phase of transition after Second World War, when a new idea of autonomy based on citizenship and nationhood is taking shape in India. This notion of citizenship is allied with western liberal democracy. Playing with the two notions of 'subject' as 'subject to' and 'subject of,' Balibar[6] shows how attaining subjectivity is intricately related to subjugation to an absolute sovereign power, so that the formation of a subject even under the most well entrenched tenets of democracy paradoxically constitutes a breach of the same democratic principles. We will see how 'Herbert', in its depiction of Naxalite movement and in its representation of state sponsored violence that emerges from behind the apparent peacemaking endeavors of modern democracy, illuminates the presence of the absolute sovereign. This logic of the sovereign hides itself behind a particular facade of political rationality that can deal with contradictions only by either complete incorporation within its folds or by annihilating its traces by brute force if necessary. When Binu, Herbert's Naxalite nephew gets shot by the police late at night and is taken to the hospital to be assured by a government agent that if he gives up his activism and assists the police then the government would help him, his legs are still in chains. This shows the fallacy of democratic liberalism that can assure security only after the subject has been subjugated to its power by submitting to a particular political rationale. Later when the Rationalists arrive to blast Herbert's claim to mysterious power of talking with dead spirits it apparently seems they are secular and liberal activists against obscurantist mysticism, but this actually shows another facet of an intolerant state mechanism rallying against that which it cannot explain or accommodate by its rationality. A particular form of rationality then becomes the godhead. Any threats to the body of this sovereign can be logically terminated - a point that is illustrated in the film poignantly through the state sponsored murder of Binu, and Herbert's forced suicide to escape humiliation by the Rationalists.

Herbert is born in an independent nation as a free subject. Just after his first birthday, his father passes away. His father Lalitkumar belongs to the colonially educated nouveau riche middle class who profits enormously from the uncertainties of the market during the Second World War. The money that he amasses by selling scrap iron during the war, is used mostly to take on the mores and manners of a highly anglicized middle-classness. Lalitkumar's business of film production is partly to acquire a greater cultural capital as a patron of arts and partly to facilitate his extra-marital affairs with Miss Ruby, an actress he promotes and casts in his film.

After death, Lalitkumar and his wife continue to haunt, symbolizing the lingering traces of the colonial past. It is, as if the life of the new-born Indian democracy is haunted by the maladies of its colonial past, the effects of which are not acknowledged though it always remains inside. We also see how Lalitkumar and his wife observe and capture every moment of Herbert's life. The dead father's camera appears always present yet passive instrument, which captures Herbert repeatedly. The constant presence of the camera in the film suggests that the subject is always and already framed, as is Herbert by his circumstances and realm of ideas and association in which he is brought up. Herbert is that living dead - dead living - the dangerous dead human bomb which disturbs our everyday peace with warnings that what we see as independent and autonomous are not simply so. The subject acts through his cathexis - asserts his autonomy through his existential beingness. If it is imperative to be subjected to dominant power structure in order to gain subjectivity then Herbert is the subjectless subject. He declares the impossibility of the finality and wholeness of the project of subjectification.

Even his English name is a marker of impossibility - a reminiscence of shadows of colonialism. One of his father's friends on his first birthday half jokingly comments that his name reminds one of Herbert Spencer. Herbert's name in this film is a caricature of developmental normativity of life, which the sociologist Herbert Spencer, the champion of Darwinian notion of struggle for existence, had proposed.

Herbert, however, refuses to pursue this developmental programme. This refusal needs to be understood in the context of the Naxalites' principle to fight out the maladies of colonialism, its education and ideologies which formed the mind-set of the educated Indian middle classes. They called Indian democracy 'semi-colonial, semi-feudal'. Herbert's avoidance of study, his purposeless loitering in the attic, his secret collection of pornography, his eventual taking up of communicating with the dead, all point towards a refusal of colonial structures of reasoning which regularized school going, salaried job, encouraged one's control over his body and mind giving a purpose to life etc. Much of the Naxalite discourse was also against a certain opportunistic purposefulness. The activist youth who came from the middle classes very often believed in self-less sacrifice and becoming declassed by sharing life with agricultural and industrial laborers - stepping into other people's shoes for a radical transformation of this world of bourgeois opportunism.

Herbert's fractured gibberish in English, his rage against English education that treats all types of miracles and mysticism as false is an effacement of his identity which is given from above by his parents - by his postcolonial bourgeois legacy. He is that element of uncertainty which modern bio-power attempts to control by programming human behavior for future sustenance and survival of the species-being. He performs the lack on which the modern bio-political regime is founded. With similar interest, he reads Marxist revolutionary literature and books on spirits and the afterlife. Herbert in the film stands for repetition of the negations, not that of positions. First he repeats the negation of the colonial past which constituted the postcolonial nationalist English educated bourgeois structures of reasoning and then he repeats the negation of Naxalite ideological armed violence which constituted modern neo-liberal logic of secured survival and avoidance of violence. Herbert speaks to the dead. He makes money by fulfilling desires of those who want to know the afterlife of their dead near and dear ones. The desire for overcoming death is connected to instincts for adherence to ideas/ideals that would assure a sense of continuity in the face of death. Death then is the forgotten and excluded other of the ideologies, which however is its very foundation. Death represents that abyss of meaninglessness excluding which ideologies are grounded - it is the mark of undecidability on which decidable social and political meaningfulness is grounded. Herbert engages with death in his youth when he discovered a skull from a locked store room and it was suggested that one of his predecessors was a *Tantric,* a man who possesses mysterious powers by practicing a supernatural cult of spirits. Then when his friend commits suicide after humiliation in love he dreams of being surrounded by skulls. Love, like religious and political sentiments, is also adherence to ideas to avoid death and therefore grounded upon death. However, in our political culture the primordial void of death is avoided by an act of meaning making. Revolutions need to have a goal in real life to turn down order which is temporary to bring about a continuous never ending future of finality. Often ideas of changes are directed towards a permanent changelessness forgetting that the only form of finality and changelessness is death. Ideas are embodied and thought of as immortal and this happens at the cost of forgetting the political and individual bodies through which they come into being - bodies which are contingent and mortal. Bodies move and change but leave their traces on ideas and as ideas undergo change travelling from one place and time to another they carry the traces of earlier bodies. Herbert's talking with the ghosts is an ironic commentary on how traces continue to haunt even after the apparent political death of an ideology.

No longer a person of little self-worth, Herbert, whose very out-dated Westernized name implies an excessive, not necessarily useful quality, assumes a definitive value tangible in terms of the exchange of money that each of his interactions with the dead bring him. From the novel of the same name written by Nabarun Bhattacharya, on which the film 'Herbert' is based, we learn that much of Herbert's financial transactions with the living via the medium of the dead take place during 1991- 1992, and therefore his narrative assumes a particular cogency. This is the time when India goes global through a set of economic reforms. Words like neo-liberalism, globalization, market; stock-exchange get inserted within the everyday rhetoric of an increasingly consolidating middle-class. "A year went by. 1992 brought along an abundance of scandals, cases of pilfering, and wickedness" and again "In Mumbai, a man by the name of Harshad Mehta was waiting for a telephone call from Delhi to sanction his plans".[7] The Harshad

Mehta scandal and the consequent irregular movements in the Mumbai stock-market become in *Herbert* a symptom, a tangential sign of the disruptions brought on by the influx of global capital and India's own troubled mergence into the circuit of a New World Order of finance after decades of closed economy. In short, this is a world haunted by myriad apparitions amongst which Herbert's 'conversations with the dead' constitute a tiny site of traffic. Unlike Harshad Mehta's skill in conjuring vast, astronomical but ultimately spectral profits for the general investing public, Herbert must content himself with 100-rupee notes pressed into his hands by sometimes-satisfied clients. Not bad still for a man who until recently had been so bereft of dignity that he could be thrashed by his cousins on the slightest pretext. In another way, Herbert's world is spectral. A sense of it can be gleaned through the constantly flickering television sets that animate a force-field of visual desires with the advent of cable television and the mushrooming of cable dish antennae sets on roof-tops. The image of the fall of the pigeon net and erection of dish antennae in its place in the film seems violently surreal. Indeed, Herbert's one place of solace and retreat, which is the roof-top, is invaded by the whirring images and electro-magnetic currents of the dish antennas. A way of life dies and is replaced by a new pattern so quickly that the former is almost forgotten. 'Herbert' does present a cluster of events and happenings that agglomerate and crystallize at particular junctures of time. What is present are 'structures of feeling', which as Raymond Williams suggests "can be defined as social experiences in *solution,* as distinct from other social semantic formations which have been *precipitated* and are more evidently and more immediately available".[8] The provocation of art for Williams lies in the degree to which art manages to tease out the emergent, whose characteristics remain dissolved within the residual and hence cannot be fully and clearly identified.

Interesting to note here, the entire narrative of the film is charged with a certain element of cyclicality - a coming back of events. The two aspects of this cyclicality are on one hand, a coming back of events with new meaning-as occurs in detective fictions-and on the other hand, a jarring effect when events do come back to us - when we know the absurdity and irony of the previous meaning. The second aspect is nonetheless connected with the first but it breaks our illusion of moving towards positive connections like a detective narrative and instead suggests a movement from meaningful towards the absurd. The opening scene on which title cards flow shows a board of balloons to be blasted by air gun bullets fired for practicing aim. At the end of the film we learn that this same board was used by the eponymous hero Herbert to advertise his supernatural feat of conversing with the dead and reporting their affairs in the afterlife to relatives and friends. On the same board where multicolored balloons hang for people to aim and play was once scripted the words : 'Dialogues with the Dead, Proprietor : Herbert Sarkar'. When threatened by members of the West Bengal Rationalist Society to stop his hoax of claiming that he could communicate with the dead, Herbert cries in uncontrollable rage : "If talking in English could only stop the brawl...then there would be no problems. White people screwed us day and night...they couldn't stop it. White people left, these people came. So many doctors and lawyers were convinced...yet these bastards think it's a big fraud." The irony of these sentences is unfathomable when read in the light of the entire narrative of the movie. The movie is not simply about communicating with ghosts - it is also about communicating with one's own past. In the period of a neo-liberal economy, the movie puts forth the question of ideology and its assumed absurdity with respect to this economy. With sudden eruptions of violence in our otherwise peaceful city we realize that still some people raise arms for a cause they believe. The usual way of understanding them by existing power mongers is to mark them as primitives, as inassimilable elements of a past, which cannot negotiate with this existing and emergent world order. They are either attempted to be accommodated in these global structures of reasoning or eliminated in a spree of cleansing. Faith, belief, adherence to unbending moral ideas - all these are stroked out of the sphere of the political. Politics after World Wars becomes an exercise to maintain peace, to maintain a certain order, which would maintain the flow of capital.

The Naxalite uprising embodied by Binu or an isolated individual like Herbert who claims to possess a capacity for supernatural communications - constitute threats to the governmental rationality that must be terminated. Binu, the youngest cousin of Herbert came to Kolkata to study Geology. Motivated by Naxalite ideology, Binu decided to immerse himself fully in the armed struggle following the release of an impassioned pamphlet by the legendary Naxalite leader and intellectual Charu Majumder. One night, while stenciling a picture of Mao on a city wall, Binu is shot by the opposite party. While chained to a hospital bed and suffering from a punctured lung, he confides a secret to Herbert, rather incoherently : "Herbert Uncle, the worship room...behind Kali's picture... diary...diary". The police search the house but to no avail. They do not find the diary. We can talk about the irony of a Maoist revolutionary hiding his diary behind the framed painting of the Goddess in the traditional Hindu prayer room. The visions of the emergent and new, are housed in the most traditional of Hindu upper caste architectural space. This again suggestively connects the religious and the ideological. Naxalites thought what they were doing was rational and spoke against religion as a misguiding false consciousness. However, they remained oblivious to deep structures of the human mind - how ideas go through hypostases and are embodied by the self which then acts as a dynamo. Likewise, we shall see how the armed struggle of the middle class Naxalite youth for the cause of proletarian revolution, though thought as a past phase of the history of Bengal, remains hidden as a structural imperative of present day politics in West Bengal. Within political slogans of not bringing back the seventies, lies dormant its possibility of eruption. In an autobiographical essay, Nabarun Bhattacharya writes : "yet still I feel somewhere seventies is still there".[9] Binu dies and the secret of the diary fades away till one day it is resurrected through a dream that Herbert recognizes as a vision from the world of the dead. Memory is not fully elided therefore but assumes a complex form. What also starts in the wake of the successful discovery of the hidden diary is Herbert's own commerce with the dead, till he is visited by the members of the West

Bengal Rationalistic Society, bent on exposing as a deception and fraud all acts connected with the 'supernatural'. Their visit leaves Herbert a shattered wreck of an individual. The fear that they induce in him is not merely a result of the possibility of being unmasked as a fraud or the humiliation that might follow as a consequence, there is something much more intense and deeply ingrained than that.

Let us focus on one particular moment of exchange between Herbert and the rationalists. Herbert says : "You don't know a thing. Aren't you ashamed to come and create trouble?" One of the rationalists say in response "Cops will drag you away...handcuffed". "I did not lie...Never harmed anyone... There are ghosts...there will always be Ghosts. I saw Binu in my dreams. The police shot Binu dead!" Herbert began to scream and cry loudly. In the face of the threat of the police Herbert's only form of defense is the affirmation to a lie that has now become an essential truth for him. The deception becomes much more acute; the ghosts become a value system, a possibility of alterity that provides the only valid realm of experience for a marginal figure like Herbert in the city. Ultimately the lines of flight created through the artifice of Herbert's performativity are captured through a rationalist mechanism of statist power. We use the term statist consciously, for how else do we conceive of the Rationalist Society if not in terms of an active bourgeois civil society functioning in the best interests of the state. The fear of the police that they bring to bear on Herbert is not an accidental one. The police, the state, and the rationalists all become part of a continuous series and mechanism of power that entraps Herbert as indeed it had once entrapped Binu.

We live in the era of security linked to bio-power, where the logic of development is inextricably bound to its ability to identify threats which can curb its growth. Threats never really disappear but are reactivated and given newer meanings in the corpus of security, as is happening presently with a reactivation of the Naxalite fear of disorder and violence. Brian Massumi sees the logic of late modern capital as inextricably linked to a constant articulation of everyday precariousness and threat to sustain consumption.[10] One might draw on this and suggest that not only capitalism, but the very art of governance, of governmentality, depend on how well the level of threat can be maintained in order to have the apparatus of security working. Herbert commits suicide, principally in order to avoid being arrested and is taken to the crematorium where it is decided that his body would enter the furnace, along with his bedding and mattress. Shortly after this is done, the sound of a massive explosion is followed by the disintegration of the furnace walls leaving the entire crematorium in darkness. The cyclical repetitive structure of the film suggests a repetitive nature of violence lying dormant within the facade of an apparent peace. At the end of the film, after we see that police have failed to detect the cause of the explosion, we learn that the mattress had contained dynamite that Binu and his Naxalite friends had stuffed in to avoid detection decades before. We do not really know for what purpose the sticks of dynamite had been stored - perhaps to create a general anarchical uprising in the city, perhaps for something else altogether, but the instant of their explosion is resonant with latent energies. The explosion marks what we would call a *scandal* of translation between an over-determined past event and its continued resonance in the contemporary. The materiality of life itself in the city, like the innocuous mattress with its deadly sticks of dynamite becomes historical traces for thinking resistance, for formulating agency that scars the smooth texture of the linear historical terrain of capitalist development. At a contemporary juncture when resistance is increasingly becoming impossible as an ideological project - when every aspect of life and political existence seems to have become enmeshed in terms of grids of discourses through which power operates - the possibility of explosion lies hidden inside the commonplace, inside apparently harmless passive victims of power like Herbert.

Throughout the film, however, each moment of Herbert's life doesn't influence him in a positivist, linear, logic of progression but in terms of gaps and fissures, losses and isolations that create his subjectivity. His birth and death are connected intricately in a logic of becoming which however acts through a constant denial of being instead of asserting and positing it - it is a hauntological connection and not an ontological one.

'Herbert' compels us to rethink our political subjectivity as a negative outside produced by existential political and social conditions rather than asserting subjectivity simply as an effect of those conditions or even as the cause of them. Both Herbert and Binu offered resistance against the legacy of colonial structures of reasoning but Herbert's resistance exposes the existential nature of it more than Binu whose Naxalite teleology of a classless society seems forgetful of the fact that resistances are implicit to any hegemonic power structure and not only a conscious act of the subject. It moves beyond the intentionality of the subject. We see in the film how euphoria about the radical Marxist movement spread from Binu's father to Binu and Herbert, who initially enjoyed the mere excitement of it with child-like curiosity, uttering slogans like "Lenin! Stalin! Mao! Ho! Red Salute! " This euphoria however is not simply a romantic utopia, but is foregrounded in more sinister circumstances of post-independence nihilism, corruption, poverty and crises. However such existential compulsions have to be thought beyond teleology. Just after Binu makes fun of Herbert's faith in ghosts and spirits we see him venting out his faith about a classless future society. He believes it with a rigour similar to Herbert's faith in ghosts. However, he believes that he is rational and Herbert is not. He forgets that even rationality is existentially determined by one's own political and personal history that is full of gaps and fissures. Herbert mocks not only postcolonial democratic rationality but also the Naxalite structure of teleological reasoning. He turns into a human bomb after his death even without knowing - his protest is unintentional. He explodes without intention to show how explosions are imperative to any structure which thinks itself to be absolutely rational and conscious about its future. His explosion was rooted to the background of the Naxalbari movement though not determined by it. He therefore forces us to rethink the significance of such a resistance in our culture of apparent political peace and perfect balance. The movie 'Herbert' renders unavoidable thinking of the Naxalite movement in our times.

Notes and References :

1. Partha Chatterjee in "The World after the Great Peace" in *The Politics of the Governed* (Delhi : Permanent Black, 2004) writes : "Some of us believed in our callow youth that the decade of the 1970s would be the decade of liberation. It now appears that even American Banks had the same dream. For the time being at least, the bankers' dream has turned out to be true. If you have an American.

   Express credit card in your pocket, you would feel sufficiently liberated to shop to your heart's content in any country of the world." (83).

2. Anil Acharya, "Bhumika" ("Introduction") in *Sottor Dashak* (Kolkata : Anustup, 2010), xi.
3. Michel Foucault. *The Birth of Biopolitics : Lectures at the Collège de France, 1978-1979.* Ed. Michel Senellart. Trans. Graham Burchell. New York : Picador, 2010.
4. Kathleen Stewart. *Ordinary Affects.* Durham, NC : Duke University Press, 2007.
5. Kathleen Stewart. *Ordinary Affects.* Durham, NC : Duke University Press, 2007.
6. Etienne Balibar, 'Citizen Subject' in *Who Comes After the Subject* edited by Eduardo Cadava, Peter Connor and Jean-Luc Nancy (New York : Routledge, 1991), 33-57.
7. Nabarun Bhattacharya. *Herbert.* Trans. Jyoti Panjwani. New Delhi : Sahitya Akademi, 2004.
8. Raymond Williams. *Marxism and Literature.* Oxford : Oxford University Press, 1977.
9. Nabarun Bhattacharya, 'Petrol Diye Agun Nevanor Swapno' ('The Dream of Putting Down Fire With Petrol') in *Shei Dashak (That Decade)* edited by Pulakesh Mondal and Jaya Mitra (Kolkata : Papyrus, 1994), 82.
10. Brian Massumi. "Everywhere You Want to be : Introduction to Fear". *The Politics of Everyday Fear.* Ed. Brian Massumi. Minneapolis : University of Minnesota Press, 1993.

Naxalism in Cinema : The Absent Community

M. K. Raghavendra

Background :

Naxalism as a phenomenon developed and spread in India in the 1970s and may be roughly equated with Marxist or Maoist inspired violent radicalism - whether agrarian or urban. The figure of the Naxalite did not exactly proliferate in Indian cinema either in the 1970s or later but Naxalism has been a romantic notion for film-makers outside the mainstream, especially those with radical sympathies. Consequently, there are a number of films made when Naxalism was a current issue in which either a Naxalite features or the film is implicitly sympathetic to political violence. Since the Naxalite is the closest that India has to the political revolutionary, whatever understanding is reached here about his or her representation could have some significance for our grasp of political cinema in India, its successes and failures.

The kind of political cinema produced will evidently depend on the milieu that produces it and, by and large, I propose that the milieus may be classified as under : a) a country after a revolution as in the former USSR and Cuba, b) a liberal-democratic milieu in which dissent is tolerated as in western Europe and countries like India and Japan c) countries under repressive regimes in which political film-makers often work clandestinely as in Latin America. These categories have been denoted on the assumption that film-making is within the milieu being depicted. This qualification is necessitated by film-makers like Costa Gavras, who have been 'international', making films on political issues in different parts of the world - e.g.: Czechoslovakia in 'The Confession'

(1970), Uruguay in 'State of Siege' (1972) and Chile in 'Missing' (1982). Another film-maker to have gone 'international' is the Italian Gillo Pontecorvo who made 'The Battle of Algiers' (1966) which was commissioned by the Algerian government. Pontecorvo also directed the Frantz Fanon inspired 'Queimada!' (1969) which is about a nineteenth century slave uprising on a sugar producing Caribbean island. Since this is an examination of how revolutionaries or revolutionary action tends to be represented in Indian cinema, it may be useful to compare films made in India with those from the other liberal democracies where radical criticism - even if it is not encouraged - is not punished as it is under repressive regimes. Before we look at some Indian films which include the motif of Naxalism or may be taken to be sympathetic to its cause, I propose to begin by examining three films from other democratic milieus which are about Marxist or Maoist activists and violent radicalism.

Violent Radicalism : Godard, Fassbinder and Ôshima :

The first film to be examined is Jean-Luc Godard's 'La Chinoise' (1967) which may roughly be taken as being located at the point at which Godard took a decisive step towards becoming political. There have been many artists who became political in the course of their careers - Badal Sircar is an example - but Godard's case is different in as much as he appears poised in the act of making a political choice. In films like 'La Chinoise' (and the earlier 'Le Petit Soldat' - 1963) he seems to be aware that the forces of the right and the left are not very different in their methods but still throws his lot with the latter. 'La Chinoise', set in contemporary Paris, takes place in a small apartment and is structured as a series of personal and ideological dialogues between five French university students - three young men and two young women - belonging to a radical Maoist cell. The heroine Veronique, an advocate for violent revolution, meets philosopher Francis Jeanson on a train to Paris. They get into an argument during which Veronique supports blowing up the universities. "And then, what?" asks Jeanson and Veronique has no answer.[1] But Godard suggests that the lack of an answer to this question justifies and actually confirms Jeanson in his inaction. Veronique later volunteers to carry out a political assassination and bungles it, killing two people instead of one. Still, at the end of 'La Chinoise', Godard appears to be supporting Veronique because, he seems to be asserting, even mistaken action is better than no action. But important from our perspective is the fact that 'La Chinoise' revolves around a community of radicals who are engaged in revolutionary action with the participants in the group constantly working out between themselves the steps they need to take in order to be effective politically.

The second film to be examined in this context is Rainer Werner Fassbinder's 'The Third Generation' (1979), a film about a bungling terrorist group, which was made two years after the death of the leaders of the Baader-Meinhof group, who had been widely regarded with sympathy in Germany. This film bears some resemblance to Godard's 'La Chinoise' (1968) in that it is about a terrorist group that botches an assassination attempt. But while Godard's viewpoint is that even misguided action is better than no action, Fassbinder's film is more ambivalent. The 'Third Generation' has a number of characters; apart from the members of the group there is the businessman Lurz who regrets early in the film that he has not been selling computers to the security services - because there have been few terrorist attacks. The film proceeds on the basis of Lurz's formulation that 'terrorism is a creation of capitalism, intended to force the state to take extreme measures to protect itself.' Not aware that their group is funded by Lurz, the film concludes with the group kidnapping him and making a video of the businessman announcing the radical purpose behind his abduction.

The plot of the film has all the makings of satire but Fassbinder takes the film to another level through his portrayal of the group. The members of the group are as assorted a bunch as one might imagine, each one with his/ her own preoccupations with only a general notion of the subversive ends they hope to attain. There is a huge amount of 'noise' in the film in as much as persons are talking at cross-purposes and reciting literature at each other. The television is always playing and people are perpetually moving in and out of the space of the action. My own sense is that Fassbinder chooses a terrorist group as his subject because, living with danger and death, such a group should be united by a single powerful objective. We would expect such a group to exemplify individuals driven by purpose. When Fassbinder shows such a group run on the lines of a standard non-government organization he is calling into question the notion of 'purpose' - can like-minded radicals undermine the structure of the state without being perpetually distracted as individuals? Fassbinder's film deals with a community of radicals as does 'La Chinoise' but where 'La Chinoise' is optimistic, The 'Third Generation' is deeply skeptical about the ends of violent radicalism. The key difference perhaps arises out of Godard's protagonists being 'innocent' in some sense and it is one of the conventions of political cinema that only an innocent life can be politicized. Fassbinder came from a milieu in which the classes that should rightly have been 'revolutionary' had collaborated with the monstrous politics of Nazism. He may therefore have found 'innocence' an elusive quality to detect and could, perhaps, not be hopeful about the intrinsic value of politicization.

The third film to be examined is Nagisa Ôshima's 'Night and Fog in Japan' (1960) which is different - a personal political statement on the condition of the organized left in Japan. Nagisa Ôshima is the most important director of the Japanese 'New Wave', the directors who rose to prominence in the late 1950s and early 1960s, the generation after Akira Kurosawa's and one which took an adversarial position vis-à-vis traditionalists like Kenji Mizoguchi and Yasujiro Ozu. The films of the 'New Wave' have perhaps a counterpart in New German Cinema because both came out of military defeat - although one senses no 'post-war guilt' in Japanese cinema. The story of the film is revealed in several flashbacks which are motivated by a central wedding ceremony in which two former Communists Nozawa and Reiko are brought together. An intruder at the wedding is a former comrade who assails all those present for abandoning their ideals. In flashbacks, personal and political wounds are reopened and focused on are Nozawa's subjective experiences in both 1950 and 1960. The memory of a young student who committed suicide is reconstructed as a criticism of the authoritarian leadership of the Communists in 1950 which ruined the movement. A former student leader who is now a Communist functionary, is especially taken to task for his doings. While one also does not get a sense of political issues except in local terms in 'Night and Fog in Japan' and an ignorance of post-war Japanese politics can leave one handicapped, there is the general sense to be gained from the film of the Communists forming a community perpetually trying to find its way politically and constituted by different kinds of individuals. The difference in Ôshima's film is that while the films by Godard and Fassbinder deal with terror and subversion, 'Night and Fog in Japan' deals with a Communist party which was in national politics.

The three films just examined are hardly alike because they take different positions vis-à-vis political action. If Godard is optimistic but clear-eyed, Ôshima's film is about political disillusionment and Fassbinder is preoccupied with how political subversion can itself be subverted by capitalism. But the films have one aspect in common which is that they see a community - however fragile it may be and with all its rivalries and bickering - as a necessary first step in radical action. It will now be interesting to look at a handful of Indian films dealing with Naxalism - India's counterpart to the movements described in the films - to compare the representations.

Representations of Naxalism :

Indian films of the 1970s and 1980s in which Naxalism is invoked - overtly or covertly - fall broadly into three groups. The first group may be represented by Mrinal Sen's three Calcutta films of the period : 'Interview' (1970), 'Calcutta 71' (1972) and 'Padatik' (1973) and the second by two films of Satyajit Ray's Calcutta trilogy - 'Pratidwandi' (1970) and 'Seemabaddha' (1971). The third group is represented by some key films by Shyam Benegal and Govind Nihalani - Benegal's 'Ankur' (1974) and 'Nishant' (1975) and Nihalani's 'Aakrosh' (1981) and 'Party' (1984). While there have been other films by directors like

Buddhadeb Dasgupta - 'Dooratwa' (1978), 'Grihayuddha' (1982) - and Sudhir Mişhra - 'Hazaaron Kwaishen Aisi' (2005) - which invoke Naxalism, I will restrict my attention to the three groups indicated above since the latter films roughly bear out the same observations.

Mrinal Sen's films of the early 1970s perhaps represent the most strident endorsement of militant radicalism in the period and 'Calcutta 71' is perhaps the most important of the three films. 'Calcutta 71' brings together three stories said to pertain to 1933, 1943 and 1953 but relevant to our purpose is only the contemporary fourth story that 'contextualises' the others. We see the Maidan at dawn, a young woman treads softly on the grass in the early morning air presumably waiting for her young man, we hear gunshots disturbing the quiet and a brief voice on the radio announces the death of a twenty-year-old boy in an 'encounter'. The three other stories that 'Calcutta 71' tells separately do not pertain to the present and the director is evidently using the device just described to locate them historically and make them relevant to the immediate period.

Sen's telling of the three stories is faithful to the tenets of realism but the devices that he employs to frame and link these stories are either frankly didactic or satirical. Between the individual episodes he has a boy - a mere head against a dark backdrop - acting as a chorus. The boy declares that he is only twenty years old, but that for thousands of years he has been witness to poverty, misery and death and that he has also seen deception and exploitation. Sen concludes 'Calcutta 71' with a contemporary piece set at a party involving the city's bourgeoisie. A public servant is being entertained by an upper-class host who keeps pictures of starving people in his living room - as a gesture towards the famine of 1943. Drunken revellers express 'solidarity' with the poor as pulsating lights illuminate a noisy musical band. At the end of this episode we see the boy, who has been performing the task of the 'chorus,' standing up - now evidently bleeding from a gunshot wound. This connects with the earlier episode where the death of the boy in an encounter was announced. We then see brief segments from the earlier stories to establish the connection with the present. We also see documentary footage of the police firing; we see the boy being shot down once again and killed on the Maidan. We then, expectedly, hear the voice on the radio announcing the boy's death.

Mrinal Sen leaves us in no doubt as to where his political sympathies lie but I find it pertinent that the only image of Naxalism that he provides pertains to a young man who is already dead, although still resolutely standing up and addressing the audience. Of course, 'Calcutta 71' uses the motif of Naxalism only to address political issues that are not immediate but there is no representation of *Naxalism as a viable proposition* even in the other two films. In 'Padatik', which is about a Naxalite youth seeking refuge, the protagonist is on the run and the film revolves around the relationship between him and the upper-class woman who shelters him. One might propose that, taken together, Naxalism in Mrinal Sen's three Calcutta films is represented as a lost - if still morally attractive - cause and this is singular considering that when the films were made, Naxalism was not yet completely spent as a political force.

Satyajit Ray's two films also show sympathy for the figure of the Naxalite although he proceeds very differently from Mrinal Sen. Unlike Mrinal Sen who uses a number of devices to drive home a political message, Ray's is a more openly middle-class approach. Ray deals with a class he is familiar with and he restricts his view to the experience of the class. Since Ray has apparently no intimate experience of Naxalism or Naxalites, he declines to put into his films the kind of rhetoric that Mrinal Sen uses freely. Where Mrinal Sen's viewpoint is that the ruling class is so abhorrent that militant radicalism is even morally correct, Ray's is apparently that decent and liberal-minded persons of his class will be naturally sympathetic to Naxalism.

The first film in Ray's Calcutta trilogy 'Pratidwandi' is about an unemployed young man named Siddhartha in contemporary Calcutta, his attempts to find employment, those he meets and his efforts at connecting with members of his family. Siddhartha has a younger brother named Tunu who is single-mindedly committed to political causes and with whom Siddhartha cannot communicate. Although

Siddhartha is alienated from Tunu, he shows his own political inclinations in the key interview scene in which he is asked what he regards as the most important event of recent decades and he cites the Vietnam war - the resistance of the Vietnamese to America rather than the landing on the moon, which is what his interviewers would like to hear.

One senses from 'Pratidwandi' that Ray's position is somewhat like Siddhartha's - that while he is sympathetic to the Naxalite cause, he still finds himself far from it. If this is his emphasis, 'Seemabaddha' has a slightly different one because its protagonist Shyamal is a former radical who has now become a successful company executive. The moral centre of 'Seemabaddha' is his sister-in-law Tutul, who admired what he once was and who still looks up to people capable of selfless radicalism. She sees Shyamal display his penchant for parties, clubs and beauty parlours. At the climax of the film Shyamal's life is thrown into crisis when he is forced to engineer a union strike as a result of which people are killed. It is obvious that the once idealistic Shyamal has sunk morally and Tutul watches it all. In this film and 'Jana Aranya' (1976), in which the middle-class hero pimps in order to become successful at business, Ray's position has apparently become more inimical to his own class and we take it as a leftward public journey of sorts but at no point is Ray affirmative about radical action. Whatever positive counterpoints are offered, they are innocuously on the periphery.

Ray and Mrinal Sen were perceived to be at political loggerheads in the 1970s but they are alike in their sense of Naxalism : they view it as morally attractive but neither has much faith in its viability. The films by Godard, Fassbinder and Ôshima discussed earlier take different moral positions vis-à-vis violent political action - with Godard and Fassbinder representing the polar opposites of optimism and deep scepticism - but all three filmmakers see political radicalism as having the propensity to create a viable (but perhaps not harmonious) community around it. This is in contrast to Satyajit Ray who views Naxalism as a state of political consciousness - a private one - and not as something around which an alternative community can be fruitfully imagined and constructed. Where even people given to religion or trade unionism can see belief or class solidarity as a basis for erecting communities, sympathy for violent radicalism does not seem to have a similar effect. Judging from the films Naxalites either die[2] or fade away alone.

The third group of films came from a different kind of milieu from the other two in as much as it did not have to deal with Naxalism on a day to day basis. Since the country had generally become politicized in the 1970s, the films draw upon the ethos to deal with political violence in a more abstract way. Shyam Benegal, who made the first of these films 'Ankur' (1974) came from the advertising industry - as unlikely a source for radical film-making as any - and this will give the reader a sense of how politicized the middle-class had then become. These films are really an extension of the middle-class cinema of directors like Hrishikesh Mukherjee who had made 'Namak Haraam' (1973), which is set in a trade union milieu. 'Ankur' is set in Andhra and is about a cowardly landowner named Surya who seduces his dalit servant Lakshmi. Lakshmi's husband Kishtaiah is a simpleton and a deaf-mute. Kishtaiah is wayward and given to drunkenness and deserts Lakshmi, which is when Surya and she come together. But Kishtaiah returns abruptly after Lakshmi becomes pregnant and believes the child is his. When he strides purposefully towards Surya to give his master the glad tidings, Surya is frightened and, almost in panic, has Kishtaiah beaten and humiliated. All this is watched by a village boy and the film ends with this boy hurling a stone at the landlord's window and the screen gradually turning red. As will be evident from this description, 'Ankur' subscribes to a fairly simple politics but it can be taken to be sympathetic to political violence. Andhra also saw Naxalite activity in this period and the film is perhaps feeding off this recognition.

Perhaps a more powerful film than Benegal's 'Ankur' or 'Nishant' (1975), which followed, is Govind Nihalani's first feature film 'Aakrosh'. Nihalani was Benegal's cinematographer and 'Aakrosh' - scripted by Vijay Tendulkar - may be regarded as belonging to a similar kind of dramatic political cinema although it is derived from Marathi theater, which had become radical at the time because of playwrights like Tendulkar and Mahesh Elkunchwar. 'Aakrosh' is structured as a thriller set in a small town in Maharashtra. A tribal named Lahanya Bhiku has just been arrested for the murder of his wife Nagi. A young lawyer named Bhaskar Kulkarni takes up the task of defending him and, since Lahanya refuses to speak even in his own defense, decides to investigate the case on his own. He discovers that many of the respectable people in the town - all members of the Officer's Club - have raped and murdered Nagi and that they will do anything now to prevent the truth from coming out.

'Aakrosh' also introduces a peripheral 'Naxalite' (played by Elkunchwar) who is in touch with the tribals but who is later abducted by the villains and presumably murdered. This figure of the murdered Naxalite which we also found in 'Calcutta 71' reappears once again in Govind Nihalani's 'Party' (1984) based on a play by Elkunchwar. In this film members of the cultural glitterati spar with each other at a party and reveal their sordid selves. Absent from the party is an immensely talented writer-poet named Amrit who has been working with the tribals. The film ends with a nightmarish epilogue in which Amrit is shown to be brutally murdered by the police at around the same time that the party is in progress.

Assessed together the three groups of films all show sympathy for violent radicalism although they take different paths. Mrinal Sen is didactic and rhetorical while Ray tries to see it from the liberal perspective of his own class. Nihalani's 'Aakrosh' identifies, as Ray's 'Pratidwandi' does, with the liberal although the liberal lawyer in 'Aakrosh' tries to become involved more strongly than does Siddhartha in 'Pratidwandi'. More important than their differences however is the fact that the films all identify more with the apolitical middle-class than with the revolutionary left and this becomes apparent because there is no community around either the Naxalite or the oppressed whom they are working for. 'Aakrosh' is especially culpable here because the tribals do not emerge as a cohesive group capable of communicating or transacting with each other and there is a stronger community constructed around the upper-class villains than around their marginalized victims. Seen in the context, the figure of the dead or dysfunctional Naxalite becomes significant; it is not farfetched to propose that many of the films take comfort in it.

The Nation and the Alternative Community :

It is evident that we need to speculate about why non-mainstream cinema, although sympathetic to radical causes, is unable to imagine a community around radicalism and Naxalism. The most obvious explanation is that Naxalite organization always went on behind closed doors and was outside the reach of the personal experience of artists and film-makers. But this explanation is evidently untenable because cinema is unable to even *imagine* Naxalism as an ongoing project when it has no problems with similarly imagining the criminal underworld - which is also outside the reach of the personal experience of artists and film-makers. A more satisfactory explanation is perhaps that since the communities imagined by 'Third World' texts tend to allegorize the nation in some way[3], it will be difficult to imagine another one created with the deliberate aim of subverting the nation-State as Naxalism set out to do. The last proposition just offered evidently needs more explaining.

The cinema just described represents the closest India has to an official national cinema. The growth of cinema in the former colonies went through several stages. In the first stage - between 1910 and 1915 usually - there was an explosion of locally produced cinema that was soon wiped out by mass-entertainment from the West.[4] Even in India, which was to later dominate its domestic market, 85% of the screen-time in the 1920s was occupied by foreign imports.[5] Some of these local commercial cinemas reasserted themselves later but they also provoked reactions of a predominantly negative kind among Third-World critics and theorists and the critical writing or the theoretical speculation that Hollywood generated was absent. It was perhaps as a response that the first wave of 'national' film-makers emerged from the former colonies : Youssef Chahine from Egypt, Satyajit Ray from India,

Lester James Peries from Sri Lanka, Leopoldo Torre Nillson from Argentina, TG Alea and Humberto Solas from Cuba and Fernando Birri from Brazil. The 'national' film-makers were largely from the Western educated elite of the former colonies and their films were often designated as representing national cinema.

To explain national cinema's allegorical role though an illustration, the central monument in Indian cinema, Ray's 'Pather Panchali' (1955), could not perhaps have been made before 1947 although it is an adaptation of a much older work. Unlike in the novel, every event in the film is directed towards Apu's development as an individual and towards his eventual maturity. Many of the most memorable sequences in the film have to do with Apu's encounter with modernity - the telegraph wires, the train - and Ray's 'realism' conveys the acute sense of indigenous objects arriving for the first time, as it were, before the technology of cinema[6]. The film exhibits a certain pride at indigenous reality being captured by technology, a pride that could not have been felt by a colonized culture. Since Apu's is the 'new' consciousness through which reality is experienced it is in the analogous position of the young Indian Nation apprehending its own reality - through the use of a modern apparatus and India's encounter with 'modernity' was a key preoccupation of Nehru's India of the 1950s.

While Satyajit Ray may have been our first 'national' film-maker, the Film Finance Corporation under the direct influence of Mrs. Indira Gandhi took upon itself the role of promoting 'national culture' and 'healthy entertainment' and films like Mrinal Sen's 'Bhuvan Shome' (1969) and Mani Kaul's 'Uski Roti' (1970) were financed, with the government's interventionist role in film culture becoming official in 1971 after guidelines were issued by the I & B Ministry.[7] This being the case, film-makers who are not 'commercial' in India have depended on state patronage - usually through awards, showcasing at the IFFI and television rights. This does not imply that film-makers must tow the official line; the state hardly frowns upon social/ political criticism and public pronouncements make it seem that the film-maker needs to actually function as a kind of public conscience.[8] The nation-state, to be fair, does not publicly defend its worst doings and rewarding cinema - and the arts - for being critical of it then becomes a kind of phony atonement on the part of the state. But the criticism is always in the tone of an insider - pointing out where things may be going wrong.

The argument here is that the 'national' status of the cinema dealt with here - however violent its polemics it may be - means that its role is essentially constructive and on behalf of the nation; whenever it is required to imagine a community, therefore, it has unhesitatingly imagined one within the national mainstream. This does not mean only the rich or the middle-classes because even the poor and the marginalized are accommodated as equals within the scheme of the nation. One way of doing this, for instance, is to deal with tribals or the marginalized during British rule as in BV Karanth's 'Chomana Dudi' (1975) or Mrinal Sen's 'Mrigayaa' (1976) even while admitting their exploitation by native landowners and/ or the upper castes/ classes. Since the British are designated as the primary common adversary, the implication is that all 'Indians' will be equally involved in the independent nation regardless of the relationships existing among themselves.

Another possibility is to cast an actor with a cosmopolitan 'Indian' presence as the marginalized - e.g. Nandita Das as a slum-dweller or a dalit - without attention to the local characteristics that mark people. But this notion that everyone is equally 'Indian' within the nation widely informs the arts. In Salman Rushdie's novel *Midnight's Children* (1981), when midnight August 14th 1947 confers miraculous powers equally on both the upper-class protagonist and a beggar girl, the implication is the independence means the same thing to all Indians regardless of where they are placed. In effect, therefore, cinema and the arts are wittingly or unwittingly imagining a national community in which everyone is an equal stakeholder. This is evidently an insidious myth and one that Marxist-Leninists will contest. It is perhaps because Naxalism is actively engaged in resisting the democratic nation, because Naxalites have taken it upon themselves to subvert the nation-state that they can neither be included within the national community nor granted another legitimate one of their own. This is only a hypothesis but it may also explain several aspects of the 'socially conscious' cinema produced in India.

Notes :

1. This may find an echo in Bertolt Brecht's ballad about the child Jakob Apfelboeck who murders both his parents but does not know what he should do thereafter. See *Apfelboeck, or the Lily of the Field* from Bertolt Brecht, *Manual of Piety/ Die Hauspostille,* translated by Eric Bentley, New York : Grove Press, 1966, pp. 19- 24.
2. The dead Naxalite seems a more popular motif in cinema and literature than the active one. Another pertinent film is Govind Nihalani's 'Hazar Chaurasi Ki Maa' (1998) based on the novel by Mahasweta Devi. See Mahasweta Devi : *Mother of 1084.* Translation from Bengali by Samik Bandyopadhyay, Calcutta : Seagull Books, 1997.
3. According to Frederic Jameson, unlike in the developed countries, the difference between the personal and the public has not emerged in the newly independent countries of the Third World and private stories have public connotations. Consequently, all 'Third World' texts are national allegories. See Frederic Jameson, 'World Literature in the Age of Multinational Capitalism', from Koelb, Lokke (eds.) *The Current in Criticism,* West Lafayette (Ind.), Purdue University Press, 1987 pp. 139- 158.
4. For a detailed account see Roy Arnes, *Third World Film Making and the West,* Berkeley, CA : University of California Press, 1987, pp. 55- 57.
5. Ibid, p. 57.
6. Ashish Rajadhyaksha, *Indian Cinema in the Time of Celluloid : From Bollywood to the Emergency,* New Delhi : Tulika, 2009, pp. 161- 1.
7. Ashish Rajadhyaksha, Paul Willemen, *Encyclopedia of Indian Cinema,* New Delhi : Oxford University Press, 1994, pp.150- 1.
8. For instance, the President of India frequently makes demands for cinema's social responsibility. See "Patil urges industry to promote social responsibility via films" www.businessofcinema.com 3rd September 2008, accessed on 4th September 2011. http://www.businessofcinema.com/news.php?newsid=9737& page=2

Reading 'Red Alert - The War Within' : A Convenient Reality

Amitava Nag

The Primordial Representation :

> A young man on the run jumping off a wall, running through the lanes - dingy and dark, pursued by the police (the Calcutta police in white uniform), finally shot in an open space - a field preferably. The timing is sometimes around midnight, but more often than not it's almost dawn punctuated by the signature tune of Akashvani[1] beginning the news bulletin.

The above cinematic shot is not of one single film but of many which somehow or the other focussed on the Naxalite movement that germinated in West Bengal in the spring of 1967, spread rapidly for the next few years, culminating in bitter bloodshed in the metropolis of Calcutta. Calcutta, first hit by the transfer of power from her to Delhi by the British in 1911, then by the ill-fated partition of undivided Bengal during the Indian Independence of 1947 was dealt its penultimate blow by the Naxalite movement of 1967. Though the movement started in Naxalbari (a village and a development block in northern part of the state of West Bengal[2]), in no time it was spearheaded by the elite middle-class who followed the line of Mao Ze-dong. A revolutionary movement which was operated in the village and the rural belt of West Bengal, Bihar, Andhra Pradesh, Kerala and Punjab[3] soon spilt over in the city of Calcutta. There are many, students in large numbers primarily, who joined the armed revolution - the situation became alarming and the state using its machinery - the armed police, brutally devastated the movement. Hence it was a common reality of the Calcuttans to wake up to the Akashvani tune and listen to the early morning bulletin airing the news of discovery of yet another anonymous dead body somewhere in the city. The particular shot mentioned in the beginning of the article taken from Mrinal Sen's 'Calcutta 71' (1972) acts as an iconic symbol for the represntation of Naxalite movement of the 1960s and '70s. Similar sequences were found in Sen's 'Mahaprithibi' ('World Within, World Without', 1981), even references in Gautam Ghosh's 'Kalbela' (2009) and Suman Mukhopadhyay's 'Herbert' (2005) - both these films were shot around thirty five years after the Naxalite movement but set in the turbulent '70s. This angry Bengal is represented again in Mrinal Sen's 'Interview' (1970) - the last sequence where the protagonist flings a stone to break open the showcase of a shop and wearing the suit of the mannequin. This disrobing of the 'official' uniform is symbolic in the attempt of rejection of bureacracy and/or governance. In effect, Mrinal Sen's *Calcutta Trilogy* ['Interview, Calcutta 71 and Padatik' 1973)] is replete with visual markers which identify the movement on the streets of the city and the state repressal in trying to curb it.

The more prevalent and vast operational manouevering of the armed battle in the rural circuit was less known by the media, the middle-class intelligentsia (predominantly the Calcutta-bred Bengalis) and hence less depicted in cinema.

Thus, the representation of the Naxalite movement of the '70s in Bengali cinema (predominantly because of its effect on Calcutta) or by the Bengali directors is what is being perceived by the middle-class and for their consumption only. Even in the films of the diplomatically 'apolitical' Satyajit Ray (the interview scene of 'Pratidwandi' ('The Adversary', 1972) or in making the boyfriend character of Sharmila Tagore, a Na67xalite, in 'Seemabaddha' ('Company Limited', (1971)) or the *enfant terrible* of Indian cinema Ritwik Ghatak [notably 'Jukti Takko Gappo' ('Reason, Debate and a Story', 1974)] there had been a streak of sympathy that presumably emerged from a sense of empathy for the elite middle-class educated Naxalites with whom all these directors and the Calcuttans shared a common space - more mental than physical. Hence it's no wonder, that the films made by them having the Naxalite reference had mostly been non-analytical, veering on being sentimental and implicitly supporting the cause. This, in contrast with the few books written from completely reverse perspectives primarily by the police have also been partisan.[4] It comes as no surprise that the police reports in most cases were doctored and the confessions by political prisoners in police custody were manufactured by the police - whether in the pre-Independence militant freedom struggle, or the post-Independence armed Communist movement.

Cinema is the latest and most sophisticated art form. Along with the financial and economic grandeur that comes with it, no wonder, there are multiple dialectics to define cinema as a vehicle for shaping and propagating mass culture. In the Western and developed countries where differences in class, religion and language are less, cinema can act as ideological badnwagons - for the elite vis-a-vis the working class. However, in Indian context, where the rubrics of an unified nation state is diverse and difficult, cinema shares an intriguing space between 'art' and 'entertainment'. Yet, it has always been a tool for the middle-class educated intelligentsia - to promote and evolve their aesthetic sensitivities and sensibilities. The 'evil' vs 'good' polar opposites, henceforth have always been depicted from the stand-point of this middle-class[5], the way they want the other classes to be portrayed. Also interesting is the feminist critique which essenially points that the notion of such violence or struggle is inherently grounded in a 'male'-psychic world. Inspite of being positioned on the Western audience bred on Hollywood films, still Laura Mulvey's stance that eventually the audience gaze in cinema is a 'male' gaze which is active (as opposed to a 'passive' female gaze) still holds true for an Indian audience[6]. Therefore, these depictions of mass struggle and revolution is fragmented in its reality and biased in its opinion.

This is a rudimentary basic to understand the cinema of India - that a cinema of the 'poor' is also a cinema for and by the 'middle-class' - the reason why 'Peepli Live' (2010) inspite of its superlative facade falls short of the actual peasants' expectations AND the film had to be baked in satirical nuances for the 'middle-class' audience to marvel at the supposed comic reliefs[7]. To mark this as unholy will be simplistic, its better to understand this phenomenon in its complexity and re-look at the cinema of this land from these perspectives.

The Shift in the Movement :

Over the last around 40 years since the first spate of the Naxalite movement was crushed, the movement itself changed colours as well. What remained quite a 'city' event as well (and thereby probably losing touch with the peasant majority for which it was supposed to fight for), over these years, Naxalite movement had spread to multiple states but its penetration in the cities declined with it. The movement which was so long termed predominantly as the 'Naxalite' movement stepped out of its geographical bondage and embraced an ideological one, eventually the movement being termed as the 'Maoist' movement in recent times. The transfer from *Naxalism to Maoism* henceforth safeguarded the notion of internalising violence through armed struggle against the state as a tool for claiming social justice.

In his seminal book *In the Wake of Naxalbari* (published by Subarnarekha, 1980), Sumanta Banerjee mentions

> But at the lowest rung of the rural hierarchy were the rural laborers or landless peasants.... Besides poverty, the rural poor also suffered from social exploitation and oppression, since a large number of them also belonged to lower castes [a form of class and social division in India] and the aboriginal community.

The discontent of the rural poor as reflected by an individual (Sumanta Banerjee) was a reality which the Indian Government also couldn't choose to be oblivious of. This is obvious from a report submitted by a special committe set up by the ministry of home affairs to investigate the reasons for agrarian unrest. This report of 1969 was titled *The Causes and Nature of Current Agrarian Tensions.* It was freely circulated, though unpublished till much later, in a 1986 OUP book edited by A.R. Desai. The report said,

> The basic cause of unrest, namely, the defective implementation of laws enacted to protect the interests of the tribals, remains... Unless this is attended to, it would not be possible to win the confidence of the tribals whose leadership has been taken over by the extremists.

In the next four decades of Indian history, there had been a steady decline of morality in the ranks of bureacracy (this I have discussed in the next section in detail) marred by rampant corruption thereby ensuring that 'the defective implementation of laws' was never 'attended to'. The confidence of the poor (tribal or otherwise) slowly eroded and armed violence against state was what we all come to see this day, so much so that the current Prime Minister, Manmohan Singh, has described the Maoist uprising as 'the biggest internal security challenge ever faced by our country'. There are little doubts that the Maoist revolution has threatened the country's security.

It has to be acknowledged that the main support base of the 'Naxalite' movement transformed from an elite class to the nation's poorest and most deprived classes in the 'Maoist' movement. Theses landless and tribal people are ousted from their homes by up-coming industrial projects, and denied access to their traditional forest resources. With general conscious-level increase due to the media, these people recognize the face of their exploitation by landowners, money lenders and the police. Hence there is no surprise that these people have thronged themselves under the Maoist movement which in the last two decades or so has resorted to guerilla activities. These Maoist groups have network with similar revolutionary organizations in neighbouring states. Therefore to curb such outfits (not one but many) becomes difficult for the Government of India alone thereby elevating it to a stature as described by the Prime Minister.

It should be borne in mind that the Maoists do not yet control any large area comparable to the `liberated zone' that the Chinese Communists could establish in Yenan within a decade or so in the 1930-40 period. The Maoist movement having spread in different states henceforth have bottled themselves up in their rural underground shelters - the link and camaraderie with the worker class in the organized industrial and the unorganized sectors failed to be set up. This ensured that with increasing civilian killings by armed personnel termed 'revolutionary' by the Maoists and banished as 'terrorists/extremists' by the Indian government, the Maoists revolution truly and steadily lost its base amongst common people - both in the rural India as well as its elite urban counterpart.

This shift is important since the cine-going India who thronged the multiplexes and guaranteed the revenue of the Box Office slowly but surely discontinued to relate with the Maoists. So what was a natural and experienced reality of Naxalism in the city in the '70s by the middle-class, soon became an unknown reality to them in today's world - relying only on heavily biased A/V media. Hence the empathy of the middle-class soon got eroded. The anger of the '70s world-wide subsided in the next two decades. For India as well, the effects of Globalisation ensured embracing the West more than cultivating the indigenous. Slowly but steadily the Indian youth aligned them more with the Western capitalist culture - the larger Indian cities marked with malls and flyovers and an entire generation looking forward to emulate the notion of prosperity through the concept of credit economy. By and large this consumerism made most of the middle-class youth to look at themselves and their fellow class people rather than across classes. The primary reason why so many city-bred youth were lured by the idealism in Marxist philosophy in Naxalite movement of the '70s was that they trusted their ideological conscience in caring for classes poorer than them in most aspects. The ideological shift thereby removed the elite middle-class from the realities of Maoist struggle apart from occasional and grave incidents.

Also contributing to the middle-class alienation is the lack of confidence in armed revolution against the State to bring in equality. There had been trends which show that internal squablings and resorting to petty tactics of unarmed civilian killing as a mark of muscle strength had weakened the basic cause of such movements. As Sumanta Banerjee notes

> The history of the last four decades of the Naxalite movement in India is a painful record of attempts - both heroic and loutish at times - to bring about a revolutionary transformation in the benighted economic and social living conditions of the Indian poor. The chronicle of courageous battles against a vicious state machinery followed by self-sacrifice by thousands of guerrillas, and patient efforts by dedicated cadres to initiate land reforms and social changes in their areas of control, has often been marred by "lumpen" acts like extortions from petty traders and contractors, and ruthless killing of innocent people suspected of being police informers[8].

For any film-maker to make a film on the Maoist revolution is doubly difficult hence - on the one hand the najority of her audience will find it difficult to relate with the reality and on the other, she herself will also primarily have to rely on secondary and tertiary sources of information.

'Red Alert - The War Within' - Displaced Realism :

Released on July 9, 2010, the film Red Alert - the War Within[9] raised interest primarily due to two statements made public by individuals related to its making. Anant Mahadevan, the director claimed

> The film is set in India but then it could have been anywhere else in the world as well, whether it was Cuba or Ireland! Whenever a revolution has taken place somewhere, there are men like Narsimha who get trapped.[10]

If this generic sweep at the nature of revolution tend to catch the eye, the claim by one of the actresses in the film, Bhagyasri seemed profound

> The movie will draw home a lesson to all. Also, the government will come to know that they must provide education and infrastructure in naxal-hit areas..rope in private sector to build industries, thereby providing employment to the poor people in there.[11]

This statement seemed quite ordinary yet logical, there is little confusion in 'what to do', probably many-fold more the enigma surrounding the 'how to do'.

The film starts off by stating 'The film is based on a true story against the backdrop of the naxalite movement'. Within the first part itself there were debates raised - the Maoist leader suggesting the difference between terrorism and revolution as one that's directed against the "state", the other, against the "system" and an "educated" comrade saying 'Words have the power that guns don't.' However the entire reel time we found their actions opposite of their statements (due to lack of conviction?) - blowing up police stations and other national properties.

The film took no pain in showing the intrinsic causes behind the Maoist revolution. There were two - Narsimha and Lakshmi who joined the Maoists by accident and for taking revenge against being raped, respectively. But apart from these the multi-pronged poverty of the poorest strata of India, the exploitation either direct or indirect (by displacing them off their land to build Bauxite and other ore industries) was never apparent. The director wanted to be balanced - on one hand he tried to show sympathy towards the Maoists, and on the other, he wanted to be rational in justifying the governance. What slipped through somehow is the reflection of abject poverty of morality in the ranks of bureaucracy which ascertains that 'Rs 15 of every Rs 100 spent for the poor reaches them.[12] Also pertinent is the brutality with which the Maoists mastermind their sustenance by collecting levies from ordinary citizens and also getting funded by the corporate[13].

So in essence the film became a general gang-war movie devoid of the Maoist specifics in detail and authenticity. There were ambushes, fierce gun-fights, mass slaughter at the pretext of basic rights for the poor. That is primary the reason why apart from Narsimha and Lakshmi all the other Maoists seemed face-less, distant. Only the latter two seemed real - the 'ordinary' human being. Though extremely controversial for her overtly political standpoint and raw snide at the Government, yet Arundhati Roy's Outllook India article 'Walking with the Comrades' may help in getting one perspective of the Maoists - their world and vision -

> Sukhiari, who as a child was abducted and forcibly married to an older man (she ran away and went to live with her sister), now organises mass rallies, speaks at meetings. The men depend on her for protection. I asked her what the party means to her. "Naxalvaad ka matlab hamara parivaar (Naxalvaad means our family). When we hear of an attack, it is like our family has been hurt," Sukhiari says. I asked her if she knew who Mao was. She smiled shyly, "He was a leader. We're working for his vision.

In another grucling truth -

> I met Chamri, mother of Comrade Dilip who was shot on July 6, 2009. She says that after they killed him, the police tied her son's body to a pole, like an animal and carried it with them. (They need to produce bodies to get their cash rewards, before someone else muscles in on the kill.) Chamri ran behind them all the way to the police station. By the time they reached, the body did not have a scrap of clothing on it. On the way, Chamri says, they left the body by the roadside while they stopped at a dhaba to have tea and biscuits. (Which they did not pay for.) Picture this mother for a moment, following her son's corpse through the forest, stopping at a distance to wait for his murderers to finish their tea. They did not let her have her son's body back so she could give him a proper funeral. They only let

> her throw a fistful of earth in the pit in which they buried the others they had killed that day. Chamri says she wants revenge. *Badla ku badla.* Blood for blood.

Or,

> Kamla doesn't seem interested. I ask her if she likes watching movies. "Nahin didi. Sirf ambush video (No didi. Only ambush videos)." Later, I ask Comrade Sukhdev about these ambush videos. Without batting an eyelid, he plays one for me[14].

The moment the characters in Mahadevan's film seemed drifting, so was the entire basis of the film - what revolution, for whom, by whom? Questions and doubts pour in from every corner. The solution at the end, hence, seemed too naïve. Like Bhagyasri's simplistic doodle, the film ends with an iota of suspense and how the Maoist chief understands the futility of armed struggle, gets a chance to flee and comes back as an industrialist with a heart of gold and bouquet of 'development' opportunities - for the poor.

Sarabjit Kaur also tries to suggest solutions thus simplistically

> To combat the Naxal movement undertaking oppressive steps by the government is, however, not a remedy to the problem. The governments at the Centre and in States should direct their efforts towards finding a long term solution to the problem. For this, they have to take such measures which will solve the problem of economic deprivation and in turn will prevent the rise of frustration amongst the indigenous population of various States affected by the problem of Naxalism....It therefore becomes pertinent for the governments-Central and State -to seriously undertake developmental activities whose benefits actually reach the poor, local masses.[15]

This is a realisation which is not new (refer to the 1969 Government report mentioned in the previous section). However fact of the matter is, the Government allocate funds for the poor development, the corruption racket eats it up, the poverty inflates leading to unrest amongst the poor and they taking to arms - the Government then tries to curb the movement even more brutally leading to another masacre. This is indeed an vicious cycle. Venkateswar Reddy, alias Telugu Dipak, one of the Maoist leaders of West Bengal suggests

> Yes, dialogue should happen. We can have talks around partial demands. The conflict could be postponed. The intensity of conflict should decrease. If such talks happen and our leadership takes a decision, the cadres will fall in line.[16]

Sumanta Banerjee perhaps sums up the Maoist struggle to a degree of rationality -

> To put it in stark terms - while generations of heroic revolutionaries may remain committed to the strategy of a "protracted war", the vast masses of the common people may not always be prepared for it. Although sympathetic to the revolutionaries who uphold their cause, all of them cannot be expected to join the revolution and adhere to the discipline of revolutionary cadres. They vacillate when offered sops by the state, or may even squeal when coerced by the state. They are caught in the crossfire between two maximalist positions - one adopted by the revolutionaries who are determined in their well-meaning goal of smashing the present iniquitous socioeconomic order and replacing it with a "people's democratic state", and the other taken by a stubborn ruling class equally determined to continue with the status quo and suppress any resistance to it. Of the two, the communist revolutionaries who claim to look after the welfare of the poor and the oppressed, are expected to be more humane in their choice of tactics and genuinely democratic in obtaining popular consent for them - particularly when such tactics affect the vast masses of uninvolved citizens. If in their drive for retaliation against enemy offensive, they stoop to the level of the police or security forces and indulge in

> indiscriminate attacks on soft targets (e g, blowing up railway stations, or school buildings, or killing innocent tribal people) totally indifferent to the problems faced by the common people as a result of such actions, they become indistinguishable from the vicious terrorist acts by sectarian coteries like the Liberation Tigers of Tamil Eelam of Sri Lanka, and the various Islamic fundamentalist outfits in west Asia - who have killed more innocent civilians than the armed minions of their respective states whom they target as their enemies.[17]

The reason for quoting so much in this section is primarily to drive home the point that the topic of the maoists are so varied and different now than ever before. Their are sides - the government, the maoists, the general mass and so forth. With high quantity of low standard media threatening the existence of the middle-class urban population there is no wonder that confusion will only prevail. For the middle-class film-maker and his middle-class audience, hence, its extremely difficult to build a stance of their own and ground the film's reality on that. In most such cases, the director tries to be street-smart in the guise of being diplomatic.

So it comes as no shock that Red Alert in trying to claim rationality of reasoning, in actual, lacked the conviction and courage to deal with this complex problem. To eulogize or to disprove - both need sensitive handling and honest vision. However, to dilute a particular set of problems in lure of generalizing it across lands and time (refer to Mahadevan's claim) is in essence - commericalization of the issue in discussion. The Indian bureacracy has commercialized the Naxalite / Maoist struggle for the last four decades. The media and the elite middle-class has supported this process. This is why in the films made on the same we find that particular voice of conscience that suits those the films are made for. The brutal honesty and rawness of the Maoists as depicted in Arundhati Roy's reportage is a reality that the urban elite find difficult to comprehend. The sheer disavowal of the middle-class sensitivities and ethics is something that we are not familiar with. If these details are so difficult to avail, the whole process of a middle-class understanding gets a beating. This article hence is also crippled by a perceived reality remote from the essayist's existential experience (this is a problem which was less in Calcutta of the '70s when the first lot of cinema on Naxalism were made as mentioned in the beginning of this article).

Unfortunately perhaps, there is no other choice apart from the fact that any cinema of the third world countries like India will be driven and consumed for the urban middle-class elite - for their own romantic misgivings, relatively oblivious of the ground reality of over a third of its population.

Notes and References :

1. All India Radio (abbreviated AIR), officially known as Akashvani, is the radio broadcaster of India and a division of Prasar Bharati. For details read here http://en.wikipedia.org/wiki/Akashvani (accessed on September 20, 2010)
2. http://en.wikipedia.org/wiki/Naxalbari (accessed on September 20, 2010)
3. Sumanta Banerjee, Naxalbari (1967): The Naxalite Movement in India, http://venus.unive.it/asiamed/eventi/schede/naxalbari.html (accessed on September 20, 2010)
4. A notable exception will be *The Naxalites through the Eyes of the Police*. Select notifications from the Calcutta Police Gazette. 1967-1975, Edited by Ashoke Kumar Mukhopadhyay; Dey's Publishing, Kolkata, India; 2006 - since the editor Ashoke Mukhopadhyay's pure academic interest in the matter led him to collect the relevant documents of that period from the Calcutta police archives and present them as information rather than trying to colour them with his own interpretation and views.

   Equally interesting is Mohit Sen's take where he called for saving the Naxalites from Naxalism (Mohit Sen, 'The Naxalites and Naxalism', *Economic and Political Weekly*, Annual Number January 1971, pp :195-198).
5. By middle-class I hereby define the elite and educated intelligentsia who

reside both in rural and urban India and whose subset is the great Indian 'middle-class' (defined on their economic viability).

6. Laura Mulvey, 'Visual Pleasure and Narrative Cinema', *Screen,* 16.3 Autumn, 1975, pp. 6- 18.
7. Please read the alternate debate on Peepli Live in Tehelka - http://www.tehelka.com/story_main46.asp?filename=hub180910Peepli_relived.asp (accessed on September 20, 2010).
8. Sumanta Banerjee, 'Beyond Naxalbari', *Economic and Political Weekly,* July 22, 2006 pp 3159-3163.
9. http://www.imdb.com/title/tt1245732/ - the IMDB entry (accessed on September 20, 2010).
10. http://www.bollywoodhungama.com/features/2010/07/07/6412/index.html (accessed on September 20, 2010)
11. http://www.allvoices.com/contributed-news/6200874-red-alert-eye-opener-on-naxalism-lesson-for-all-upcoming-flick-red-alert (accessed on September 20, 2010)
12. Shankkar Aiyar, 'Hope amidst despair', India Today - http://indiatoday.intoday.in/site/Story/62251/Cover%20Story/Hope+amidst+despair.html (accessed on September 20, 2010)
13. Sumon K Chakrabarti, 'Naxal leader claims corporates funding rebels', IBNLive - http://ibnlive.in.com/news/naxal-leader-claims-corporates-funding-rebels/104457-3.html (accessed on September 20, 2010)
14. Arundhati Roy, 'Walking With The Comrades', Outlook India (March 22, 2010) - http://www.countercurrents.org/roy220310.htm (accessed on September 20, 2010)
15. Sarabjit Kaur, 'Towards Understanding Naxalism', *Mainstream,* Vol XLVIII, No 12, March 13, 2010 - http://www.mainstreamweekly.net/article1953.html (accessed on September 20, 2010)
16 Soutik Biswas 'Why India Maoist leader is a 'big catch' ', BBC News, July 7, 2010 - http://www.bbc.co.uk/news/10506197 (accessed on September 20, 2010)
17. Sumanta Banerjee, 'Beyond Naxalbari', *Economic and Political Weekly,* July 22, 2006 pp 3159-3163.

Narrative Coping with Naxal Violence : 'Red Alert - The War Within' and Mainstream Hindi Cinema's Story Strategies

Bernd Zywietz

Introduction :

Rapid growing fandom and general interest in Indian movies - particularly popular mainstream Hindi cinema ("Bollywood") - made this kind of entertainment-art widely accessible (especially on DVD) in Germany and other parts of Europe. In this sense by films like 'Dil Se' (1998), 'Fanaa' (2006) or 'Rang De Basanti' (2006) Germans learn - though rudimentarily - about India's political, ethnical and religious tensions, conflicts and crisis, from struggles in and about Kashmir to communal Hindu-Muslim-violence, from police brutality and corruption to riots and terrorism. Additionally, terrible events like 2008 Mumbai attacks are extensively covered in German news media. Yet, only few have heard about Naxalites or Maoists or at least are aware that Naxalism poses the "the biggest threat to India's internal security" (according to Home Minister P. Chidambaram in 2010).

My doctoral paper is about terrorism narratives in movies from Germany, Ireland, the United Kingdom (concerning the "troubles" in Northern Ireland), and "Hollywood" - and about Indian political violence. Focussing especially on Hindi mainstream productions I came across a plethora of films - Bollywood or "middle" cinema - about Indian heroes fighting extremists or featuring the "tragic terrorist" (a grieving victim of violence itself) who finds his peace, his way back into all-Indian society or a tragic death.

However, movies about Naxal violence are rather rare, for all examples like Hindi action drama 'Chamku' (2008), tragic 'Hazaar Chaurasi ki Maa' (1998) or Malayalam 'Lal Salam' (1990). Asking a lecturer at the Satyajit Ray Film and Television Institute I got the explanation : Naxalite engagement and violence is too political, inconvenient and thereby unsuitable for conventional entertainment. But what about common films dealing with post-Ayodhya riots, everyday communal resentments or the bombings and assassinations in India and its "troubled peripheries"? Clearly the problem with Naxalite ideology goes deeper for it defies dominant national self-imaginations and narratives on the one hand and cinematic strategies to negotiate internal political conflicts, miseries and its violent outcome on the other. To outline these challenges and limitations, this article takes a closer look at the popular, yet not that successful Hindi movie 'Red Alert - The War Within' (2009) as an example for cinema's ways in coping with this ideologically delicate issue.

I. Narratives :

> It is difficult to distinguish between art and life in South Asian society; they no longer imitate each other but appear to have merged. Political philosophies, social values, group behaviour, speech and dress in society are reflected in the cinema and, like a true mirror, reflect back in society[1].

Understanding films as such a social instrument ("seismograph") or collective "reflectors" demands clarifying movies' epistemological status and "praxeo-logic": asking *how* film fiction generates, distributes and let the audience receive *what kind* - of knowledge. How is this (social, historical, political) knowledge structured? What use and with what effects do people obtain it? Film theory offers theses and concepts about the interaction between reality, politics, ideology and movies, genres, film images and cinema apparatus[2]. However, more important seem the latent tasks and functions movies accomplish and perform. People are not passive wax boards imprinted with media messages, but neither do they live free from (or outside) given (adapted or negotiated) norms, conventions and codes governing symbolic and other kinds of meaning and understanding. Thus, even the most trivial direct-to-video production contains values, a cinematic language and - on the other hand - offers a communication platform for individuals, cultural and social understandings, beliefs, assurances and (re-)integration. It movies need to if they should be *understood*. And as people who enjoy a traditional heroic story feel uneasy when the villain succeeds in the end, every narrative needs an inherent logic and closure. That does not mean that a narrative must provide a happy ending or could not transgress conventional (especially generic) standards. But *if* it does so, it has to do so in a larger, meaningful framework (e.g. the one of anti-illusionistic "thought provoking art") or else it might cause what Leon Festinger famously called "cognitive dissonance"[3], what could result in dismissing the movie as poor storytelling.

This seems - at least a bit - the case when Mayank Shekhar, film critic of the *Hindustan Times,* wrote about 'Red Alert - The War Within' :

> The film's complex subject then remains at once its only merit, and its immediate failing. [...] The backdrop is its only purpose, and doubles up for its skeletal plot. The picture probably started out with, "Let's make a movie on Naxalites. Art picture. No songs!" The rest should follow[4].

Before we take a close look at the movie and its contradictions, there is another remarkable point bothering Shekar. Concerning 'Red Alert's substantial insufficiency - according to Shekar's critique - he connects the movie's narratives with "real-life" ones :

> I suppose you may as well go back to popular narrative that plays out Maoist attacks each day as some chicken-egg catfight between bleeding heart liberals (Arundhati Roy), and a ruthlessly heartless Indian state (P Chidambaram). It's at least reductive enough to make for a good read, or watch -- from a distance, of course[5].

Unknowingly or at least ironically Shekar points out to several characteristics and functions of narratives which are important here. First : Following authors like Jerome Bruner[6] or Czarniawska-Joerges[7] narratives are fundamental concepts not only in fictional accounts but also as a general cognitive mode of organising knowledge and meaning in everyday life, while constructing something we call history[8], culture or when it comes to integrate individual and collective identity in social (and political) movements[9]. This narrative approach is flexible and in certain aspects more versatile than typical fields in film theory like Marxism, linguistics and semiotics, psychoanalysis or mere formalistic and cognitive approaches. One of his major advantages lies in bridging the philosophical and methodological-analytical gap between fictional and non-fictional narratives without entirely neglecting the differences. Thus, considering movies as narratives opens a common ground to relate factual real-world to cinematic "Naxalite"-discourses and offers a valuable set of "tools" (like analysing the acting "characters").

Second, by referring to Home Minister Chidambaram and writer-activist Arundhati Roy, Shekar in his review marks the two basic positions on Naxalism. At its core - like in any case of political violence - it is an argumentative struggle about *legitimacy*. Its outcomes are narratives about violence or counter-violence, action and reaction, law versus rights (of self-defense, political participation) etc. From an anti-Naxalite viewpoint Maoists are backward irrational offenders, who kill rightful centre and state agents and exploit peasants and adivasis for political purposes, undermining peaceful coexistence under the unifying Hindustan umbrella and blocking technological and economic development in rural areas.

A rather pro-Naxalite stand takes Roy, especially with her lengthy Outlook cover story 'Walking with the Comrades'[10], published on March 29, 2010, about three months prior to Shekhar's review of 'Red Alert'. In this decidedly subjective and sympathetic report of Maoist world in Dantewada, Chhattisgarh, recorded "comrade's" personal stories and motivations or Roy's interpretation of the bigger historical, cultural, social and political picture Maoist's engagement as a just cause.

Naxals act in self-defense or to protect the poor and marginalised. They are no stranger from outside but originate from lower castes, working and peasant classes or adivasi communities itself. Yet they are distinct : They are deeply rooted in tradition (therefore join the Bhumkal festivities) and represent an authentic, harmonic and "natural" way of life (e.g. as people blending into the woods, with fluid identities and many names). At the same time they correct "wrong" cultural and social habits and practices, e.g. by empowering women in society. Naxal's enemies are local police forces or Salwa Judum militias who burn, rape and kill; landlords, contractors or major corporations exploiting the people and destroying the land; misleading media and governments and state officials who are corrupt or suppressive and violate basic human rights. In this situation violence is the only way to gain attention, weapons are the only means to save and restore dignity :

> I feel I ought to say something at this point. About the futility of violence, about the unacceptability of summary executions. But what should I suggest they do? Go to court? Do a dharma at Jantar Mantar, New Delhi? A rally? A hunger strike? It sounds ridiculous. The promoters of the New Economy Policy - who find it so easy to say "There Is No Alternative" - should be asked to suggest an alternative Resistance Policy. A specific one, to these specific people, in this specific forest. Here. Now[11].

Against this background single narratives - individual (e.g. joining the armed struggle because of personal experience; concrete atrocities of security forces and militias), collective (tribal history, class struggles) and abstract ("evil" forces of Imperialism, Colonialism, Capitalism or Globalisation) - are interwoven into a larger narrative net with a certain point of view and character types, a cause-effect dramaturgy or an ideology. It is structured around central recurring issues and motifs (e.g. women as victims). Some of them seem crucial for narrating Naxalism, and as with Roy's text it is very revealing to analyse them in a movie like 'Red Alert - The War Within'.

2. 'Red Alert - The War Within' :

'Red Alert' is based on the *Hindustan Times* article ('Both of Us Fired. He Missed. I did Not'), published on September 7, 2007. The movie opens with a depiction of this very article as to prove not only its own narrative authenticity but also to promise some insight into the "true story" behind daily media accounts about far-off Naxalism. Main character is the poor villager Narasimha (Sunil Shetty). In underdeveloped Andrah Pradesh he cooks for a group of Maoist guerrilla and is forced to join them after they are ambushed while Narasimha delivers the food. Worrying about his wife and children back home for whom he has to raise money, Narasimha becomes engaged in the guerrilla's daily life, political lessons and training but also in raids on police stations or in an assault on a landlord (which turns out to be an ambush). He even is forced to kill a befriended comrade who turns out to be an undercover policeman. Foreign employees of a steel company are taken hostage; in reaction police retaliates by burning villages and killing people. Finally, when his outfit raids a school where security forces are stationed and a child Narasimha tries to save is shot, he breaks down and decides to leave the group. Commando leader Velu (Ashish Vidyarthi) is about to stop him so Narashima shoots him in self defense and flees. Stuck between Naxals and the police he turns to journalist Raghavan (Makrand Deshpande) and becomes an informer for grim DIG Rathod (Gulshan Grover) and superior Home Minister. Despite his plea his former comrades are gunned down. To "end the violence" he promises to turn in Maoist leader Krishnaraj (Vinod Khanna), shoots and burns the cadre in his hideout when troops arrive - or so it seems...

The end of till then rather dark and pessimistic movie is most notable and peculiar : We see Narashima, now wearing glasses and living with his wife not longer in their poor hut but in a rather wealthy home. Their children return from school (their education was one of Narashima's concerns throughout the film) while on television Narashima recognises the pronounced dead Krishnaraj as a political business man explaining his micro farming model. A flashback illuminates the plot twist : Back in Krishnaraj's hideout the communist leader declares to the bewildered hero (and the movie's audience) how he, thanks to Narashima, has realised that the armed struggle leads nowhere, causing only pain and death, and that peaceful political engagement would be the only chance to better economic conditions. "Like this we can do nothing in the next fifty to hundred years." So without hesitation he fakes his death by using his dead bodyguard's corpse and escapes through the backdoor. In his new life without hardship Narashima - as his voice over comment states - is glad that an uneducated man like him could convince an educated person to change his thinking and guide him to another way.

This epilogue is unrealistic and implausible in many ways. During the film we witness Home Minister and his Deputy Inspector being unsympathetic and ruthless in dealing with Maoist and common people alike (due to the pressure of human rights groups and the foreign press Rathod orders to sew the killed villagers' heads back on to the severed bodies, however : "Don't waste time trying to match the heads with the bodies"). Therefore it seems unlikely that small-time informer Narashima and his family not only get away unharmed, but even are enabled to live such a luxury life. The same is true for hardliner Krishnaraj's miraculous insight and his renouncing of violence, after he once scoffed at naïve, apolitical and low-ranking Narasimha's thoughts when he happened to overhear them by chance.

More important, however : beyond politically correct phrases the movie presents no substantial argument against the relevance or effectiveness of "armed defense" in this conflict. Sure, the violence causes death and destruction - even a child loses his life. Yet, 'Red Alert' fails to convince that there is any alternative (analogue to Roy's argument) as - for example - NGOs are unsuccessful in stopping the mining company and the government in establishing Special Economic Zone. Only mugging the company's convoy and kidnapping foreigners ensures public attention and needful pressure to the government.

In the end, the movie blends two typical popular narratives together you can find all over the world where foreign domination and liberation struggles are essential to a nation's history and cultural identity (e.g. in Ireland which was - like India - for so long "part" of the British Empire): The one is the prototypical story of heroic outlaws fighting oppressors, the other is about the blinded idealist, who - with good intentions and motivated by personal loss - loses the right perspective and has to be stopped or "woken up" for the sake of healing collective wounds and building a new peaceful and free future. So up to the end 'Red Alert' seems rather inevitably sympathetic to the Naxal's cause and the effectiveness of violence and threats as Roy in her article, even if the movie takes a political "safe" stance : Director Anant Mahadevan and writer Arona Raje put much effort to show good and bad sides with the comrades. Even arrogant and cold-hearted Velu shows no hatred but some respect for killed policemen : "They're our enemies just because they work for the government. If they had died for us, they would at least have had a decent funeral". Again and opposed to that, the police - foremost D.I.G. Rathod - officials or the Home Minister are only presented as too indifferent and without personal life, beliefs or any traits to make the audience sympathise with them. When it comes to the film's ending, nevertheless, the story seemed way too gloomy to the producers and to offer some positive message and to soothe the Central Board of Film Certification; we now face this closing turning 'Red Alert' in its last minutes upside down.

3. Problematic Naxalism :

Here we meet the central problem of Naxalism story material, despite its dramatic potential and the morally powerful conflicts and claims. Leftist ideology threatens "Hindi cinema's own agenda - imagining a unified nation [...]"[12]. In general Bollywood developed certain narrative strategies in coping with political violence. One is to acknowledge grievances and injustices "rebels" have experienced (or at least fight) while blaming single ruthless businessmen, unscrupulous police official or corrupt politicians, thus leaving Hindi nation itself untouched (e.g. in 'Rang De Basanti'). The other is to condemn (and quasi *expel*) separatists and other "freedom fighters" as "Others": Pakistan's agents, traitors and "terrorists" (see for example highly patriotic 'Zameen'). Commonly the term "terrorist" is in India mostly applied when labelling specific aims, motives and conflicts (e.g. Kashmiri groups). According to Nayar in his book about national martyr Bhagat Singh, a terrorist is motivated by personal hatred while a "revolutionary believes in the complete overthrow of any established government or political system that does not give equality to the people"[13]. In 'Red Alert - The War Within' 'Commander Velu asked by reporter Raghavan clarifies : "There's a wide difference between terrorism and revolution. They're against the nation. We are against the system". In other movies like 'Chamku', the difference is made quite clear, too. So despite bombing railroad tracks, killing members of the forest department or kidnapping, Naxals are no terrorists.

For a person from France, Italy or Germany this is rather strange : Before transnational Islamic terrorism became such an urgent and dominating subject, social-revolutionary leftist extremists were the paradigm for home grown terrorism in these countries. And groups like the Red Army Fraction (RAF) in West Germany or the Brigate Rosse in Italy were both deriving from the same worldwide Marxist, Castro and Mao inspired student revolts or "awakenings" that gave political birth to many of Naxal's intellectual cadres. Another point why Naxals are "terrorists" could lie in the very history of the term itself : When Russian anarchists and socialists started the first international wave of terrorism (besides radical Irish nationalists), they proudly called themselves "terrorists" to stress the political essence of their deeds and to relate to the French Revolution and its aftermath (the Jacobinian anti-counterrevolutionary *régime de la terreur*)[14].

More important than the word's usage, however, is that Naxalism with its Maoist ideology (thereby rooting in Marxism) is - despite character Velu's assertion in 'Red Alert' - inherently very well "against the nation". That is : not against the Indian nation itself but in opposition to the very notion of a nation-state as some relevant form of human society's organisation. Beginning with Karl Marx's and Friedrich Engels' *The Communist Manifesto* (first published in

London 1848) according to Marxist (informed) worldview, the central and fundamental class struggles are inter- or even supranational : the working class, the "Proletariat" (more central the peasant class for Mao), has to be united across borders like the major companies, the "Capitalists" or the "Bourgeoisie" have already done. Economical "System" and cultural, political and historical "State" or "Nation" are inseparable for, according to Marx's and Engels' Historical Materialism, economic conditions ("Basis") determine, shape and form human history and society together with its "consciousness". Arundhati Roy, in this sense and adapted for modern Globalisation, describes Naxals as heroic freedom fighters that oppose not only greedy capitalist mining companies but also defend the helpless, powerless (class) against an aggressive Indian imperialist and colonialist nation.

> Almost from the moment India became a sovereign nation, it turned into a colonial power, annexing territory, waging war. It has never hesitated to use military interventions to address political problems-Kashmir, Hyderabad, Goa, Nagaland, Manipur, Telangana, Assam, Punjab, the Naxalite uprising in West Bengal, Bihar, Andhra Pradesh and now across the tribal areas of Central India[15].

This is a powerful and highly unpleasant narrative interpretation and accusation : ideal free and equal Hindustan is a historical or "mythical" product of self-liberation and the defeat of imperial power and colonial policy. It questions modern India's moral secular authority and ideological roots and imagination. Furthermore, it complicates negotiating the Maoist issue : Neither could the Naxals be fully excluded as "foreign" terrorists, nor easily paternalistically re-included and re-integrated like radical Muslims and Hindus who just have to learn *religious-ethnical* tolerance and accept that they are "one family" under India's tricolour. National social-economical causes are much more difficult to handle, especially when Globalisation and national economic growth became (most) dominant master narratives. Therefore even established story-strategies like scapegoating single villains (e.g. the corrupt Minister of Defense in 'Rang De Basanti' who is visually equated with the British officer responsible for the Jallianwalla Bagh massacre 1919) do not work out when the very "Indian Constitution, the moral underpinning of Indian democracy [...] ratified colonial policy [...]"[16], thus allowing suppression, exploitation and marginalisation.

Dominant Hindi cinema simply can neither approve nor demonise the Maoist movement and plenty of its legitimate basic issues and claims (which are used in regular standard Bollywood storytelling either). Thus, it is vital that Naxals - as Krishnaraj in 'Red Alert', who is not responsible but embodies Maoists's leadership and policy nevertheless - by their own choice and insight renounce violence and support the democratic parliamentary state "system". In return, 'Red Alert' ignores larger political visions, reducing Naxal conflict to unspecific issues like poverty and "terrorising" policemen - "naturalised" social, economical and political *phenomena*, "visible" to the camera or "tellable" in cinema's generic language. Hence, depicting the Naxal movement is per se problematic because the larger social-revolutionary philosophy, agendas and concepts are missed or have to been *translated* : "classes" become (groups of) individuals (actors); "exploitation" turns into ambiguous dramaturgy - so when servile contractors paying tedu leaf pickers too little are now threatened and blackmailed by Naxals itself. Yet, cinema can at least address complex constellations and interrelations beyond (stereo-)typical standards as in 'Hazaaron Khwaishein Aisi' (2003): Activist Siddharth (Kay Kay Menon) recounts in a letter an incident in Bihar : After the local landlord's son has raped a village girl the furious crowd is determined to castrate him. Revolution is at hand when the powerful father suffers a heart attack.

> The lower-caste villagers who had been screaming for his blood a minute ago where suddenly overcome by some ancient dutiful urge to save him. After all, he and his family had been their lords

> and masters for centuries. [...] This strange compassion of the villagers towards their oppressor in his moment of need taught me something. What? I'm still trying to decipher.

'Red Alert - The War Within' is not concerned with such important psycho-social dynamics or even only mentions unarmed Naxal groups or a broader socialist movement. However, the movie presents another approach in balancing Maoist violence and legitimacy : Naxalism's ideo-political ambivalence, the contradiction between just cause and intolerable violence, real grievance and abstract ideals - all implemented already in the uneven story structure with its dysfunctional but inevitable ending - is projected on (or embedded in) Naxal characters, their traits and personal conditions, thereby offering another way of making *narrational* peace with the revolutionaries.

4. Flawed Idealists :

First and foremost main character Narasimha poses a challenge to the proclaimed high standards and noble motivations, on which Naxalites and their advocates rely. Narasimha, whose perspective dominates the movie, is an anti-hero - passive, frightened and clumsy. Shetty represents him most of the time with a blank insecure or astonished expression and submissive gestures towards his fellow comrades. No paragon of Naxalism spirit, he lacks not only all heroic virtues but also the political (let aside revolutionary) convictions : On the one hand Narasimha joins the ranks only involuntarily, on the other only the need for money to support his wife and children keeps him interested. His awkward asking and cautious demands for his promised payment, thus, heavily interferes with the Maoists' self-narrative, their idealistic, altruistic engagement, motivations and aims. "We are fighting for people like you", Narasimha is told indignantly, and especially Velu becomes furious when Narasimha stays persistent while a very attentive reporter witnesses the compromising hassle. But maybe Velu's family is dead - as the leader retorts-, but of course, Narasimha's is not, and if money is so much beneath them, why did the Naxals agree on the Rs. 1.500 a month in the first place? Angry but helpless Velu throws the money bill in Narasimha's face.

Despite becoming a traitor Narasimha is the only person in the movie with a real and concrete goal. He is not interested in any larger program or big time revolution but in satisfying his family's most basic needs and to enable his children a future, that is : an education. No jobs await them due to the existing conditions, he is told, but between the broader social improvement and the individual well-being is a gap too big and too well known in social-revolutionary history. The Naxal guerrilla can extort contractors and kill hostages to stop a steel mining project. But neither are they able (or interested) to soften their own comrade's hardship, nor to save innocent villagers, landless and tribals from being caught in the middle of an asymmetrical war while fighting on their behalf.

> One of the group commanders, who looks suspiciously like the author Pankaj Mishra, says reading books is all he does : "Words have the power that guns don't." The words don't match his own actions[17].

Mayank is right. His reproach, however, ignores that 'Red Alert' is first and foremost about idealist freedom fighters which try best but fail to live up to their own ideals and expectations. Velu, for example, states to fight for a classless society, but he himself acts arrogant and patronising way beyond his duty as the outfit's leader : When Narasimha dares to serve him dinner leftovers after Velu rejected food, he is deeply insulted. So even the struggle for equality creates (new) hierarchies, perpetuates higher and lower caste constellations.

Moreover, with quite tragic notion, the comrades live and struggle like a melancholic army of ghosts : They have long lost what they are fighting for and - in stark contrast to Roy's account of Naxal's existence and except of Narasimha standing in between - they no (longer) belong to the world of those they claim to represent.

Another aspect of these ambivalences and the comrades'

otherworldly existence are the females' position and fate. Already the very cast is a symbolical reference : "Saral" or "Saralaka" alias Seema Biswas played Phoolan Devi in Shekhar Kapur's 'Bandit Queen' (1994), "Comrade Radhaka" Ayesha Dharker is best known for her role as designated Tamil suicide bomber Malli in Santosh Sivan's 'Theeviravaathi - The Terrorist' (1998). These roles were especially *gendered* rebel characters, with rape, revenge and pregnancy being of great thematic and motivic significance to the stories. In 'Red Alert' both "experienced" women are joined by frightened and traumatised Lakshmi (Sameera Reddy). During a raid on a police station the Naxal outfits finds and frees the young woman. Accused by her boss of stealing for he rejected to sleep with him, Lakshmi got arrested, imprisoned and gang raped all night long by the policemen. Especially older Saral takes care of her in the camp - and presents to her rifle and olive uniform as (symbolical) tools for a new, self-determined way of life : No longer a victim's existence. "When you hold a gun it lessens your fear", Saral explains, and later : "I picked up the gun at the age of fifteen. Since then I feared no one."

Gender equality and women's empowerment by joining the ranks are revolutionary struggle's positive side effects. Arundhati Roy addresses the "feminist" side of the Naxal engagement, too. About a group of young Naxals working as village-level militia, she writes :

> They have just finished a day's work, helping to build fencing around some village houses to keep the goats out of the fields. They're full of fun and curiosity. The girls are confident and easy with the boys. I have a sensor for this sort of thing, and I am impressed[18].

Additionally, this empowerment is one of women's *narrative* roles, too. Mani Ratnam's 'Raavan' (2010) - no movie decidedly about Naxalism, but one you could interpret as such - the rebel-bandit's sister is imprisoned and raped several times. But 'Raavan' (as the title implies) is a much more traditional, almost mystical story. Thus, after coming free the dishonoured and shamed young woman drowns herself. It is not hers but her brother's to seek revenge.

Modern Naxal movement may allow women to break free from such limited, passive stereotypical roles. Yet, again, there is a price to pay, at least in 'Red Alert'. The de-gendered paramilitary life hardly allows sex, love, friendships or relations : Velu laments that he has not slept with a woman for years, and when book-loving well-educated Commander Murli (Murli Sherma) is more interested in his propaganda material, his "girlfriend" Comrade Saralaka turns away in anger : "Sleep with these posters. It'll be fun". That in the end, women liberation is not inherent to the Maoist movement at all but an independent issue of its own very own logic becomes apparent when Narasimha shoots Velu and Lakshmi takes the blame : She killed him, so Lakshmi explains, because he tried to molest her. No one doubts her, for "all men are alike". So to Saralaka not even the Maoist camp is safe for women anymore, while Lakshmi, in some sense, simply cannot escape her own story of the victimised woman, but now even hides herself and Narasimha behind it - behind a lie. But to what end? After Narasimha gives away the outfit's position to the police, Lakshmi is the group's only survivor and her (plot) journey ends as it begins : In a police cell. There she is found dead, hung herself. With the belt of her olive uniform.

Conclusion :

Between Bollywood entertainment and serious political drama 'Red Alert - The War Within' is as flawed as its characters. However, not despite but because of its shortcomings this movie - like others, too - is so interesting when scrutinizing problems which political and especially leftist violence poses to society and its ideological formation. Naxalites pursue widely acknowledged goals and oppose grave injustices. At the same time, they oppose the very nation's constitution and authority. Thus, Naxalism needs a narrative of balancing or closure - at least on (or for) the silver screen. One way is to acknowledge not only Maoist's claims, moral and - to a certain degree - intellectual integrity, but again their tragic failure. "You cannot win", 'Red Alert' states, "how much you deserve it". Therefore, leftist revolutionary violence is dismissed not just principally (for the "war" just produces instead of *martyrs* innocent and meaningless *victims*), but also functionally : it does not succeed. Yet, this message is as ambivalent as the film's dysfunctional ending for maybe violence is tragic, wrong and not successful, but it may *work*, nevertheless - at least for the moment and on an individual level. Thus it is an explanation for the Maoist threat to India, too.

References :

1. Akbar S. Ahmed (1992), 'Bombay Films : The Cinema as Metaphor for Indian Society and Politics', *Modern Asian Studies*, 26, 2, pp. 289-320, here : 289.
2. See for example Fareed Kazmi (1999), *The Politics of India's Conventional Cinema. Imaging a Universe, Subverting a Multiverse.* New Delhi / Thousand Oaks, CA / London : Sage, pp. 16 ff.
3. Leon Festinger (1957), *A Theory of Cognitive Dissonance*, Standord, CA : Standfort University Press.
4. Mayank Shekar (2010), 'Review : Red Alert', *Hindustan Times* (July 9, 2010). Online :http://www.hindustantimes.com/Review-Red-Alert/Article1-569950.aspx (retrieved May 25, 2011).
5. Shekar (2010).
6. Jerome Bruner (1991): 'The Narrative Construction of Reality', *Critical Inquiry*, 18, pp. 1-21.
7. Barbara Czarniawska-Joerges (2004), *Narratives in Social Science Research*, London : Sage.
8. See for example Hayden White (1980), 'The Value of Narrativity in the Representation of Reality', *Critical Inquiry*, 7, 1, pp. 5-27.
9. e.g. Ronald N. Jacobs (2002), 'The Narrative Integration of Personal and Collective Identity in Social Movements' in Melanie C. Green / Jeffrey J. Strange / Timothy C. Brock (Ed.), *Narrative Impact. Social and Cognitive Foundations*, Mawah, NJ / London : Lawrence Erlbaum, pp. 205-228.
10. Arundhati Roy (2010), 'Walking With the Comrades', *Outlook* (March 29), pp. 22-59.

11. Roy 2010, p. 44.
12. Jyotika Virdi (2003), *The Cinematic ImagiNation. Indian Popular Films as Social History,* New Brunswick, NJ / London : Rutgers University Press, here : p. 1.
13. Kuldip Nayar (2007 [2000]), *Without Fear. The Life and Trial of Bhagat Singh, New Delhi* : Harper Collins India (first published as *The Martyr Bhagat Singh–Experiments in Revolution.* New Delhi : Har-Anand Publications), here : p. XI)
14. Walter Laqueur (1982), *Terrorismus.* Frankfurt a. M.: Suhrkamp.
15. Roy 2010, p. 53.
16. Roy 2010, p. 53.
17. Mayank 2010.
18. Roy 2010, p. 31.

Running Away…
The Buddhadeb Dasgupta Trilogy

Shoma A. Chatterji

Introduction :

'Dooratwa', 'Grihajuddha' and 'Andhi Gali' form a loose trilogy by Buddhadeb Dasgupta. The common thread that links the films is the notion of disillusionment with idealism and political commitment and the spilling over of this discontent and restiveness into the personal lives of the subjects. Each film has an independent story sourced from an original literary piece, re-scripted to suit the needs and interpretations of the director and his medium - cinema. Each film has its independent statement, plot and theme. Each film is complete unto itself. Together, they belong to a time-space setting with the same context of extreme Leftist politics in West Bengal. The male protagonist has a background of Leftist commitment in his past. The present finds him trying to distance himself and run away from this past. This 'running away' somewhere along, becomes a running away from Life itself, and from the responsibilities and relationships that form the core of life. The three films did not follow sequentially. Dasgupta broke the 'continuity' after his first full-length feature 'Dooratwa' with 'Neem Annapoorna' (1979), a film in a different realm. He then made 'Grihajuddha' and 'Andhi Gali'.

The three films are set against the background of the Naxalite movement. The protagonist of each film is a former Naxalite, someone who was once theoretically dedicated to the building of a better world and willing, if necessary, to lay down his life for the 'cause', but who was subsequently ideologically set adrift only to return with neither design nor cathartic submission, to his middle-class moorings. The three films depict the dimming of the flame of idealism and the lighting in its place of the fire of respectability, kindled by the ardour of acquisitiveness[1].

The titles of each film, taken sequentially, suggest a narrowing of vision without a corresponding increase in focus. 'Dooratwa', meaning 'distances' suggests a constant widening of spaces between and among people engineered, almost unconsciously, by the protagonist, Mandar. He tries to bridge this 'gap' but we do not know if this attempt to 'correct' his past behaviour will colour his future. 'Grihajuddha' is translated as 'Crossroads'. The dictionary translation of the Bengali word is 'domestic conflict.' Dasgupta widens the horizons of this meaning to embrace a small world in conflict, where people meet at a certain crossroad they have been pushed into, and are vague about their bearings, about the risks involved, the lurking dangers, and about the responsibilities they are forced to take up. They are confused about which road to take next. This 'small' world is a microcosm of the larger world, where moral decay in one group of people or one individual victimizes another individual or group. The victimizer, such as Mandar in 'Dooratwa', Bijon in 'Grihajuddha' and Hemanta in 'Andhi Gali', evolve into victims themselves sucked into a vicious circle of their own making, from which exit seems difficult, though not impossible.

'Andhi Gali', Dasgupta's first film in Hindi, means 'blind alley.' Hemanta who seeks to run away from his past, is trapped in a blind alley from which perhaps there is no escape. Hemant, a symbol of the ideologically fickle middle class, is an extension of Mandar of 'Dooratwa' and Bijon of 'Grihajuddha'. The ideological Jaya, a symbol of lost innocence and purity in 'Andhi Gali', is an extension of Anjali and Nirupama in the other two films.

'Dooratwa' (1978) :

Based on a short story by Sirsendu Mukhopadhyay, 'Dooratwa' was completed in 16 shooting days on an incredibly low budget, exposing 20,000 feet of film. Dasgupta made changes in the original short story to bring it close to his interpretation of society. He did not fall into any clichéd, pedantic problem-solving, trying to offer an artificially imposed solution to the problem the film unfolded. The film bagged the National Award and a Special Critic's Award at the 1979 Locarno International Film Festival.

A Calcutta college teacher and former revolutionary of the late 1960s, Mandar marries Anjali. When he learns that Anjali is pregnant, he leaves her because she tells him that it is not his child. Anjali refuses to reveal the name of the father because she feels she is equally responsible for the pregnancy. After he leaves her, Mandar refuses to give shelter to a Naxalite on the run. Mandar forms a relationship with Nandini, a steno-typist who lives with her insane mother. But the relationship keeps him as restive as ever and winding up his relationship with Nandini, he goes to Anjali, hoping to re-build the relationship within freshly defined parameters of friendship and understanding. In the meanwhile, Anjali has taken up a teaching job and is bringing up the child single-handedly. He is a bit surprised to discover that Anjali bears no ill-feeling towards him for having divorced her. She accepts him as a friend while Mandar learns to shed his earlier prejudices that made him reject her.

On the surface, 'Dooratwa' is a simple story. A woman, whose family is helped by a friend in time of need, sleeps with him. When she learns she is pregnant, the man suggests abortion which she cannot accept. She manipulates another family friend to marry her and tells him the truth a month later. The husband lets her go but he finds that even after two long years, he is unable to forget her, or the insult of having used him to legitimize the child. He refuses to listen when she says that she had wanted him as much as she desired the baby. The elaborate introduction of the cast and characters shows that 'Dooratwa' is intended to be as much a cinematic exercise as an investigation into middle-class morality in a contemporary urban setting. It is a mature portrait of a middle class dilemma, subtle in its understanding and sensitive in treatment.[2]

'Dooratwa' does not offer answers to the questions it raises. It slightly brushes the surface of ideological confusion by letting Mandar overcome at least a part of his moral conflict that makes him take the rather unconventional step to visit his ex-wife with hopes of a possible friendship. The clash between life and ideology is presented as a human problem in the original story. Dasgupta gives it a political perspective without making it look like a strident political message or a plea for social change[3]. He tries to present people and things as they are, and the social responsibility they must face if being what they are and how they behave entails risks that might topple moral and social concerns within urban lives, creating distances ('Dooratwa') in emotional and social space between and among people and in their interactions with one another. The film has an open ending, left to the audience to read into.

'Grihajuddha' (1982) :

An interesting reality of 'Grihajuddha' is that the Left-ruled Marxist Government of West Bengal produced it while the WBFDC (West Bengal Film Development Corporation) took the responsibility of distributing the film. It is a strong yet subtly stated critique of the Establishment. So, the WBFDC developed cold feet when it saw/ heard about the film and its statement. It held back the film's release for two years. Later, it decided to release the film in theatres that previously screened either Hindi or English films from Hollywood. Unlike most of Dasgupta's films that do not do well commercially, 'Grihajuddha' was reasonably well-received. It picked up six *Ultorath*[4] awards in 1984 for Best Story (Dibyendu Palit), Best Script and Direction (Buddhadeb Dasgupta), Best Actor (Gautam Ghosh), Best Actress (Mamata Shankar) and Best Supporting Actor (Sunil Mukherjee). It won the Fipresci Jury award at the Venice International Film Festival in 1983. The same year, Utpalendu Chakravorty's 'Chokh' was awarded the Golden Lotus while Gautam Chattopadhyay's 'Nagmoti' was declared the Best Bengali Feature Film at the National Awards though both films were released earlier. Thus, 'Grihajuddha' was sidetracked at the National Film Awards for two consecutive years.

'Grihajuddha' (Crossroads) was based on a Dibyendu Palit story. This was Dasgupta, crossing Black-and-White to step into colour. He used the format of a slickly made political thriller to unfold the story of a family's victimization to corporate politics. He goes on to portray how one member, the daughter engaged to her dead brother's runaway friend, draws strength and moral courage from the very oppression they are victim to. The story is built around a few individuals whose lives are trapped in an urban corner where all the exit points have suddenly been closed. This is tragic as each one is fighting a war (griha meaning 'home' and juddha meaning 'war') and is seeking his/ her own way out of this war. If one is fighting a war for love, another is fighting a war for integrity, and a third is forced to wage a war for basic survival. Somewhere along the way, these separate, individualistic 'wars', congregate and the difference between them is nothing more than a confused blur.

'Grihajuddha' (Crossroads) begins with the 'accidental' death of the chief labour officer of a private steel company in Barrackpore following his detection of serious corruption within the management. He reports the matter to the authorities in New Delhi but the management learns of the secret report. The officer resigns and dies an 'accidental' death soon after. Soon after this so-called accident, Probir Dutta, the intrepid young secretary of the company's trade union, gets to know the truth about the officer's death. He calls a workers' meeting intending to expose the management. Before he can do this, he and his close friend Bijon are attacked by hired killers. Probir is killed. Bijon manages to escape. Bijon breaks the news to Probir's family and absconds.

Probir's family comprises his aged parents, two grown-up sisters and a small brother. They are compelled to leave their suburban home to settle in a backstreet home in Calcutta. Nirupama, the elder sister, in love with Bijon, waits for his return. A young reporter Sandipan is assigned by his paper to do an investigative story on the series of mystery deaths and their links to the company. He doggedly collects bits and scraps of information that, when pieced together, provides a likely answer to the question - who are the killers? He tracks down one of the suspects, Sital, goalkeeper in a small-time football team. His conversations with Sital reveal that the management has used Sital with the lure of money or a job and Sital who now wishes to concentrate on living a normal life through football and a job is intent on distancing himself from his criminal past.

In its attempt to compromise the bereaved family of Probir and the insistently questioning Nirupama, the company offers her a job. Though Nirupama is by now aware of what led to her brother's death, she is forced by circumstances to accept the offer with the hope and confidence that Sandipan will continue his crusade to discover the truth.

In the meantime, Bijon, who had done well at faraway Nashik in Maharashtra comes back. Bijon is now a successful salesman and no longer cares for the revolutionary ideals he stood for in the past. His youthful anger against the Establishment has disappeared in the face of material success, leaving him content on the one hand and cynical of those who still stand by their faith in radical social change on the other. He rents a flat in one of the city's better parts and proposes marriage to Nirupama. She accepts and requests Sandipan to be a witness to their registration. As he proceeds for the wedding on his two-wheeler, Sandipan is hit by a car and is killed on the spot. A shocked Nirupama who refuses to accept Sandipan's death as a mere accident, asks Bijon to postpone the wedding. He is very angry. Nirupama, realizing that this is no longer the man she was once deeply in love with, turns him away. The break makes her realize that she has an inner strength she was never aware of, a capacity to defy she never recognized. The film ends with the elimination of Sital when he is killed in a deserted playfield during his workout in the breaking hours of the day.

Dasgupta gives celluloid credibility to the middle class milieu in 'Grihajuddha'. The inquisitive neighbours leaning out of the rooftop, the tipsy husband tottering back home, the distressed family huddling together in their dingy dwelling reveal Dasgupta's commendable concern for detail. Based on a contemporary short story called 'Maachh' (Fish), structurally, the film runs along two levels almost like parallels on a single plane[5]. One consists of a young and crusading journalist's attempt to investigate two murders committed by the management of the factory. The other explores the inner journey of Nirupama, the sister of one of the murder victims, in her separate search for truth on the one hand and her love for Bijon on the other. The two strands meet at one point, move together for some time and then go their separate ways after Sandipan is killed. Sandipan functions as the common link between these two levels. His death could have been the climax but Dasgupta saves the film from this clichéd end and lets it move on for some more time to end in a freeze shot of the footballer against the soundtrack of the breaking of a glass pane.

The most striking element of 'Grihajuddha' lies in its 'absences.' The adversaries in the film are never really visible but make their presence strongly felt by the power of their absence. Their names and identities are never articulated because they represent a collective strength - a power they can abuse and misuse when they feel these are being questioned and threatened by people they consider below them. Dasgupta exercises excellent control by presenting the murders mostly in 'absence' with only one direct confrontation when Probir is beaten up and dies as a result. The stylistic presentation of the footballer Sital at the end of the film is a case in point. Sandipan's death is almost glossed over by the camera and that heightens the shock and the intensity of the death.

Dasgupta's statement on 'Grihajuddha' is perceptive and forceful. "In 'Grihajuddha'," he says, "my intention is to portray an average man with contemporary sensibilities, aware of the world around him, left with no choice but to be committed. But the atrocities practiced by big capital frighten him and force him to abandon his commitment. Predictably, he tries to justify his veering away from his original stance. The metamorphosis is tragic because it makes him stand up against his own people. This, to my mind, is the tragedy of the present times and of many a sensitive, present-day individual"[6]. Though Dasgupta uses the masculine pronoun 'he' to make his statement, it is Nirupama who emerges triumphant, by refusing to surrender to a man she can no longer recognize as the one she once loved, though she is aware that with this, she has possibly signed off hopes of a marriage in future. She refuses being either a victim or a martyr. The victims are all men, including Sital, the pawn who fails to realize his dreams of a normal life, and

Bijon, the man who has made it good, only at a price he can never hope to regain. He is the worst victim. His 'success' is tinged with his failure to make his lady love accept him as life partner.

'Andhi Gali' (1984) :

'Andhi Gali' is the final part of the director's trilogy. Based on 'Gharbari' (Homes and Houses) penned by Dibyendu Palit, 'Andhi Gali' draws its substance from another intriguing aspect of urban reality. Palit's story appeared in the Pooja special of a Bengali journal. Dasgupta had already made two films based on Palit's stories, 'Sheet Grishmer Smriti' and 'Grihajuddha'. Dasgupta picked 'Gharbari' and moulded it to fit into his celluloid interpretation. Palit's story is rooted in contemporary Calcutta but can equally apply to any middle class situation in any city. Dasgupta gave the film wider human and social significance than one finds in the original Palit story. Two memorable films released in the same year as 'Andhi Gali' were Gautam Ghosh's 'Paar' and Biplab Roychoudhury's 'Ashray', also in Hindi.

'Andhi Gali' focusses on the conflict between political commitment on the one hand and self-pursuit on the other. "Once in a while, there comes along a film which moves startlingly close to life, reality and the truth as we see them - flawed, distorted but strangely attractive"[7]. This is an ideal one-liner that defines 'Andhi Gali'. The film holds a mirror to the urban hell called 'society'. In its reflection we see the ugliness we have created for ourselves. The film is bitter, cynical, dark and pessimistic. Dasgupta is disenchanted with the moral degradation of the urban middle class. Yet, he also believes that there possibly is a way out. A dead end does not necessarily mean that there is no escape. If one goes beyond the cinematographic frame and the narrative space to explore Hemant's past, 'Andhi Gali' evolves into an indictment against urban young men who once felt committed to the ideology of the Left and when they felt they could not cope, they tried to escape, only to discover that there was no escape. Relationships at the individual level demand the same sense of commitment and loyalty that political commitment to an ideology does. Leftist or Rightist inclinations do not matter. Hemant discovers this with a sense of shock. But it is too late. Mandar and Bijon make similar discoveries in their lives.

Like its predecessors, 'Andhi Gali' points a finger - albeit an invisible one - at the Leftist movement in West Bengal, underscoring through its male protagonist Hemant, its tendency to breed men who turn out to be complete failures in their personal lives once they quit the movement. Yet, ironically, for men like Hemant, Bijon and Mandar, there is just no turning back. The film opens in Calcutta in 1973 when Hemant belongs to the political wing of an extreme Left party. He is captured one morning in the school where he teaches. The police put him in a van along with his comrades. Somewhere along the way, the van stops at maidan. The prisoners are asked to get off and run. The police begin to shoot in what is notoriously known as an 'encounter' killing.

Hemant escapes by the skin of his teeth and runs for his life. We see him five years later in Mumbai, where, having shed his political leanings, he is trying to run the cut-throat race of material success. He has become what the Marxists call 'the bourgeoisie.' But he is still trying to run away from his past fears that have spilled over into his present life, threatening to disturb and disrupt its emotional balance. His value system is warped. He is blindly groping for a way out of the mess and morass his life is reduced to, constantly manipulating and using his innocent and naïve wife Jaya as scapegoat. Jaya is no scapegoat. She pays the price for his manipulations - giving him the right to sell off her ancestral home and her jewellery, till it comes to a compromise on her values - so different and distanced from his. Till Jaya remains oblivious of this difference, she allows herself to flow with the tide. This helps her cope with the tragedy of losing the child she was bearing. Motherhood might have rescued her from the perennial loneliness in the spacious space of their brand new apartment. When she realises that Hemant is more dictator than husband, more rapist than lover, prepared to stake his wife to achieve his material ends, she puts her foot down in the only way she can - she jumps off the balcony of the multi-storied apartment they live in, onto the flat ground of the compound below.

Jaya's voice still remains one of the most strident and strongest 'silent' voices of women in cinema. Jaya disproves her father's dying statement to Hemant. "I am worried about Jaya" he says, adding, "She won't protest. She just accepts everything"[8]. This underscores the unpredictability of naïve, simple and innocent women like Jaya. It is also a pointer to how her father, who has brought her up singly, has failed to understand the rebellion this young daughter is capable of. Jaya is a much-misunderstood woman. Her father has not understood her. Her husband has never cared even to make the attempt.

In a desperate attempt to persuade Jaya to get back to the job she has just given up, Hemant sets up a series of events. It is a prelude to a 'punishment' he has planned for quitting the modelling job that paid the hefty installments on the apartment he has bought. On a bright Sunday morning, he takes her to a restaurant. When they come back, he bursts out in rage and in a fit of mounting violence, rapes her. Her response to this brutal rape is a quiet, "you are not human." It is the final straw in a marriage that began to die the day Jaya lost her baby. She refuses further humiliation of her body, mind and dignity. When her quiet anger leads her to the final leap off the balcony, it is a punishment-in-reverse. Hemant loses everything he has - the wife who served as his ladder to the top and the house he dreamt of that is no longer his. He suffers the ultimate ignominy of being informed of his wife's death by neighbours knocking at his door as Jaya's broken body lies in a heap below while he sleeps on late into the morning in their bedroom, oblivious and unrepentant of what he has done.

A precursor to Jaya's concern about her personal autonomy and her discomfiture with the modelling assignments she does not wish to do come across once. At one point, she asks Hemant, "How long should I continue to do this work? You should have asked me first." This simple question followed by a normative statement throws up four things. One, she is unhappy with the work she has been forced into. Two, she is unhappy about her husband not having had the decency of asking her permission before assigning her to such work. Three, Hemant is an arrogant, manipulative and abusive husband. He takes her too much for granted and his earlier involvement with extreme Left Marxism has not stripped him of his patriarchal and feudal mindset, everything that Marxism claims not to be. Four, Hemant ignores the anger and the protest hidden in the question he ought to have taken as warning of his wife's growing discontent and the dangers lurking therein. He pays a price heavier than the one Jaya has to pay. The only difference between Jaya's tragic end and his lies in that he has chosen to shape his destiny himself, while he has not permitted Jaya any space for making choices. Yet, she turns the tables on him, leaving Hemant to grope and run alone in the hope of seeing some faint ray of light in the 'blind alley' of his own making.

For a moment, one might feel that Jaya's suicide is rather drastic and 'convenient' a closure for a razor's edge film like this. All Hemant wanted was a decent home. Then one realises to one's horror that one's own sense of right and wrong has been dulled to such an extent that compromises like the one Jaya is asked to make are 'minor' and 'acceptable.' This is what Dasgupta tries to point out. Jaya symbolizes what we all want to be - the ideal human being, the perfect woman. Hemant, like us, is full of imperfections. This makes it easier for us to identify with him. We are never able to hate him. Hemant, like Mandar and Bijon, is a man who has lost his roots and floats in an undefined urban and social space, trying desperately to hang on, to belong, to anchor himself anew to fresh roots, to build and re-build relationships, but failing all the time.

The Women :

The women in the three films emerge as much stronger individuals than the men. Anjali in 'Dooratwa' knows exactly what she must do with her life, though her pregnancy is a sort of sacrifice of values and morals for her family. Instead of using her pregnancy as a means of emotional blackmail of the ones responsible - the family benefactor and the family itself, she accepts the change and the responsibilities that come along with it. Her manipulation of Mandar stems from a sense of 'belonging.' When it backfires, she takes the rejection in her stride and carries on with life as if nothing happened. She moves on, and when Mandar comes back and knocks on her door, she welcomes him with the dignified distance that defines her persona.

Though Mandar, the protagonist, is a man, Anjali, the woman, slightly marginalized within the cinematographic space by Mandar, comes across as the stronger of the two. She is much more in control of her life than he is. She is firm in her decision of keeping the baby, of not asking Mandar to stay on, of bringing up the child all by herself, of refusing to abort the baby when the man responsible asks her to. Then why does she stoop to deceiving Mandar into a marriage of cheap, political convenience? Because basically, she is as conventional as the girl next door and is aware of the support she needs from a man to bring up the child. She is no sexually permissive woman who is promiscuous. The pregnancy happened through circumstantial pressure, and instead of turning her back on it, she takes it on as her sole responsibility. Yet, she is no dumb woman who readily accepts the victimization of being a single mother, or be frustrated by the divorce thrust on her by her husband. Mamata Shankar essays the character with the restraint it needs and in this, she gets able support from Pradip Mukherjee who portrays the perennially confused and insecure Mandar. Though he speaks of women's liberation in the classroom, at the personal level, Mandar is unable to accept that his wife is expecting someone else's child and has married him by deceit. He is completely disillusioned with the Leftist movement he was once so involved in. Yet he lacks focus in life -political, personal, emotional or any other.

Mamata Shankar as Nirupama somehow offers a kind of continuity from Anjali in 'Dooratwa', as if Nirupama is a logical extension of Anjali if not the same woman in a different time-space-incident setting. Nirupama is as low-profile, as subtle and as quiet as Anjali is. She changes along with changes in the social, familial and political environment of her life. The sudden responsibility thrust on her of having to turn sole breadwinner for the family following the tragic death of the elder brother she idolized so much is something she finds difficult to begin with, but learns to cope in her own simple and unobtrusive way. Every experience makes her stronger than she was before, the final turning point coming with the death of Sandipan and her acceptance that the man she once loved is certainly not the one she would like to spend her life with. Mamata essays the same restraint she essayed in 'Dooratwa', along with the same silences. As the only female character of note in a film almost entirely peopled by men, Nirupama stands out not by her beauty, her sensuousness or her seductive qualities, none of which are even touched upon in the film, but by her subtlety and her growing strength. Her strength is wonderfully counter pointed by the weak Bijon portrayed by Anjan Dutta. Sandipan, portrayed brilliantly by director Gautam Ghose, comes across as a strong complement to Nirupama. Both the men offer two different kinds of contrasting characterization to Nirupama.

Jaya's suicide is not a defeatist act of self-destruction. It is political act of attack, of not compromising with her moral values or contributing to the moral decay. The lighting produces the claustrophobic effect of a blind alley even when the couple shifts into the sparse, spacious flat in the skyscraper. The slow emotional metamorphosis of Jaya as she moves from her cheerful, simple, vulnerable mode into deep depression is expressed through her mobile face and her body language. Once, the camera captures her in mid-shot as she curls up into a foetal position on the staircase of her home, perhaps an expression of her wish to go back into her mother's womb. Her body language changes and so does her way of dress - she stops caring about her hair, about wearing ironed saris, she stops smiling and even stops talking. "Why should death be looked upon as the end of life? It could also be a process of realization," asks Dasgupta. "Jaya is a concept. She is ideal and ideals always die," he sums up.

Conclusion :

In this trilogy, the protagonists either wage their individual crusades or carry their individual crosses. But in dealing with the individual as the focal point of his films, Dasgupta never loses sight of the broader social perspective[9]. His 'individual' is an integral part of the social organization and his/ her crisis emerges from his/ her dichotomy between his/ her persona and the society he/ she belongs to. His films try to resolve this contradiction. The process is not withdrawal but attack.

The trilogy demonstrates Dasgupta's concern about depicting the social forces that go to shape the destinies of individuals rather than trying to explore the psychology of individual characters. He never lets his characters to be reduced to cliché, cardboard characters used to mouth their own ideologies or simply to make a point. The distances created by Mandar in 'Dooratwa' are sustained, or perhaps heightened within the inner conflict in 'Grihajuddha' and stretch towards an unknown infinity in 'Andhi Gali'. The inner conflicts of Mandar, Bijon and Hemant are not identical, but the consequences they encounter in ideological terms, are. Is this because these men are lesser than they believed themselves to be? How does one explain their moral cowardice and decay once they have quit their political commitments in the past? Or, has their disillusionment with the movement they once believed in has led to disillusionment with themselves? Are these three men symbols of the ideologically fickle middle class of Calcutta in the 1970s? These significant questions are universal and timeless. They mark this Dasgupta trilogy as the most outstanding political and social statement of the times they reflect.

Notes :

1. John W. Hood (1998). *Time and Dreams : The Films of Buddhadeb Dasgupta,* Seagull Books, Calcutta, p.18.
2. Swapan Mullick (1981). 'Dooratwa', *The Statesman* (March 27, 1981) Calcutta.
3. Ibid.
4. *Ultorath* is a noted Bengali film monthly brought out of Calcutta which instituted awards though these awards are no longer given since the magazine has fallen into bad days.
5. Dhruba Gupta (1984). 'Grihajuddha', *Cinewave,* No.6 (April-Sept., 1984).

6. Vidyarthy Chatterjee. 'Struggle Within' in Pradip Biswas (ed.) *Buddhadeb Dasgupta : Cinema of Imprinted Times,* Aurora Film Corporation, Private Limited, p.27.
7. Deepa Gahlot (1984). 'The Urban Hell', *Filmfare* (January 1-15, 1984,) pp. 76-77.
8. John W. Hood, op.cit., p.32.
9. Mriganka Sekhar Roy (1990). 'Weaving Image with Metaphor - An Interview with Buddhadeb Dasgupta', *Deep Focus, A Film Quarterly* (Vol.III, No.1, 1990), pp. 62-65.

Representing a Fragmented Society : 'Hazaar Chaurasi ki Maa'

Sukanta Acharya

'Hazaar Chaurasi ki Maa' (1998) (Hindi; English : The Mother of 1084) is an Indian feature film that deals with the life of a woman who loses her son, a Naxalite, to the violence that is a result of his adopted ideology.

The film is directed by Govind Nihalani and is based on Magsaysay and Jnanpith award recipient Mahasweta Devi's Bengali novel *Hajar Churashir Ma.* The screenplay is written by Nihalani and the dialogues by Tripurari Sharma. The film stars Jaya Bachchan as Sujata Chatterjee, Anupam Kher as Dibyanath Chatterjee, Milind Gunaji as Inspector Saroj Pal, Seema Biswas as Somu's mother, Joy Sengupta as Brati Chatterjee and Nandita Das as Nandini Mitra. It marks Jaya Bachchan's return to acting after a gap of 18 years. In 1998, 'Hazaar Chaurasi Ki Maa' won the National Film Award for Best Feature Film in Hindi.

Dibyanath Chatterji, his bank-employed wife, Sujata, and youngest son, Brati, live an affluent existence in Calcutta, West Bengal, India, circa early 1970s. Sujata is a quiet, devout Hindu, religious, and compassionate woman, and Brati has finished his school and is now attending college. His parents are proud of him, and keep track of his progress. Then their world is shattered during the early hours, when they are informed by the police that Brati has been killed. Sujata goes to identify Brati's body, mourn, lament inconsolably. They know now that their lives will never be the same again - for by the police they will be called the mother and father of corpse No. 1084. Sujata struggles to understand Brati's passing, meets his friends one by one, comes to know that Brati had a girlfriend, Nandini Mitra, and that's when she finds out that Brati was part of a rebel group often referred to as "Naxalites", a militant leftist group. As she delves deeper and deeper into Brati's life, she begins to understand her son's struggle, and decides to continue to further this.

The Bengal Renaissance in Question :

The film opens with some issues that interrogates the so-called modernity in West Bengal that issued from the Bengal Renaissance at its heart - Kolkata, the capital of the State and within the city itself the canvas selected for the film is only a part of the city space - from Bhowanipore, that inherits the cultural legacy of the Bengal Renaissance to southern Jadavpur that in the context of the film is on the fringe of the city and in many senses, outside it. In theoretical terms, if Bhowanipore as late as in early 1970s still carried forward the Renaissance legacy of modernity, was modernity itself, southern Jadavpur not only did not share this cultural legacy, people living there represented the other : migrants from erstwhile East Bengal who were still grappling with meeting their bare material needs to live in a society that was humane. This brings in more fundamental questions : if the social and the cultural space between Bhowanipore and southern Jadavpur, not to talk about the city of Kolkata as a whole, or for that matter, larger entities like the State of West Bengal and India, could be analyzed as one society in the same manner as Classical theorists talked about the word 'society' in universalistic modern terms.

Language of Modernity :

Over a century ago, Nietzsche (1887, 2003 : 151) berated the modern scientist's narrow "factualism" and "renunciation of all interpretation," and a few decades later Weber (1919, 1958) declared the age of the generalist to be over. Extreme specialization, self-enclosed disciplinary jargons, and narrowly focused technical work have since transformed these prescient visions into observable realities. Responding to the dominant forms of a theoretical- empirical work and a historical "general theory" in post-World War II American social thought, C. Wright Mills (1956 : 183-4) asked : "Where is the intelligentsia that is carrying on the big discourse of the Western world and whose work as intellectuals is influential among parties and publics and relevant to the great decisions of our time?" In his view, professional social science was guilty of "pretentious triviality" and incapable of grasping the growing threats to freedom and reason. About the same time, Raymond Aron (1970b : vi, 332) argued that classical social theorists shared "a certain solidarity" deriving from their "global historical interpretations of the modern age": a broad vision which has been regrettably lost (Aron, 1969 : v-xviii; 1970a : 7-9, 332-3; 1970b : v-ix, 331-2).

From this perspective, classical social theory provided comprehensive analyses of the core features, central processes, and imminent threats and possibilities of modernity and such broad and wide-ranging discourse is still useful and needed today. Classical social theory is primarily a theory of modernity and that the classical tradition of modern social theory raised fundamental questions concerning the nature, structure, and historical trajectories of modern societies. By putting modern societies in broad historical perspective, by emphasizing the linkages between their differentiated social institutions, and by expressing the potentialities for normatively guided social change, classical theorists such as Marx, Durkheim, Weber, and Dewey developed a discourse that facilitated comprehension and discussion of, and posed responses to, the rise of modernity and its problematic social conditions.

The Chatterjee Household :

The play of modernity's operative aspects and consequences inherited from the Bengal Renaissance are acted out in Dibyanath Chatterjee's household : it is taken as the spectacular stage. Every member of the household is a successful member of the modern professions. The male members of the household have the additional quality of having the right kind of mediations in their own associations and outside that makes 'success' as the inevitable outcome. All members of the family are not only highly educated, but they have also earned fame for themselves, so much so that they are known for their talents as individuals and as a family. To cut a long story short, the family represents everything that modernity stands for, in the areas of education, culture, way of life, affluence, in the context of post-colonial Kolkata, that the Bengali bhadralok at one time loved to call the second largest, greatest and glorious city of the British empire. It is pitiable, however, that in the world-views of the members of this family, except Sujata and Brati, vices that go with a modern way of life, like patriarchy, promiscuity, greed and the like, also crept into the inner psyche of the family that no longer pricked their consciences. With their virtues and vices, the Chatterjee family stood for the normal citizens who could represent and be represented in a polity that they thought fit to call a democracy.

The cultural site of the Chatterjee household, or of Bhawanipore where it is located or for that matter the larger canvas between Shyambazar in the north and Bhawanipore in the south that contained the metropolis that was Kolkata and the exclusion of every other area, geographically close by that it may be, but culturally not worthy of inclusion, interrogates the truth of the Bengal Renaissance and its relevance. The yardstick by which many writers on Bengal's recent history tended to arrive at a judgment on this would fall apart if we consider the following from societies that seemed to set the standards for these writers.

As Clifford Geertz has poetically noted, "all modern nations-even Norway, even Japan-contradict themselves : They contain multitudes" (Shweder, Minow, and Markus 2002, back cover). These "multitudes" challenge the structure and practices of the nation state (see Shweder, Minor, and Markus 2002) but may invigorate democracy's best promise when difference engenders serious engagement and debate.

Managing difference is becoming one of the greatest challenges to multicultural countries. From Britain, France to Sweden, Brazil to Bolivia, Indonesia to Malaysia, the work of managing difference calls forth a new educational agenda. Children growing up in these and other settings are more likely than in any previous generation in human history to face a life of working and networking, loving and living with others from different national, linguistic, religious, and racial backgrounds. They are challenged to engage and work through competing and contrasting models, such as kinship, gender, language (monolingual and multilingual), and the complicated relationships between race, ethnicity, and inequality, in new ways. It is by interrupting "thinking as usual"-the taken-for-granted understandings and worldviews that shape cognitive and metacognitive styles and practices-that managing difference can do the most for youth growing up today.

Negotiating differences requires energy-the kind of energy that can be recycled and harnessed to bolster a cornerstone of human intelligence : the ability to consider multiple perspectives (Piaget 1936; Gardner 1999; Vygotsky 1978). Taking multiple perspectives, reversing mental routines, and articulating multiple hypotheses from a common set of facts and working through the logical and rational vectors that would best explain those preexisting facts are crucial features of human intelligence. When distinct cultural models and social practices are deployed to address a common set of problems, youth gain the cognitive and metacognitive advantages inherent in examining and working on a problem from many angles. Freely, fully, and respectfully arguing within a framework of difference is likely to better equip youth to deal with the complexities of the day.

The problem is that between the Chatterjee family of Bhowanipore and the largely migrant society that inhabited southern Jadavpur the difference that exist in the storyline of the film is not manageable in the sense that the scholars under reference above are arguing for : not manageable through engagements, debates, negotiations, working and networking, taken for granted understandings and shared world-views that exist across the differences they have at the back of their minds and their writings.

The consequence is that any idea of political representation that offers itself or challenges the idea that the Chatterjee family believes in and lives by in the context of the film even by one of its members, namely, Brati Chatterjee who engages in exploring an alternative idea of political representation in association with his friends who live in southern Jadavpur, had to be annihilated along with his friends, by a section of inhabitants of southern Jadavpur in collusion with the armed forces of the state.

The homogeneity of the ruling coalition represented by the Chatterjee family it did not hesitate to breach the codes of family life. At the beginning of the storyline in the film, the character Sujata, Brati's mother, receives a call from someone who asked her to come immediately to Kantapukur for identification of dead body number 1084, which to the knowledge of the police forces concerned, was Brati Chatterjee's. But, since in law it required identification, some one from the Chatterjjee family had to give credence to this information as evidence.

When the whole family woke up to this event, Sujata was grappling with what Kantapukur stood for, gets a clarification, and decides to go there herself. Dibyanath quickly engaged his elder son Jyoti to work a way out of the impasse by disowning Brati from the family connection in every possible way. He refused to go to Kantapukur himself, not allow Sujata to take his car anywhere near Kantapukur, lest it is identified and try his networks and make sure that Brati Chatterjee's name does not slip into the media and the public domain in any way. A father and brother's behavior on hearing the news of their son's and brother's assassination| When Sujata lay bedridden in the aftermath of her younger son's death, Dibyanath made sure that the last traces of Brati's association with the Chatterjee family were removed from the building that housed it. In other words, Brati was cast out of the power elite that till then ruled Bengal and dominated its culture and society.

South Jadavpur - Other Possible Modes of Political Representation :

The site of other possible modes of political representation and contestations between them could be viewed at south Jadavpur when Sujata crossed the threshold of the confines of the social and cultural barriers of the Chatterjee household and met Somu's family and explored information from them. She came to know that it was in

Somu's residence that Brati spent his last night along with his four friends that it was in the foreground of this makeshift dwelling unit that large number of people, who gathered with arms to the level sufficient to assassinate the few young people that Brati and his few friends were with a common purpose or intention : to stamp out the mode of political representation that Brati and his comrades offered - the so called Naxalbari line of violent revolution that called for destruction of all so called bourgeois institutions of political representation.

It was not the case that the people of southern Jadavpur who organized themselves for the purpose of killing Brati and his friends at Somu's residence or any section of it, had any personal enmity with Brati or any or all of his friends. In fact, as Sujata learned from Somu's mother, almost all of these assassins were personal acquaintances of members of Somu's family. Still, it was on their side that policemen in plainclothes fought shoulder to shoulder with the purpose of the common mission of eliminating those who converted to the Naxalbari line of political representation that refused to compromise with the so called bourgeois mode of political representation.

The strategies and tactics of these people, as part of a larger political configuration in West Bengal, was to strike a balance between the Naxalbari mode of political representation that refused to compromise with the so called bourgeois mode of political representation and the bourgeois mode of political representation inherited from the so called Bengal Renaissance. When this was their strategy, that is constructing a Leninist Party organization and function in accordance with its premises and principles, there was nothing wrong in having a few policemen in plainclothes for a tactic to assassinate those who offered the contending mode of political representation, namely, Brati and his friends who believed in that mode of political representation.

Political Representation :

There have been a number of important advances to the concept of political representation. In particular, these advances call to question the traditional way of thinking of political representation as a principal-agent relationship. Most notably, Melissa Williams' recent work has recommended reenvisioning the activity of representation in light of the experiences of historically disadvantaged groups. In particular, she recommends understanding representation as "mediation." In particular, Williams (1998, 8) identifies three different dimensions of political life that representatives must "mediate:" the dynamics of legislative decision-making, the nature of legislator-constituent relations, and the basis for aggregating citizens into representable constituencies. She explains each aspect by using a corresponding theme (voice, trust, and memory) and by drawing on the experiences of marginalized groups in the United States. For example, drawing on the experiences of American women trying to gain equal citizenship, Williams argues that historically disadvantaged groups need a "voice" in legislative decision-making. The "heavily deliberative" quality of legislative institutions requires the presence of individuals who have direct access to historically excluded perspectives.

In addition, Williams explains how representatives need to mediate the representative-constituent relationship in order to build "trust." For Williams, trust is the cornerstone for democratic accountability. Relying on the experiences of African-Americans, Williams shows the consistent patterns of betrayal of African-Americans by privileged white citizens that give them good reason for distrusting white representatives and the institutions themselves. For Williams, relationships of distrust can be "at least partially mended if the disadvantaged group is represented by its own members" (1998, 14). Finally, representation involves mediating how groups are defined. The boundaries of groups according to Williams are partially established by past experiences - what Williams calls "memory." Having certain shared patterns of marginalization justifies certain institutional mechanisms to guarantee presence.

Williams offers her understanding of representation as mediation as a supplement to what she regards as the traditional conception of liberal representation. Williams identifies two strands in liberal representation. The first strand she describes as the "ideal of fair representation as an outcome of free and open elections in which every citizen has an equally weighted vote" (1998, 57). The second strand is interest-group pluralism, which Williams describes as the "theory of the organization of shared social interests with the purpose of securing the equitable representation ... of those groups in public policies" (ibid.). Together, the two strands provide a coherent approach for achieving fair representation, but the traditional conception of liberal representation as made up of simply these two strands is inadequate. In particular, Williams criticizes the traditional conception of liberal representation for failing to take into account the injustices experienced by marginalized groups in the United States. Thus, Williams expands accounts of political representation beyond the question of institutional design and thus, in effect, challenges those who understand representation as simply a matter of formal procedures of authorization and accountability.

Another recent way of envisioning representation was offered by Nadia Urbinati (2000, 2002). Urbinati argues for understanding representation as advocacy. For Urbinati, the point of representation should not be the aggregation of interests, but the preservation of disagreements necessary for preserving liberty. Urbinati identifies two main features of advocacy : 1) the representative's passionate link to the electors cause and 2) the representative's relative autonomy of judgment. Urbinati emphasizes the importance of the former for motivating representatives to deliberate with each other and their constituents. For Urbinati the benefit of conceptualizing representation as advocacy is that it improves our understanding of deliberative democracy. In particular, it avoids a common mistake made by many contemporary deliberative democrats : focusing on the formal procedures of deliberation at the expense of examining the sources of inequality within civil society, e.g. the family. The benefit of Urbinati's understanding of representation is that it emphasizes the importance of the domain of opinion and consent formation. In particular, this contemporary addition to the theoretical literature poses an agonistic conception of representation, one that emphasizes the importance of disagreements and rhetoric to the procedures, practices, and ethos of democracy. Her account expands the scope of theoretical discussions of representation away from formal procedures of authorization to the deliberative and expressive dimensions of representative institutions. In this way, those who recommend adopting an understanding of representation as advocacy provide a theoretical tool to those who wish to explain how non-state actors "represent."

Moreover, some conceptual advancement has helped clarify the meaning of particular aspects of representations. For instance, Andrew Rehfeld (2009) has argued that we need to disaggregate the delegate/trustee distinction. Rehfeld highlights how representatives can be delegates and trustees in at least three different ways. For this reason, we should replace the traditional delegate/trustee distinction with three distinctions (aims, source of judgment, and responsiveness). By collapsing these three different ways of being delegates and trustees, political theory and political scientists overlook the ways in which representatives are often partial delegates and partial trustees.

Other political theorists have asked us to rethink central aspects of our understanding of democratic representation. In Inclusion and Democracy Iris Marion Young asks us to rethink the importance of descriptive representation. Young warns that attempts to include more voices in the political arena can suppress other voices. She illustrates this point using the example of a Latino representative who might inadvertently represent straight Latinos at the expense of gay and lesbian Latinos (1986, 350). For Young, the suppression of differences is a problem for all representation (1986, 351). Representatives of large districts or of small communities must negotiate the difficulty of one person representing many. Because such a difficulty is constitutive of representation, it is unreasonable to assume that representation should be characterized by a "relationship of identity." The legitimacy of a representative is not primarily a function of his or her similarities to the represented. For Young, the representative should not be treated as a substitute for the represented. Consequently, Young recommends reconceptualizing representation as a differentiated relationship (2000,

125-127; 1986, 357). There are two main benefits of Young's understanding of representation. First, her understanding of representation encourages us to recognize the diversity of those being represented. Second, her analysis of representation emphasizes the importance of recognizing how representative institutions include as well as they exclude. Democratic citizens need to remain vigilant about the ways in which providing representation for some groups comes at the expense of excluding others. Building on Young's insight, Suzanne Dovi (2009) has argued that we should not conceptualize representation simply in terms of how we bring marginalized groups into democratic politics; rather, democratic representation can require limiting the influence of overrepresented privileged groups.

Moreover, based on this way of understanding political representation, Young provides an alterative account of democratic representation. Specifically, she envisions democratic representation as a dynamic process, one that moves between moments of authorization and moments of accountability (2000, 129). It is the movement between these moments that makes the process "democratic." This fluidity allows citizens to authorize their representatives and for traces of that authorization to be evident in what the representatives do and how representatives are held accountable. The appropriateness of any given representative is therefore partially dependent on future behavior as well as on his or her past relationships. For this reason, Young maintains that evaluation of this process must be continuously "deferred." We must assess representation dynamically, that is, assess the whole ongoing processes of authorization and accountability of representatives. Young's discussion of the dynamic of representation emphasizes the ways in which evaluations of representatives are incomplete, needing to incorporate extent to which democratic citizens need to suspend their evaluations of representatives and the extent to which representatives can face unanticipated issues.

Another insight about democratic representation that comes from the literature on descriptive representation is the importance of contingencies. Here the work of Jane Mansbridge on descriptive representation has been particularly influential. Mansbridge recommends that we evaluate descriptive representatives by contexts and certain functions. More specifically, Mansbridge (1999, 628) focuses on four functions and their related contexts in which disadvantaged groups would want to be represented by someone who belongs to their group. Those four functions are "(1) adequate communication in contexts of mistrust, (2) innovative thinking in contexts of uncrystallized, not fully articulated, interests, ... (3) creating a social meaning of 'ability to rule' for members of a group in historical contexts where the ability has been seriously questioned and (4) increasing the polity's de facto legitimacy in contexts of past discrimination." For Mansbridge, descriptive representatives are needed when marginalized groups distrust members of relatively more privileged citizens and when marginalized groups possess political preferences that have not been fully formed. The need for descriptive representation is contingent on certain functions.

Mansbridge's insight about the contingency of descriptive representation suggests that at some point descriptive representatives might not be necessary. However, she doesn't specify how we are to know if interests have become crystallized or trust has formed to the point that the need for descriptive representation would be obsolete. Thus, Mansbridge's discussion of descriptive representation suggests that standards for evaluating representatives are fluid and flexible. [For an interesting discussion of the problems with unified or fixed standards for evaluating Latino representatives, see Christina Beltran's *The Trouble with Unity.]*

Mansbridge's discussion of descriptive representation points to another trend within the literature on political representation - namely, the trend to derive normative accounts of representation from their function. Russell Hardin (2004) captured this trend most clearly in his position that "if we wish to assess the morality of elected officials, we must understand their function as our representatives and then infer how they can fulfill this function." For Hardin, only an empirical explanation of the role of a representative is necessary for determining what a representative should be doing. In *Ruling Passions*, Andrew Sabl (2002) links the proper behavior of representatives to their particular office. In particular, Sabl focuses on three offices : senator, organizer and activist. He argues that the same standards should not be used to evaluate these different offices. Rather, each office is responsible for promoting democratic constancy, what Sabl understands as "the effective pursuit of interest." Sabl (2002) and Hardin (2004) exemplify the trend to tie the standards for evaluating political representatives to the activity and office of those representatives. In 'The Good Representative', Suzanne Dovi (2007) identifies three standards for evaluating the performance of democratic representatives : those of fair-mindedness, critical trust building, and good gate-keeping.

Political Representation in Hazaar Chaurashi ki Maa :

In 'Hazaar Chaurashi Ki Maa', even theoretical explanations of 'political representation as advocacy' was not given the social space from where it could operate as an alternative to the power elite that took shape in early 1970s in West Bengal. This was in consonance with Christina Beltran's interpretation in her The Trouble with Unity. It is true that in a society of fragments that West Bengal was at the time that the storyline describes, the interests that Brati and his friends sought to articulate were not crystallized, making political representation rather unclear at least to sections of people in southern Jadavpur and elsewhere in the metropolitan city of Kolkata and its fringes. This problem was compounded by the character of the state apparatus that was by no means as if we could assess the morality of elected officials, and understand their function as our representatives and then infer how they can fulfill this function.

The consequence was two-pronged. On the one hand, social fragments in the sense outlined above could by no means be governed by laws meant for a liberal society. On the other hand, law-enforcing agencies of the state constructed on the assumed homogeneity of society, fall into pieces and function without an internal normative coherence. In other words, what in liberal democratic parlance is known as 'rule of law' and in post-colonial countries like India is one of the corner-stones of the Constitution, in effect fall through in its functioning.

In consequence, elections to the decision-making bodies of the state are held, candidates are declared as elected representatives of the people, the law-enforcing and other agencies of the state are authorized to act in accordance with laws enacted by the legislative bodies of the state. This results in bestowing on the functionaries in law-enforcing and other agencies extraordinary discretionary powers and they exercised these powers on the instruments handed down to them by the physical apparatuses of the state.

The patron-client relations that develop between the socially and culturally degenerate power elite and the functionaries of the law-enforcing and other agencies of the state not only work to each other's benefit that is visible to other fragments in society, are seen in disgust by them. But they can do little to counter this unholy nexus, because apart from some skin-deep ideas that they romanticize upon to write their posters and raise their slogans, they fail to work out methods for their own defense or to counter the brutality of the so-called law-enforcing agencies and their functionaries. Breaking away from their intellectual, social and cultural backgrounds, only Brati and Nandini bet on their lives to take on a pedagogic role in a semi-literate subaltern bhadralok social fragment. They fail in their effort because they do not have at their disposal means to cultivate a normative homogeneity of society at large. In effect, democracy remains a façade on a population that is disenfranchised.

The Culture Carnival :

Everything is for consumption in the huge drawing room of the Chatterjee family. The occasion is a prelude to the matrimonial ceremony of Tuly, Brati's elder sister. She was already engaged to Tony Kapadia who is in intercontinental business and has powerful connection both in Kolkata and overseas. Dibyanath had a special liking for Tony for his connections from which he benefitted in his business and he also shared his views on patriarchal and adulterous passions and pursuits. More to the point, he liked the fact that it was Tuli, his younger daughter with whom the matrimonial alliance was arranged, who not only shared his views on patriarchal and adulterous passions, but also helped him actively in his adulterous adventures with the former typist of his office. The drawing room with about fifty guests was full with decorations, food items and the other accessories bequeathed to this section of society by their former colonial masters. Sujata, as usual, remained on the sidelines.

Conclusion :

'Hazaar Chaurashi ki Maa' comes full circle in a concluding cinematografic setting another two decades later where Sujata has retired from service and is in full time service for the protection of human rights. Apparently, she is in an NGO that fights for the protection of human rights among the subaltern bhadralok who in more senses than one have been enfranchised. It would not be wrong to assume that the lack of normative homogeneity that left them disenfranchised several decades back and unfit for receiving pedagogic lessons from the literati in society, have given way to their enfranchisement. Sujata devotes herself to this mission in order to accomplish her son Brati's mission. Nandini meets her here and reveals that she has taken a similar role for the tribals, who are still largely disenfranchised.

References :

Nietzsche, Friedrich, *The Genealogy of Morals,* translated by Horace Barnett Samuel, New York : Courier Dover Publications, 2003.

Weber, Max (1919) 1958, 'Science as a Vocation', in H.H. Gerth and C.W. Mills, *From Max Weber : Essays in Sociology,* New York : Oxford University Press.

Mills, C Wright, *The Power Elite,* New York, 1956.

Raymond, Aron, *The Elusive Revolution : Anatomy of a Student Revolt,* New York : Praeger Publishers, 1969.

Shweder, Richard A., Martha Minow, and Hazel Markus, editors (2002), Engaging *Cultural Differences : The Multicultural Challenge in Liberal Democracies*, New York : Russell Sage Foundation Press.

Piaget, J. (1936), *La Naissance de l'Intelligence chez l'énfant*, Delachaux et Niestlé, Neuchâtel.

Howard Gardner (1999), *Intelligence Reframed : Multiple Intelligences for the 21st Century*, New York : Basic Books.

Lev S. Vygotsky, (1978), *Mind and Society*, Cambridge, MA : Harvard University Press, pp. 79-91.

Melissa S. Williams (1998), *Voice, Trust and Memory : Marginalized Groups and the Failings of Liberal Representation*, Princeton : Princeton University Press.

Nadia Urbinati (2000), 'Representation as Advocacy : A Study of Democratic Deliberation', *Political Theory*, 28 : 258-786.

Rehfeld, Andrew, 2009a. *Political Representation : An Explanatory Account*. Manuscript. Department of Political Science, Washington University in St. Louis. Rehfeld.

Andrew, 2009b, 'On Quotas and Qualifications for office' in *Political Representation and Democratic Self Rule*, eds.Ian Shapiro, Susan Stokes, and Elisabeth Wood. New York : Cambridge University Press.

Iris Marion Young (2000), *Inclusion and Democracy*, Oxford University Press.

Suzanne Dovi (2009), 'In Praise of Exclusion', *Journal of Politics*, 71 (3): 1172-1186.

Jane Mansbridge (2004), 'Representation Revisited : Introduction to the Case Against Electoral Accountability', *Democracy and Society*, 2 (I): 12 13.

Jane Mansbridge, (2009), 'A Selection Model of Representation,' *Journal of Political Philosophy*, 17 (4): 369-398.

Russell Hardin, (2004), 'Representing Ignorance,' *Social Philosophy and Policy*, 21(1): 76-99.

Andrew Sabl (2002), *Ruling Passions : Political Offices and Democratic Ethics*. Princeton University Press.

Intersection of 'Middle Class Bhadralok' and Naxalite Movement : A Montage of Selected Movies

Monalisa Basu

Movie is a multilayered reflection of a variety of events which is represented by the directors and often that adds some new dimensions to it as director's perception and understandings are also impounded on the subject consciously or unconsciously. This often helps us to read the nature and impact of those social events which are apparently not so perceptible. In tune with the theme of the book, I will try to analyse in this article the impact of Naxal movement on movies by keeping my primary focus on bhadralok middle class i.e., how has this class made a specific framework within which the movement itself was ultimately limited and how have these movies on Naxal politics reflected the impact of the movement over this class. There is a crisscross zone in-between 'bhadralok middle class' and Naxal Movement and how does that get manifested through movies will be briefly analysed here by concentrating on four selected movies which directly or indirectly deal with the movement - 'Pratidwandi' (1972) by Satyajit Ray, 'Padatik' (1973) by Mrinal Sen, 'Anu' (1998) by Satarupa Sanyal and 'Hazar Chourasi ki Maa' (1998) by Govind Nihalni. First three movies are made in Bengali whereas the fourth one is a Hindi movie.

Middle Class Bhadralok :

Bengal more specifically Calcutta was the main epicenter of the emergence of middle class bhadralok during the British rule in India. Some scholars have made distinction between the 'Middle class' and

'Bhadralok'; but in terms of their origin, features, social role and position they are more similar than different from each other and there are many overlapping zones in between them. Amit Kumar Gupta in the introduction of his book, Crisis and Creativities : Middle Class Bhadralok in Bengal 1939-52 (2009), wrote that by the term 'bhadralok' reference is given to the cultural background of the class and by the term 'middle class' the economic position of that class is acknowledged. In this article we will use the term middle class bhadralok to denote a single class who has some common and distinctive features.

Calcutta became the heart of Bengal and was just after London among all cities of British Empire in the early 20th Century. Calcutta had remained the capital of India till 1912 and economically, politically, culturally and most important, intellectually, Calcutta was the centre of the whole circle. It became a city of migrants due to its growing opportunities in employment and education. In this background one emerging feature was the rise of an elite group - a group of Bengalis who claimed and was given recognition as superior in social status to the man of the fellows. This elite group was known as the 'bhadralok', literally the 'respectable people', the 'gentlemen' (Broomfield 1968 : 5). By following Broomfield, we can say that this bhadralok class is different from the rest of the society in terms of their deportment, speech, style of housing, dressing, eating habit, occupation, association, and urge for education and fundamentally, in terms of their cultural values and sense of social prosperity. The most vital attribute of this class was their social honour and that is why Broomfield called them 'status group' (Broomfield 1968 : 12). However, scholar like S. N. Mukherjee has differed from this view and referred to bhadralok as social-class as they play an important role in economic change and social mobility in Bengal (Mukherjee 1977 : 24). One important line of distinction between the bhadra and abhadra was the mental stigma of the class against the physical labour. In Broomfield's language "The basic and most rigidly maintained between bhadra and abhadra, between high and low, the respectable and the others, was the bhadralok's abstention from manual labour and their belief in inferiority of manual occupation" (Broomfield 1968 : 6). Caste is also an important factor as most of the members of bhadralok class belonged to the three upper castes of Bengali Hindu Society -Brahmin, Baidya and Kayastha. Another important feature is that, unlike in many other parts of India, the high caste people of Bengal were not directly related to land or agriculture. Either they had sold their land or if they even possessed, they had engaged agricultural labour to till the land. This emerging new class was the first and fast to learn the language of the ruler that was English and became the main force of British administration, bank, hospital, school, college etc. Macaulay in his famous Minutes (1835) wrote about this class that "...who may be interpreters between us and the millions whom we govern". On the one hand, their English education helped them to be an important part of the British administration, and also the horizon of Western philosophy and literature were opened to them on the other hand. It is important to remember that all members of this class were not very educated; actually this class had a fetish for education. In the Simon's Commission Report (1928) it was written that these educational institutions like Presidency College, English University, and Inns of Court in London etc were considered as a gate to the society of bhadralok (Report 1928 : Vol-VIII : 24). This educated middle class bhadralok now became conscious of their language - an elegant, literary Bengali - Sadhu bhasa - developed parallel to the enrichment of Chalit bhasa and bhadralok speech became different from the non-bhadralok as the former strove to avoid unrefined diction or apabhasa. This group with their sense of superiority developed a conviction that they had a vital role to play both in the political process and cultural uplift of Bengal as well as of India. They started to take an active interest in analysing Indian culture and religion in the light of Western philosophy. They became the agent of protest and brought various new values in the society through various reform movements. This process gave birth to what we call the 'Bengal Renaissance'. Binoy Ghosh observed that in the 19th century the movements for social renaissance and against superstition were led by this middle class (Ghosh 1973 : 9). Joya Chatterji wrote, "Since the late nineteenth century, the bhadralok had regarded themselves as a group that was 'cultured', by the early twentieth century, they saw themselves, more specifically, as heirs to a particular cultural heritage, the Bengal Renaissance" (Chatterji 1994 : 155). Since then this class has engaged itself in different social and political activities. In 1876 Indian Association and in 1885 INC were formed under the initiative and the leadership of this class. The first major success of them in politics was the agitation against the partition of Bengal since 1905 and final reunification of Bengal in 1912. By the beginning of the 20th Century, involvement of middle class bhadralok in politics became most dynamic and obvious - swadeshi-boycott movement, moderate-extremist rift, rise of revolutionary terrorism etc were the outcome of their involvement. Another unique feature of the class is the inner contradiction and duality of their nature. Joya Chatterji made an interesting observation in this regard when she analysed some novels of the 19th century - "The Bengali Hindu persona that emerges out of Renaissance writing is thus full of contradictory essences; it is simultaneously courageous and timid, vigorous and passive, other-worldly and venal, spiritual and hypocritical, cultured and imitative" (Chatterjee 1994 : 163). This class is marked by the lack of physical strength and vigour. T. B. Macaulay to describe the stereotype feeble character of this emerging middle class bhadralok wrote, "Courage, independence, veracity, are qualities to which his constitution and situation are equally unfavourable" (Macaulay 1843, III : 345). Bankimchandra Chattopadhyay in one of his famous writings Babu sarcastically described the same class as 'He whose strength is in his one time in his hand, ten-times in his mouth, a hundred times behind the back and absent at the time of action is a babu' (Chattopadhyay 1874 : 11). In Pather Dabi Saratchandra Chattopadhyay depicted the nature of this emerging class through these protagonists of the novel, Apurba - a good natured, sentimental young man who is also weak, indecisive and fearful and the hero of the novel Sabyasachi is just the opposite, the ideal expected character who will liberate the nation.

Impact of the Middle Class Bhadralok on the Naxalite Movement :

Bhadralok politics is a typical characteristic of the Bengal politics since pre-independent era and that has been continuing even after independence. With the gradual collapse of the one party domination at the Centre and emergence of many non-Congress governments at various state levels including West Bengal, a steady erosion of the bhadralok politics is marked throughout India since late 1960s. But surprisingly, in spite of the coming of the Left parties, that is, the parties of the proletariat, into power, the actual nature of the politics of Bengal has not changed in reality. In other words, we can say that the composition of ruling party of West Bengal has changed in 1977, but not the features of bhadralok politics as such. In West Bengal, the Left Front came to power in 1977 and continued for more than three decades with the help of the radical philosophy of Marxism and very successfully connected themselves with the rural masses. The trend of the urban educated bhadralok leadership based on radical philosophy of the mass has become a distinctive feature of the Bengal politics. On the other hand, Naxal movement which is the most drastic and militant movement of India since independence, is viewed by many as altogether different from all previous movements of India, particularly after independence. Started as a peasant movement, supported and joined by urban educated youth, based on radical ideology of Mao, executed through new lines like action squad, guerilla warfare, annihilation of class enemies etc, the movement has become a sui-generis. But the movement, though started as a peasant movement, ultimately became a movement of the urban educated people, not only in terms of the leadership but also in terms of the participation, strategy, line of action and media attention. Asim Chatterjee, most popular leader of urban youth of the time, later observed that there were two distinct lines of thought - path of Naxalbari and path of Naxal movement. In a semi-feudal society the base of class struggle is the fight for land and that gradually helps to develop the class consciousness and mass-organisation which will ultimately reach to the level of armed struggle to capture power. This was the path of Naxalbari (Chatterjee in

Goswami 2006 : 147). On the other hand, another line of thought developed which rejected all the needs and demands of the people, of mass- organisation and mass-movement and adopted the direct line of annihilation of class enemy. This is the path of Naxals and unfortunately, the urban youth shifted from the first line to the second (Chatterjee in Goswami 2006 : 147). According to Chatterjee, this was the fourth phase of the movement and this line was even imposed over the peasants in the name of 'Red guard Action' (Chatterjee in Goswami 2006 : 148). This phase got an immediate hype and popularity in media and mind of people, created huge fear psychosis. Chatterjee wrote that Naxalbari became an image of revolution; the real Naxalbari went behind the veil of over-imagination (Chatterjee in Goswami 2006 : 149)[1]. Even if we look at the composition of the leadership of the movement without any exception as such we will find that the movement of the marginal peasants was under the guidance of the bhadralok of the society. In reality, bhadralok class of Bengal particularly supported both the philosophy of status-quo and radicalism on the basis of the need of the situation in order to continue the leadership. Though apparently Naxal movement may be different and very fundamental in nature, but that does not ultimately refute its middle class bhadralok character at all.

When the basic frame of the movement itself was limited within the edge of the bhadralok politics, it is very natural that its impact on movie is not an exception. In fact, majority of the movies which have dealt the movement directly or indirectly, have focused on the movement mainly from the urban view-point. Through these movies hardly the real issues of the movement like the demand of the tribal peasants, their frustration, agitations, sacrifices etc have got proper reflection; rather most of these cinemas have dealt with the frustration of urban youth, their anger against the education and employment system, their insecurities, ideological confusions, police oppression on them and the problems of their family as well as their society to handle them and the movement. All four movies that I have chosen for this article, though directed by four different renowned directors, two of which made in early 1970s and other two at the end of 1990s, addressed their subject form different perspectives, but have remained same in dealing with the basics of the movement. In other words, these movies have dealt with people who basically belong to the Bengali middle class bhadralok community and all their psychology and sentiments are projected from different angles. Siddhartha Chatterjee in 'Pratidwandi', Sumit of 'Padatik', Brati and Sujata of 'Hazar Chourasi ki Maa', Anu and Sugato in 'Anu' - all belong to this type of families. In spite of their many differences their families fundamentally adhere to basic common natures of middle class bhadralok. These families of movies economically belong to lower middle class (Sumit's family in 'Padatik') to upper middle class (Brati's family in 'Hazar Chourasi ki Maa'), but culturally they are more similar to each other that is to say that they all belong to bhadralok class - their earnings come from jobs, not from land; whatever is their economic condition they are inclined to modern education (Siddhartha of 'Pratidwandi' left his medical study, Brati of 'Hazar Chourasi ki Maa' was a student of a reputed college); all of them speak the same urban polished language called bhadra language; main protagonists are all conversant with English language (in 'Padatik' Sumit was reading book of Lenin and Frontier, which were in English, in 'Pratidwandi' Siddhartha went to watch an English movie); their dress code, hairstyle, body language, social interactions etc, all typically correspond to the already described features of middle class bhadralok. None of the character of any of the selected movies used any rural dialect; all the male and female persona in spite of their variation in economic background from higher to lower middle class, wore the contemporary, urban clothes which were no way close to tribal peasant mass. Audience has no confusion in identifying them as urban youth brigade of the movement for social change! We also know that this class is distinctively marked by its domicile character - more concerned with family and its well-being than any major rebellious and radical activities. They are basically conservative in nature, more keen to maintain status-quo. There is a Bengali proverb which says that the top-most and the lowest can mix with each other without much hesitation, but the middle always keeps a safe distance.[2] This is an ideal example to describe the Bengali middle class bhadralok mentality that usually prefers to stay within the boundary and prefers to preserve the threshold. That is why Sumit's father in 'Padatik' who was a low paid private firm worker grumbled on his son for his so-called revolutionary activities and ideological inclinations. The same grouchy mentality about ideology of social change and radicalism was reflected through the dialogues of Siddhartha in 'Pratidwandi' to his younger brother, who was actively involved in radical political activities. In other two movies the central characters are women - Ananya in 'Anu' and Sujata in 'Hazar Chourasi ki Maa' who were also similar as both of them were happy in their make-believe world. Anu was helping her elder brother and her love interest Sugato without being much involved in political ideologies whereas Sujata the mother of Brati in the other movie firmly believed that she knew her son Brati best. She was also very proud of him. She was happily holding her private and public life. We see the mental vacillation and hypocritical observance of radical philosophy without much change from within as they love to fantasize the romantic ideological stands. We also see their final submission to the existing traditional value system at the time of countering the reality. This is also part and parcel of this middle class mentality. In 'Pratidwandi' Siddhartha had mental appreciation for the mass revolt of Vietnam but could not participate in revolutionary practice like his brother and in the climax of the movie the rebellious act he could manage to do was dismantling the interview board though finally he surrendered himself to the most dissatisfactory job which he was not ready to accept earlier and left Calcutta. This nature was most pronounced in Sugato's character in 'Anu'. The main protagonist of the Naxal movement in this movie was Sugato who always talked about freedom and equality of all including women and of a new society after ground-breaking change through their revolution. But such a symbol of emancipation and egalitarianism finally could not accept the mark of those wounds on the body of his wife Anu, which were the result of the gang rape as revenge by the people whose search for Sugato was in vain. The typical orthodox values that consider woman as a mere body or sex object, which emphasize the virginity and chastity of a woman/ wife as most important, ultimately determined his behaviour with his wife when he faced the hard core reality and through this Sugato reconfirmed his typical middle class bhadralok mentality.

Many more examples we can draw from these movies to show that ultimately like the movement itself movies also have hyped the urban aspects of the movement and thus in spite of strong alternative potentialities, like the movement itself most of the movies including these selected four have remained confined within the frame of middle class bhadralok politics.

Impact of the Naxalite Movement on Middle Class Bhadralok :

We have already come know the fact that these selected four movies particularly represent Bengali middle class bhadralok families and surroundings. All their conservatism with apparent bounteous mentality was going well in parity with their middle class values and identity. But in all these four movies the main characters gradually changed their stands and beliefs as slowly as they were exposed and ultimately collide with the realities of their social surroundings. And needless to say that the common social surrounding in all these movies was the radical Naxal movement of 1970s to which all these characters opened up directly or indirectly.

In 'Pratidwandi', Siddhartha Chatterjee, a high caste Brahmin, 2nd year medical student was compelled to discontinue his study due to the sudden death of his father which brought economic limitations to his family. He being the elder son felt the responsibility of earning livelihoods for the family and started searching jobs regularly. Though in the interview board when he was asked to mention the most important event of the century, instead of man's land on moon he said it was the people's revolt in Vietnam and didn't get the job, in his daily interactions with his brother who was a radical activist Siddhartha remained just a curious spectator from outside. The middle class hesitation in every regards, from leaving the city for job to viewing the opposite sex, was full in him. He, like typical elder brother, didn't prefer the intimacy of the boss with his sister and also went to meet him - dreamt of killing the boss, but in reality he maintained his bhadralok middle class dignity and talked to him politely even about his own chance of getting a job. But his inner frustration was brewing and that was fueled by his younger brother who uncomprehendingly pointed out that Siddhartha was actually doing nothing and standing no where. As a typical city dweller, who is comfortable in living in the city only, Siddhartha did not like the idea of leaving Calcutta even for a job. In the climax of the movie, he went for an interview as his last try in Calcutta and at the end he lost his nerves and jeopardized the whole interview board and that for the first time not in dream but in reality! He became a rebel character at that moment, lost the last chance to get a job in Calcutta, left the city to join a new work in Balurghat and again started dreaming of his resort through his relation with his girl friend. How a top to bottom middle class bhadralok has become a momentary insurrectionist under the influence of Naxal movement is very nicely depicted in the movie.

In the movie 'Padatik', Sumit the hero was actively involved in the radical political activities, a fugitive from police and had taken shelter in a flat arranged by his group. Sumit belonged to a lower middle class family where he had the responsibility to earn the livelihood of the family but by ignoring that he joined the rebellious activities of his time by going against the wish of his father. Sumit's father more specifically represents the mentality of middle class bhadralok through his attachment to family, domestic life and his aversion to radical politics. He was the single bread-earner of the family, also looked after many of the household activities due to his wife's illness, never supported Sumit's political stand. Even he never tried to get any information of his son when he was in hide-out. Once he even angrily advised his son that in his youth he also had studied Lenin and many revolutionary books but to practise that in reality instead of taking the responsibility of family was not pragmatic. But that middle class character of father suddenly changed at the end of the movie when Sumit from his hide-out came to visit his mother at her death-bed. Despite mother's death, Sumit's father very calmly told him to leave the place quickly before anybody gets information about his coming. He exempted him from his mother's last rites so that he must not be caught by the police due to any delay. The last few statements of Sumit's father unpredictably brought out a different personality out of his typical middle class bhadralok personality. When Sumit was about to leave, his father told him that he was suspended from his job as he did not compromise with his authority on the right of the workers to strike! And in the climax scene father, by breaking all his middle class bhadralok mediocre mentality, advised his son to 'be brave' - ironically, as if a spark of revolutionary fire was transferred from the typical father to his rebellious son, who had been confused for the time being during his hide-out and recharged himself! Through the movie it becomes clear that in this alteration of the mind-set of the father from a conservative to silent rebel no doubt the role of the catalyst was played by the Naxal movement.

In the movie 'Anu', the hero Sugato and the leading female protagonist Ananya both belonged to usual middle class bhadralok Bengali family. Sugato the radical activist was the love interest of Anu who initially was neither involved nor interested in the movement or in its ideology. Gradually, she learnt and realised various ideological stands like socialism, feminism etc from Sugato only. Her life changed drastically and directly when she was gang-raped by a group of people out of revenge who were searching Sugato but failed to know where he was from Anu. That incident changed her whole life - she suffered a lot from her wounds, lost her elder brother in encounter, Sugato was sent to jail, her parents could not cope up with the social taboo about a raped victim and finally she left her house, even Calcutta forever and became a school teacher in suburbs and started to stay alone with the hope that Sugato would be released and come back to her one day. But the movie has another sharp bend when Sugato was traumatized and mentally shocked by seeing her wounds when he came back and started to stay with Anu after marrying her following eight years of his long imprisonment. This mental block went to the extent that he failed to accept her physically as her wounds reminded him about the lustful use of her body by the rapists! Anu immediately refused to stay with him when she came to know about this from his diary and as she said that would be more insult to her than the incident of rape itself. In this movie the impact of the movement on Anu is very direct and clear as on the one hand she became aware of the real significance of the concepts like rights, freedom and equality from her constant interaction with the Naxal activist and his lover Sugato and on the other she was exposed to the hard core realities of life because of the consequences that she had to face for being the girl friend of a Naxalite. Her long fight within all odds made her a symbol of revolt against the traditional system and mind-set of middle class bhadralok and transformed her from a naïve, innocent, simple girl to a mature, complacent, struggler for justice.

In the movie 'Hazar Chourasi ki Maa', there is another depiction of the middle class bhadralok family who economically belonged to the upper middle class, had a proper house to stay in a good locality, both of the parents were working, had a single son Brati who was a good student and studying in college and overall this family portrayed a picture of a happy middle class bhadralok family. But the picture was torn one fine morning when they suddenly came to know that Brati was killed by police in encounter as he was actively involved in Naxal politics. His mother Sujata went to the morgue to identify the number 1084 as the body of his son and from there a new journey started for her. The whole movie is actually a journey of Sujata who came to know about an absolute different reality of his son's life and the surroundings. Her world was shattered not only because of her son's death but more so as she found some completely different image of Brati's life and of the tangible world within which they all were living. Initially it was very difficult for her to digest them all and here Brati's girlfriend Nandini's interaction with Sujata was most remarkable which brought the final transformation in her outlook. A typical mother of upper class bhadralok family gradually established the link with all the threads that were left in-between by her maverick son due to his sudden death. The movie ends with abrupt death of Sujata as her appendix burst in a party where all his relatives and friends were celebrating their normal life even after such an abnormal death of Brati. Death of Sujata in the claustrophobic middle class artificial celebration of life has become truly symbolic at the end of the movie. A true relation between the mother and the son was planted after his death through Sujata's new findings about reality and coming out of her enwrapped middle class values and beliefs.

In all four selected movies the directors have upheld this transformation knowingly or unknowingly. Whatever may be there in the mind of the directors and their main focus, the impact of Naxal movement on the mentality of middle class bhadralok and its transition are quite visible in these selected four cinemas.

Conclusion :

It often seems to be wrong to analyse any social issue or movement from a single dimension and to put it within a particular bracket. The Naxal movement also does not fit within a single frame of the middle class bhadralok politics in an absolute manner. It bears some distinctive features that make it close to the bhadralok politics and at the same time it has many characteristics that prove otherwise. For example, it has challenged the existing historical understanding based on the values of Bengal Renaissance and brought the issue of margins at the centre. Today, politics of Bengal is challenged by fragmented forces like tribal, peasants, and people of neglected areas like hill and forest. Claims of universality and all grand narratives have been declining in the face of such challenges particularly after 1990. Naxal movement can be considered as the early beginning of such challenges. It had attacked several meta narratives like universal claims of liberal capitalist reform, Euro-centric Marxism, Bengal Renaissance, unadulterated domination of bhadralok class in politics etc, sometimes consciously and sometimes spontaneously. There is no denying the fact that the Maoist and tribal activities that have become major sign of today's new trend of 'fragmentary postmodernism' in politics had acquired its initial voice through the Naxal movement. But ironically, most of the movies on the subject have failed to discover these multilayered dimensions of the movement and greater part of them have remained limited in exploring the alternative potentiality of the movement by going beyond its popular urban face value. That may be the result of various factors like - all the directors of the chosen movies are urban middle class bhadralok people, they have to look at the commercial purpose of the movie at the ultimate level and cannot go beyond a perimeter of experiments, their target audience is not the rural mass but the urban educated intellectuals etc. In spite of much debate and controversies about Naxal movement, the need for studying the movement in general and the movies in particular, from diverse multifaceted perspectives, by searching into its complex position, has not ended even after forty years of its outset.

Notes :

1. In Arjun Goswami's edited book, *Uttal Shat-Sottar,* Asim Chatterjee wrote in his Bengali article : *Naxalbari sudhu ek bidroher bhabmurti hoe daray, prakito Naxalbari ei atikalper arale dhaka pore jae.*
2. Bengali proverb : *Uttam Nischinte Chole Adhamer Sathe / Tini-i Madhyam Jini Chalen Tafate.*

References :

Broomfield, J. H. (1968), *Elite Conflict in a Plural Society : Twentieth-Century Bengal,* Bombay : Oxford University Press.

Chatterjee, Asim 'Uttal Shat Dasaker Yubo Andolan' in Goswami, Arjun (ed.) (2006), *Uttal Shat-Sottar : Rajniti, Samaj o Sanskriti,* Kolkata : Chayanika.

Chatterjee, Joya (1994), *Bengal Divided : Hindu Communalism and Partition : 1932-1947,* Cambridge University Press.

Chatterjee, Partha (1997), *The Present History of West Bengal : Essays in Political Criticism,* New Delhi : Oxford University Press.

Chottopadhyay, Bankim (1874), 'Babu' in Lokarahasya, *Bankim Rachanabali,* Vol. II.

Ghosh, Binoy (1973), *Metropolitan Mon Madhyabitto Bidroho,* Orient Longman.

Gupta, Amit Kumar (2009), *Crisis and Creativities : Middle Class Bhadralok in Bengal 1939-52,* Orient Blackswan.

Mukherjee, S.N. (1977), *Calcutta : Myth and History,* Kolkata : Subarnarekha.

Reports :

Macaulay Minutes (1835).

Simon Commission Report (1928) Vol. VIII.

Historical

Reappearance of the 'Uncanny' : Naxalite Memory in Malayalam Cinema

Darshana Sreedhar. M

> The beholder feels an irresistible urge to search such a picture for the tiny spark of contingency, of the here and now, with which reality has invested the subject, to find the inconspicuous spot where in the immediacy of that long forgotten moment that the future nests so eloquently that we, looking back, may discover it.
>
> Walter Benjamin, 'Little History of Photography' (1931)

The 'tiny spark of contingency' and the 'inconspicuous spot wherein the immediacy of that long forgotten moment of future rests', Benjamin uses to mark out the indexicality of image may not be that impossible to capture after all. The specific context which I would deal here would explore such moments when such 'long forgotten moments' frozen in the repository of the collector memory are triggered back to life. The turbulent phase of 1970s Kerala, when the panacea offered by an ideologically motivated group of comrades found its support among the oppressed tenants and peasants of the tribal belt, did jolt the hitherto acknowledged modes of resistance against oppression and denial of rights. I would trace how these moments drift through a temporal realm, in which past and present inextricably fuse with one another and mark a different trajectory of return; what was thought of as an answer to the 'endless sufferings' of the subjected sections of society unfortunately could not come into fruition. After going through a transitory phase of amassing popular support, it got intertwined with the factionalism which has been the tragedy of all uprisings against the institutionalized state and subsequently trimmed down to a slow death. My attempt would be to re-read the historical trajectory that Naxalism traversed and its depiction in a recent Malayalam film, 'Thalappavu' (2008), largely facilitated by the dense discursive space in Kerala, along which the renewed memory of one of the leading figures of Naxalism, Varghese was recreated. His alleged encounter death gathered significance in the early 2000s, with the confession of Ramachandran Nair, the retired head constable who gave a confession on his role behind Varghese's death. The long-buried details of Varghese's killing lit the fuse to public protests revolving around repression and human rights violations perpetrated by the State. Traumatised by guilt, constable Nair penned a confession shortly after he shot Varghese in a fake police encounter in the forests of Wayanad back in 1970. The letter he claimed was handed over to the slain Naxalite leader's compatriot, A. Vasu gathered dust until it surfaced in the memoirs of another Naxalite leader, K. Venu, published in a local journal in 2000[1]. Following the murder of landlord Vasudeva Adiga and a suspected police informer Chekkoo at Thrissileri in Wayanad in 1970, and the subsequent police crackdown, Varghese and his comrades retreated into the Thirunelli forests. They were eventually tracked down by CRPF personnel, with the help of Sivaraman Nair, who was the caretaker in a safe house for Naxalites run by an elderly widow Ittichiri Manayamma. In the contemporary world where murders are wrapped in the foil of encounter deaths, the revelation of Ramachandran Nair assumes importance. The official version claimed Varghese to have died in a police encounter, which in turn was confirmed by Kozhikode Revenue Divisional Officer (RDO). After a lapse of 29 years, in 1999, Ramachandran Nair approached the Kerala High Court with a prayer seeking inquiry into the death of Varghese. He later filed an affidavit in the court to that effect, stating that he had shot Varghese under pressure from his superiors B. Vijayan and K. Lakshmana, then DIG and Dy. SP respectively of Kozhikode, the accused in the infamous Rajan case involving the disappearance of an engineering student in police custody during the Emergency[2]. Rallies and protests took place in different parts of Kerala to put pressure on the Government to transfer the case for CBI investigation. Constable Nair's letter represents possibly the first known case of a subordinate functionary going on record with an admission of a custodial killing carried out on the orders of a superior officer. In the meanwhile, Ramachandran Nair came up with his memoir, *Njan Jeevichu Ennathinte Thelivu* (An Evidence to Prove that I have Lived), relating the events which unfolded the 'actual chronology'. In such a cultural cauldron, the discussions on Naxalism saw resurgence. It was as if the ghost of Varghese was hovering on the crevices of the society to avenge the injustice done to him.

Each time an event erupts, hope and anxiety accompany it. Many initially outside its compass are rapidly moved to intervene, in attempts to support it, to redirect it, or to squelch it. An event starts out of apparent uncertainty and foments a wider band of uncertainties as it expands and morphs[3]. Events emit contagious and infectious energies. The sheer sense of apathy with which CPI (M) reacted to Thalasssery-Pulpalli incidents, the first in the series of uprisings was one such. The government of the day, which drew flak for condoning the event, was headed by Achutha Menon of the CPI in partnership with the Muslim League, whose leader, C.H. Mohammad Koya, was then the home minister. It seems to be not just ironical but cynical that CPI (M), which credits itself with the first demand for a probe into the killing, raised by E.M.S. Namboodiripad as leader of the Opposition in the state assembly on Varghese's murder, tried to stall the selfsame demand, when Chief Minister of CPI(M) E.K. Nayanar in 1998, rebuffed the demand by prominent personalities as well as by 'Niyama Vedi', an organization of lawyers against human rights violation, for a full-fledged inquiry into the circumstances that led to the killing of Varghese[4]. 'They (Marxists) applauded the revolutionary spirit of the youngsters involved and argued with righteous indignation that the motive should not be doubted...and proclaimed it their bounded duty to get the prodigals back to the fold'[5]. At the same time, as a rejoinder they added, '...these incidents (Pulppali-Thalasseri) would only help ruin the revolutionary movement and sustain and strengthen the bourgeoisie-capitalist system' - a statement which encapsulates the duplicity inherent in their position. But, as the issue gathered momentum, the CPI (M) leadership faced pressure from party fora to relent to the probe demand[6]. All these contradictory veins and shifting alliances form the part of the life narratives by former Naxalites in some of the weeklies like *Malayala Manorma* and *Madhyaman,* published almost the same time as the appearance of Ramachandran Nair's statement.

The memoirs of some of the cadres involved in the Puthupalli police attack case like Ajitha, Philip M. Prasad, K. Venu et al became the fulcrum around which the patches of memory on Naxalism were superimposed. Ajitha's memoir[7] and Ramachandran Nair's memoir had referred to Varghese's death and is a prime source material to the script of the film under consideration. Before getting into the film straight away, I will outline the pegs along which the films drew its narrative, through a brief sketch of Pulppalli-Thalasseri revolt which triggered of similar uprisings in Kerala, drawing inspiration from the Naxalbari movement.

The corrupt and inefficient governance and the apathy of the administration in redressing the grievances of the masses had its own share in the mass uprising. This coupled with the authoritarian style of the administrative functioning alienated the poor peasants and exacerbated the intensity of suffering of the unfortunate lot. It was amidst such growing impatience over such a pitiable state that the anonymous letter addressed to Kunnikkal Narayanan, detailing the oppression meted out to the settlers in Wayanad, largely by the State in collusion with the police became the spark for the uprising in Pulpalli. The police atrocities started with the takeover of the *oottupura* (dining space) of Sitadevi temple by Malabar Special Police (MSP) camp as their temporary base. This was thought to be a ploy for the forceful evacuation of the *porambokkukar,* settlers from the land, which the temple management alleged them to have occupied. The cruelty and torture unleashed by them was solely intended to upset the sanctity of the otherwise sacred temple and allow the temple management to have their freę way. Apart from constrains imposed on the people, the police worked hand-in-glove with the landlords of the area and terrorized people into passivity. This became the spark for the intervention of the group led by Varghese, Philip M. Prasad, Ajitha, Thettemala Krishnan Kutty, Kissan Thomman, Joseph, Sukumaran et al to attack Pulpalli police station and a few land lords who made the life of the peasants miserable. It had the whole hearted support and cooperation of the beedi workers and weavers of Kannur. Thalassery-Pulppali became a source of inspiration for many such local uprisings organized by the peasants against the ruthless landlords in many other parts of Kerala, like for instance in Kuttiyadi (1969) and Thirunelly (1970). Right from the pre-production phase, the broader framework which governed the discursive space of 'Thalappavu' was the renewed memory of the failed revolution and its contemporary relevance, post the confession of Ramachandran Nair. Both visual and print media were primal in bringing anew the forgotten matrices and shifting the tenor of the debates on State containment and combing of 'non-state actors' by bringing a humane face to those involved with its radical politics.

The Visual Depiction of Pulpalli-Thalesseri :

Like photographs, films appears to inhabit a present instant, more towards Siegfried Kraceur's understanding of it as capturing the transience in the visible world around us, with its 'involuntary gestures and other fleeting impressions'[8]. Thus film in many ways continues with the tradition of photography and as Benjamin puts it, it is suffused with the evidences of optical unconscious[9].

Here I wanted to discuss how the visual depictions on Naxalism transcended the immediate context of its production and entered into an autonomous realm which could withstand the hegemonic ideological construction. These images were originally meant to counter the spread of Naxalism, to show how the transgressors were brought back to the fold. So when the Naxalites were captured alive, they were projected as living embodiments of sinful existence. Varghese, who challenged the establishment by evading the eyes of the MSP (Malabar Special Police),

Picture I- Ajitha exhibited outside the police station[10]

became for them an irritant who has to be brought to book at any cost. When the State found that Varghese's dead body stubbornly refused to give away any traces of compromise, Ajitha (the only woman comrade among the revolutionaries) became a natural choice. The malicious move, meant to tarnish her image and brand her as a whore is played out in the picture I. It would give a clearer picture when read alongside her memoir :

> I was in sari. I was asked to take it off. Under it I was wearing trousers. They made me remove the woolen jacket too that I was wearing over the blouse. Then, I was asked to walk out of the station in trousers and blouse. They made me stand on the platform of the flagstaff in the police station courtyard and paraded me to thousands of people who had thronged around. I trembled with humiliation and helplessness. The police proclaimed that I had moved around in forest in this attire with

> my comrades. Their zeal to portray me as a whore was blatant. *Journalists without wasting a moment began clicking away.*

Picture I, photographed by K. Aravindan in 1968, got published in almost all the newspapers and magazines of the time immediately after the Putuppally comrades were arrested. The title, 'The poster woman of Kerala's Naxalite movement' 'encapsulated the immense possibility inherent in the image, its circulation and reception. More than Ajitha's identity as a torchbearer of women in Naxalism, the image mirrored the 'humiliation and helplessness' that marked her body. Images in that way transcends the significatory purpose and becomes an actor on the historical stage[11]. The print media cashed on Ajitha's arrest reaffirming Anderson's formulation that in the age of print capitalism, newspapers are 'one-day best-sellers'[12]. To imbue 'ephemeral popularity', the image of Ajitha exhibited as a spectacle in midst of the jeering remarks of

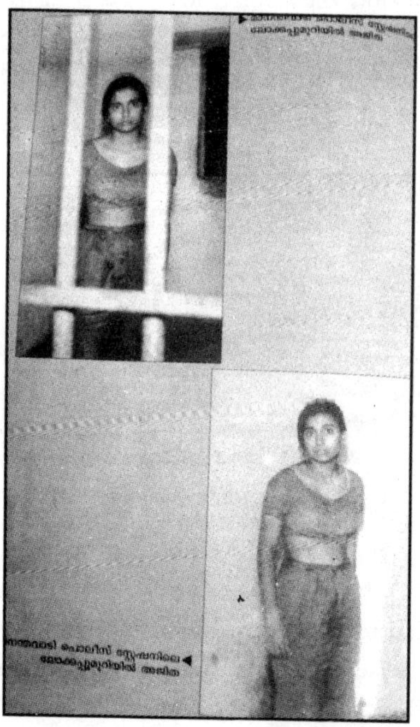

Picture 2- Ajitha, inside the lock up

men, was strategically used by the media[13]. The circulation of the images of the captured Naxalites was widely disseminated as a visible marker of the State's success in containing the menace of Naxalism (picture 2). Susan Buck-Morss' theorization that the image has the potential to move beyond the schematics of representation and thereby negate the immediate context of its production seems to be apt to recall in this context. The way objects could be conceptualized as 'image-trace' could be substantiated in the way the image outlives the moment and carries the trace of the moment in the image body. In this case, the image of the humiliated image of Ajitha went on to add to the simmering fire raised over alleged human rights violations of the State in containing Naxalites. The spectral presence of the historical moment, memories and a quality of being intensely present mark these images and gets reflected in the film 'Thalappavu'. As an evidence of the gruesome murder, the 'gouged eyes' of Varghese took a signification which went far beyond the depiction of Pulpalli-Talessary as a failed Naxalite uprising. It became a constant reminder of the blindness of the state to the hard life of the oppressed sections and how it could pave way for an armed retaliation by the cadre.

Picture 3- Publicity posters of 'Thalappavu'

'Thalappavu', starring Prithviraj was a directorial debut of Madhupal, who has been in the silver screen in Malayalam from the early 90s. It has resurrected the memory of Naxalite leader Varghese and pumped fresh adrenaline into speculations and contestations that lie forgotten in the trashcan of history. More than the efficacy of the script which re-constructed in a meticulous way the Naxalite uprising in Kerala in the 1970s, it was successful in initiating a debate among different political factions and civil society on the uncomfortable truths it carefully straddled. Babu Janardhan who proved his mettle in script writing with films like 'Vasthavam' and 'Achanurangatha Veedu', brings backs the memory of Naxal Varghese through the character of Joseph and with it a plethora of half baked truths.

Picture 4

The opening credits of the film assemble the scattered newspaper reports on Naxalite uprising in Kerala in the 1970s and State combing meant to contain its pernicious reach. The photograph of *Sakavu* Joseph on the foreground sets the mis-en-scene for the movie. The newspaper reportage on Naxal Varghese's death is accompanied by the photographs of Joseph, exposing the torture he had to succumb to, before being shot at close quarters. Side-by-side is juxtaposed, the box column news of Raveendran Pillai's photograph with the caption, 'With the memories of Joseph, Raveendran Pillai in Court'. This immediately brings to me Barthes' evocation in *Camera Lucida* on photography as a medium in which signifier and the referent are collapsed onto each other. Photographs assert the referent, such that they mark its existence in that (past) moment when the person, the thing, was there in front of the camera[14]. Not just in translating the historical happenings into the celluloid, but also in conjuring up the 70s setting, make it all the more like a documentary fiction. But such a reading gets contested straight on as one see the text following the credits : "The story and the characters in the movie is (are) entirely imaginary. Any resemblance to any incident or personality is purely accidental or coincidental". This, in one way goes against the publicity posters which acclaimed 'Thalappavu' as a film where "History becomes Film and Film made into History". The notion of 'history' evoked here becomes problematic as the contrary pulls to align with a past that is gone and at the same time the reluctance to categorically take a position to disavow it, puts it in a strange situation.

Picture-5

The movie begins with the extreme wide shot of the approaching convey of police jeeps, followed by the medium close up of a person giving off the location where Joseph is hiding. The sound track captures the voice-over-commentary of Christ's betrayal by Judas. As the commentary concludes with Jesus' words, "The one who has dipped his hand into the bowl with me will betray me", the camera slowly pans over to a shot where Joseph is trapped by police on a tip off by one of his closest comrades. The narrative then moves onto the most crucial shot of the whole movie, the moment of Joseph's execution at the hands of constable Ravindran, who is given orders against his will to be the death's messenger. Unlike the linear progression of the narrative logic, the plot unravels in a back and forth manner, transcending time and space and constantly making use of the mis-en-scene to work out the symbolic association of Joseph as Christ figure, equating his death with the sacrifice he willfully chooses to redeem humanity. The sound track captures this mood quite poignantly, with the church bells chiming and a dissolve bringing into the frame the parallel action; the past interactions between Raveendran and Joseph. The gesture of Joseph holding out his hand as if to beckon Raveendran close to him is the shot that recurs throughout the narrative. Not only does it bring the haunting memory of the death of Varghese to Raveendran in spite of the lapse of years separating the two time periods, but also brings back the interactions both of them shared outside the bounds of formal relations, the most evocative one being the bus trip to Wayanad. The diagetic space is dense with a recapitulation of Ramachandran Nair's memoir, the primal connection being his account of the last moments of Varghese. "He requested me give him a signal when he is about to be shot, so that he could die as a *yadarthe viplavakari*[15]. The thunderous shout of *Viplavam Jyikkatte* (Long Live the Revolution) that rose above the gun shot reverberated in the Thirunelli forests became a priced moment captured in 'Thalappavu'. Nair recreates the sequence of events:

> Lekshamana told us that Varghese was going to be shot. DIG Vijayan was standing nearby. Then Lekshmana ordered those of us who were willing to shoot Varghese to raise their hands.

> Rappai and Sreedharan raised their hands. Haneefa hesitated but finally raised his. I did not. The dissenter was then chosen to perform the deed. Varghese was sitting between two rocks. He was calm but alert, as though he was waiting for something to happen and wondering why it wasn't happening. I went up to him and rested the nozzle of my rifle on the left side on his chest. Then I remembered his request. I sounded a signal with my tongue. 'Long Live the Revolution,' he shouted and I pulled the trigger. He fell over[16].

This brings me to think more on how individual recollections evoke traces of forgotten moments which then gets re-crafted into the cultural scripts or templates. This is all the more relevant in the contemporary society in the grip of memory boom, expressed in myriad ways creating 'multiple sites of memory', *Les Lieux de Memoire*, as Pierre Nora[17] puts it. When the present slips into a historical past, it is also the point of revisiting the crystallized memory, where remnants of what has been forcefully waded away returns. Memory thus remains in permanent evolution, open to the dialectic of remembering and forgetting, unconscious of its successive deformation, vulnerable to manipulations and appropriations, susceptible to being long dormant and periodically revived. It thus nourishes recollections that may be out of focus or telescopic, global or detached, particular or symbolic. In one way, one is reminded here of Maurice Halbwachs notation of memories as 'multiple yet specific by nature'[18]. Relating his miseries and inadequacies, Raveendran says at one point, "...life has never been the same for me after... it has not moved on ever since that day ...I am still paying the dues for the inadvertent mistake of mine...I have lost 35 years of my life...I am still living in that moment". The disjointedness of his narrative and the lasting traces left by Joseph's murder had indeed 'killed' Raveendran. Not only was he deserted by his family, but this also turned him to an alcoholic. The failure of the uprising thus got transposed onto Raveendran's personal life, where he is left with only the frozen memories of Joseph to give him solace. The colleagues who once shared the work space with him started to keep a check on his movements under orders from the superiors. The life under strict surveillance had taken a toll on him, when he lost track of the last counts of hope. Even at the moments of extreme crisis and dejection, Raveendran finds solace only in the memory and presence of Joseph. It seems as if everything has been frozen for him to that moment. The ghost of Joseph, with blood stained hands haunts him, a grip so strong for Raveendran to let go.

The activist interface with the peasants has been thought of as a guiding principle in bringing about an armed insurrection. As Charu Majumdar states[19], "In the days to come, these poor and landless peasants will shine like bright stars giving inspiration and lighting the way forward for the revolutionaries". To see everything through the eyes of the landless peasants was thought of as a first step which would enable one 'to adopt the class outlook of the downtrodden'. This to a great extent acts a defining principle in construction of the peasant figure in its pure, unmediated sense in the film. Whether it is Samuel or Johny or the other unnamed multitudes who crowd the canvas of the *kodiyetta karshakar* (landless peasants) in the sequence set in Wayanad, one finds a conscious attempt to frame an idyllic life, which is faced with imminent destruction by the malicious hands of the land lord, Krishnadeva Saiver. Saramma, whose husband was killed by Saiver was raped and coerced into becoming his *veppatti* (kept woman). His Rule of Law was what dictated the lives of many. Women were treated solely as sex objects and those who disobeyed his orders were brutally erased. If Mathan and Johnykutty were found hanging, it was the punitive justice of Saiver that took their lives.

Naxalite annihilation practice could be seen as something that undermines the feudal code of power. Ranajit Guha's idea of 'peasant consciousness' seems here a handy tool to look at the peasant uprisings. Even if the peasants may not be conscious of what they were doing, it certainly enabled the re-formation of the peasant. "...(T)he peasant creating a new sense of self...Killing his enemy could help the peasant define himself anew; and the greater the violence and display with which he did it, the greater the distance he put between himself and his previous identity as a subordinate"[20]. The peasant uprisings in Nilampur in 1970 which drew inspiration from Pulpalli-Thalesseri were organized by the peasants without much ideological support from the activists. This shows how 'the notion of resistance to elite domination' relied on horizontal mobilization and how the inherent violent streak it carried took disastrous proportions when the destined time comes. In Ranajit Guha's contestation of Hobsbawm's idea of 'pre-political', one could see a remarkable shift from the conceptualization of peasant insurrection as spontaneous and unpremeditated. Guha posits instead, that at the heart of any peasant insurgency, there is an attempt to reflect on the destruction of the social symbols of prestige by the rebels. "It is this fight for prestige which was at the heart of any insurgency. Inversion was its principal modality. It was a political struggle in which the rebel appropriated and/or destroyed the insignia of enemy's power and hoped thus to abolish the marks of his own subalternity"[21]. The rebels in 'Thalappavu' destroys the land deal documents which was confiscated by Saiver. Alongside the death of Saiver, there is also a symbolic destruction of power when the documents are destroyed by the rebels. Another striking image is how Saiver is killed by Joseph. The courtyard which had borne the brunt of Saiver's cruelty now becomes the site of his murder. Thus the semiotics of domination and subordination gets destroyed. Another interesting note is the similarity in the evocation of names and other details which the film borrows from the history. If the recreation of Varghese as Joseph is not just coincidental, Ramachandran Nair becomes Raveendran Pillai, Thirunelli as Cherunelli, Vasudeva Adiga becomes Krishna Deva Saiver and many more.

Death seems to me a predominant trope throughout the film. The martyrdom of Varghese is the subtext here and the cold-blooded murder of Varghese by the establishment is denounced with all vigor. Towards the concluding section of the film, one see Raveendran slowly coming back to the life he had desired for long, when his daughter comes back to stay with him after her mother's death. But the happiness is cut short by the revelation that she had been a prostitute all this while and she retorts in anguish her "right to live her life" to a crowd of men who demands that she be thrown out of the neighborhood. Lost for words, Raveendran is accosted by Joseph's ghost who instills in him the confidence to reveal the truth behind the police fabrication of his death. Raveendran appears before the court with his version on Joseph's death as if it was the sole purpose for which he had been living for that long. But what could finally rescue Raveendran from the life of pain and misery, caught in the inescapable labyrinth of events is the possibility of death. Even in his last moments, it is Joseph, with his brooding, slightly forbidding, heavy-lidded face and a bleak, unforgiving knowledge of the present who accompanies him with a lighted torch. The final shot of the film is the retrieval of the candle in a coconut shell by Janu as she sweeps Raveendran's courtyard after his funeral. If till then, one thought the re-appearance of Joseph as part of Raveendran's fictive imagination, with this twist one is pushed into what Paul Ricoeur says about 'returning to the past its own future', which gives the historical period the sense of a transferential function, whereby the past dissolves in the present, so that the future becomes (once again an open question) instead of being specified by the fixity of the past.

Crystallized precipitations of diffuse longings and scattered hopes are knitted together with consummate skill, where the use of the other mediums of representation like newspapers, print and visual media adds self referentiality to its production. The system stood accused of greed, willfulness and irrationality through the Christ-like suffering of the hero and his selfless heroism in midst of intrigues and callous indifference. The victory of 'good' over 'evil' is re-enacted in sentimental spectacles full of tears and moral tones. The film also explores different cinematic modes : documentary, melodrama, black and white frames et al. The camera eye view, because of its constantly varying vantage has the privilege of seeing that to which the audience have no access. Also notable is the wandering long duration shots, voyeuristic gaze of the camera at moments of violence, frequent dissolves and fades that create time lapses, prevalent grey tone of the film, haunting sound track, frequent use of flashbacks et al. In the scene where Joseph is about to be shot, one can see an absence of cuts for more than 4 frames. The distant placing of the camera from the incident as it unfolds, so close enough for its meaning and horror not to be missed makes the viewer positioned as a helpless bystander, cognizant of the event, but powerless to do anything about it.

The filmic depiction of Joseph, singularly aimed at the portrayal of Varghese- like hero, the incorruptible, selfless ideologist who sacrifices his lot and plunges into the embers of revolution in a different register, a far cry from the passive, tamed antihero figure the state projected him to, had contributed much to the reception of the film. Here, Varghese's death takes a new life, one that is freed of opportunism and compromise. The 'weapons of torture' could not weaken the determination of the protagonist. He relentlessly refuses to name his accomplices. I strongly feel that, for Varghese, death was a redeemer; the only possibility he was left with. Where the opportunists rule the roost, he could not have withstood the pretentious existence (which advertently or inadvertently most of the Naxalites ended up with). Among Varghese's compatriots, most of them have shed the idealism of Naxalbari and had moved on. When Vasu became an active trade union leader, Ajitha preferred to work for women's rights and Phillip M. Prasad is an advocate and a devotee of Satya Sai Baba. The torchbearers of the Naxalite movement, who believed that class enemies did not have the right to live, have found their respective slots in bourgeois society[22]. Yet, the resurrection of the radical ghost of Varghese has opened up many truths which has hitherto straddled between memories and forgetting. Varghese is sure to remain as a beacon of hope to revolutionaries to come, 'as a volcano carrying deep within the potent embers of a fierce eruption' More than that, to go by Ajitha's memoirs, his leadership qualities and tactics have been looked at with askance by his own comrades. He was seen as a threat not just for the State, but more to his party, for the same ideologists for whom he became a sacrificial goat. Thettamala Gopi who became instrumental in trapping Varghese, incidentally was once the right-hand of Varghese. Varghese's death was marked by the same sense of dauntless energy which has been his distinguishing mark and is sure to remain in the memory of Malayalees as a last glimpse of a revolutionary with a humane face.

"History is hysterical : it is constituted only if we consider it, only if we look at it- and in order to look at it, we must be excluded from it." For Raveendran Pillai, this 'exclusion' becomes impossible as he is condemned to live in a perpetual present. The only glitter of hope emerges at the last minute immediately before his death when like a candle that burns faster but brighter, he claims to see more things in that limited time than anyone would possibly be able to imagine. Like pervasive melancholia which comes from a cramping sense of guilt, past cannot be shed that easily. Like a disowned self dogging steps of a patient who cannot own up his or own illness, the past trauma haunts. Yes, that is the only solace which Raveendran yearns for. Ramachandran Nair died in before he could testify before the court and the final verdict, which could have eased him from the guilt-ridden life, also came much later.

Notes :

1. Menon, Venu, 'Confessions of a Cop', *Outlook* Magazine, November 23, 1998.

   http://www.outlookindia.com/article.aspx?206579. Accessed on 23/1/10.
2. T. Ramavarman, '40 Years later, Ex IG found Guilty of Naxalite's Murder', *Times of India*, October 28, 2010.
3. Connolly, William, 'The Contemporary Condition : The Politics of the Event', http://contemporarycondition.blogspot.com/2011/04/politics-of-event.html. Accessed on 6/11/11.
4. Ibid.
5. Ajitha, *Kerala's Naxalbari : Memoirs of a Young Revolutionary*, translated by Sanju Ramachandran, Sristi Publications, 2008.
6. Ibid.
7. Also, Ajitha, *Ormakuruppukal*, DC Books, 1982.
8. Siefgried Kraceur, *Theory of Film : The Redemption of Physical Reality*,

(ed) M. Bratu Hansen, Princeton, 1997.

9. Benjamin, Walter, 'Little History of Photography', *Screen* (1972) 13 (1): 5-26.
10. The first three pictures are reproduced here from Ajitha (2008).
11. W. J. T Mitchell, *Iconology : Image, Text, Ideology* , University of Chicago Press, 1998, p. 9.
12. Anderson, Benedict, *Imagined Communities : Reflections on the Origin and Growth of Nationalism*, Verso, 1991.
13 Nayar, Pramod, 'A Naxal Remembers', DNA (Daily News Analysis),June 22, 2008.http://www.dnaindia.com/lifestyle/books-and-more_a-naxal-remembers_1172667. Accessed on 12/10/11.
14. Barthes, Roland, *Camera Lucida*, tran. Richard Howard, New York, 1981, p-65.
15. Ibid.
16. Ibid.
17. Susannah Radstone et al (eds), *Regimes of Memory*, Routledge, 2003.
18. Ibid.
19. Charu Majumdar, 'A Few Words about Guerilla Actions' in Suniti Kumar Ghosh edited, *The Historic Turning Point : A Liberation Anthology*, Volume 2, Calcutta,1993.
20. Sanjay Seth, 'From Maoism to Post colonialism : The Indian Sixties and beyond', *Inter Asia Cultural Studies*, Volume 7,Number 4, 2006.
21. Partha Chatterjee edited, *The Small Voice of History*, Permanent Black, New Delhi, 2009.
22. Ibid.

'Thalappavu' : When the Ghost Haunts the Conscience

Arya Aiyappan

Life, a masterstroke by our supreme maestro artist on a canvas, captures a multitude of colours in various hues and cinema, the seventh art doles out, both the effervescent and throbbing spirit of this life in every frame. Life and art sharing a bond of mutual dependence are engaged in a constant exchange of culture, stemming from the incessant urge to commune. Art in its varied forms like painting, music, sculpture, dance, drama and cinema, partake of the imperative essences of life, inclusive of its diverse manifestations as social, cultural, political, economic or historical. Cinema, one of the novel art forms of the age, unquestionably enjoys a reciprocal relation with life.

Tracking the history of Indian cinema throws light on the inception of serious or art cinema in the 1960s, along with the growing popularity of the French New Wave cinema. These movies upholding an anti-mainstream aesthetics were also frequently disposed towards an anti-establishment ideology. Many moviemakers influenced by this new wave or termed otherwise aimed to transform cinema into a social vehicle, while a few decided to cash on the opportunity to experiment with new ideas and novel subjects. The initiation of middle cinema, drawing artistic elements from both popular cinema and serious cinema and juxtaposed between them helped forge a new aesthetic philosophy in the history of cinema. With a plethora of genres (popular, serious and middle) and each as diverse as the name it bears, there persists some pertinent differences between them.

Treading new grounds, eminent filmmakers like Satyajit Ray, Mrinal

Sen and others influenced by the milieu, came up with remarkable contributions to cinema. Every social, political and cultural movement which has had an impact on our motherland, be it the independence struggle, political insurgencies, socio-cultural revolutions, religious extremism, terrorism and Naxalism have always arrested the attention of the filmmakers.

Terror, bloodshed, strife and an endless saga of agony and pain encapsulates in a nutshell, the relentless struggle for power. Equating victory with loss on the balance of power, calls for a review of the Naxal movement in the history of Kerala in India. Naxalism as a movement has been through many a rough patch. Nonetheless, its defining note as an alternative movement in opposition to the mainstream politics has time and again gained currency among the masses and artists alike. Claiming to be the watch guards for the toiling downtrodden of India, this movement has always ushered in a new era of rejuvenated hope together with an added sense of curiosity and quixotic mystery engulfing the otherwise mindless violence.

Consequently, when filmmakers in Kerala responded to the Naxal movement through their artistic manifestations, it was not a shocker out of the blue. Among the movies made in Malayalam, some foreground the political dogma of the Naxal activists, while others cloak the ideology under a veil of passive proposition. If 'Kabani Nadi Chuvannappol' by P. A.Backer, 'Amma Ariyaan' by John Abraham and 'Aparahnam' by M. P. Sukumaran Nair were some of those prominent movies on Naxalism conforming to characteristics of serious cinema, 'Ithiri Poove Chuvannapoove' by Bharathan, 'Aaranyakam' and 'Panchagni' by Hariharan were those clearly meeting the requirements of a popular or commercial cinema.

The sixties witnessed an upsurge of the Naxal movement in Kerala, which rocked the political climate of the state, only to gradually fade into oblivion in the eighties. The northern districts of Kerala - Wayanad, Kannur and Kozhikode, were searing with Naxal activities. Enthused by the Naxalbari armed rebellion of the peasants under the able leadership of Charu Majumdar and Kanu Sanyal, the intellectuals of the day following the ideologies of Mao Tse-tung organized a string of revolts to fight for the cause of the helpless farmers and adivasis. Wayanad with a remarkably large adivasi population was at the helm of the Naxal attacks modelled along the lines of the Naxalbari episode. These armed struggles did not spring up from the class discrepancies operating between the landlords and peasants alone, but also acquired its impetus from the inhuman conditions of bonded slavery to which these hapless poor were subjected to, due to the meagre wages and scarcity of alternative employment avenues.

The revolutionary fire kindled by the intellectuals, disillusioned with the ideologies of compromise propagated by the Indian National Congress and the passive revisionist propaganda of the CPI (M), took to the Naxal path of radical rebellion. Pullpally and Thalassery were the first places in Kerala destined to get a taste of the Naxalite revolts as early as 1968. The exploitation of the migrant farmers and the high-handedness of the officers of the special Police Camp triggered the Pullpally attack, followed by the Thalassery attack in support of the problems endured by the beedi workers.

Unfortunate as it may appear, the initial embers of active rebellion died out, attributable to unforeseen state of affairs, in spite of the active leadership provided by Areekkal Varghese, Kisan Thomman, Thettamala Krishnan Kutti, Kunnikkal Narayanan, Mandakini, T.V. Appu, Philip. M. Prasad, Kuruchiyan Kunjiraman, Ajitha and others. The Thirunelly attack of 1970 unleashed much terror in the region by murdering a landlord, nevertheless when the iron hands of the government and law caught up with them, Varghese was the first casualty. The mystery clouding his death remains an enigma till date evoking suspense and awe.

The revolutionist Naxalite movement did stir up considerable changes in the socio-political atmosphere of the state regardless of its waning popularity. Unable to mobilize public support coupled with the lack of coordination were the major hitches, repeatedly, culminating in the untimely end of the armed revolution. Often these isolated revolts directed against the repressive systems of power like the police stations could hardly achieve any concrete long-standing objectives. In the face of the stiff opposition and stringent government policies and measures, these isolated armed struggles could garner neither a fertile ground nor a congenial environment. Analysts have dubbed the Naxalite movement in Kerala as a political infatuation of the middle class youth of the 1960s, as one of the former Naxalites, K. Venu echoes :

> The Naxalites [in Kerala] failed to realize the realities of Kerala and the impact of the progressive policies.... They failed to understand that the driving force of armed struggle as envisaged by Charu Mazumdar - the class rivalry of poor, landless peasants against the landlords - was already satiated to an extent in Kerala through social reforms, (though imperfect) land reforms, the crumbling of the landlord-tenant link, the organisation of the working class and the spread of literacy that made old-world-style exploitation impossible (Philip 9).

The age-old theory of an "annihilation line" popularized by Charu Majumdar proved fatal, backfiring to the very followers of the dictum in the state of Kerala. The government and the various systems of power resorted to miscellaneous means crushing the rebellion by nipping the bud in the nascent phase itself. Rebounding on the Naxalites, many of the key intellectual figures had to sacrifice their lives for the cause or were branded as terrorists and murdered mercilessly, under the guise of encounter. Though divided factions still haggle over the impact factor of the movement and its consequences, the image of one personality is conspicuous amongst the outcry, much for the scintillating suspense gripping his entire life and even more controversial death.

It would be a folly to overlook or even dismiss the services and sacrifices rendered by the revolutionary hero Areekkal Varghese, a local prototype of the Latin American hero Che Guevera. Having let loose bloody battles against the oppressive structures of authority, the spirit of Varghese still haunts the tribal settlements of Thirunelli forests in Wayanad, instilling a glimmer of hope in the hearts of the thousands of impoverished.

Varghese, a staunch Naxalite, fought relentlessly against the oppressive measures and atrocities perpetrated by the landlords and the police officers on the adivasi people of Wayanad in the 1960s. Lending active support to the Naxal movement, the name of Varghese stands out tall and large not only for the stories of his daring feats, which have travelled far and wide, but also for the maze of puzzles shrouding his death which have gained much currency over the years.

The fag-end of the sixties witnessed some of the bloodiest episodes that have gone down in the annals of the history of Kerala as a black blotch, which many would consider otherwise. Varghese, one of the key figures of the radical Left fought against the atrocities and exploitation of the illiterate Adivasis. With his gang of armed Naxalite supporters, Varghese set out on a mass killing splurge with many landlords finding themselves under the knife. He spearheaded the Naxalbari movement in Kerala by gathering the support of some of the local masses in his mission to wipe out both the system and its representatives of power (police stations, the politicians and the feudal landlords). However, as fate would have it, Varghese's grand mission was cut short when the state decided to curtail his activities at any cost.

Surprising as it may seem though the stories of his brave feats have become a part of history, his death has evoked much curiosity among the people. Considered an integral part of the folklore of Thirunelli, Varghese met with an untimely death, which can be termed as 'brutal' if the word could capture the gruesome experience without any loss of intrigue whatsoever. As the legend goes, the Central Reserve Police raked through the Thirunelli forests and came across Varghese and his fellow members, but luck favoured the Naxalites as they dodged their way ingeniously out of the peril looming large upon them. The rest of the action that transpired culminated in his gory death still reverberates in the Thirunelli woods. Many versions of the episode have been doing rounds with many loose ends left dangling hither and thither.

In the year 1998, one of the retired police constables, P Ramachandran Nair, associated with the Varghese encounter, broke his silence and confessed that they had shot the Naxal leader Varghese in the Thirunelli forest, when he was defenseless. In his plea presented before the Kerala High Court he had sought a fresh inquiry into the episode which was strategically closed by the Mananthavady police as clear case of 'encounter' with the autopsy report issued by the RDO of Kozhikode validating the above. The police record states that when they detained Varghese, in retaliation, he fired at the police Superintendent, who fired back in self-defence resulting in Varghese's death in the encounter.

Ramachandran Nair's prayer before the court of law stated that he had to execute the orders of his senior police officials DSP Lakshmana and DIG Vijayan, under threat to his own life. The constable's confessions had given a fresh lease of life to the case with many activists and former Naxalites coming to the forefront demanding a fresh investigation into the otherwise open and shut case.

The old man's detailed account of the horrendous incident as cited in illustrious newspapers and websites has brought to the notice of the public eye many facts hitherto kept under wraps. As per the retired constable's detailed confession, Police received information about Varghese's hideout. He had taken refuge in the house of Ittichiri Maniyamma, a supporter of the Naxals along with her caretaker, Sivaraman Nair. When the police force surrounded the house a voice from indoors enquired, "Who's there?" and when intimated about their presence, an enraged voice hollered, "Nair, have you betrayed me?" When the cops barged in, a calm and composed Varghese accosted them with his arms flung out, "Don't worry. I'm unaccompanied and unarmed." They led Varghese through the street and nestled him into a jeep, with his wrists tied with a rifle sling.

DSP Lekshmana and DIG Vijayan joined them on their way to Manathavady. Ramachandran Nair could hardly forget the last few moments he spent with Varghese and the strange request he had made, "They are going to kill me. One of you will have to do it. I have one request. Before I am killed, give me a signal so that I can shout a slogan."

The police then blindfolded Varghese and Nair remembers their brief encounter when he shared his food with Varghese and offered him a beedi. Nair in his plea has not glossed over any minute detail when he remarked, that at 6:30 p.m., "Lekshamana told us that Varghese was going to be shot. DIG Vijayan was standing nearby. Then Lekshmana ordered those of us who were willing to shoot Varghese, to raise their hands. Rappai and Sreedharan raised their hands. Haneefa hesitated but finally raised his. I did not." Nair's desperate efforts to reason with and request his superior regarding producing the convict before the court of law was brushed aside by Lekshmana with a sharp reminder, "Policemen could die in accidents." Nair quickly sensed the threat. "Varghese was going to die anyway. If I died, my family would be helpless."

Ramachandran Nair was the unfortunate one called upon to carry out the ordeal and Nair could hardly wipe out from his memory the gruesome episode, until he breathed his last recently, "Varghese was sitting between two rocks. He was calm but alert, as though he was waiting for something to happen and wondering why it was not happening. I went up to him and rested the nozzle of my rifle on the left side on his chest. Then I remembered his request. I sounded a signal with my tongue" and "'Jai Mao', he shouted and I pulled the trigger. He fell over." To give the semblance of an encounter, another officer subsequently fired a shot in the air and placed the gun in Varghese's motionless hand. Thus they executed the horrendous encounter drama to perfection.

Varghese's brothers, Thomas and Joseph, had revealed to the world then that they were informed about his death through encounter the next day. Nonetheless, they could not assuage their doubts about the encounter episode when the body was brought to the Government Hospital, Mananthavady, for identification. "There were wounds and marks of physical assault on various parts of the body. The police were of the stand that the body could not be released".

Nair's confessions virtually unlocked the Pandora's Box leaving many questions unanswered. The CBI conducted an inquiry into the case and the high court in a landmark judgement found the police guilty of faking an encounter drama. The prime accused in the charge sheet filed by CBI, Ramachandran Nair passed away in 2006, and even with the final verdict out, the ripples raised by the storm are yet to subside. One of the former activists Ayinoor Vasu remarked :

> Naxalite Varghese was the captain of the Thirunelli action. In fact, he was shot dead by the police in the forest before I was caught, but the media published that he was shot dead in an armed encounter with the police. The general public believed that. Recently, after 30 years, the policeman who was forced to shoot Varghese pleaded guilty after his retirement. The truth was that the police caught Varghese, questioned him in custody, took him to the interior of the forest and shot him dead (Pallath 4).

The embers may have died down and the luminaries have also opted for better and safer pastures, but the political ideology with a radical romantic outfit does invite much attention and appreciation in the celluloid medium, rooted in the socio-political milieu of any nation. 'Thalappavu' (The Headgear), debut movie by actor-turned director Madhupal in 2008, is rooted in the folklore of Thirunelli, where once the Naxal hero Varghese had deadly clashes with the system seethed in exploitation. The disclaimer defending its fictional status does not hold against the basic thread of the story revolving around the dubious mystery of the Varghese murder. Even though the names are altered, with the police constable's role essayed by Lal named Ravindran Pillai instead of Ramachandran Nair and Prithviraj's role as the Naxalite leader named as Joseph instead of Areekkal Varghese, one cannot help but draw parallels between the real incident and reel rendition of the same.

The framework of the movie clearly encases the 'Varghese encounter death drama' episode in line with the confession given by the old cop Ramachandran Nair. The movie follows the similar sequence of events culminating in the dissenter cop Ravindran Pillai (Ramachandran Nair) being burdened with the task of shooting Joseph (Varghese). So too Joseph's final outcry of the slogan is in keeping with the real life account, save for the minor aberrations. Many vouchsafe for Varghese's final outcry as "Jai Mao", clearly in line with the influence of the

Maoist ideologies on the Naxal leaders as against the movie rendering of "Inquilaab Sindabad". Similarly, there are discrepancies regarding fastening Joseph to a tree before facing the gunshot and the reference to the setting as Cherunelly instead of Thirunelly. However, these changes do concede to the narrative requirements to portray a riveting drama than a documentary and the validity of the disclaimer.

'Thalappavu' gives a clear insight into the entire gruesome chapter in the history of Kerala, but from a different frame of reference. The central focus is on the plight of the police constable and the trauma he endures, unable to relieve himself from his own gnawing conscience. The movie is set in Wayanad and Kuttanad in Kerala and the story keeps alternating between the past and present, with the filmmaker's attempt to place the Naxal movement within the context of the latter half of the sixties with pointers towards the decadence of the modern society.

The Naxalites moved by the plight of the browbeaten, take to an armed rebellion against the landlords and the police officers, who have let hell lose in Wayanad. The movie moves through diverse terrains of experience, displaying different phases in the life of the constable, shifting from his adolescent days to adulthood to old age, spanning over 50 years. Madhupal, the filmmaker, has given prime importance to the emotional and the human angle in the entire course of events.

The movie unfurls from the point-of-view of the ageing constable who gunned down Joseph and for no fault of his was deprived of all relations. However, what makes the movie different is that the director fastens all the threads together to present a rounded picture before the spectators. The murder of Joseph is a pivotal angle in the movie, but the events that lead up to this have been deftly brought together as an effort to showcase a movie than a documentary. Therefore, the introduction of the various subsidiary characters in the storyline is to cater to the entertainment factor of the narrative like the rendition of the budding romance, between the adolescent Ravindran and Saramma and the cruel hands of Fate tearing them apart. Likewise, the filmmaker has fleshed out together various episodes, like Pillai's marriage with Karthayani and their blissful marital days, the Joseph encounter episode, his subsequent addiction to alcohol, estranged relations his family, and the loneliness, engulfing his life forever till his death, all embellish the cinematic value of the story. His chance encounter with the Naxalite leader Joseph and their growing understanding and reverence for one another is the thread linking all these episodes.

Joseph comes across as the voice of insurgence, raised in the spirit of fiery rebellion to seek redress for the grievances of the poor and needy. His deeds materialize his altruistic life philosophy, which goes down well with Ravindran Pillai, whose kindness and generosity begets a friendship association based on mutual respect. Ravindran the simpleton is unable to grasp the lofty radical ideas propagated by Joseph and his comrades, but can see through the underlying righteousness they strive to disseminate through their political ideology. In the words of the filmmaker Madhupal, the movie seeks to explore, "the friendship between a person who is killed and the man who killed him. The film will explain what I mean. We live in this world where no one is sure about what will happen to our lives in the next moment. 'Thalappavu' deals with such uncertainties in human lives."

Pillai's strange encounter with his childhood sweetheart under hideous circumstances in Wayanad throws light on her transformation from a coy young girl to an impassive woman, who having lost her husband, honour and happiness has sought refuge in the radical ideas publicized by the Naxalites. The crimes perpetrated against the tribal communities include bonded labour, abuse of women and enforced silence through vicious violence or even murder. These episodes not only unearth the disconcerting side, but also subtly situate the context, which enabled the Naxalite faction to gain a fertile ground in Wayanad.

Even when the film-maker portrays the Naxalites as revolutionaries desperate to cleanse the society of all its ills, he does not hesitate from showing Ravindran Pillai, a representative of the exploitive power system as expressing his sympathies with the activists. Pillai comes across as a ploy in the hands of the despotic power regimes, unable to piece together the happiness vanishing from his life and finds himself at the receiving end. Regardless of our mounting sympathies for the

Naxalites, Pillai, whose wife and children have abandoned him is the one more sinned against than sinning.

All the events that happen in his life in connection with the Varghese encounter episode are nothing but a figment of the imagination of the scriptwriter and the director, who have fused together fact and fiction in the movie. Therefore, in comparison with the other movies made in Malayalam, like 'Kabini Nadi Chuvannappol' and others, 'Thalappavu' at times takes a singular stand with regard to the aspects of justice in relation to the crux of the story, which revolves around the ideologies of the Naxalites and the movement per se. Consequently, while earlier movies have frequently accorded a political treatment to an inherently political theme, 'Thalappavu' has given a completely distinct non-political treatment to a political theme, even when the political background looms large. The apparent mystification is evident as the frame of reference keeps vacillating between the agony of the constable and the Naxal movement in the early half of the seventies.

The filmmaker frequently reinstates the fidelity to the actual episode, with the cop coming across as a tormented soul, who has been unable to communicate his plight to anyone, let alone his loving and understanding wife. He is always misjudged for his deeds and lives with the anguish buried deep in his heart as a loner. With the focus clearly on Pillai's life, the director now and then gives more room for the depiction of the discoloured and wretched lives of Pillai's children, the son who assaults his father and the daughter, who fends for her family by indulging in the sleazy flesh trade. The movie-maker has opted for a different mode of presentation, laying more emphasis on the expressive aspects to present an engaging story, in all probability to avoid the label of being a movie conforming to the genre of serious cinema. All said and done, the theme and its treatment is quite in keeping with the style enunciated by the filmmakers experimenting with the genre of middle cinema, which toes the line between commercial cinema and serious cinema.

Nevertheless, the movie addresses some of the crucial issues associated with the Naxal movement in context of Kerala back in the

1960s and tries to draw a parallel with the conditions prevalent in the modern day. The ghost of Joseph stalks the townships and reasons out with an ageing Pillai that their aggressive modus operandi rooted in armed revolution was the right step to do away with the administrative and political institutions steeped in corruption and injustice. Emancipation substitutes exploitation as their watchword, in their constant endeavour to create a classless society. Unwilling to tolerate the growing oppression both active and passive, Joseph's words clearly resonate the ideas of the inspector general of Nagpur, Prabhat Ranjan, "Naxalism is a philosophy. The armed struggle attached to it is just an offshoot. Killing a Naxal would not solve the problem because the ideology is transmissible in the society. We need to counter the ideology and not the carrier. We need to have a dialogue with the people and get closer to them" (Bose).

With its overriding affecting tone, 'Thalappavu' cloaks the leftwing extremist violence under a romantic guise and raises pertinent question through the words of the Naxalite leader Joseph. These are in line with Prasenjit Bose's idea of the state as "semi-colonial and semi-feudal under neo-colonial form of indirect rule, exploitation and control" (Bose 30). Joseph's justification for their guerilla warfare espouses the widespread disillusionment among the exploited sections, who could savour freedom only through Naxalites's proposal for a substitute system of governance. Seizing power through the barrel of a gun, would advocate their belief in the theory of, "kill one and frighten thousands". Joseph indirectly labels the Indian independence as formal and nominal thereby justifying their violent deeds as unavoidable to cleanse the society through radical social revolution. Armed rebellion is exalted as the promising strategic solution for emancipation through which he rationalizes the cold-blooded murder of the local landlord Krishnadeva Saiver.

In a powerful conversation Joseph's ghost reasons out with an aged Pillai as to why he could not tolerate any injustice be it the corrupt police or the present day government officials. He throws light on the chaotic state of the country when even an apolitical man like Pillai would understand what their movement signified. "A proactive nation alone can beget a fortified democracy. There is no point in complaining against exploitation. You should question them and die if needed and kill if needed."

The cult of violence that Joseph preaches often encases a rationale, which Pillai cannot overlook or for the matter dispense with. Burdened with the guilt, he gives vent to his frustration by openly confessing to the media the heinous crime carried out in the name of Joseph encounter. The ghost of Joseph signifies Pillai's pricking conscience, which is yet to come to terms with the horrendous reality engulfing him. The film ends with the old cop waiting for the ghost of Joseph to escort him to the tranquil world of virtue, where his soul would be liberated from the torment by fire and overriding guilt. Their walk together is evocative of Pillai's recognition that the Naxal faction and its ideology is far better when compared to an unjust system cruel to the core and working against the cardinal tenets of democracy. It is subtle vindication of the Naxal ideology, but not at the cost of the brutal violence.

The evocative use of pertinent symbols like the frequent toll of the church bell, the blood dripping from Joseph's hand and the portrait of Christ's crucifixion are clear paradigms enabling a semiotic reading of the telling representation. Joseph's sacrifice is compared to Jesus' crucifixion to forge the image of a saviour of the browbeaten and the helpless. When Joseph's ghost escorts a dying Pillai, the latter's choice of moonlight over candlelight condenses the waning popularity of Naxalism in the modern society. Sensing the zeitgeist, Pillai realizes that Naxalism has had its run, wherefore the Naxal proposition to wipe out the oppressive darkness will no longer hold firm in the modern world steeped in corruption and nepotism.

One cannot though overlook the minimal obstacles. Harping much on melodrama, the main thread repeatedly slackens and the seriousness and integrity of the pivotal argument goes for a toss. The filmmaker's Leftist inclinations seep in through his conscious effort to back the Naxal ideology as the right alternative to an oppressive system steeped in ruthless exploitation. Pillai's reflections on the Naxal activities clearly echo these turbulent thoughts, "They were good people. They killed Saiver because of their helplessness."

'Thalappavu' treads the unbeaten path by analyzing a concept from a different dimension and for bringing Naxalism back to the limelight. Typical of a middle cinema, the movie leaves many a question unanswered; the film-maker without taking a predisposed stand has opted for an open ending, even when he displays mixed emotions onscreen. However, the film-maker has employed mainstream artistes like Prithviraj, Lal, Rohini and others to enhance its reception factor. Definitely not an adaptation, the movie offers an interpretation into the complex psyche of the human minds through its trip down the memory lane of history.

Harping on those bruises, which are still fresh and sore though decades have passed by, the movie does not delve deep into ideology, than on the repercussions. Therefore, he has excluded the courtroom proceedings and key intellectuals like Ajitha, Vasu and others, which would have lent another dimension to the otherwise poignant story. Giving the film-maker a benefit of doubt, his efforts mark an attempt to render a real life incident in a manner, which has not been explored until date, from the perspective of the traumatized constable, Pillai (Nair). This is a conscious effort on the part of the film-maker to avoid the previous representations of the Naxal movement and the Varghese episode in Kerala.

The much-awaited judgement on the Naxal Varghese encounter case came on October 28, 2010 with the court sentencing DSP Lakshmana for life imprisonment. Many a heart heaved a sigh of relief, with justice finally delivered after 40 long years. Hailed as the first encounter case in the history of Kerala Police, the verdict appeases several tortured souls but ambiguities still prevail. Intriguing as it may seem, the masterminds behind the Varghese encounter are still in their safety nets and even the movie though silent on that, takes note of their conspicuous absent presence. It is in these circumstances that a critical analysis of 'Thalappavu' stands a chance, when numerous passionate moviegoers are left conjuring a possible ending had the movie been made after the verdict was passed.

Filmography :

'Thalappavu' (The Headgear). Dir. Madhupal. Perf. Prithviraj, Lal, Atul Kulkarni, Dhanya Mary and Rohini. 2008.

References :

Philip, Lalu John. 'Naxalism in Kerala', 10 May 2010. http://knol.google.com/k/naxalism-in-kerala#

"Before I am killed, give me a signal so I can shout a slogan." Rediff. 13 Nov. 1998. 10 May 2010. http://www.rediff.com/news/1998/nov/13keral1.htm

"Naxal leader Varghese was murdered in 1970, says CBI." 10 June 2007. 15 Apr. 2010.

http://naxalwatch.blogspot.com/2007/06/naxal-leader-varghese-was-murdered-in.html

Pallath, J. J. "INDIA : Tortured in 1969 and Still Suffering - The Story of Torture Victim Ayinoor Vasu." *Human Rights Solidarity*. 26 May 2003. 12 June 2010.

http://www.hrsolidarity.net/mainfile.php/2003vol13no03/2277/

"Prithvi's Naxal Attack." *Cine Fundas.com* 12 Sep. 2008. 8 Aug. 2010. http://www.cinefundas.com/2008/09/12/prithvis-naxal-attack\

Bose, Soumittra S. 'Mass Contact Crucial for Countering Naxal Ideology', *The Times of India*. 25 Aug.2010. 19 Sep.2010. http://timesofindia.indiatimes.com/city/nagpur/Mass contact-crucial-for-countering-Naxal-ideology/articleshow/6429893.cms

Bose, Prasenjit, Ed. (2010), *Maoism : A Critique from the Left*. New Delhi : LeftWord Books.

Subramanian, S. 'Naxalism -Fact, Fiction and Future', 3 Aug. 2010. http://www.aapssindia.org/articles/art3/factfiction.html

K. S. Subrmanian (2007), *Political Violence and the Police in India*, New Delhi : Sage Publications.

Mohit Sen, 'The Naxalites and Naxalism', *Economic and Political Weekly* (Jan. 1971). 195-198.

Pradip Basu, Ed. (2010), *Discourses on Naxalite Movement (1967-2009)*, Kolkata : Setu Prakashani.

Sumanta Banerjee (2002), 'Naxalbari : beyond Past and Future', *Economic and Political Weekly* (June 1, 2002).

Naxalite Movement : As Captured by Films

Indrani Bhattacharya

Indian politics witnessed all kinds of revolts, upheavals and struggles. Some had been temporary, some long lasting, some went international, some died into oblivion. But if we look back to history, the Naxalite Movement is possibly one of the history's longest movements; even from international perspective. It is the most significant movement after Indian independence, although it respects Telengana and Tebhaga movements as its pioneers. Despite its ups and downs in various times, an underlying, sometimes fragmented stream of its ideology in the urban intellectual society, its tactics in its direct war against the state, its somewhat uncanny power of mobilizing the different groups within its fold, are still giving Indian Government a serious thought.

The Naxalite Movement owes for its name to a small North Bengal Village of Naxalbari, Shiliguri subdivision, West Bengal. What started as a peasants' meeting and turned to a police inspector's killing by enraged farmers resulting in a mass murder of nine innocent victims by the police next day, changed the scenario of Indian politics for ever. The Naxalites follow May 25, 1967, as Naxalbari Day. The Naxalite Movement greatly influenced the future of the leftist politics in India, Bangladesh, and Nepal. The Naxalbari incident sparked numerous ideological debates.In Bengal, the Naxalbari wave shook the traditional base of society, politics, and culture. The movement is still very much relevant and alive in controlling the socio economic and political scenario in some parts of India. With its agenda of seizing state power or "dictatorship of proletariat", as they may call it through armed struggle or "direct action" in their own register, the Naxalites are still seeking a restructured society. The movement is also unique in that it tends to mobilize the most subdued and socially marginalized sections and on the other hand, its influence on the very urban intellectual society had always remained enormous, especially on those who dwelt their youth in the roaring decade of '60s and '70s.

The undivided CPI (ML) did not have any officially declared cultural group, and the protagonists like Charu Mazumdar himself once said that organizing the farmers and workers with the means of "party line" was the most important thing to do, as the movement was at its height. But, individual's sympathy for a bunch of young enthusiastic self-sacrificing people, respect and awe towards the arrogance of challenging a mighty force with hardly anything more powerful than a dream and faith of changing the society in a different way, gave birth to numerous cultural and social activities, like music, literature, theater performances, film, with a compelling feeling of capturing the time through different art forms. The party did not directly control the forms of art or media (except party news bulletins and slogans). Rather, party workers, supporters, and sympathizers created and nurtured these media forms (songs, and literary works) individually or collectively, in accordance with their own ideological views.

The suddenness of the movement changed the form of theatrical presentation altogether. A physical stage, lights, microphones, and make-up became less important. Class oppression, genocide, and police torture became common themes. Writers also adopted imagery from international historical events such as the French revolution, and the struggle in Vietnam. It was not only a bunch of enthusiastic youths who burst up with fresh political ideology and themes like feudal oppression, armed struggle, government-organized genocides, Naxalites' call for "red terror", and torture of political prisoners; popular established names like Manish Ghatak, Birendra Chattopadhyay, Satyajit Ray, Samaresh Basu, Sunil Gangopadhyay, Ajay Das, Utpal Dutt, Jochhan Dastidar, Mrinal Sen, Mahashweta Devi, Buddhadeb Dashgupta also could not turn their faces from the Naxalite movement's re-evaluation of the existing socio-political system, and became creative in their respective fields. The Movement created new famous names like Indu Saha, Nabarun Bhattacharya, Kamalesh Sen, Srijan Sen, Amal Ray, and so on. As Gautam Ghose says in an interview in the documentary, 'Memories of Spring Thunder': if he was not born in that period, he might not become a film director at all, he would have ended up perhaps as any normal fellow with a higher middle class background.

While discussing about film, we can not really overlook the literary world depicting that time. Between 1967 and 1970, subject matter remained primarily rural. Writers talked about zamindars, moneylenders, and the "revisionist" character of the other communist party leaders, who in forming the West Bengal government abandoned their earlier promises. After 1970, the conflict shifted towards urban areas and the enemy became the police, CPI (M), and Congress Party members. From 1970-1971 the city and suburbs witnessed the mass killing of alleged Naxalites. Much of Naxalite literature feature prominent female characters, not only as mothers, sisters or lovers, but also as communist party workers. Writers like Mahashweta Devi (*Hazar Churashir Maa, Sarsatiya, Chetti Munda o Tar Teer* etc.) demonstrated that caste struggle and class struggle were identical in the context of village society. Samaresh Basu (*Oder Bolte Dao, Siddhanta, Gantabyo, Mahakaler Rather Ghora* etc.) viewed the Naxalites as lost, violent youths driven by irrational passions while Sunil Gangopadhyay (*Kendrobindu, Payer Talar Mati* etc.), Samaresh Majumder (*Kalbela*), portrayed the era in a more positive light. Nabarun Bhattacharya (*Herbert*) shows how it can inspire a person to dream and protest in the midst of all human helplessness. Some of these above-mentioned works got a life on screen by the directors like Gautam Ghose ('Kalbela', 2007), Govind Nilhani ('Hazar Chaurasi ki Maa', 1998), Suman Mukhopadhyay ('Herbert', 2005).

A film, unlike some other individualistic art form, needs more means, resources and a considerable assemblance of like-minded people, which probably caused to produce a very small number of films, directly depicting Naxalite Movement, in comparison to other branches of art, like literature and music.

Indian communists never seriously developed the use of film as a political medium. In certain films by individual directors like Satyajit Ray ('Pratidwandi', 1970), Mrinal Sen ('Interview',1970), 'Calcutta '71' (1972), 'Padatik',1973), Buddhadeb Dasgupta ('Grihajuddha', 1982), Gautam Ghose ('Hungry Autumn', 1974, 'Kalbela', 2007) we find glimpses of uncertainty and unrest, mode of protests of what we know as Naxalite Period. We also find relatively recent films with new faces as directors like Shatarupa Sanyal ('Anu',1991, 'Atotayee', 2002), Nirmalya Bandopadhyay ('Ujan Beye', 2002), Amar Bhattacharya ('Memories of Spring Thunder',2006), talking about the movement.

Having its root in a single district in West Bengal, the movement expanded its activities covering over 160 districts across 14 states in all these years since 1967. The root causes are so substantial even today that it never lost its relevance. Intellectuals from other states were not to remain silent. The turbulence of the time, the questions, raised on the very basis of social structure, the uncertainty and unrest, emergency and state oppression, Bangladesh war, Soviet-China relationship, international political scenario, all had tremendous impact on the society in general. Marathi theatres did a lot to shape Hindi films to what it is today. Hindi movies partially or directly based on the Naxalite themes are not hard to find. All are, feature films, with very less commercial success, but interesting in its aspects and execution of plot with a limitation.

'The Naxalite' (1980) by K. Abbas made a sensation in the critic world. Main stream "commercial" movie star Mithun Chakraborty played the character of the protagonist. Director Govind Nilhani's film 'Hazaar Chaurasi Ki Maa' (1998), based on the novel, *Hazar Churashir Maa* by Mahasweta Devi, starring Jaya Bachchan, Anupam Kher, gives a very sympathetic portrayal of a Naxalite killed by the state. 'Hazaaron Khwaishein Aisi' (2005) is directed by Sudhir Mishra. Set against the backdrop of the Indian Emergency, the movie tells the story of three youngsters in the '70s, Kay Kay Menon, Shiney Ahuja, Chitrangada Singh played the main roles. A thought-provoking film, 'Lal Salam',

Posters from 'Hazaaron Khwaishen Aisi'

Posters from 'Hazaar Chaurasi ki Maa'

directed by Gaganvihari Borate, is based on true incidents relating to socio-economic problems in tribal society and thus the role of revenge and power through arms. Sharad Kapoor and Nandita Das acted in this film. Ananth Mahadevan's 'Red Alert - The War Within' (2010), literally abuses the Establishment and lays the blame squarely on the government for fostering inequalities and injustice for the unprivileged classes thereby leading to the 'Maoist-Naxalite movement'. The protagonist's role is played by Sunil Setty. 'Raavan' (2010), a much anticipated film by Mani Ratnam, but, personally, I do not see 'Raavan' as an essentially Naxal-themed movie, 'Raavan' seemed to be set in an indeterminate region and time zone. Not once the protagonist mentioned to be a Naxal. His politics seemed more personal than political. A twenty minute documentary, 'Guns and Daughters', by Shikha Trivedi captures real stories of women, taking part in this struggle. 'Flames of the Snow', a documentary by two Indian film-makers on the Naxalite movement in Nepal, was widely released in Kathmandu this year.

All these above-mentioned movies had a poor run in theatres mostly due to its "non-entertaining and serious" theme and art cinema qualities. However, these had been considered by many critics to be masterpieces in terms of novelty of theme and unconventional treatment. Even the main stream actors with maximum mannerisms, came out of their shell in these films. Almost all the leads were showered with praise for their performances. If one looks at the two posters I used here, will be able to find these movies' actual character. Or better to say, none of these Hindi movies actually could break out from the stereotype of what we know as "bollywood masala" movie. Even a hauntingly serious movie like 'Hazar Chaurasi ki Maa' could not avoid using a romantically intimate scene from the movie for publicity. In the 'Hazaaron Khwaishein Aisi' poster, the boldest word is "LOVE", not "POLITICS", to name only a few common scenario in Bollywood-made Naxalite movies.

If we try to reassemble the ideas we got from our study, a pattern is not hard to find. Bollywood never kept its silence when it comes to militancy; in movies like 'Roja' (1993), 'Black and White' (2008),

'Lamha' (2010), to name only a few, while dealing with so-called "jihadis", somehow kept a sympathetic outlook towards them and portrayed them as victims of the communal and political injustice. The Naxal-oriented movies were no exceptions. In almost all the movies, you find an enraged youth, taking arms against the establishment; and to be honest, very few films occasionally have grasped it as a collective protest. Mostly, some deprivation in the protagonists' own lives caused them to rage a war. Again, however sympathetic, the directors never forget to leave their own statements in these films; which invariably is, violence can do no good after all. Almost in all of these films, there has to be a character, who at the end, succeeds to convince the protagonist to leave arms and to admit that this path was never right. We somehow get a logic behind this almost common treatment of these films. All these militant groups are enemies of Indian government, and to release a movie, one can not really ignore the red eye of censor board. Other than a few independent documentaries, no feature film successfully depicted the movement with authenticity. Other than a very insignificant number of "partisan movies" made in South India, almost all are directed and acted by mainstream movie personalities.

The aim of this paper is an attempt to find disentanglement of cinema and a chapter of history. The history of Naxalite movement in general, some unresolved debates, passion, obligation of different types, ideology, stories of broken dreams, almost the power of a terminator of resurrecting itself again and again, are what Naxalite movement is known for. I want to explore the mood of this historical chapter in this paper with the aide of mainly three films - all documentaries, and all made long after the first temporary setback of the movement. 'Memories of Spring Thunder' (2006), directed by Amar Bhattacharya, 'Ujan Beye' (2002) by Nirmalya Bandopadhyay, 'Guns and Daughters' by Shikha Trivedi.

'Bosonter Dinguli' (2006), ('Memories of Spring Thunder'), is a Bengali documentary film directed by Amar Bhattacharya, who himself was an active party worker and accused by police and government as a central leadership of an underground militant Naxalite fraction of late

'70s and '80s. The title, 'Memories of Spring Thunder', reminds the very statement the Beijing Radio broadcasted on July 5, 1967, after the May 25 incident in the Naxalbari area, Darjeeling, West Bengal same year. The Beijing Radio described the incident as "spring thunder over India", and thus the title comes. The film is a documentary and tells the history of the Naxalbari Movement in a chronological order. The journey begins in 1925, that is, with the birth of Communist Party of India (CPI) and other than a few lines or news clippings of recent times, it generally portrayed the scenario till 1972.

The film starts with a very powerful drum beating, which is generally used for declaring war against enemies in indigenous society. Then the orator goes back to the history of mankind and birth of Marxism as a philosophy, October Revolution and the birth of Communist Party of India. Communist International song in the background signifies the internationalism of communist parties of the world. And the journey has to be through war and the goal, seizure of power, what the marching sound suggests. The beginning of the main part starts with a Bengali statement, "*October biplober kamaner awaj deshe deshe Marxbaad pouche diyechilo...*" (the roar of cannons of the October Revolution reached Marxism to various parts of the world). This is what the protagonist of the Naxalbari Movement, Charu Mazumdar once wrote in the Party Programme of CPI (ML) in 1970.

In an interview, Harvansh Singh, (a veteran leader of CPI, Kanpur Branch) tells us about the foundation of the Communist Party of India in Kanpur. Then the film shows the Telengana Movement, its rise and fall. Some rare footage and Andhra leader K. Seetharamaiah's interview have been used. The unavoidable international incidents caused CPI to split into two different parties, CPI and Communist Party of India (Marxist). The background music changes every time with the mood of events in the film. Some footage and still photographs of important radical international and national political events made the film more interesting and made it easier to understand the youth of the generation in 1960s. Then the party splits again, mainly on the basis of whether to follow the conventinal parliamntarian path or elction boycott and armed struggle. Radicals announced the birth of the third Indian communist party, Communist Party of India (Marxist-Leninist), on May 1, 1969. Right from its birth, the film follows the journey to its temporal setback in 1972, with massive arrests, genocides and death of the leaders.

Some interviews are especially of valuable historical and research importance. For instance, Khokan Mazumdar was an eye witness of the 24th May incident when inspector Sonam Wangdi was targeted by the furious peasants in the Naxalbari area. He was the only leader who was present at that time. He was also a witness of another important incident, the death of Babulal Bishwakarmakar, the first noted martyr of CPI (ML). Mazumdar was a part of the same action squad in which Babulal was a member at that time. Krishnabhakta's interview adds special value to this film. He says about his journey to China with important political documents, Charu Mazumdar handed over to him. His execution of a 72 days' excruciating walk amazes us. Student leaders of that time, Shaibal Mitra, Nirmal Brahmachari, Asim Chatterjee all have contributed to this film with their valuable experience and comments about the movement. Prof. Suniti Ghose, the politburo and central committee member, and also editor of Liberation, the central party organ of CPI (ML) in '70s, shared his experience of the party congress held in Kolkata with an unmatched secrecy in 1970. Pavan Singh, son of Sonamati Singh, one of the innocent victims of police

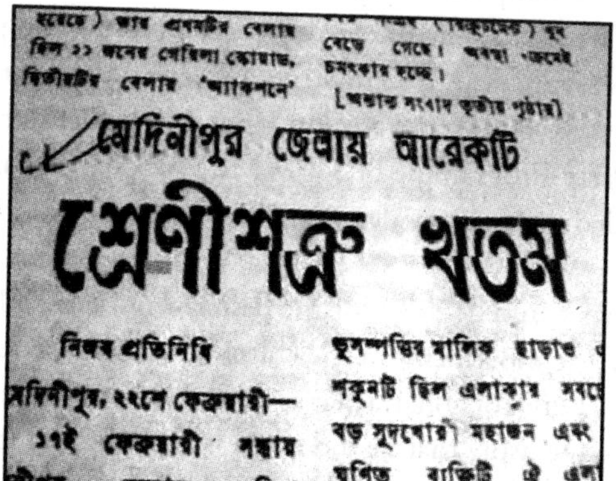

[অন্যান্য সংবাদ তৃতীয় পৃষ্ঠায়]

মেদিনীপুর জেলায় আরেকটি

শ্রেণীশত্রু খতম

নিজস্ব প্রতিনিধি

মেদিনীপুর, ২২শে ফেব্রুয়ারী—

১৭ই ফেব্রুয়ারী সন্ধ্যায়

ভূসম্পত্তির মালিক ডাকাত

শকুনটি ছিল এলাকার সবচে

বড় সুদখোর মহাজন এবং

ঘৃণিত ব্যক্তিটি ঐ এলা

Deshabrati, the Bengali organ of the West Bengal State Committee, CPI (ML)

firing in the Naxalbari incident, shares his story of a haunting memory of his mother's death. Most of the interviews used in this film, are the sole interviews of these important people which had ever been preserved. "All the characters in this film, played their own role", as the director says.

One particular scene makes its entry thrice in this film. The beating of drums by indigenous peasants, declaring war against enemy. Its first usage captures the mood of the whole film, the rural nature of the struggle. The second time appearace of the same peasants takes place side by side with a series of international movements by radical youths, denoting the fiery era of '60s. Then the final appearance of those peasants declares the beginning of the Naxalbari Movement in 1967. As Prof. Tarun Sanyal later in this film says that this movement was the last spring of the past century. Formation of AICCCR and with their ideology of armed struggle and election boycott was indicated by an axe sited on the screen, symbolizing the direct action policy declared by them. In this film, only three scenes have been enacted : The scene where the indigenous peasants are running, with their arms, the scene of the killing of women and children by police in the Naxalbari area, and the last scene, suggesting the undaunting spirit of the movement. Although the collection of evidential visual documents and interviews took years of research, the easy manner of story telling and good editing make the film concise and compact. A beginner or learner of Indian politics and a veteran will find it equally interesting. Certain terms and phrases show the director's sympathy towards the movement. For example, the director calls it "October Revolution" (not November), the same term used in the Party Programme of CPI (ML) by Charu Mazumdar. The Naxalites killed have been described as "martyrs" in the script all through.

A few things could be done for the betterment of the film. I thought the impact of the movement on the cultural ground portion could be a little shorter. Director Bhattacharya has a very good collection of interviews, it's a treasure that he did not want to hide and it is a fact that if he had not used them in this film, we could not see them either. The first song written on the Naxalbari incident was "O naxal naxal barir maa..." and it was written by Dilip Bagchi, the then secretary of Students' Union of North Bengal University. He sang this historical song himself in this film. Amal Ray, who performed the first street play on Naxalbari incident, gave his interview here. Ajit Pande, Ajay Das, Pratul Mukhopadhyay, Gautam Ghose, Buddhadeb Dashgupta, Nabarun Bhattacharya, Meghnad, Kamalesh Sen, Prof. Tarun Sanyal all attributed their valuable comments about the influence of Naxalbari Movement on their personal lives as well as on art. Gadar's live performance is another good clipping which is from the personal archive of the director. Those who know about the Naxalbari Movement might

Memories of Spring Thunder : A moment captured from the film

be interested to know that one of the main figures of the Gopiballabhpur struggle, Lebachand Tudu and his wife Koni Tudu made an appearance in this film and sang a communist song in their own language. The background music is adequate to its forefront theme.

Some rare still photos and news have been used in this film from personal collection of Bhattacharya, and some had been collected from other resources; for instance the government archive, police files, and personal collection of active CPI (ML) cadres of '70s. For example a Food Movement martyr, Nurul Islam's still photo, a photo of the first United Front Ministry, courtesy government archive, another picture capturing Utpal Dutta, standing side by side with Charu Mazumdar and Souren Basu, is from the director's personal collection which, he said, he first time used in some of his articles in various news papers after colleting it from Naxalbari area. Saroj Dutta's wife Bela Dutta and Charu Mazumdar's daughter Anita Mazumdar's interviews are two historically important interviews giving statements which are still not supported by the police and government. Saroj Dutta is still "untraced" as the police report says, but Bela Dutta confirms his murder by the police and Anita Mazumdar is the only living member of Charu Mazumdar's family, who last saw him alive in Lalbazar police custody and in the hospital after his death. She confidently says that Charu Mazumdar was murdered by police and it was not a normal death, although police report declares it to be one.Overall it is a good attempt to preserve the history and without doubt it can be said it has elements which can no longer be found elsewhere. Interviews of important personalities, who are no longer amongst us, had been taped or videoed.

Sound quality is sometimes poor, the crew had to work with very insufficient resources as they say they were doing this for years and never actually thought of making a film, they only thought of preserving the history. Certain clippings, which were collected from History Channel or other documentaries, have English subtitles, whereas the other parts don't. I, personally would have appreciated it to have an English subtitle as it contains historically important events and it has research value. The editing of this film is good, except a few long interviews. It is a political documentation, not a propaganda film. Although it shows the director's sympathy towards the movement but it is definitely not a propaganda

A still photograph used in this film. From the left : Kumkum Bhattacharya, Nirmal Guha Roy, Utpal Dutt, Charu Mazumdar, Pabitra Sengupta, Tapas Sen and Souren Bose

film, it does not instigate against or enforce any view. If we could see some more interviews of people from the other side of the story, like from Anti Naxal Cell, police, Congress and other "democratic" communist party leaders of that time, it could be more interesting. But as it was not an investigation story and neither the director had any intention to establish any particular opinion, those did not seem to be absolutely necessary. Naxalbari Movement inspired various feature films and a few documentaries as well. But as far as I can gather, no film broadly talked about the movement in general, they portrayed some incidents, studied and elaborated the same. This film tells the history in a chronological manner in a story telling format, supported by authentic evidence. Overall, the film is a good documentary, capturing important events supported by relevant interviews.

'Ujan Beye' (2002) (Across the Tide) is a Bengali documentary film on Kashipur-Baranagar genocide, directed by Nirmalya Bandopadhyay. He never claimed himself as an activist, but definitely shows his sympathy towards the movement.The title, 'Ujan Beye', comes with a metaphoric usage of the river Ganga, flowing relentlessly and showering off the bloodshed of those days, as the script suggests. The prelude talks about the Naxalite Movement in short. Some very good footage and rare photographs have been used to make it authentic. Then the story moves forward the bloody genocide allegedly arranged by Congress party and a direct involvement of police made it possible. The camera wanders across the roads of those localities, as if still haunted by memory. We come to note the break-through of this genocide; people claimed it was purposefully "designed" by Congress party and the professional criminals, raised under party flag. The director raises questions on the official claim of "spontaneous rage" of the common people against the militant Naxalites. The massiveness of the incident and the usage of weapons like fire arms, swords, police rifles, and bombs clearly show that it was hardly possible to be "spontaneous". The film then concentrates on two survivors, Ganesh Biswas and Debashish Ghose. Both were CPI (ML) activists and they recollect how and what actually happened that day. A local doctor says in his interview that he heard police firings that day although no police force came to stop this atrocious violence, he also claims to have seen police men patrolling with some local goons that night. In short, the film clearly states that police and administration supported this heinous deed. Some stories and experience actually gave a chill across the spine. The film also catches our attention towards the psychological impact the affected families are still bearing with. Some saw their houses burnt, sons butchered.

The film deals with a particular incident, and has its investigative qualities. Although the director shows very clearly his sympathy towards the victims and definitely took interviews of those who all abhorred the Kashipur-Baranagar genocide, he never lost his track as an investigator, and also talked to people, who never supported the movement. So, it was not a one-sided story presented in front of us. He interviewed Jyoti Basu, Siddhartha Shankar Ray, Tarun Sanyal, Asim Chatterjee; four personalities, with different relationship with the event. Jyoti Basu, who later became CPI (M) MLA of that area, went vocal in the state legislative in a demand for an investigation. Siddhartha Shankar Ray, infamous with his reputation of being extremely harsh on Naxalites, confidently says that it was the rage of the common people of that locality, who, he claims, actually felt relieved after the end of a terror era. Tarun Sanyal is not with any of the above-mentioned parties. He clearly says he never supported the movement, although he saw sincerity in the youths involved. Asim Chatterjee tells us how the party planned next events after hearing about the incident a few days' later.

The film is, overall a good attempt, has its worth in establishing a convincing background and although the director leaves it on the viewers what to conclude, it's not hard to see what he aimed at. He did not use any hypothetical conclusive statement; instead, he raised questions, which the events answer themselves. Only a few things which I would like to mention here do not go with the mood and quality of the film. A background song has been used which is totally out of the story, and causes a momentary distraction. The script went very melodramatic sometimes, especially while introducing us with the locality of Kashipur-Baranagar. A film of this genre does not really have any place for an introduction of the river Ganga as "holy water" or describing the place "holy" because religious figures like Ramakrishna and Vivekananda once resided there. Otherwise, the film is a good research work.

'Guns and Daughters' is an English documentary film on women participants of the Naxalite Movement, directed by Shikha Trivedi, backed up by NDTV production.The film captures real stories of women, taking part in this struggle, their disappointments, broken hearts, and uncertainties. It also shows the real story of late Anuradha Gandhy, a central committee member of CPI (Maoist), who was

Guns and Daughters

married to Kobad Gandhy, an eminent Maoist leader himself. The film actually has two different stories under its wings.

The first half of the story is a story of disappointment met by the female Naxalites of present times. Here we have to remember that in urban Bengal, the picture of a "Naxalite" is somewhat very different than what the present days' underground groups are. In the poorest of villages, women join the Naxal groups, not being driven by any idealistic dream; the sole driving force is poverty and deprivation. Sometimes an urge to get noted in a male dominant society and to create a new identity for themselves, make them choose the life of a "Maoist". They are trained in the deepest of forests across Chattisgarh, Bihar, and they take part in the "war against state" side by side with their male comrades. But the story does not end that way. During different encounters, sometimes these women are arrested alive, most surprisingly in most of the cases; they are tested pregnant while taking to police custody. Their life as an alleged "terrorist" and of a single mother begins. If they are fortunate enough, their parental families come forward to help them. Extremely poor, they have to sell every possession to parole their daughters. Right from the moment she gets arrested, party turns its face off from that unfortunate woman, Roma, a human rights activist, says, these young women get sexually used. Babita joined CPI (Maoist), stayed five years in forests, never heard of Chairman Mao or Naxalbari, the only thing she says that she was promised to be provided with substantial needs by the party workers. Vijay Veenit a local journalist explains the situation more clearly. He says that these women can not contact their party again, as the party thinks they might have become police informers. We see a militant woman, Lucky, who took active part in a 2007 "action".

Then the second part of the story begins with Anuradha Gandhy's life. She, born and brought up in a privileged family in Mumbai, never had an uncertain future awaiting her. A bright youngster with brilliant academic background, fell for the movement in '70s, with an idealistic driving force of changing the world and make it a better place. She became an active party worker, later on married to Kobad Gandhy, an eminent Naxalite leader, both led a life with simplicity, practiced what they believed and said. The director asks questions about her choice of "armed struggle". P.A. Sebastian, a lawyer, and a friend to Anuradha, determines the essential difference between "violence in offence" and "violence in defense", and Anuradha chose the second path, he says. Alpana Chowdhury, a journalist, describes the couple's simple life style in Nagpur, where Anuradha was a trade union leader. Late '90s she disappeared in the forests of Bastar, cutting herself off from the outside world. Her friend says, answering the director's question, that Anuradha never had any regret for anything she did with her life. Anuradha's brother says, he feels kind of "relieved" that now, after her death, at least they can talk about her openly.

Very different in their backgrounds, very different causes as the mobilizing fore, stories of these women surprise us. Bengal, with its long radical history, will find Anuradha's story more familiar and the stories of those village women, shocking. We get to see glimpses of lives, torn in what someone has described as "India's very own civil war" - where some are drawn unknowingly into taking sides, and some make a conscious choice. But as this documentary says, "...today there are ideas of many India at war with each other. And in any war, women are the worst off..."

With the ever changing character of Indian politics and perspective towards social order, law and justice, and with the Naxalites, still a burning issue, India is more likely about to see more films on it.

References :

Bhattacharya, Amar, ed. 1992, *Naxalbarir Probhabe Shilpo Sahityo Chalacchitro* (Art, Literature and Film under the Influence of Naxalite Movement) Kolkata : Naya Istahar.

Dasadhikari, Swapan, ed. 1996, *Sottorer Shohid Lekhak Shilpi Sankhya* (The Martyrs Writers and Artists of '70s) Kolkata : Jalarka.

Ghose, Nirmal, 1988, *Naxalbari Andolon o Bangla Sahityo* (Naxalite Movement and Bengali Literature), Kolkata : Karuna.

Acharya, Anil, *Sottor Doshok*, (The '70s), vol. 2, Kolkata : Anustup.

http://www.impawards.com/404.html (posters)

http://en.wikipedia.org/wiki/Naxalite

7. Bhattacharya, Indrani., 'Naxalite Movement Media', *Encyclopedia of Social Movement Media*. Ed. John D. H. Downing. 2010. U.S.: Sage.

   http://www.ndtv.com/video/player/ndtv-special-ndtv-24x7/guns-and-daughters/111088

   http://naxalrevolution.blogspot.com/

The Naxalite Movement : In Reality, Reel and People's Perception

Manoj Kumar

The spark of revolution that emerged from an obscure, remote area of Naxalbari in Siliguri of West Bengal in May 1967 engulfed nearly 13 states of India[1]; West Bengal, Andhra Pradesh and Bihar being, comparatively, more affected where landlords with feudal mind-set, and rapacious and exploitative moneylenders were attacked by revolutionary peasants when the latter ran out of their patience and, of course, lost hope of getting equitable distributive justice in feudal-bourgeois-dominated political system, structures and processes. The ideals and aspirations of the Indian national movement, democratic provisions of the constitution of India, and the promises made by the ruling party failed to keep the toiling masses of the country in peace as the provisions, policies and principles of the constitution remained mostly on the paper than implemented causing frustrations and disappointments among the marginalized sections of Indian society who had hoped to gain and improve their life from the implementations of various ameliorative measures, particularly land reform measures which remained largely unimplemented. Those who had served the British regime by becoming pillars of its ruling system at the expense of interests of Indian people, after India's political independence in 1947, joined the Congress party and began sharing power with the post-independent Indian government. Erstwhile zamindars and their kith and kin joined politics and administrative services and they made their best efforts to, first, prevent the enactment of land reforms act and then to circumvent and defeat its provisions in which they could succeed to a great extent. Most of the former zamindars retained large tract of land in some fictitious names[2] and continued to maintain their hegemonic positions in society. The dream of landless and poor peasants to own land and have the status of landowners shattered causing intense resentment among them against the prevailing political system that prepared a propitious ground for the Naxalite organizations to mobilise them against the rural oppressive force, feudal landlords.

The rural areas were chosen to be the main centres of armed peasant struggles as the level of oppression and exploitation in rural regions were deemed to be at the peak and, secondly, the state control in these areas were considered to be, relatively, weaker compared to the urban locations. This rural based armed struggle of peasants was adopted on the basis of analysis of Indian society as semi-feudal and Indian state as semi-colonial which was similar to the characterization of Chinese society and state during pre-liberation phase (before 1949). On the basis of this similarity, the revolutionary strategy, adopted in China under the guidance of the Maoist philosophy for the success of Chinese revolution, was found to be suitable for the successful struggle and liberation of Indian people as well[3]. The peasants of the Naxalbari region began agitating under the leadership of the 'Naxalbari Krishak Sangram Sahayak Samiti' which was later transformed into the All India Coordination Committee of Communist Revolutionaries (AICCCR). When the movement intensified, the need for a revolutionary communist party was felt that gave birth to the Communist Party of India (Marxist-Leninist) [CPI (M-L)] in April 1969. The party adopted annihilation of class enemies as tactical line while rural based armed struggle and formation of base areas with the ultimate aim of encircling the cities and seizing state power as the broad strategy for revolution. Agrarian revolution became main content of the People's Democratic Revolution. The emphasis was laid on use of traditional arms that the peasants possessed. The annihilation of class enemies was overstressed. As a result, a number of landlords and rapacious moneylenders were annihilated by the armed squads and many of them fled from their villages for fear of their life. Those who stayed in villages (especially in areas that were under influence of the Naxalite Movement), tried to compromise and agreed to the dictates of the Naxalites. Indiscriminate murders were committed in distant villages to claim the particular areas to be under the influence of the Naxalite movement. These armed activities had spread rapidly to different parts of the country with some pockets of West Bengal being most affected. However, as the movement grew intense within a short span of period, similarly, it declined also soon (by the mid-1970s). The difference within the party on issues of annihilation as tactical line, liberation of Bangladesh, death of Lin Piao and repressive measures adopted by police and the army deployed for the liberation of Bangladesh, were among the major causes for collapse of the movement and dissension within the party resulting in fragmentation of the Naxalite organization and emergence of a number of factions.

The movement became weak but remained alive in varying intensity in different parts of the country. During nation-wide emergency period, a severe state repression was launched against the movement and a large number of cadres were killed by the police and paramilitary force. Many of them were arrested and imprisoned. A number of innocent persons were harassed, tortured and put behind bars in the name being the Naxalites. After the Janata government came to power and formed government at the centre, ban on the Naxalite organizations and their activities was lifted and most of the Naxalites were released from prisons which provided the Naxalite movement with a new lease of life, strength and impetus. The Naxalites began reviewing their ideology, strategy and tactics based on independent analysis of the Indian situation. As an outcome of the review process, the emphasis was laid on the development of mass movement by mobilizing the peasants and workers for ultimate seizure of state power so as to accomplish the task of the transformation of Indian society along humanist lines. Different factions started coming together and forming a new party or organization with an aim to expand the area of their operation and to strengthen the radical peasant movement. Thus, the process of consolidation began which made the movement stronger.

Pursuant to the policy of converting Naxalite movement into a people's movement to achieve the goal of establishing people's democracy in the country, a number of mass organizations were formed to operate on surface among the people and spread the revolutionary message which was considered to be an essential strategic policy for success of the people's democratic revolution. The decade of 1980s witnessed the greater level of increase in the activities of the Naxalites. Many Naxalite organizations were operating in different parts of the country but main organizations among them were : the Communist Party of India (Marxist-Leninist) Liberation [CPI (M-L) Liberation], People's War Group (PWG), Maoist Communist Centre (MCC), Communist Party of India (Party Unity) [CPI (M-L) PU]. Despite realizing the need of making concerted efforts for common cause, they continued to remain fragmented because of their differences on strategic-ideological and organizational issues, indulging often in inter-factional fraternal killings while describing each other as being renegades and revisionists. One of the surface organizations of the CPI (M-L) Liberation, the Indian People's Front (IPF), which was formed in early 1980s, grew powerful in a short span of time and started participating in elections that antagonized political parties as the latter felt threatened and began conspiring to suppress the movement of armed peasants in 1980s. Because of their internal and factional differences and animosities, besides encountering state repression, they lost many cadres making them ponder over the importance and need of unity among different Naxalite organizations and to wage struggle to achieve their common objectives. The need of unity among them emerged also because of growing offensive capability of private sena[4] in Bihar where feudal forces were stronger and more oppressive compared to other states. By the mid-1990s, one of the major groups, the CPI (M-L) Liberation, came overground and began participating in elections since 1995 while dissolving its political mass front, the Indian People's Front (IPF). Other underground Naxalite organizations criticized this party for adopting constitutional path and for disbanding its armed squads which, in the opinion of underground organizations, had encouraged and strengthened the private senas resulting in increased attacks by the reactionary forces on the support base of the Naxalite movement (who were generally rural poor belonging mostly to the lower castes and classes) and described it as being the sarkari Naxalite (governmental Naxalites), especially after it (the Liberation group) began participating in parliamentary politics using the constitutional-legal means and methods. However, the party claimed to be open to use of all possible means- legal and illegal, overground or underground activities, as warranted by the situation[5]. Though it disbanded armed squads but retained the smaller squads in order to meet the emergency needs. In the late 1990s and the early 2000s, the CPI (M-L) could effectively challenge the growing power of the Ranvir Sena in areas of Bhojpur district with the help of these small armed squads.

Various armed peasant organizations began discussing on the need of uniting together for the common cause against the common enemies, particularly to challenge and check the growing strength of the private armies of feudal-landlords in regions of Bihar. Towards the late 1990s, serious efforts were made by different organizations to resolve their inter-factional differences and join together in struggle against the feudal forces by launching campaign to create awareness among the members of the Naxalite organizations about the goal of their revolutionary activities and the need of unification, including organizing meetings for constructive discussions on the issues of their disagreement[6]. In January 1998, the CPI (M-L) People's War Group (PWG) and the CPI (M-L) Party Unity (PU) merged and formed the CPI (M-L) People's War. As a result of the continuous discussions and efforts to unite, in September 2004, the CPI (M-L) People's War and the Maoist Communist Centre (MCC) along with other smaller organizations merged together and formed the Communist Party of India (Maoist) [CPI (Maoist)]. The formation of this new party was a historical turning point in the history of the Naxalite Movement in India as this unification accelerated the pace of the movement and expanded its area of influence. Newer areas came under the influence of the Naxalite activities involving nearly thirteen states and over 170 districts of the country. The regions of Chhattisgarh, Jharkhand, Orissa, Andhra Pradesh, Bihar and West Bengal witnessed rise in activities of the Naxalites. The issues of rights of tribal, in the current phase, have been one of the major issues of the movement. The incidents occurring in tribal- dominated areas of Chhattisgarh and Lalgarh became usual part of the national news related to the growing activism of the Maoist movement which led to the severe state repressive measures in these areas. The efforts have been made by the civil society to restore peace by bringing the representatives of the Naxalites and government on a negotiating table as observed during 2004-2005 in Andhra Pradesh but without any fruitful result worth the name. The present nature of the movement is described as being a phase of anti-state resistance based on the issue of forest rights of tribal people more than the struggle against rural based feudal forces as the power and dominance of the latter have substantially declined because of the movement's focus on the anti-feudal struggle[7].

Generally, the research conducted by the different organizations and institutions described and interpreted the movement as the product of the socio-economic problems and suggested institutional reform initiatives as well as the use of physical force to resolve the Naxalite-related problem but the government focused on the latter measures more and the reform policy, largely, remained as paper tiger. The Naxalite movement caught the attention of literary personalities, film-makers, dramatists, besides its presentations and projections in media in different ways. Most of the news reports and interpretations of the nature and pattern of the Naxalite movement are similar, in features, to those of the government's projections of the movement. The news covered regarding the 'encounter' deaths of the Naxalites are generally the police and official version and anyone having a normal common sense will be able to figure out (by reading the news reports) whether such encounters are real or fake. This phenomenon is nothing new. Fake encounters have been adopted as a state's strategy to commit extra-judicial killings with an aim to suppress the voice and agitations of poor peasantry and working class for raising the demands that have guaranteed in the constitution[8].

The Naxalite movement has influenced Indian cinema since the 1970s in different forms and degree. A number of films have been made on themes of the Naxalite movement directly or indirectly. The themes of the films in which poor peasant/s challenging horse-riding upper caste (and class) zamindars (with surnames, such as, Thakurs, Choudhary, etc.), challenging their right to oppress and exploit, including right to caste-based oppression are shown reflect the influence of nature and purpose of the Naxalite movement and, in general, the movement of peasants against the feudal landlordism under the guidance and leadership of communist philosophy and parties. All the films made on Naxalism focus, broadly, on the resistance against social inequality, corruption, poverty, injustice and associated socio-economic evils for creation of a just society based on egalitarian principles. The negative aspects of such films are noticeable when film-makers and directors try to present it in distorted forms while mixing romanticism and other orientations for commercial purposes and not intending to highlight the naked reality of the Indian society that the Naxalite Movement focuses on. Generally, the depiction is oriented towards abrupt and temporary expression of resentment and frustration of some youth and people against the existing socio-economic evils with not a strong will as has been observed, in reality, in the practice of the Marxist-Leninist and Maoist philosophy of social transformations. This could be understood from the critical interpretation of the story of some films made on the themes of the Naxalism.

'Calcutta 71' is a first important movie on the Naxalite movement based on four stories (by different writers) and directed by Mrinal Sen which was released in 1972. The film highlights the misfortune and suffering of the middle class family while focusing on the deeds of corrupt politicians and resistance against such evils for a better society[9]. Through this movie, the poverty has been shown as the root cause of all the evils in society (such as, exploitation, oppression and other ills) including the indignity of a fellow human being that results in outbreak of agitations and conflicts within socio-political structure. It was made at the time when people of Calcutta were passing through a difficult time with routine killing of people, Naxalites' rejection of parliamentary path of politics, clashes between different factions of the communists, particularly the Communist Party of India (Marxist) and the Naxalites. The film presents not only the criticism of the contemptible gap between rich and poor, between the oppressor and the oppressed but also resistance against such social system.

'The Naxalites' (*Mera Inquilab*) made in the 1980 and directed by Kwaja Ahmad Abbas[10] is the second major film on the issue of the Naxalite Movement that reflects the deprivations and vicissitudes of people in Indian society. The sight of starving peasants, inhuman torture of a man by the policemen, a man selling his mother on the street as a prostitute, and an orphan living in a cemetery who lost his parents to the famine and is traumatized by memories of his mother selling her body to survive, reflected the pathetic condition of Indian masses through this movie which is bound to generate turbulence resulting in violent rebellions to break away from the shackles of centuries of oppression and establish an egalitarian society. No substantial difference has been noticeable in the condition of Indian poor which is one of the major reasons for the movement to remain alive aiming at humanist change in the nature of socio-economic order in India. The people's awareness of being unfairly treated and denied justice prepare them for revolt and revolution and they become psychologically tuned to sacrifice everything, even their own life for the sake of a just society. It could be said that brutality breeds hatred and brutality while justice and fairness create humanist sentiments. The one whose hopes of a better future and dreams of an improved life shatters is unlikely to think of anything than revolting against the system. The essence of the movie was expected to awaken the dormant conscience of people to fight against unjust social order heavily loaded with feudal tendencies and create a better humanist society. However, it is difficult to measure the impact of the movie on psyche of Indians. Docile mentality and rapacious nature of major portion of population of the country have been constantly impeding the desired social change despite a number of attempts in this direction by few conscientious revolutionary personalities and dreamers of a peaceful, harmonious and exploitation free society. However, it is unfortunate that even after more than four decades of the Naxalites' activities could not convey the revolutionary message to people of the country as a result of which people have different kinds of perceptions regarding the nature and purpose of the radical peasant movement which is also one of the reasons responsible for the failure of the movement.

'Hazaar Chaurasi ki Maa' (Mother of 1084) movie made in 1998 and directed by Govind Nihalani is based on a novel, Hajar Churashir Maa, written by an eminent literary personality, Mahasweta Devi in Bangla language. The film deals with the life of a woman who loses her son who had become the Naxalite. The plot of the movie is - A young man who belonged to an affluent family and was pursuing college education was killed as a consequence of his association with and participation in the Naxalite Movement and parents are called to identify the dead body of their son (corpse no. 1084) that makes them deeply aggrieved. They begin enquiring and come to know about the cause for which he was struggling. They too realize the genuineness of the cause and decide to advance the struggle for a better social order[11]. Other important film 'Hazaaron Khwaishein Aisi' made in 2003 and released in 2005 on the Naxalite theme directed by Sudhir Mishra is focused on the life and ambitions of three youth studying together but having different ideas and dreams in their life[12]. The story of the movie reflects on the environment during 1970s, when the country was undergoing intense social and political changes. One of the youth belonging to a well off family, driven by the strong revolutionary urge to bring about radical change in the society of Bihar along the principles of humanist goals and eliminate social evils, like caste discrimination, joins the radical movement while others get engaged in improving their individual status in society. However, youth with revolutionary spirit finds himself disillusioned, leaves the path of radicalism and decides to pursue his career whereas his lady-love who initially was not interested in such radical activities decides to stay back and serve the people.

The film 'Chamku' directed by Kabeer Kaushik was released in 2008 that deals with the theme of Naxalism in which the Naxalite encounters disillusionment and tries to get away with radical activities but his situation does not allow him to do that[13]. Generally, the movies related to the Naxalite movement are art films which do not run well in theatres like those of commercial films even if the film is of not only social value but important from artistic point of view. 'Red Alert : The War Within', a movie (released in 2010 and directed by Ananth Mahadevan) on the Naxalite-related issues deals with the story of a cook who becomes Naxalite and encounters a confrontation with group leaders that make him run from militants and law[14]. There are other films, like, 'Lal Salam' directed by Sanjiv Karambelkar, 'Janda' by Kodi Rama Krishna, 'Rakta Charitra' by Ram Gopal Varma and other regional-linguistic films ('Tiladanam' in Telugu directed by KNT Sastry, 'Panchagni' in Malayalam) that deal with the issues associated with the Naxalite Movement[15]. Besides these, there are other movies that deal with the issue of the Naxalism but most of the films get into complex trap of doing justice with the socio-political reality and serving commercial interests and that is where the possibilities of distortion and distraction in the essence of the theme and purpose of filming such issues start getting affected. Most of the films on the Naxalite Movement have been made on the basis of considerations of its potential to sale and run in cinema halls which make the film-makers tamper the essence of the issue.

At the time when a number of issues related to socio-economic evils, corruption and scams of various kinds are in news and form the part of serious public debates. People perceive the Naxalite movement in different ways. There are many who feel that the Naxalites are fighting for justice and dignity to common men which the state machinery has not been able to ensure whereas a substantial number of people have mixed reaction and opinion on the issue. Many times, the Naxalites are bracketed with terrorists. Even one very senior police officer who had served in the Naxalite affected regions had explained about the Naxalite activities and described them as members belonging to a criminal group that is more organized and operating under the cover of Maoist philosophy[16]. The feeling of love and hate towards the movement reflects construction of people's perception influenced by many factors, such as, their level of awareness about the movement, their own caste/ class background (generally, persons belonging to the upper castes and classes have negative opinions about this movement), their personal positive experience, etc. However, it is widely perceived even by the government representative and national leaders that the Naxalite movement is the product of socio-economic problems and necessitates reforms measures besides other measures related to law and order.

Notes and References :

1. See Basu, Pradip (2000), *Towards Naxalbari (1953 -- 1967): An Account of Inner-Party Ideological Struggle*, Kolkata : Progressive Publishers; Ram, Mohan (1971), *Maoism in India*, Delhi : Vikas Publications; Johari, J. C. (1972), *Naxalite Politics in India*, Delhi : Indian Institute of Constitutional and Parliamentary Studies; Gupta, B. D. (1974), *The Naxalite Movement*, New Delhi : Allied Publishers; Ghosh, Sankar (1974), *The Naxalite Movement : A Maoist Experiment*, Calcutta : Firma K L Mukhopadhyay; Mohanty, Manoranjan (1977), *Revolutionary Violence : A Study of the Maoist Movement in India*, New Delhi : Sterling Publishers; Sen, S., Panda, D. and Lahiri, A. (eds.) (1978), *Naxalbari and After : A Frontier Anthology*, volumes I & II, Calcutta, Kathashilpa; Jawaid, Sohail (1979), *The Naxalite Movement in India : Origin and Failure of the Maoist Revolutionary Strategy in West Bengal 1967-1971*, New Delhi : Associated Publishing House; Banerjee, Sumanta (1980), *In the Wake of Naxalbari : A History of the Naxalite Movement in India*, Calcutta : Suvarnarekha; Banerjee, Sumanta (1984), *India's Simmering Revolution : The Naxalite Uprising*, London : Zed Books Limited, for details for the causes leading to emergence of the movement and various aspects of the early phase of the movement.
2. Land was transferred in the name of cats, dogs, servants and unborn child to evade the acquisition of surplus land (excess land than allowed by the ceiling laws), including other manipulative methods, such as, installing idols in temples as land could be retained in the name of maintaining and

looking after the affairs of temples and idols of deities. Within the same premises of 'a temple, many idols were installed so as to claim for retention of land in excess of ceiling limit.

3. In the Chinese situation, guerrilla warfare was adopted and found to be more effective revolutionary strategy while laying emphasis on development of peasants-workers' consciousness and mass movement. In India, annihilation of feudal-landlords in countryside constituted the main tactical line of the agrarian revolution, a principal axis of the Naxalite movement. The killing of innocent persons in the name of class enemies was considered as an important qualifying criterion for being accepted and recognised as a true communist. In the killing frenzy that began in late 1960s and early 1970s, a number of innocent persons were murdered which created an impression among the people regarding the movement as being terroristic and murderous in nature and not revolutionary. Such impression, later, became one of the reasons for decline of the movement. During one of the interviews that I conducted during my field survey from 1999 to 2003 in Naxalite affected areas of Bihar, one of the ex-Naxalites in Mushahari block of Muzaffarpur district revealed that when the members of dalam (armed group) used to take shelter in villages, during their stay, they used to ask the host about the presence of oppressive landlords with feudal tendencies in those areas and, many times, host suggested the name of persons with whom he did not have good terms and wanted to settle his personal scores. The host utilized such occasions and instigated members of the armed squad to annihilate persons who were his personal foes in the name of annihilation of exploitative and oppressive feudal class enemies. This phenomenon earned a bad name and image for the movement, besides, creating confusion and feeling of aversion in the minds of people, including the Naxalite activists towards the nature of movement. Many important cadres left the organization and the movement because of intra-party differences on such issues leading to weakening and decline of the movement. However, a combination of many other reasons, besides this, was responsible for the weakening of the movement.

4. When the Naxalite movement grew intense in Bihar in post-emergency period (post-1977) after the release of Naxalites from prisons, lifting of ban on the Naxalite organizations and Naxalites' emphasis on developing

mass movement with the help of open fronts, the landed gentry interest groups felt threatened and could no longer rely only on the support provided by the state police force. The changed situation made them form their own armed militia groups, mostly along the caste lines to protect their interests and maintain hegemonic status quo in the society. This phenomenon of forming private armies along caste lines began in the late 1970s and converted the class struggle of the Naxalites into a caste violence as whenever the class struggle grew stronger and intense, caste factor came on the way and the people were mobilized and polarized along their caste lines that resulted in occurrence of caste based violent incidents. The main private armies that emerged in the areas of intense agrarian struggle in Bihar where the feudal oppression was at its peak, were the Bhoomi Sena of Kurmi landlords, the Kunwar Sena of Rajputs, the Lorik Sena of the Yadav caste, the Sunlight Sena of Rajputs and Brahmin landlords, the Brahmarishi Sena, the Savarn Liberation Front and the Ranvir Sena of Bhumihar caste landlords, besides many other smaller private armies. The Ranvir Sena was the most dreaded and powerful among them all. However, most of these private armies weakened by the end of 1980s due to attacks launched by the Naxalite organizations and their (private armies') own internal weaknesses while the Ranvir Sena declined in the early 2000s. See Singh, Kumar Narendra (2005), *Bihar Mein Niji Senaon ka Udbhav aur Vikas*, New Delhi, Vani Prakashan for details.

5. Interview with the CPI (M-L) Liberation's senior leader and Central Committee member, Mr. K. D. Yadav and Central Committee member, Mr. Prabhat Kumar Choudhary, 13-14 December 2002, Patna at the party office, Birchand Patel Road.
6. Interview with one of leaders of Lok Sangram Manch, Patna, 17 December 2002. Also see, Samkalin Bahas (in Hindi), an irregular journal, Patna, Rashtriya Press, November 1996, a journal that carried viewpoints of various organizations.
7. Informal interview with the leaders of the open organizations of the CPI (Maoist), Patna, July 2010. However, the open fronts deny having any link with the underground organization.
8. Killing radical peasants and their associates in the name of being Naxalites is an open secret. Those police involved in such killings are

commended for gallantry awards and recommended for promotions instead of identifying and subject them to the provisions of law. Surprisingly, recently, one police officer, Mr. Lakshamana, who was responsible for encounter death of a Naxalite in Kerala in the early 1970s has been convicted by the court of law on the basis of the confession made by a constable who shot the Naxalite dead on the order of this police officer. This is unique as it has been observed that the state and its judicial organ make every effort to implicate the Naxalite activists in false cases and protect its police officers forgetting its constitutional duty of providing justice to all on the basis of the principle and fundamental right of every citizen of the country to avail the privilege of 'right to equality' irrespective of difference in their status and identity in society. The implication of Dr. Vinayak in fabricated police case (he was accused of having links with the Naxalites and assisting them) and his imprisonment for nearly two years is one such recent instance.

9. 'Calcutta 71- An Outstanding Film', http://www.boloji.net/cinema/calcutta71.htm, 28 May 2011; CALCUTTA 71 (Dir. Mrinal Sen, 1972, India) - 'Calcutta was passing through a terrible time...', 1 January 2010, http://omarsfilmblog.blogspot.com/2010/01/ calcutta-71-dir-mrinal-sen-1972-india.html, accessed on 28 May 2011. The director of the film was influenced by the European modernists such as, Godard and Brecht, including the idea of Eisenstein and realized the need and possibilities of utilizing art as a tool for the propagation of ideas and initiating change in society. He argued for state-sponsored alternative to commercial cinema so as to focus on the social-political reality of society and the country.

10. K. A. Abbas has been the progressive literary personality, film-maker and an existentialist who holds the hierarchical social structure as the responsible factors for ills in society and seems to be intending to provide stimulus for chance process at grassroots level. He tries to expose the failure of the Indian democratic system and judicial organ of the state by focusing on the depiction of multifold problems, particularly, lack of basic amenities to people, such as, clean drinking water, homelessness, cruelties and atrocities perpetrated by the police force, incompetent bureaucracy and colonial influences in Indian society, including the tightening grip of the oppressive forces and suffering of toiling masses.

See 'The Naxalites - Khwaja Ahmed Abbas, Mithun- A classic movie from the 1980's', http://naxalrevolution.blogspot.com/2008/09/naxalites-khwaja-ahmed-abbas-mithun.html, 28 May 2011.

11. 'Hazaar Chaurasi ki Maa', http://en.wikipedia.org/wiki/Hazaar_Chaurasi_Ki_Maa, 28 May 2011.

12. 'Hazaaron Khwaishein Aisi', http://en.wikipedia.org/wiki/Hazaaron_Khwaishein_Aisi, 28 May 2011.

13. 'Chamku' (film), http://en.wikipedia.org/wiki/Chamku_(film), 28 May 2011.

14. 'RED ALERT' - A film on Naxalite movement, http://www.glamsham.com/movies/scoop/09/oct/14-red-alert-a-film-on-naxalite-movement-100910.asp, accessed on 28 May 2011 'Red Alert Movie Review : Red Alert - Topical,finely crafted & performed', http://www.indiaglitz.com/channels /hindi/review/11340.html, 28 may 2011.

15. 'Rakta Charitra', http://en.wikipedia.org/wiki/Rakta_Charitra, accessed on 28 May 2011, http://www.rakthacharithra.co.cc/2009/12/first-look-ramgopal-vermas-new-film.html, 28 May 2011. Also see Telegraph (Calcutta, July 2011), http://www.telegraphindia.com/1100711/jsp/7days/story_ 12670028.jsp, accessed on 28 May 2011; http://www.totaltollywood.com /articles/tiladaanam.html, accessed on 28 May 2011; Srinivas, S. V., Telugu Cinema : N.T. Rama Rao and After, http://www.bfi.org.uk/features/imagineasia/guide/contemporary/telugu.html, accessed on 28 May 2011; 'Geetha in Malayalam Cinema - Her Notable Malayalam Movies', accessed on 28 May 2011, http://box4.chakpak.com :9080/articles/?p=20765.

16. Interview with one senior Police officer of the Inspector General designation serving in the State Secretariat during my field survey in November 2002 on the conditions of anonymity.

Filming the Young Brigade

Praskanva Sinharay

A Tale of Three Monkeys :

One must be familiar in India with the tale of three monkeys who preach a slogan each 'Bura maat dekho' (Never see 'wrong'), 'Bura maat suno' (Never listen 'wrong'), 'Bura maat kaho' (Never say 'wrong'). But interestingly hardly has anyone enquired that who these monkeys are, who has given them the authority to advice or whom do they represent. As a student of politics, these three musketeers could never convince me of their teachings because I have always found their words ambiguous. The big question that stands before us is that who decides what is 'right' and what is 'wrong'. Here I can't help recalling a scene from one of my favourite films 'Hirak Rajar Deshe'(Kingdom of Diamonds) by Satyajit Ray where the Shiksha Mantri (Education Minister) visits the pathshala (school) ran by Udayan Pandit, the teacher. The minister learns from the teacher that it is a *Hitopodesh* (Moral Science) class that day and asks sarcastically, "*Hitopodesh*? Kar upodesh? Hitahiter bichar kore ke? Jano na toh! Jaar naam nai, tar kathar o kono daam nai... hitahiter bichar koren Hirak Raj!"[1](Moral advices?? Whose advices? Who defines morality?... You don't know? A person who doesn't have a name, his words too don't hold a claim... you better accept that morality is defined by Hirak Raj!"). The tale of the three monkeys is a similar case. If we keenly watch their story, particularly mark their words that they preach through the prism of politics, we can find that these monkeys are real loyal pets who have been the mouthpiece of the state, the authority, of those who are in power. The Indian State decides and the monkeys preach. That what is defined politically 'right' by the state is right and that what is declared politically 'wrong' is wrong. The equation is very simple- either you are with the state or you are 'wrong'.

Fortunately, some people consciously chose to be 'wrong' throughout ages in history of human civilization and revolted time and again against the established order set and maintained by the state. Their unhappiness towards the established 'thesis' gave birth to an 'anti-thesis' which brought forth a new dawn- a 'synthesis'. This is the core of Marxian dialectical materialism. Marxian philosophy has argued that in all stages of history, the 'anti-thesis' has always been tagged 'wrong' by the 'thesis' but at the same time the 'wrong' has been an inevitable necessity for civilizational progress. Marxism as a school of thought has always catalyzed such 'wrong' and initiated a movement from the municipal level to the international level by continuously laying emphasis upon the unified interests of the working class under the direction of the vanguard communist party in order to overthrow the bourgeois state putting an end to the socio-political and economic exploitation, breaking up its bureaucratic military state apparatus for the establishment of transitional 'socialist' state ultimately culminating into 'communism' where classes shall no longer exist. "For Marx, the state belongs to the superstructure. So in course of history each mode of production gives rise to its own specific political organization to further the interests of the economically dominant class"[2] Those who challenged these specific political organizations produced in the course of history by each mode of production were declared 'wrong' by the dominant economic class as their interests were hampered. The history of India is no different. The glorious history of the Great Revolt of 1857, the Santhal Rebellion, the Sanyashi Revolt, the Tebhaga and Telengana movements have shown how the common man became conscious of his class and position in the existing socio-politico-economic framework and led a unified revolution against the state. Each and every time the state reciprocated mercilessly and coerced these movements because, as the monkeys will tell you, these were politically 'wrong'.

A wrong was repeated in West Bengal, India in the late 1960s and

1970s. The streets of Calcutta reverberated with slogans 'Aamar naam, tomar naam...Vietnam, Vietnam' and 'Naxalbari Lal Salaam'. Vietnam resisted US imperialist attack and set forth an example before the world. The dream of a proletarian revolution that leads to a classless society germinated on Indian soil once again in 1967 when the local tribal people attacked a landlord and seized the land in Naxalbari village in the state of West Bengal. "This phase is marked by a certain shrillness of rhetoric and a high degree of esoteric polemics based on the tenets of Marxism-Leninism-MaoTse-tung Thought."[3] The objective of the movement as defined by the ideologue Charu Majumder was the 'seizure of power through an agrarian revolution' by eliminating the male-dominated feudal order in the Indian countryside to free the socio-economically oppressed masses from the clutches of the exploitative landlords and to replace the existing system by redistribution of land to the actual tillers through land reforms. "This was the phase when the movement had cast its magical spell all around among idealist youth and the call to make the 1970s the decade of liberation was taken very seriously by a large number of its followers."[4] The movement received huge mass support from the urban educated students, youths and intelligentsia of India, particularly Bengal, leaving a long-lasting impression on the socio-cultural and politico-economical spheres of the country.

The Naxalite movement had impact over all the socio-political and cultural sectors of the country including films. Independent India was only twenty years old in 1967 when the movement sparked for the first time. The Indian government was struggling with its nation-building process. The socio-politico-economic structure was semi-feudal and semi-capitalist and the civil society was underdeveloped. And the charismatic Nehru who diplomatically and convincingly manipulated the various civil society apparatuses in the process of nation-building was already dead. Films in India, post-independence, reflected the socio-political trajectory bridging cinema and the course of nation-building. They talked about the hopes and aspirations of an emergent India free from the ravages of British colonialism. Films played the appropriate role of a civil society instrument capable of socio-politically and culturally hegemonizing the masses in favour of the state just as they do, according to the political ideas of Antonio Gramsci, in advanced capitalism. But films in India exhibited a bit vacuum after the death of Nehru and his euphoric ideas of socialism. The creative search to develop and expand the horizons that not only fulfill the peoples' aesthetic needs and aspirations but also reflect historical progress and development lost direction in the haze of immediate commercial concerns. This period marked a phase of moral confusion and political incoherence. Films failed to address the historicity of a certain phenomenon acquainting people with the course of history and help them grasp the link between the past and the present. The Naxalite movement filled up the vacuum and supplied resources, fuel and energy once again to the Indian cine-world. After all "Marxism and films share one thing in common : they are both interested in masses."[5] Films now had with them a strong ideology to deal with and crucial issues to address. Filmmakers like Ritwik Ghatak, Satyajit Ray, Mrinal Sen, Govind Nihalani, Tapan Sinha and others tried to address direct issues centering the movement. A fresh air was introduced in the films of India, post- Naxalite movement, and now there was a concrete socio-political trajectory to focus on. Films started challenging the state by upholding the issues of the exploited, the oppressed, unemployed, tribes, women, of love and relationships, government and reforms, human rights, etc. Daily life of a common man, the regular ups and down and the various paradoxes that existed all around him started getting filmed. Films now were capable of providing an intellectual and moral leadership to the cause of a revolution by counter-hegemonizing the working class in response to the already existing hegemony of the state by its civil institutions. As Mike Wayne opines, "Marxism raises questions about relationships at every level of social order. It reminds us that how important socio-economic relations are and any authentic Marxism understands the complexities of the cultural arena within those relations. Marxism demands that we historicize everything rather taking it to be a natural immutable fact. It refers not only to past and present but also future."[6] Films from now onwards tried to address the historicity, of acquainting the people with the course of history and the history of socio-economic exploitation. With a social responsibility on them, films in India now were interested in masses. One of the finest filmmakers in India Satyajit Ray believed that "films cannot change society"[7] but they can aid a revolution when it takes place and they can also continue with the hang-over of the revolution stressing upon its basic tenets. This was evident in Indian cinema, post-movement. Here now follows the discussion on how the young brigade who participated in the Naxalite movement marking it as one of the salient features has been filmed in Indian cinema.

The Idealist Youth—Brati :

Ideologically strong as it was, the movement received participation from the peasant class and support from young Bengal, the urban educated student community and a part of the intelligentsia. One can remember that the protagonist of 'Jukti Takka Ar Goppo' asking the young Naxalites in the jungle that, "Ami jante chai je tomader modhye ki pranshakti kaj korche?"[8] (I want to know the immense force that drives you ahead). The role of ideology had been strong and filmmakers have tried to discover this in their various projects. The youth of Bengal dreamt of a classless society where there shall be no exploitation, oppression, corruption, injustice and poverty. They dared to dream to change everything around them, uproot the existing social order erasing the colonial and feudal hang-over and ignite the aspirations of the working class for their emancipation. This ideological thrust that the young Bengal received has been filmed by Govind Nihalani in 'Hazar Chaurasi Ki Maa'. We hear the character of Brati, the idealist youth who says his mother, "Maine ek sapna dekha hain Maa, koi chota sa nahi, bahoot bada- kranti ka sapna"[9] (Mother, I have seen a dream, not a small one but a gigantic dream-the dream of revolution). Young Brati is only a brilliant student and a national scholarship holder for his father, family and society but he wants to change everything around him along with his fellow comrades who dream alike. Being disgusted with his surrounding socio-politico-economic scenario that begins with the oppression over his mother within the family, he wants to champion a revolution that he has dreamt of for establishing a classless society, sacrificing all the comforts of life. He spends time at his upper middle class house and at the slum at his friend's place with equal ease. He wants to de-class himself. One can see his determination when he leads the confrontation with the local party-backed goons and shouts the slogan 'Naxalbari Zindabad'. The determination and conviction that works within him shakes the viewer. Brati confronts his father who mocks at his beliefs as he feels that people around him do nothing but pontificate about changing the system and he is sick of that. Marxism as a doctrine influenced the ideological stand of thousands of youth like Brati who felt suffocated in the existing semi-feudal, semi-capitalist Indian society. The young brigade of India, particularly Bengal, proliferated in thousands to the call of Naxalbari in order to bring about a new world as Brati dreams- 'a world of equality, peace, justice and dignity to everyone'.[10] The movement was not only marked by rejection of the ruling ideology but a thorough critique of all the established ideologies. Charu Majumdar became a youth icon. The youth, especially the students, were not only concerned and fighting for those issues that directly affected them but they made alliances with the working class and the peasants in order to reach their desired end. The doctrine of jeopardizing the capitalist state by politically assimilating the village masses made a huge appeal to the youth section. They worked in the countryside to politically socialize the peasants and the workers to grow within them a class consciousness. The youth of the period started believing that 'power flows from the barrel of a gun'. The call for revolution was in the air and the youth couldn't stop themselves from dreaming of a whole new world. They consciously accepted the 'annihilation line' of Charu Majumdar, took up arms and justified their act of popular violence which they feel is 'just' in response to the oppressor violence. The young brigade felt that violence has a liberating purpose- as a means to win revolution. It was their belief that the state must be confronted directly with all diverse forms. It is very wrong to say that in revolutionary struggle there is no place for ethics. It is rather erected on the basis of Marxian dialectics- what class is directing violence against whom? Why is it being waged, in whose interests? These are the basic questions, which decided the justness and unjustness of the use of violence during the course of struggle. The justness of violence, more particularly counter-violence, against the state atrocities as well as the exploitative feudal landlords and bourgeoisie penetrated the young hearts. The perennial exploitation and state-sponsored violence over a certain class of people invited the use of counter-violence. However, Brati had a dilemma regarding the application of violence. Even few of his fellow comrades felt the same that periodic violence was a premature political move. The killing of a traffic guard pains Brati and intensifies the dilemma. He feels that the annihilation line shall provide them nothing positive in the urban areas rather shall bring negative results. Extensive campaigns on the party line and political socialization of the masses can bring them the desired results. He debates on this with his fellow comrades which remains inconclusive. The question of anchoring to violence remains till last a pertinent question- 'what is the right to violence?'

The Rudderless Man—Siddhartha :

The ruling ideology could not convince the huge section of young India who did not participate in the movement but were direct victims of the post-independent suffocating phase of socio-economic exploitation in the country. It is often found in the developing societies that modernization creates aspirations among the urban educated groups for better employment and good prospect which the existing economic and political system fails to provide. "Decremental deprivation is caused by a situation where value capabilities decline with no corresponding diminution in people's aspirations. Here takes a positive loss of value."[11] Apart from the films that had been made in direct context of the movement, the nature of films as a whole, post-movement, metamorphosed, where film-makers started challenging the establishment and dared to dehumanize the state. This state of decremental deprivation has been sarcastically addressed in 'Jukti Takka Ar Goppo' when we hear the character of Nachiketa says, "Ami abak hoye bhabi, ei amar moto kato chhele kono prospect samne na dekheo...!"[12] (I think that young people like me don't see any prospect before them but..!). Then the protagonist sarcastically repeats and mocks the very word 'prospect'. Films thus reflected the ideological paradigm shift from Nehruvian socialism, nation-building task to the leftist ideology. The role of the young brigade depicted in films attained primacy and films, like politics, accommodated the new voices, alternative thoughts and fresh ideologies. The youth of Bengal started getting ideologically inclined towards communism. There was poverty, there was hunger, there was no employment, women were restricted to the kitchens and there was extensive insecurity. The cluelessness and uncertainty of the common youth were evident. The youths were like the rudderless ships who vacillated aimlessly. Siddhartha Chowdhury, the protagonist in the film 'Protidwandi' (The Adversary) by Satyajit Ray represents this huge section of young India. Siddhartha is smart, intelligent, educated who fails to continue studies in medicine due to economic instability after his father's death and has strong and honest ideological convictions which he follows to his maximum extent. He is a blend of mutually opposing characters. He is both bold and coward. He answers in a job interview at a private sector enterprise that the most significant event in the period 1960-1970 was the 'Vietnam War' which unpredictably revealed the extraordinary power of the ordinary Vietnamese people that takes one's breath away and later laments before his friend saying that answers must be calculative in an interview. Ray in this film has raised a legitimate question : do you need to be a communist in order to admire Vietnam? If the common people feel the need for resistance against the injustices, uncertainties and whims of the capitalist order, if they start to challenge injustices, if they oppose exploitation in every possible form, social, economical, political or psychological, should they be marked as communists? It appears as if either you are with the 'state' or with the 'communists' (read 'extremists') and the monkeys will mark you 'wrong'. In 'Protidwandi', the vacillating character of Siddhartha supports his younger brother for the latter's decision of joining the Naxalite movement but he himself tries to fit within the system. He gifts his brother a book on Che Guevara at the cost of his own medical books and is proud of his brother's strength. He himself can't pursue it due to the numerous pull factors. He loves his family, his mother, brother, sister and his love. He cares for them and behaves like a watchful guardian trying to be a silent protector. He also suffers from the colonial hang-over which is evident when we see him imagining himself dressed in western outfit at the tailor's corner, smiling at the hippies at the park and fearing the death of a revolutionary as described by his brother. However, the Marxian ideology is deep-rooted within him and he cannot compromise with the rampant oppression, corruption, exploitation and injustice. He bears an inherent hatred deep in his heart towards the owner class. The scene where he converses with his sister's boss and his helplessness and anger on the road after he comes out of that house confirms it. He is not against women empowerment but against the bourgeois liberal culture that is exported along with capitalist democracy. His dialogues with his sister show it. Perhaps he was rightly anticipating in the imaginative sequence in the roof when his sister confesses about her dancing lessons that in practice, commodification of women's body is the only vested interest of the bourgeois culture behind the veil of 'empowerment' and 'equality'. He, though pained, respects his sister's decisions in her life. Siddhartha all throughout remains a vacillating person, aimless and confused in an intimidating society and finally violently protests against the authorities in his last bid to secure a conventional job. The scene of his protest against the inhuman treatment of the authorities is sensational and nerve-tingling which has been re-used in 'Kalbela', another film on Naxalite movement by director Gautam Ghosh. Siddhartha fails to find a satisfactory answer till the end. The conviction and ideological belief centering on the Marxian philosophy that steered him fails. Similar example can be cited in case of Nilkanto Bagchi, the lead man in 'Jukti Takka Ar Goppo' who feels that there must be a way out of the suffocating socio-political system but admits at the end, "ami confused"[13] (I am confused). Such confusions exist till date unanswered.

The Emotional Girl—Nandini :

The movement was suppressed by the State Government of West Bengal and the young brigade had to surrender before the state repression. The failure also influenced film-makers and many of them have taken the initiative to analyze the causes of the failure and aftermath. Films too, as a weapon of Gramsci's war of position, identified the shortcomings of the movement, the procedural and organizational mistakes as well as the other causes of failure consequently helping the future generation to avoid repetition. The largely romanticization of emotions and dreams which indulged a massive portion of the young people to dive into the movement without any prior perfect groundwork and proper evaluation of rural as well as urban psychology has been filmed in Indian cinema. Nandini shall mark such post-movement analysis as reactionary opportunism. She is an emotional girl who passionately dives into the waves of revolution without any calculative measures. Her love Brati, in the film 'Hazaar Chaurasi Ki Maa', drives her to firmly stick to the ideology. Brati used to tell her that ideology for her is a religious experience. All that she wanted was 'land for the landless tillers' and 'freedom for the oppressed'. She bets her life for championing her dreams and takes up weapons for liberating the proletariat. She values the love and passion that worked within her and expects equal and opposite reciprocation. She recites poems and chants the words of Mayakovsky to Brati. We find her celebrating her revolutionary ideals and emotions. She narrates her initial years in the party. It was like the long-awaited end of a dark phase and she and her comrades were the first step towards the new dawn. But the failure of the movement makes her grow up. She realizes the treachery and marks the traitors like Anindya. Nandini admits that they passed out in the spirit of revolution ignoring all the ground realities and could not see their own shortcomings, their loopholes and their gradual diversion from the revolutionary path. This was all because they were not taught to disbelieve. The death of Brati and others shatters her emotions, ideals and dreams. But she stays strong and dares the police repression. The emotional girl matures but doesn't leave the cause of the revolution. Nandini is tired of seeing people around who remains ignorant of the entire proceedings during and post-movement. How can people remain silent? Don't they feel the urge to know what and why exactly happened during the movement? These questions bother Nandini. She screams at the fake normalcy post-movement and fights against the police atrocities for human rights concerns and at the same time lends her hand for the emancipation and proliferation of the tribals working within them. Her maturity inspires the audience. Nandini is not a lone example. The quotients of love, passion and emotions and lack of proper political homework marked the salient features of the entire young participants like Nandini of the Naxalite movement. The understanding of Ritwik Ghatak must be noted here. The protagonist of 'Jukti Takka Ar Goppo', Nilkanto Bagchi rightly addresses the young Naxalites, "tomader sincerity, birotto, tomader aatmatyager pratigyan eshobe amar kono sandeho nei. Kintu tomra sampurno misguided...... tomra eki sange safal o nisfal, ek sange gowar, ebong andho"[14] (I have no doubt about your sincerity, your courage, your will to sacrifice. But you all are totally misguided...you are simultaneously successful and failed, both obstinate and blind). He tried to preach the idea that the revolutionaries must not be myopic and should correctly judge the strength of the enemy before waging their battle against the capitalist state. The bourgeoisie has achieved tremendous power by assimilating large amount of resources post-1947 and again Nilkantho Bagchi advises, "Ora nei bollei chole jabe na, oder shekar ooprate hole oder shakti ebong oder durbolota bhalo kore jante hobe"[15] (They shall not leave if you treat them insignificantly, if you want to uproot them, you have to know their strength as well as weakness). The emotional young brigade perhaps needed political maturity.

The establishment remained untouched by the death of an entire young generation ranging from sixteen to forty. But the dream has not yet died. Youth of India still dare to dream for a change which the state terms India's 'gravest internal security threat' and the monkeys say 'wrong'. Even after three decades of the end of Naxalite movement, the state has to depute paramilitary forces to combat the dreamers- 'people who live with their dreams, while the rest of the world lives with its nightmares.'[16] A movement can be killed, the people can be killed, but the ideas of the youth cannot be killed. Ideas shall never be extinct. They shall continue disturbing the establishment. Naxalism as an idea, hence, still works. Films still point out the Naxalite ideology challenging the establishment. 'Rang de Basanti' by Rakesh Omprakash Mehra has shown the journey of six friends who act in a film on Bhagat Singh and gradually get influenced by his revolutionary ideals in the course of shooting the film. The six young students in a globalized state and economy with every lucrative comfort of capitalism with them identify with those revolutionary ideas, their beliefs metamorphose and they take up weapon at the end against the state corruption when their initial peaceful movement was suppressed by police. There, somehow, is an ambiguity in the message of the film. First, the 'young guns' in the film had their ideological boost from the life and actions of Bhagat Singh and the action of gunning down the minister is obvious. But the contradiction comes later when one of the key dialogues "politics join karo, police ya I.A.S. mein bharti ho jayo, badlo chiso ko" (join politics, get admitted to police or I.A.S., change things)[17] surfaces. On the one hand, they anchor to violence with no other choice left and embraces the act of annihilation and on the other hand, we see them talking about joining the civil bureaucratic institutions which are an integral part of the capitalist order. What we found is the simultaneous propaganda of two mutually contradicting ideas. However, the film had a huge impact due to the parallel show of the contemporary cool quotient, revolutionary inputs and commercial success. Another film 'Raavan' by Mani Ratnam has addressed the lives of those people who live with their dreams and are inhumanly treated by the state and her armed forces. Beera (portrayed as Raavan), the protagonist, is the messiah of the tribals. The parallel co-existence of an ethnic culture, the simple lives of the people from the jungle, their love and relationships and hatred for the urban hypocrisy and the state repression on them have been skillfully filmed. The dream of reaching a society where exploitation shall vanish must be on the move and films must play its role as an influential primary tool of cultural hegemonization. We must understand what is truly 'right' and what exactly is 'wrong', who are right- the three monkeys or Brati, Siddhartha or Nandini. Nandini says that someday people shall understand the immense love and trust that they had within them behind the virtual mirage of hatred. She dreams, "Log samajhte hain ki hamhe har maujuda chij se nafrat hain, par sayad ekdin aisa aayega jab log kahenge ki bahar se dikhne wali nafrat ke pichhe pyaar aur biswas ki kitni pyaas thi"[18]. Millions in India still today live with this dream.

References :

1. 'Hirak Rajar Deshe' (Kingdom of Diamonds), 1980, Director : Satyajit Ray.
2. Sushila Ramaswamy, *Political Theory*, Macmillan Publishers India Limited, p.109.
3. Aditya Nigam, 'Naxalbari, Narmada, Nandigram : The Crisis of High Modernism,' Proceedings of U.G.C. Sponsored National Level Seminar on ALTERNATIVE POLITICS : Another World, Other Voices, (2010), Ramakrishna Mission Vidyamandira.
4. Ibid.
5. Mike Wayne, *Understanding Film : Marxist Perspectives*, Pluto Press, London.
6. Ibid.
7. 'Ray on Ray', The Cineaste Interviews : On the Art and Politics of the Cinema, *The Cineaste* Magazine, Georgakas, Dan and Lenny Rubenstein, eds. Chicago : Lake View Press, 1982.
8. 'Jukti Takko Ar Goppo', 1974, Director : Ritwik Ghatak.
9. 'Hazar Chaurasi ki Ma' (Mother of 1084), 1998, Director : Govind Nihalani.
10. Ibid.

11. Amal Kumar Mukhopadhyay, *Political Sociology*, K P Bagchi & Company, Calcutta, p.174.
12. 'Jukti Takko Ar Goppo', 1974, Director : Ritwik Ghatak.
13. Ibid.
14. Ibid.
15. Ibid.
16. Arundhati Roy, 'Walking with the Comrades', *Outlook* Magazine, March 29, 2010, p.59.
17. 'Rang De Basanti', 2005, Director : Rakeysh Omprakash Mehra.
18. 'Hazar Chaurasi ki Ma' (Mother of 1084), 1998, Director : Govind Nihalani.

Particularistic

Rehashing Narrative Archetypes in Retrospect : In Khwaja Ahmad Abbas' 'The Naxalites' (1980)

Torsa Ghosal

Abstract :

This paper proposes to trace the archetypes drawn from the repertoire of Indian Cinema that are combined in the socio-political context to address memories pertaining to the Naxalite uprising of 1960s-70s in West Bengal by Khwaja Ahmad Abbas in his film 'The Naxalites' (1980). Visual and verbal inter-textual narrative references and the use of popular paradigms from Indian cinema are integral to Abbas' ideological stance of destabilizing semiotics in the narrative mediation. The relationship between Amarkaal and his dead mother and that between Ajitha and her brother serve as metonyms for the political upheaval. In the archetypal quest motif and yearning for the absent partners in the two sets of relationships lies the narrative force and it symbolically stands for the quest of the narrative in retrospect to reach the semantic core of causality that triggered the Naxalite movement.

Keywords : Naxalite Movement, The Naxalites, Narrative, Semiotics, Ideology, Indian Cinema

In March 2010, Kanu Sanyal, one of the forerunners of the Naxalite Movement and leader of the CPI (Marxist-Leninist) reportedly committed suicide in his native village Sephtulajote near Naxalbari. Sanyal was one of the triad, also comprising Charu Mazumdar and Jangal Santhal, who have been recognized as the pivotal figures of the Naxal movement of the 1960s following the peasant-uprising in Naxalbari in May 1967. Mazumdar and Santhal had passed away in the

1970s. Sanyal's death, in some sense, therefore can be marked as the end of an era. However, in March'10, Arundhati Roy's essay 'Walking with the Comrades'[1] based on her experiences at Dantewada drew attention to the fact that the tribal population of India have a history of resistance that persists. Thus, the violent uprisings against the State continue in India. The era has, of course, not ended.

If the newspapers even at the end of the first decade of the twenty-first century regularly report armed combats between the State military forces and peasant turned revolutionaries, the same newspapers also report the starvation, death and dissatisfaction of peasants which form the causal core of such Revolts. Today the terms Maoist and Naxalite are often used interchangeably by the media. In 2004, the Communist Party of India (Marxist-Leninist) which played an active role in the Naxalite Uprisings merged with the Maoist Communist Centre of India to form the Communist Party of India (Maoist). Whether or not one groups the uprisings at Naxalbari and the aftermath of 60s with the Maoist uprisings in the new millennium, there is the thread of causality that binds them together.

However, this chain of cause and effect is not linear. The history of the Naxalite movement in India is a series of dynamic concentric circles. If the 1960s uprisings form the outer ring of the series, the inner ring comprises the mass dislocation, oppression by feudal lords, poverty and Bengal famine that date back to 1940s.

Thus, the semantic core or the causal centre of Khwaja Ahmad Abbas' 'The Naxalites' (1980), the Bengal famine of 1940s and the post-independence disillusionment with democracy, antedates the cinematic narrative which primarily deals with the Naxalite movement in the rural Naxalbari and urban Calcutta of 1960s-70s. To reach out to the centre that lies outside the text, the narrative device available is retrospection. Yet, a traumatic memory can not be converted into a linear monolithic narrative bound by cause and effect chain because the essence of the memory can not be reported, it has to be evoked.

Therefore, the film combines visual and verbal referents drawn from popular Indian cinema to create a meta-fictional narrative format which underscores the self-reflexive nature of the traumatic memories surrounding the socio-cultural and political roots and implications of the Naxalite uprising on the 1960s-70s in Bengal. In this paper I shall attempt to trace how the self-reflexive visual metaphors and metonyms are superimposed to simulate the displaced semantic core of the narrative.

Of the multitude of characters who throng the narrative space and the varied relationships they share with other characters, two relationships in the cinematic narrative provide momentum to the plot and serve as a metonym for the socio-political crisis. The evolution and the nature of the two relationships are developed outside the time and space where the actual events of the film are enacted. Eventually, the absence of one of the characters in these relationships account for the narrative force. The first of this set is the relationship between Amarkaal and his dead mother, and the second is that of Ajitha and her brother, Comrade Suren. In the context of Indian cinema the relation between the brother and the sister and the relationship between mother and son carry with itself a host of inter-textual connotations.

By 1980s, when the film was released, the Naxalite movement in Bengal led by the Communist Party of India (Marxist-Leninist) had long passed the peak it had touched in the early 1970s. The ill-equipped armed forces of the Naxalites, especially in Bengal had been overthrown by the State by mid-70s. Charu Mazumdar had been driven to death by police persecution in 1972. Several active leaders of the movement had been arrested.

However, as Emergency was lifted and Indira Gandhi was defeated in the elections in 1977, a period of transition was ushered in. Jyoti Basu intervened to release prisoners arrested during the Naxalite movement from Bengal after he became the chief minister in 1977. In early 1980s the political situation in India was not exactly stable but then, these changes led to retrospection[2].

Late 1970s and early 1980s was also an era that witnessed the surfacing of simmering discontent in Indian cinematic narratives. In 1980 Mrinal Sen released 'Akaler Shandhane' (Search of Famine) in which the crew of a film move to a village to create the set up of the Bengal Famine of 1943 and the film revolves around the art of film making as well as its engagement with the 'real' and the 'political'. In Abbas' 'The Naxalites', Amarkaal's name evokes the title of Sen's film and both these titles allude to the Bengal famine of 1943 which was one of the historical forces that drove the peasantry to revolt.

As far as popular Hindi cinema is concerned, the major projected image of the era would be Amitabh Bachchan's 'Angry Young Man' avatar. 'Deewar' (1975), 'Trishul' (1978), 'Laawaris' (1981) and 'Shakti' (1982) were released around the turn of the decade and were well-received by the audience. The avatar of the angry young man takes on the establishment, often represented by the metonym of the patriarchal family. Amitabh Bachchan, as Vijay and Heera, the 'Angry Young Man' in these films, who hails either from the financially impaired sections of the society or has been alienated at some stage by his parents, faces the corrupt forces of the establishment. A representative of the marginal population, in 'Deewar' and 'Shakti', Vijay is killed in the course of the narrative. So, what makes the 'Angry Young Man' a popular figure in Indian cinema at this point in time? Maithali Rao in her article 'Rebels without a Cause (1976-1989)' observes :

> The Amitabh Bachchan persona of 'Deewar', 'Trishul' and 'Laawaris' is the logical successor to the Birju of Mother India. Birju's battles for justice against an entrenched order lose their 1950s rural innocence when the Bachchan protagonist takes the fight into the ghettos of an irreversibly urbanizing, increasingly criminalized society[3].

The character of Birju in 'Mother India' (1957) rebels against the tyranny of the feudal lord Sukhilal who extracts unfair revenues which finds it parallel in the Tebhaga Movement of 1946 initiated by the Kisan Sabha in Bengal for reducing the share of harvest given to landlords by share-cropping peasants. The Tebhaga movement is an obvious predecessor of the Naxalite revolt of the 1960s-70s. Thus, the vicious circle of deprivation, tyranny and oppression leading to wrath, vengeance and rebellion is projected onto the narrative life of the protagonist of the Indian popular cinema. The political is mirrored in the personal and familial. The matriarch in 'Mother India' represents the 'shakti' or the force on which the mythomotuer[4] of Indian nationalism was based. On the other hand, the distanced self-righteous patriarch played by Dilip Kumar in a film like 'Shakti', who serves the police force, acts as a representative of the State.

The rural lineage of Birju and the urbanized essence of Vijay remain central to the image of the protagonist in narratives relating to Naxalites in cinema. Though, a peasant uprising at its outset the protest was not limited to the rural spheres. The intelligentsia from urban centers like Kolkata played crucial roles in the mass uprising related to the urban and rural population alike. Urban unemployment and poverty coupled with the news of rural discontent led the urban youth to question and seek to subvert the socio-cultural centers of power, the smug and hypocrite elites.

Thus, Amarkaal in 'The Naxalites' is a kin of the brand of protagonists on Indian screen succeeding the legendary character of Birju and contemporary of the 'Angry Young Man', Vijay. Amarkaal's parents hailed from the rural Naxalbari but he spent his childhood and youth in Kolkata. Like Vijay and Birju, Amarkaal is also fated to die in the course of the narrative.

The choice of Mithun Chakraborty as the lead for the character of Amarkaal is significant. In 1976 the actor made his debut as the marginalized tribal in 'Mrigaya' and he was known to have been involved in the Naxal uprising himself[5]. For the audience the actor himself was a bearer of a certain image which enhanced the audience's sense of realism and association with the character of Amarkaal.

Amarkaal's past, present and future are by far the most problematic. His existence is dynamic and liable to change at each and every instant of time for he is not accommodated by any pre-given superstructure that dictates the society. The only constant in his consciousness is a persistent mother-fixation and his problematic response to his childhood memories. Born in Naxalbari, Amarkaal's name evokes the period in time when he was born and seals his fate. His father is said to have died while the family was migrating from the rural to the urban centre, Naxalbari to Kolkata to avoid starvation during the Bengal famine. His mother arrived in the city with the young child but had to sell her body to provide for her child. Eventually Amarkaal hardly remembers any of this. He vaguely remembers his mother and tries to trace his history from what he remembers which itself is unreliable. There is no character in the film to validate Amarkaal's disrupted narrative. Hence, he has a fluid identity. However, in order to integrate him to the narrative revolting against the State ideology, Amarkaal is attributed over a past by the journalist Comrade Bose.

It is significant to note here how the script uses inter-textual references and self-reflexivity to delineate Amarkaal's history. In the first scene when Amarkaal appears, the wall that forms his background has a couple of posters of Bengali films. At once this serves two functions- the Bengali script makes one aware of the possible location of the scene and the covert reference to films foreshadows the crucial role that cinema as a narrative form has to play in 'The Naxalites'.

Amarkaal's past is mapped in terms of the history of the character he identifies with while watching the film 'Dharti ke Laal'. When Comrade Ajoy Bose first meets Amarkaal at a court of law, from a few sketchy details, he gathers that Amarkaal can easily be swayed into affirming with the Naxal's mottos. A man like Amarkaal who desires to spend half a month in a jail so that he would get assured meals is initially perceived in terms of his functionality to the Naxalite's cause. Comrade Bose's benevolence towards Amarkaal is motivated by the political interests.

Ajoy Bose or Comrade Bose functions as a Communist journalist. In his film Abbas has sought to represent multiple aspects of the Naxalite movement which involved veteran journalists like Saroj Dutta. Dutta had played a crucial role in shaping the cultural attitudes of the rebels and Bose, though not as experienced or well-developed as a character in the narrative, tries to guide the attitude of Amarkaal. As a reporter himself Abbas was aware of the powers of the media and the persuasive power of the radical journalist Bose is traced in terms of his influence on Amarkaal.

Comrade Bose refers to a certain kind of paper that he says is interested in stories of people like Amarkaal. The newspaper he is talking about is quite obviously a Naxalite controlled media. If the state and its man-made crisis have led to Amarkaal's tragic fate, then Comrade Bose's intervention into his life is by no means a path to liberation. Both the State and the organized rebellion against the same victimize Amarkaal in different ways and treat him as a commodity to be dispossessed and possessed alternatively.

This notion of control and possession is crucial to the understanding of the function of a film like 'Dharti ke Laal' in the context of 'The Naxalites'. Comrade Bose evidently has watched 'Dharti ke Laal' before and is aware of its narrative possibilities. When he listens to bits and pieces of the Amarkaal's story he notes some apparent similarities and then uses a fictional work of art, a film, to render credibility to his subjective and assumed version of Amarkaal's history. The film, therefore, is invested with authority and from Comrade Bose's perspective it is a means to acquire complete control over Amarkaal's unknown past. Art here becomes machinery for achieving ideological control over Amarkaal's fluid identity.

The slogans painted on walls and on blackboards, the posters of Che Guevara and Mao Tse-tung on the walls, visually create the backdrop of the radical 1970s urban cityscape. The visual plays a more significant role in Amarkaal's story than the verbal. At the level of the verbal there is a significant gulf between space, time and character. Amarkaal is displaced not only in terms of space but also in time. His inability to form a coherent narrative identity is partly because he can not locate the time frame or the temporal underpinnings of the era which displaced him. As the cinematic discourse unfolds visually in time, it is used to bridge between disparate spaces and times. The character is reconstituted through visual referents, as the child lying on footpath in the film 'Dharti ke Laal'. The evoking of the past through a film is reminiscent of Frederic Jameson's notion of 'la mode retro' that evokes the past through images of the past. He connects the growth of such representation with the post-industrial capitalism or late capitalism as he calls it. The Naxal ideology seeks to resist such forms of capitalism but in retrospect Abbas gives in to such a form of discourse where the very materiality of one's past becomes affirmed and denied at the same time.

In 'The Naxalites' the visuals play a seminal part not only as connectives but as the mode of discourse itself. The first scene is eventually the final scene of the film in which the group of Naxalites including Comrade Dada is shot down by the police forces. The visuals presented a contrast between the organized and armed police forces and the bold but vulnerable Naxalites. In the scene at the University where the professor asks the class topper Anant to read a passage from Shakespeare's Hamlet, his dilemma "to be or not to be" is enunciated with the cut to the group of his classmates who are resolute to join the Naxalite movement.

During a period of change or upheaval the inherited discourses of the past seem inadequate. The verbal uses a language that has been filtered by the state and the establishment. There is a crisis at the verbal level which the visual with its photo-realism seeks to dissolve.

However, the adequacy of the visual is as much challenged as that of the verbal in the text. Whether the visuals do justice to Amarkaal's history remains a pertinent question because despite the realism and the immediacy of the visual narrative unfolding before Amarkaal's eyes the verbal is used to interpret the visual by Comrade Bose and it is the verbal meanings realized by Bose that Amarkaal internalizes. When Amarkaal kills the feudal lord to avenge his mother's death, Bose's remark that this feudal lord was responsible for his mother's death is Amarkaal's underlying assumption. Bose himself though, when he remarked, did not have facts to substantiate this claim beyond the premise that all feudal lords by the virtue of belonging to the same strata of the society must necessarily be the faces of the same crime.

The unreliability of the verbal and the visual draws upon the tension between ideology and semiotics. Louis Althusser's concept of

Ideological State Apparatus[7] explains that ideologies are product of social practices rather than history. If the language itself has been corrupted due to its contact with State Ideology the only way to resist the State would be to destabilize semiotics.

Abbas' use of archetypal characters and paradigmatic relationships is in synchronization with the narrative tendency to thrust identities and histories on characters as class representatives denying individual space. In *Differences and Repetition* Gilles Deleuze observed that society was pre-occupied with notions of sameness and identity but in the postmodern world the fractured self eludes such pre-given essence. In the Indian milieu, in this film, though the selfhood is fractured, there is a stress on homogeneity instead of highlighting the differences that emerge. The result of this process is a narrative that repeats referents from pre-existing narratives to self-reflexively forge an idea of sameness based on discourses of power and revolution.

Deleuze and Guattari in *A Thousand Plateaus*[8] address the tension in not being able to surpass authoritative 'forms of content'. They identify diverse levels of semiotics in which the privileged status of the language operates in dispersed manner. In *presignifying semiotic,* the enunciation is collective, polyphonic and expressions are multilayered and there is an affinity for 'deterritorialization'. The *signifying semiotics* is emitted by the State apparatus and is governed by the signifier. There is uniformity of enunciation, unification of expression. *Countersignifying semiotics* depends upon war machine and follows a path of active destruction. Deleuze says that 'war machine' has nothing to do with war per se but instead has to do with a particular way of occupying space-time, or inventing new spaces-times as in revolutionary movements[9]. The *postsignifying semiotics* is characterized by redundancy of consciousness and enunciation occurs in a manner such that the organization of power seems immanent and 'deterritorialization' seems absolute.

They further elaborate on the notion that though semiotics has not foregone the 'forms' they have been fragmented and mixed. The polyphonic ideals of the urban and the rural rebels, the state ideology that governs meaning and identity, the opposition to the state ideology in favor of 'becoming' of the Naxalites and the violent uprising that follows, in a way, mirror the distinct stages of semiotics in the narrative. They are fragmented and blend together.

The notion of becoming is related to Amarkaal and Ajitha. Ajitha and her brother, Suren, refer to the familial history of their father fighting for a cause. However, it was a different time, a different war. The Naxalite youth rejected the revisionist politics of certain wings of the independence movement of India. Deleuze suggests that history, that is a set of tried and tested pre-conditions, has to be left behind in order to 'become', that is, to create something new :

> English Romanticism is permeated by reflections on Cromwell very similar to present-day reflections on Stalin. They say revolutions turn out badly. But they're constantly confusing two different things, the way revolutions turn out historically and people's revolutionary becoming. These relate to two different sets of people. Men's only hope lies in a revolutionary becoming : the only way of casting off their shame or responding to what is intolerable[10].

1970s to 1980s saw plethora of art addressing the turmoil in Bengal. The plot of 'The Naxalites' bears strong resemblance to the plot of Asif Currimbhoy's play 'Inquilab' (1971). The character of Amar, a young student of Calcutta University who has joined the Naxalite movement, in the play bears resemblance to several characters in Abbas' film and the peasant uprising in the village in the play is parallel to the representation of the revolt in Naxalbari in the film. However, a more interesting point of convergence of the two texts is the dramatization of the relationship between the mother and the son.

In 'Inquilab', Professor Dutt's elder son, Amar's elder brother has been lost for many years but the mother continuously yearns for her absent son and seems to believe that he will return. In the film, Amarkaal, of course, does not hope that his mother will come back but then he identifies his mother with any compassionate female figure including the psychiatrist. The novel *Hajar Churashir Maa* by Mahashweta Devi penned in the 1970s also explores a mother-son relationship in the context of the Naxalite movement.

There could be multiple ways of looking at these mother-son relationships but in a country like India where the land itself is given a naturalized maternal identity one of the possible readings is that the mother-son relationship serves as a metonym for the relationship of the peasant with the land and the son feels it is incumbent on him to protect this symbolic mother figure.

The figure of the mother in the 1970s cinema takes a cue from earlier representation like that of 'Mother India' and in the context of the social turmoil the figure poses problems beyond the realm of the purely symbolic transcendent maternal figure. In 'Deewar' the famous dialogue "Mere paas Ma hai" harps on the concept of possession but the suffering or ailing mother figure who has brought up her children also exhibits a degree of independence. It is the son who strives for patriarchal approval and tries to reconstitute a patrimonial lineage. In 'Shakti' as well as'Trishul' the marginalized son's need for paternal approval is embedded in his unconscious which is a metonym for his desire to be integrated into the society. In 'The Naxalites', Amarkaal's inability to obtain approval from the State, the symbolic patriarchy, leads him to the father figure of Comrade Dada. Comrade Dada also becomes a father-figure for Suren. For Ajitha, the figure of the brother, in the absence of the father, fills in as the filial symbol.

For Amarkaal, along with a sense of responsibility for the mother-figure there are inherited shame and guilt which he has to redress. Besides, his choice of the grave as a shelter in the absence of a home is the external representation of his internal yearning for the womb from which he has been displaced. In fact, Amarkaal dies with the word 'Ma' on his lips.

The grave also serves as a symbolic for the shelter of the marginalized who has found no space in the urban cityscape. Amarkaal tells a police officer that he lives in the graveyard for there is no other place for him to go to. This scares the officer which foreshadows the threat that Amarkaal will embody as a representative of the marginalized when he joins the Naxalites.

The emotional excesses in feelings such as fear, repulsion, indeterminate narrative form and identity, unstable consciousness attributed to the character of Amarkaal is representative of the political situation as well. Amarkaal feels responsible as an agent in his mother's death. The psychiatrist suggests that he should be taken to Naxalbari to understand that it was not he but external agents that brought about his mother's demise.

With the possibilities of the Green Revolution around the turn of the decade in the 1980s there was a re-surfacing of the agrarian myth. The lush green footages of the rural landscape in Abbas' film are his version of the pastoral albeit lacking the tranquility that such a landscape mythically guarantees. The feudal lords and the state administered police forces are the invaders who have destroyed the mythic space, molested the mother earth - though the landscape itself which is sought to be protected with its idyllic qualities lies beyond the narrative. Even the rural space that Amarkaal's corroborated past refers to was one of drought and deprivation. Hence, that which is to be protected is more imagined than real. The imagined space, for Amarkaal, is also akin to the womb of the mother before she had sold her body to provide for him.

During the Bengal famine of 1943 the members of IPTA (Indian People's Theatre Association) traveled around the country collecting funds for survivors of the famine. Abbas was influenced by the IPTA and 'Dharti ke Laal' recaptures the famine inflected condition of the rural world that forces the villagers to migrate.

The other kinship, besides that of Amarkaal and his absent mother that drives the plot of the film, is one between Ajitha and her brother. The quest motif is inherently a component of the brother-sister relationship. Ajitha's stint with the movement is as much motivated by ideological reasons as it is by her quest to believe in and act for what her brother barters his life for.

The relationship between the sister and the brother has a complex cultural implication as well as history in the context of Indian cinematic narratives. Ritwik Ghatak's 'Meghe Dhaka Tara' dramatized the relationship between Neeta and her usually absent brother as the sole orifice for Neeta's escape from a troubled life. The final line of the film 'Dada, ami bachte chai' meaning 'Brother, I want to live' is a poignant summation of the existential crisis of Neeta as well as her psychological dependence on her brother.

While the relationship between two brothers took a competitive form in films like 'Deewar' and 'Trishul', the relationship between the brother-sister was predicated on a notion of search for a sort of complementation. 'Hare Rama Hare Krishna' (1971) is one such popular Hindi film developing the narrative in the terms of the brother's search for the lost sister.

Though Ajitha is romantically attached to Anant who hails from the upper middle class with his father working as a police officer and as a prototype of the privileged and refined culture, Ajitha's allegiance to her brother is far more important for the course of the narrative. As she watches her brother depart on his mission she remarks that even her way lies out there.

Ajitha's quests on both the personal and public front are thwarted. In Abbas' eponymous English novel the letter that Ajitha sends to her comrades before being hanged says :

> Comrades, reconsider what you are doing - You have killed enough - and sufficient number of you have been killed. Some at hands of Naxalites. Think whether it has led us to the goal of revolution....

Mass-awakening and mass organization was the goals of the movement, according to Ajitha, from which the Naxalites have deviated. This is the manner in which even Abbas accounts for the failure of the movement. This critique is foreshadowed in the trial of the feudal lord. When Comrade Dada asks the peasants to find out a method of punishing the feudal lord they come up with solutions like murder and molestation of the feudal lord's daughter - both of which eventually remain allied to methods used by the feudal lord to exercise his tyrannical control. The understanding that violence can not redress violence is implicit but Comrade Dada can not come up with any other solution either.

The film, therefore, through ambivalent human relationships, archetypal of Indian cinematic narratives, puts the Naxalite movement and its methodologies into perspective. In the preface to the novel *The Naxalites* (1979), Abbas wrote :

> All characters - and incidents - in this novel are fictitious, but none - is entirely imaginary[11].

The repetition of accepted paradigms in rehashed form carves out a distinct space for itself. Abbas' vehicle for critiquing political and ideological stance of both the government and the Naxalites faced censorship issues.

The availability of archetypes in the cinema of the past few decades to Abbas allows him to create a collage narrative. The juxtaposition of existing narrative tracks to create the concentric narrative cycles represents the tension in existing forms of discourse in the context of the Naxalite movement. There is an interplay and transaction of meaning taking place at different levels of the narrative. As Thomas Brockelman observes, the collage narrative is both 'representational and anti-representational'.

The intellectual montage technique that juxtaposes shots with contradictory meanings has been a vehicle for leftist ideology from the works of Sergei Eisenstein. Abbas does not use intellectual montage in the same sense as that of Eisenstein. On the other hand he draws upon archetypes and juxtaposes them rather than juxtaposing shots. The note of uncertainty coupled with the futility of the agendas of all the parties involved in the crisis expands the scope of the narrative. The ideal of change and equality is exalted but with a note of skepticism.

About three decades after the release of the film, the issues that the narrative raises continue to remain pertinent. The meaning and the possibilities of the Naxalite movement of 1970s has evolved due to overlapping movements in the country and continues to evolve. The archetypes and the cycles of the narrative persist even as they are rehashed in newer contexts.

Notes :

1. Arundhati Roy (2010), 'Walking with the Comrades', retrieved from http://www.outlookindia.com/article.aspx?264738, accessed on August 1, 2010.
2. Sumanta Banerjee (1989), 'Retrospection', *Thema Book of Naxalite Poetry*, Kolkata : Thema, pp. 107-9.
3. Maithili Rao (2003), 'Rebels Without a Cause' in Gulzar, Govind Nihalani, Saibal Chatterjee (Ed.), *Encyclopaedia of Hindi Cinema*, New Delhi : Encyclopaedia Britannica (India) Pvt. Ltd. and Popular Prakashan Pvt. Ltd., p. 98.
4. Anthony D. Smith (1986). *The Ethnic Origins of Nations.* Oxford : Blackwell Publishing, p. 229.
5. Newsofap.com (July 10, 2010), Mithun Chakraborty Talks about His Relationship with Naxalites, http://www.newsofap.com/newsofap-19617-34-mithun-chakraborty-talks-about-his-relationship-with-naxalites-newsofap.html, accessed on August 2, 2010.
6. Frederic Jameson (1991), *Postmodernism, or, The Cultural Logic of Late Capitalism*, Durham, NC : Duke University Press, p. 19.
7. Andrew Levine (1993), *The General Will : Rousseau, Marx, Communism*, Cambridge : Cambridge University Press, pp. 115-7.
8. Gilles Deleuze, Felix Guattari (1987), *A Thousand Plateaus : Capitalism and Schizophrenia*, Minnesota : University of Minnesota, pp. 148-9.
9. Antonio Negri (1990), *Control and Becoming : Gilles Deleuze in conversation with Antonio Negri*, Martin Joughin (trans.), retrieved from http://www.generation-online.org/p/fpdeleuze3.htm, accessed on August 14, 2010.
10. http://www.generation-online.org/p/fpdeleuze3.htm
11. Khwaja Ahmad Abbas (1979), *The Naxalites*, New Delhi : Lok Publications.
12. Charles R. Garoian, Yvonne Gaudelius (2008), 'Introduction' in *Spectacle Pedagogy : Art, Politics and Visual Culture*, Albany : State university of New York Press, p. 5.

Works Cited :

Books :

Asif Currimbhoy (1971), *Inquilab*, Kolkata : Writers Workshop.

Mahashweta Devi (1975), *Hajar Churashir Ma*, Kolkata : Karuna Prakashani.

Films :

Dev Anand (1971), 'Hare Rama Hare Krishna', Produced by : Dev Anand

Khwaja Ahmad Abbas (1980), 'The Naxalites', Produced by : International films

Khwaja Ahmad Abbas (1946), 'Dharti ke Laal', Produced by : IPTA Pictures

Mehboob Khan (1957), 'Mother India', Produced by : Mehboob Productions

Mrinal Sen (1980), 'Akaler Shandhane', Produced by :D.K Films

Prakash Mehra (1981), 'Lawaaris', Produced by : Prakash Mehra

Ramesh Sippy (1982), 'Shakti', Produced by : Mushir Alam and Mohammad Riaz

Ritwik Ghatak (1960), 'Meghe Dhaka Tara', Produced by : Chitrakalpa

Yash Chopra (1975), 'Deewar', Produced by : Trimurti Films Pvt. Ltd.

Yash Chopra (1978), 'Trishul', Produced by : Yash Raj Films

'Red Alert': Dialectics of Engagement and Ambivalence

Ketaki Dwivedi

Abstract :

The uniqueness of New Cinema lies in its firm rooting in the prevailing socio-cultural context and ethos that reflects the hopes and aspirations, conflicts and contradictions of its people. After the euphoria of independence and Nehruvian socialism died, cinema's search, to develop and expand the horizons, that not only fulfils the people's aesthetic needs and aspirations but also reflects historical progress and development, found new life and direction as the 'new cinema'.

Keywords : New Cinema; Third Cinema; Naxalism

Cinema, like other general art, is an artistic genre, a politico-economic institution as well as a medium of expression for mass communication with a set of ideological propositions. Political philosophies, ideologies and values, group behaviour and power-struggles taking place in the society are reflected in the cinema, and like a true mirror, it reflects back in the society. It is therefore, possible to view the cinema as a legitimate metaphor and subtext of the society, polity as well as conflicts and contradictions taking place in society. According to Mike Wayne (2001), all films are political, but not in the same way. This work attempts to examine a film as a text and situate it in a wider genre of third cinema- a cinema that is 'engaged', committed and has politics as its primary constituency.

Third Cinema and the New Indian Cinema :

Scholars of Cinema have categorized cinema as : First Cinema- the dominant, mainstream commercial, Second Cinema- the art, authorial and Third Cinema (Wayne 2001, p. 2). The most advanced and sophisticated body of political films which the medium has produced to date is Third Cinema. This cinema, emerged in the 1960s and 1970s, and according to Teshome Gabriel's book, Third Cinema in the Third World, emerged primarily in the Third World and has since been frequently conflated with Third World Cinema. Third Cinema, as Gabriel insisted, is not a cinema defined by geography; it is a cinema primarily defined by its socialist politics (Wayne, 2001, 1).

Third Cinema is a political cinema about much more than politics in the narrow sense. It is a cinema of social and cultural emancipation and one of the arguments is that such emancipations cannot be achieved merely in the political realm of the state. Socio-economic and cultural emancipation needs a much more fundamental and pervasive transformation, and if cinema is to make its own, relatively modest contribution, it too must feel the heat of such transformations, not only as films, but in its modes of production and reception. Third Cinema is such a cinema, or at least it is as close as we can get to such a cinema for such profound transformations.

On all the social indices, whether measurements of poverty, inequality, longevity, diet, access to technology, medicine and cultural or social capital, it is clear that there are fundamental divisions of wealth and opportunity between nations and regions as well as within nations and regions. A government programme here, some aid there, operates very much at the margins of this situation which in all its fundamentals, stays static, or more accurately, gets worse. It would be a modest contribution to changing consciousness and raising awareness if we had a film practice that could be adequate for addressing such crises. Above all, the term third cinema also designates a body of theory and filmmaking practice committed to social and cultural emancipation. This body of filmmaking is small, indeed tiny in terms of world cinema output. Yet Third Cinema films are amongst the most challenging films ever to be made, their political and cultural significance amplified by their proximity and intervention into the major historical processes of the epoch. Yet at the level of theory, Third Cinema is a concept in need of development in the face of its underdevelopment; a concept in need of clarification in the face of confusion and misunderstanding; a concept in need of defence in the face of contesting and indeed hostile theories and politics (Wayne, 2001, 2-5).

Fernando Birri (1997), the Argentinian film-maker called for a cinema 'that awakens/ clarifies and strengthens a revolutionary consciousness; a cinema that disturbs, shocks and weakens reactionary ideas; a cinema that is anti-bourgeois at a national level and anti-imperialist at an international level'. Third Cinema seeks to develop the means for grasping history as process, change, contradiction and conflict : in short the dialectics of history. Also, Third Cinema explores how culture is a site of power and political struggle.

Closely related to this form, content and mission of third cinema is the 'New Indian Cinema'- identified with the emergence of a certain aesthetic sensibility, a political awareness and engagement with Indian political realities, and a new style of film-making. Some would trace the beginnings of the New Indian Cinema to India's emergent art cinema, led by the Bengali directors Satyajit Ray, Ritwik Ghatak and Mrinal Sen. Satyajit Ray's 'Pather Panchali' based on many of the themes that engaged contemporary popular film-makers of the time, such as loss of social status, economic injustices, uprootment set within a naturalistic, realist frame. In contrast to Ray, his contemporaries Mrinal Sen and Ritwik Ghatak set out to expose the dark underside of India's lower middle-class and unemployed (as also, issue of rural social structure, migration and partition). More specifically, Sen pioneered a phase of didactic political cinema at the height of the Maoist-inspired Naxalite movement of the early 1970s- marked by the trilogy 'Interview' (1971), 'Calcutta 71' (1972), and 'Padatik' or 'The Guerrilla Fighter' (1973). Unlike the popular cinema, the New Indian Cinema is almost always concerned with the common man and is much more overt in their revolt against established traditions (Vasudev, 1986) as well as their explicit support to the subaltern perspectives.

The Question :

The lineage of Naxalite movement is traced to the Naxalbari uprising of May 1967 in West Bengal, which was a localised struggle against oppressive agrarian relations. The movement is now nearly five decades old. It has its victories as well as criticisms to its credit. Looking back at the late 1960s, when the Naxalite movement started, and taking stock of the major developments in the four decades that followed, it can be acknowledged that Naxalbari was a watershed in the recent history of India - in more than one sense. Most of the progressive trends in social activism today (like the growth of voluntary organizations working among the underprivileged and powerless, or the role of the media in exposing atrocities on dalits, tribals and the landless, or the affirmative actions by human rights activists as agents of entitlement, acting on behalf of the dispersed social groups) can be traced indirectly to the issues raised by, or associated with the Naxalite movement in the 1960-70 period. For the first time in post-independence India the movement asserted the demands of the poor and landless peasantry in a way that shook the then atrophied Indian political scene. The movement sensitized the society to their desperate efforts to escape the intolerable conditions of economic oppression and social humiliation (Banerjee, 2002). The movement has shaped thousands of activists and inspired people a hundred times more in number.

It has, therefore, been successfully and extensively eulogized as part of the cultural productions which reflect these sentiments and aspirations, but has also canonised it in the form of a separate genre, referred to as 'Naxal literature' (*Naxal sahitya*) and 'Naxal or red genre' performing arts and dramas. At the cultural level, movement has attempted to give a big blow to bourgeois art, literature and cinema. As mixture of fiction and 'testimony', the stories, autobiographies, poems and narratives present symbolic reconstruction and provide a fertile ground for innumerable symbols and agents of protest from the communities, members from colleges and schools as well as other white-collar sections of society. In May 1977, while inaugurating a camp for radical cultural activists at Olarikkara, Kerala, the noted dramatist N. N.

Pillai declared that 'there is only one solution, and that is revolution.' The convention had issued a manifesto of revolutionary writers and artists which stressed the need for transforming the production relations of the capitalist system and its ideological and cultural meanings. The concluding paragraph of the manifesto read : 'it is the responsibility of revolutionary artists and literary men to discern between progressive and decadent forces in history, to stand with the forces that make progress, to assess their growth, to assimilate them, and to be honest to one's times. Only thus shall we be able to realize the idea of a militant cultural front and to fight by means of new artistic- literary creations the cultural domination of the ruling classes' (Sreejith, 2010, 5333).

The ripple-effects of Naxal movement are prominently visible in the Indian film fraternity- both in Hindi and vernacular. Both the mainstream as well as neo-realist cinema, and more so the neo-realist cinema, have intermittently tried to engage with the Naxal issues though with varying treatment, intensity and approaches. Film fraternity somewhat seems to share the intention of engaging in an important and necessary civic action. They however, confer variable and blurry meanings to their involvement with the movement- in between human duty and classical political or activist choice. But more importantly here, in so doing, they also attribute to themselves a particular responsibility, in the name of their artistic identity and by virtue of the access to public arenas which their specific professional positions opened them, implying to intervene and speak out on these societal questions. As artists and film-makers they claim to have a particular sensitivity and as representatives of a 'popular culture,' they have access to a mass audience. They thus claim to speak, not only in and for the milieu to which they belong, but also and above all to and for much larger populations. P. K. Nair, veteran film scholar and founder of the National Film Archive in Pune, points out- 'our filmmakers have been handling political themes for many years'. Films like Mrinal Sen's 'Calcutta 71' (1972), portraying the brutal manner in which the police dealt with the Naxalite youth; Khwaja Ahmad Abbas' 'The Naxalites' ('Mera Inquilab') (1982), which followed the trail of the Naxalite movement in West Bengal; 'Hazaar Chaurasi ki Maa' (1998) based on a story by Mahesweta Devi and directed by Govind Nihalani; 'Lal Salam' (2002) by Sanjiv Karlambekar portraying the exploitation and consequent reassertion by tribals; and more recently, 'Hazaaron Khwaishein Aisi' (2005) directed by Sudhir Mishra; and 'Rakta Charitra' (2011) by Ram Gopal Varma have tried to approach the issue (Akhtar, 2010). These films have not only approached the issues of Naxalite movement with sensitivity, but also have critically engaged with the course and effects of the movement on the youth- both rural and urban, the peasants as well as the working class. They have successfully chronicled the courageous battles against the brutal state machinery followed by self-sacrifice by thousands of guerrillas and incessant efforts by dedicated cadres to initiate land reforms, to hike wages to and social changes in their areas of control.

The film under discussion here is 'Red Alert - The War Within', released in July 2010 directed by Ananth Narayan Mahadevan and screen-played by Aruna Raje. The film was screened at the 6th Stuttgart Film Festival in 2009. The film received the Director's Vision Award at the Festival and Best Actor Award (Sunil Shetty) at South Asian International Film Festival (SAIFF).

The film 'Red Alert - The War Within' ('Red Alert' henceforth) is a narrative of a common man and his close encounter with the Naxal movement. The film opens with the rhetoric : a war where everyone is right. The title of the film 'Red Alert - The War Within'- works at two levels of dialectics. While on the surface, it denotes the war-like situation within a country i.e. the government waging a war on its own citizens. In the deeper level, the title suggests a psychological battle of the protagonist with himself, i.e. which side to choose.

The film relates that the failure of the democratic system to properly represent the rural poor has given the Naxalites their own opportunity to do so. India's political institutions have neither given the rural masses the means to express discontent nor any resources to address poor living situations and economic disparities existent within their communities. The state has in no way tried to prevent the rampage by the multinational corporations, neither from rummaging through the forest areas to acquire lands and extract buried wealth, nor has in some way attempted to cushion the blow of commercial interests on rural and tribal ways of life. The film attempts to suggest that the revolutions are predominantly made of displaced and dispossessed peasants, disillusioned and unassimilated rural youth.

The Plot :

'Red Alert' tells the story of Narsimha (Suniel Shetty), a farm labourer living in a hamlet in Andhra Pradesh (more specifically, Khammam district), who is impoverished, heavily under debt and desperately in need of money. He gets to work as a cook and on the ill-fated day, he suddenly finds himself embroiled in a conflict between Police force and armed group, which calls itself *dalam* (group). After being rescued by members of *dalam*, he serves as cook for the group. From being a mere cook to actually training in weapons to being witness to shootouts, Narsimha finds himself unwillingly being sucked into the movement. He undergoes constant anxiety as which side he should be - on one hand are the sympathetic Naxalites who are fighting for the poor and for a good cause, and on the other hand, is the system comprising of government and the police i.e. the enemies of these dalam. Narsimha time and again questions : 'aren't the police, the government and those killed by Naxals our own people? How can they be enemies?'

Another important character is Laxmi (Sameera Reddy). She is found and rescued by the *dalam* from police custody where she was repeatedly gang-raped by men in Khaki. She stands as a testimony of police excesses meted out to women who dare to complaint against the men in power. Unlike Narsimha's dilemma and reluctance, she is quick to accept and join the dalam, its ideology as well as the operations. The other characters of importance are dalam leader Velu (Ashish Vidyarthi), Sarala (Seema Biswas), Radha (Ayesha Dharkar), Deputy Inspector General Rathod (Gulshan Grover), journalist V. K. Raghavan (Makrand Deshpande), and main ideologue of the group, Krishnaraj (Vinod Khanna).

Narsimha unwillingly becomes part of the *dalam's* operations like attack on police station for arms and weapons. He is ordered by *dalam* leader Velu to kill one of the members of dalam itself for being a mole as well as to carry out an attack on school. Due to an accident during the operation, a child gets killed in cross-fire. It is here that Narsimha decides to leave the *dalam.* A confrontation with Velu and consequently his death forces Narsimha to run for life from both - the police and the Naxals. Narsimha with the advice and help of journalist Raghavan decides to become police accomplice against the *dalam.* They are successful at cracking down the dalam and annihilating every member, except Laxmi. Laxmi was captured alive and she killed herself in the custody. At the end, Narsimha agrees to collaborate with the police to kill the main ideologue Krishnaraj. Narsimha carries out the operation successfully and strikes bargain with the Police. Towards the end, Krishnaraj masquerading as social activist reappears in a television interview. In the flashback, it is shown that Krishnaraj was convinced by the arguments of Narsimha about the futility of violence as a means to achieve the goal and had decided to leave the path of violence and thus escaped with the help of Narsimha. The conclusion of the film suggested that the movement needs to renounce the means of violence while retaining its noble end, i.e. people's welfare.

Thematic Analysis of the Film :

The film with its nomenclature and thematic presentation claims to belong to the genre of Naxal Cinema. The film can be analysed on following thematic issues :

Representation of the Repressive State Apparatuses and Ideological State Apparatus :

The film can be read through Louis Althusser's (1971) essay 'Ideology and Ideological State Apparatuses'. He mentions that state apparatus in question whether Repressive or Ideological, 'functions' both by violence and by ideology. The repressive state apparatus i.e. the government, the administration, the army, the police, the courts, the prison etc. and the ideological state apparatus i.e. political, communication and cultural instruments are explicit in the film (Althusser, 1971, 143-144). The concept of repressive state apparatus is violently visible in the film. The way police behaves, tortures and controls are examples of it. The film explicitly addresses the issue of violence perpetuated by the state and its unwillingness to engage in a dialogue with the revolutionaries. The film reflects the fact that the plain clothes sleuths are deployed to apprehend and kill Naxalites, their sympathisers, and whoever else is perceived as obstructing the anti-Naxalite operations of the police. Such anti-Naxalite police operations include the much criticized 'greyhounds', a specially trained and equipped anti-guerrilla commando wing of the Andhra Pradesh police force. Notorious for its ruthless killings of Maoists and their sympathisers, mostly in fake encounters - it best illustrates the government response to the Maoist insurgency. Also, the misplaced priority and allegiance of the state has been very well exposed in the film when the *dalam* kidnaps foreign businessmen to bargain for their demands. Instead of carrying out a dialogue, the police in response massacres innumerable innocent villagers and farmers.

The social system which the revolutionaries are out to overthrow is not only challenged by police, but also the challenges posed by the ideological state apparatus i.e. the politics, its ethics and its philosophy. The politicians, suggests the film, lack the slightest vestige of moral authority to face the Naxalites or any other principled political dissenters, and have given up the task of meeting the Naxalite challenge politically. Political authority has been transformed into facilitators of corporate interests, opting for the dictates of international capital which only make things much worse.

Further, the abdication of all responsibility by society as a whole to engage the Naxalite movement in a rational debate about its methods and its means, its theory and its practice, its analysis of society's problems and its idea of their resolution is suggested by the film. The blame is put on what is usually called public opinion though in a subtle way it watches in silence as the battle between the two guns goes on.

Another issue effectively addressed by the film is role of media as the ideological state apparatus. Raghavan, a journalist, is the representative of the media in the film who concocts to have sympathy with the cause and ideology of the dalam. Raghavan eventually helps Narsimha to conspire with the Police and politicians to wipe out the dalam for his own petty interest. This becomes obvious when Deputy Inspector General Rathod promises him of exclusive report and says : 'after all you also need to become editor'. The media's position on the movement has been like running with the hares and hunting with the hounds.

The film can also be seen through Anthony Giddens' propositions pertaining to key aspects of nation-states like permanent existence of class conflicts and monopoly over the means of internal and external violence (Dwivedi, 2010, 270). Any challenge to the nation-state's monopoly is crushed by the elaborate system of army and police.

Naxalism-Terrorism Debate :

The film attempts to engage with the Naxalite-Terrorist debate which is itself the central theme of the film : it tries to break the myth that Naxalism is terrorism and that the Naxalites, in particular the CPI (ML) (People's War), employ terror as a political instrument and that it is not a political movement. Thus, in the conversation between Velu and Raghavan, Velu sums up : 'We are revolutionaries and not terrorists. Terrorists are against the country, we are against the system!'

The film also brings home the serious debate that Naxalism is primarily and centrally a political movement, a movement concerned with fighting and altering the existing status of and relations between classes in society. Armed revolution/violence is one of the means it employs. The film portrays that the movement's social base is the poor and the oppressed but it is not in the sense that all the poor and the oppressed are its supporters. Also, though the movement does not take approval from those people for its strategies and decisions or operations, its politics indeed is oriented in their favour and the considerable support it has is among them.

Issue of Support Base :

The film is successful in bringing the point to the fore that the movement does have a popular support, and even the economic and social causes they espouse are effective. Whether it is bargaining with the local traders on wages or price of goods or bargaining with the government for right on the natural resources and forests, the film depicts an active role of the comrades. It rightly portrays the attitude of the Naxalites : we are the people and the people are us. But at the same time, the movie also portrays that the people enter the picture only in the form of a gullible mass whose problems are 'used' by the terrorists to further their own strategy which is violence. In fact, the film neutralizes its stance by suggesting that its 'ideology is only a pretext for terror'. However, the reality is not just located somewhere between these contrasting notions, but rather it swings between them. The Naxalites do not just 'use' the people. They have genuine sympathy for and identification with them (which does not preclude lording it over them on occasion); they genuinely reflect the aspirations of the people, though as narrated by the film, there is nothing to justify the misappropriation of the aspirations of people for a permanent justification of all their politics. The struggles led and waged by the Naxalites and even part of the violence - real or imagined employed by them has definitely benefited the poor and the oppressed immensely.

At the same time, the film presents a critique of the red movement itself. According to the film, the quantum of injury it is causing in the process to the people as well as to democratic civilization is something to be concerned. The Naxalite movement's worst criticism is setting up of parallel adjudicatory and executive mechanism; the revolutionaries adjudicate matters not only between the oppressed and the oppressors but also between different sections of the oppressed or the middle classes. Their procedures and their norms are allegedly determined by whatever political consciousness the local activists possess plus raw weapon power. Their administration of justice and their executive directives are sometimes more harsh and brutal than those of bourgeois law, apart from being amenable or liable to the common ills of power.

This issue is portrayed very vividly by the *dalam* leader Velu's autocratic and undemocratic actions, undertaken without *dalam's* consensus.

Secondly, it is a truth that any armed political militancy is perpetually involved in the brutal acts of weeding out agents of its enemy within its social base and this is to such an extent that it is found killing more of its own people than the enemy. This finds clear portrayal in film as well - the Naxalites have killed more of the poor and the rural middle classes than the landlords, the other exploiters or the police. This is a very unpleasant fact about political terror which its practitioners and sympathizers are hard put to defend, except to point - for the benefit of whoever is willing to find that a satisfactory reply to the promise of what the people will attain after the liberation. This stance is repeatedly defended by the main ideologue Krishnaraj. He repeatedly announces that he does not care about the ethics of the means, it is the goal that is more important. However, towards the conclusion, was the admission made by Krishnaraj that the violence unleashed by the movement and the counterinsurgency forces, the number of those killed, imprisoned, and those who vanished or were forced to go underground was indeed the flip-side of the movement.

Sumanta Banerjee's argument finds relevance here. According to him, "while generations of heroic revolutionaries may remain committed to the strategy of a 'protracted war', the vast masses of the common people may not always be prepared for it. Although sympathetic to the revolutionaries who uphold their cause, all of them cannot be expected to join the revolution and adhere to the discipline of revolutionary cadres. They vacillate when offered sops by the state, or may even squeal when coerced by the state. They are caught in the crossfire between two maximalist positions - one adopted by the revolutionaries who are determined in their well-meaning goal of smashing the present iniquitous socio-economic order and replacing it with a 'people's democratic state', and the other taken by a stubborn ruling class and state equally determined to continue with the status quo and suppress any resistance to it. Of the two, the communist revolutionaries who claim to look after the welfare of the poor and the oppressed, are expected to be more humane in their choice of tactics and genuinely democratic in obtaining popular consent for them - particularly when such tactics affect the vast masses of uninvolved citizens". In their drive for retaliation against enemy offensive, they must not stoop to the level of the police or security forces and indulge in indiscriminate attacks on soft targets like schools buildings, or killing innocent people (Banerjee, 2006, p. 3162).

But notwithstanding all this, the Naxalites do fill the space that really exists in Indian society and democracy for a popular and effective counter-weight to the force of the state's bureaucracy and the police, and the social power of the dominant classes. The film portrays the case of Laxmi as well as other women comrades where the group is their only hope and security against the oppressive system.

Concluding Observations :

In its conclusion, however, the film appears voluntarily apartisan, its political engagement is coloured with major ambivalence : the political and the civic intentions of the film ends up being 'neutralized'. Deliberate attempt has been made to combine several paradoxical elements to produce a non-engaged apolitical film. It can be argued that the politics of Naxalism is diluted and compromised in the cinema so that it would be palatable and acceptable for a wider audience. The conclusion of the film in fact seems to strip the film of its ideology and its genre as 'red film'. Also, certain characters in the film like Velu, Sarala and Radha required more space, voice and much nuanced portrayal in the film as they are representative of multiple voices. Since, the film (due to its complexity and contemporary relevance) required a layered and configurative story, i.e. the use of multi-narratives (instead of relying on single dominant narrative of Narsimha) would have been appropriate.

It is an established fact that cinema and its whole system comes under the corpus of cultural ideological state apparatus or it can be said that there exists a Cinematic State Apparatus containing censorship, spectatorship, authorship, funding, motivation for representation, aesthetics, profiteering etc that play important role in political economy of the film. It becomes pertinent for social scientists to see how a film or even a genre like the 'red film' eventually is weeded, sieved and censored by the state to make it suitable for viewing for the audience. Madhava Prasad (1998) thus argues that the Hindi film never unequivocally gives the masses what they want because, films by its very capitalist nature, its modern technologies and dominant ideologies are first and foremost at the service of the nation-state and a powerful coalition of ruling elites (Banaji, 2006).

What is sadly missing in the film, is that it neither has the quality of narrative for acquainting the people with the courses of history of the movement as was successfully portrayed by 'Hazaar Charasi ki Maa' and 'Hazaaron Khwaishein Aisi', nor could the film portray the intensity and realism of characters as dealt by 'The Naxalite' and 'Lal Salaam'. Despite the film's claim to have been inspired by a real event, its topical and current relevance, it fails to establish a correlation between the text and context like the film 'Calcutta 1971'. The lacunae primarily have to do with either the lack of perspective or 'apolitical' and distant positions on the part of many film-makers to see things in their socio-political context. This perhaps explains the reason why significant events like protest /uprising against politician-corporate nexus or violation of human rights by corporates never find place in the mainstream cinema. Even if few realistic films are made addressing such issues, they get a very limited audience.

The film neither can be clearly placed in mainstream/ dominant category nor can be seen a third/ neo-realist cinema. The issue that it claims to espouse is topical and political, but it lacks the ideological rigour and engagement of the third cinema. In its attempt to 'neutralize' and diffuse a rather charged issue it ends up as reactionary, non-committal; the Third Cinema on the other hand refuses to be non-partisan, distant - it is passionate, angry, often satirical and always complex. It can be observed that the dilemma of the filmmakers is precisely the dilemma of protagonist, i.e. whose voices and interests to represent.

References :

Aruna Vasudev (1986), *The New Indian Cinema*. New Delhi : Macmillan.

F. Birri (1997), 'Cinema and Underdevelopment', in M.T Martin (Ed.), *New Latin American Cinema, Theory, Practices, and Transcontinental Articulations*, Volume One. Detroit : Wayne State University Press.

K. Balagopal (1997), 'Naxalite Terrorists and Benign Policemen', *Economic and Political Weekly*, 32-36 (Sep. 1997), pp. 2253-2260.

Ketaki Dwivedi (2011), 'Anthony Giddens : Structuration, Nation-State and War, Modernity' in Pradip Basu (Ed.), *Avenel Companion to Modern Social Theorists*, Kolkata : Avenel Press.

Louis Althusser (1971), *Lenin and Philosophy and Other Essays* (Part-2), London : Monthly Review Press.

Madhava M. Prasad (1998), *Ideology of the Hindi Film : A Historical Construction*, New Delhi : Oxford University Press.

Mike Wayne (2001), *Political Film : The Dialectics of Third Cinema*, London : Pluto Press.

Sumanta Banerjee (2002), 'Naxalbari : Between Past and Future', *Economic and Political Weekly*, 37, 22 (June 2002), pp. 2115-2117.

Sumanta Banerjee (2006), 'Beyond Naxalbari', *Economic and Political Weekly*, 41, 29 (July 2006), pp. 3159-3163.

Shabina Akhtar (2010), 'Code Red', *The Telegraph*, Sunday, July 11, 2010.

Shakuntala Banaji (2006), *Reading 'Bollywood': The Young Audience and Hindi Films*, New York : Palgrave Macmillan.

Solanas Fernando and Octavio Getino (1976), 'Towards a Third Cinema', in Bill Nichols (Ed.), *Movies and Methods : An Anthology*, Berkeley : University of California Press.

Sreejith K (2005), 'Naxalite Movement and Cultural Resistance Experience of Janakiya Samskarika Vedi in Kerala (1980-82)', *Economic and Political Weekly*, 40, 50 (December 10, 2005), pp. 5333- 5337.

T. H. Gabriel (1982), *Third Cinema in the Third World*, Ann Arbor MI : UMI Research Press.

Film and Naxalism : A Case Study of 'Hazaaron Khwaishein Aisi'

Radhakanta Barik

A city with cosmopolitan outlook in the early 19th century having a personality of its own, expressed in poetry and historical essays with a high degree of human rationality, got colonialised. But at the same time, western influence sharpened rationality of Delhi intelligentsia. Human creativity gets articulated in poetry which has urban rationality : this embodies the concept of individuality which is the product of urbanization and industrialization. Only an individual can dream and dreams can be articulated in poetry. Poetry in India is a public activity unlike the western society; poetry is recited in public and appreciated by the public. Intellectual tradition of Delhi gets expressed in some of the best poetry from where the title of this film has come. A city does not recognize the caste and community identity but only individuality and class which are the products of enlightened consciousness of urban people. Only in a city an individual can dream if he or she is not controlled by any tradition and dreams are the basis of innovation and creativity. The title 'Hazaaron Khwaishein Aisi' implies that the city of Delhi provides space for an individual to have thousand dreams which are different from those of other individuals. The city is a pinnacle of human creativity and innovation.

The city of Delhi has experienced historical turmoil with the partition of India and the city's personality got disoriented with the partition. Partition psychology dominated the city for two decades where people started thinking in terms of 'us' and 'them' and the city suffered intellectually. But the city being the national capital of India got its energy back from the intelligentsia who migrated from other small cities. The city provided cheap physical space and intellectual space for their creative interaction. Only in 1970s this city created an environment where individuals started dreaming which was possible in the university which becomes a society of its own. Students from all over India came and studied; most came from smaller towns and other urban conglomerates such as Calcutta and Madras and Bombay. These three cities have already experienced urban renaissance which came in conflict with colonial modernity. These children came with dreams to Delhi University where they felt as part of the universe while their broad outlook with deep reading and discussion gave them an opportunity to think boldly. University provided space for them to discuss ideas and ideologies and various advanced ideas in sociological imagination got discussed in class rooms. Students carried those ideas to their hostels and coffee rooms which became the active centres of debates and discussions. Delhi University was proud of some best coffee houses in Delhi while people from other walks of life started coming to these places and discussed various issues. Artists, writers and political thinkers started congregating here and Delhi University provided space for working out some latest sociological ideas. This was not confined to only academic debates and discussions; but it went beyond the academic world and they got engaged with the outside world and related their ideas with outside reality. Here ideology started mediating between individual ideation and social reality.

1970s is the most creative phase in the second half of twentieth century. This is the time when international student community was the most active leaders in the political and intellectual sphere. Most of the Western cities were vibrant with political ideas. They were debating the issues related to state and authority. They were discussing the issues affecting the global world. They were emotionally and intellectually involved in the issues of Africa and Asia. Their internationalism shaped their intellectual debates where issues of Algeria and Vietnam became their own problems. This brought the issue of colonialism and imperialism to sharp focus. They wanted to debate these issues in a much more open and free environment which was restricted by the states of the western world. This led them to challenge the authority of state. At the same time they wanted to discuss the issues related to Asia and Africa as their own. Here they started in problematizing the ideology of Marxism. International communist movement got split into some groups. They started looking critically on Marxism which was getting practised by Soviet Union and China. In China, Mao Tse-tung led a cultural revolution where urban students went to countryside and worked with the rural people. European intellectuals wanted to undergo catharsis. Some of them went to Latin America and participated in the revolution led by Castro and Che Guevara. In such an intellectual environment Delhi being capital of India experienced intellectual and political tremors. Any earthquake creates ripples on sub-terrain level of the earth which happens in Delhi. The university provides space for freedom to discuss but this freedom led them to the countryside. Some of them went to the most backward and difficult terrain like Bhojpur of Bihar. This is dominated by high caste feudal lords where dalit labourers work in semi slavery stage. Their labour and women were exploited by the high caste landlords.

It is interesting to note that left movement in Bihar has a widespread history. It took the land question and rent question during national movement but did not take the caste question seriously. A new group of Marxists came out of this movement who questioned both the caste and land questions. They are popularly known as the Naxalites as this movement got started in 1967 in a region called Naxalbari in north Bengal. It spread to Bhojpur and Srikakulam of Andhra. They disagreed with other Marxist groups who wanted to lead a peaceful struggle. This new group initiated armed struggle. They wanted to abandon the path of peaceful social change which happened during the freedom struggles. These conventional Marxists had commitment to mass movement in a peaceful manner. They wanted to lead almost a simple Gandhian life and work with masses. They believed in mass struggles in both cities and villages. But the Naxalites believe in armed struggle in rural India which should lead the movement and cities would join afterwards. These armed struggles took place in some pockets of eastern India but also created a ripple in Delhi University. Students started discussing these issues and wanted to experience the armed struggles. They left the college hostels one night and went to Bhojpur of Bihar. Within the various Communist Party circles of Bihar there was a discussion about the armed struggle against the high caste landlords. A known leader S.N. Singh supported the extremist path of political movement against oppression. He gave a call for annihilation of class enemies. This was supported by some students belonging to Delhi University.

It is interesting to note here that some of them had not seen villages in their childhood. They had read about them from the Indian literature. They tried to relate to rural India in a romantic manner. Some of them were from the elite schools of India which are popularly known as Public Schools. These Public Schools such as Doon School and Mayo College have their history. These schools have a rigorous artistic and intellectual tradition where students get involved in both physical and mental activities. They play on best musical instruments and are trained by some outstanding teachers. They read some of the best classics in the world such as Shakespeare and Dickens. They stage the plays written by Shakespeare and Kalidasa. These plays help them to experience various emotional and intellectual turmoils when one wants to experience separation and union. They are good in both western aesthetics and Sanskrit aesthetics. They appreciate the Indian and western aesthetics in the same spirit. They enjoy cricket and football. Their aesthetic sensibility shapes their mental outlook which liberates them in one way. Their intellectual evolution does not get limited by the Indian tradition. They do not feel embarrassed by discussing love and sex with their counterparts. Such students come from the best Public Schools of India and study in some of the best colleges of Delhi University where they plan their life as to when and how they would want to go abroad either on scholarship or parental money. They think of two jobs in India - either IAS or as executives in the private sector. They have a strong school and college bond which shapes their networking in India and abroad. They use it whenever it is required either in business or administration. This works as cultural capital which nourishes their mobility in Indian state or business. Networking helps them to get things done by the police or civil administration whenever required. Such a group, backed by social and cultural capital of Indian society and having talent to enter into civil service and private executives, desired to leave this comfort zone and went to the villages of Bhojpur. They experienced psychological problems to adjust in those new surroundings. But some of them worked in the difficult terrain without any inhibition. It is the interesting part of this story.

The joint family structure provided space for their activities without any financial consideration. They start dreaming to involve in various literary and artistic activities as well as full time left wing politics. There is a scene of joint family where Gita lives. As she gets into the house, she is welcomed by her parents and aunts and uncles. There is a dining table with more than a dozen chairs which the family uses at dinner time. This is the time for fun and frolic among themselves. The young children do not have any worry about every day life in these houses. They do not take the responsibility of bringing vegetables or milk. They are free to dream and think boldly. They are encouraged by their elders to pursue their dreams. Such social support works in Indian society to allow people to pursue politics. Many of them joined politics as a profession and hold some key positions in the dominant political parties and Indian cabinet. They know left wing politics does not make an easy profession. They have to depend on family support for getting engaged in Marxist politics. Marxist politics is for those people who are dreamers and have passions. They are ready to sacrifice their careers. Moreover they can marry and leave their children back at home without any botheration. They can work in the field without getting worried about their own immediate family or their old parents. Here Gita and Sidharth have a child whom they have left with the joint family to take care of. She is able to remain active in various social works in distant villages of Bihar. Her boyfriend also does not have to bother his child's education or day to day problems. He is able to pursue his extremist politics and have to face lot of hardships while staying in field and there is a possibility of getting injured and jailed by the police firing; and this happened to Sidharth. His family and Gita's family are able to provide security to him in both social and emotional sense. Once Sidharth decides to change his political life and later decides to take to a professional career. These families try to provide financial support for his medical education abroad.

This is the backdrop of the story of film which is based on a love story of a girl and two young boys. Gita is being loved by Sidharth and Vikram. Sidharth is from an established family. His parents come from different religious and linguistic backgrounds. But Sidharth is unable to speak his mother tongue and speaks English. Vikram is from the small town Meerut where his father is an honest Gandhian Congress leader. They study in Delhi University. While studying they become very friendly with each other. This is an inner circle but there are other friends and once they visit to the rural hinterland they decide one day that they want to realize their freedom. Here the girl does not take interest in their adventurous Naxalite politics. She decides to go abroad and study for her Masters. In the meantime she gets married with an IAS officer. This marriage is an arranged marriage and she does not feel fascinated with the life of the IAS officer husband. She is extremely bored and alienated. One day she meets her friend Vikram who is working as a middle man and earning a lot in a party. Her friend tells her that the other friend Sidharth was in Bhojpur. After that incident, she does not take interest in her married life and decides to go out of the marriage. Then, one day she decides to go to Bhojpur to meet her boyfriend. They decide to live there and work for people. She works for women of the poorer section of the society. Her boyfriend works with the Naxalites. They have a child out of this relationship. They work for the common people both in politics and social work and enjoy this activity. A group of Naxalites decide to kill some members of the landlord's gang which this boy questions. He puts a question to his other comrades that violence should not replace mass movement. Despite his opposition to violence, their group decides to kill landlord's people. In the meantime Emergency is declared which turns the state into a police state. The police decides to attack the Naxalites brutally and both of them become victims. They get injured and wounded seriously by police firing. They get admitted to a hospital where the police guards them. The girl's former husband decides to rescue her and bring her back to Delhi. But nobody helps her boyfriend. This boy's father decides to inform Vikram who is well-connected with politicians and civil servants to help Sidharth. He goes to Bhojpur to help Sidharth. There he becomes a victim of the police conspiracy. He gets admitted to the hospital. In the meantime Sidharth returns to Delhi, decides to change his path and go abroad to study. Vikram gets so seriously injured that it results in loosing his memory. But the girl decides to go back to Bhojpur with Vikram. They decide to live in Bhojpur and do social work there and keep in touch with Sidharth who sends letters to them from abroad.

This is the main text but there are sub-texts. There is a description of the Emergency. This is the time when the ruling Congress Party loses its old ideological fervour. They decide to recruit youths who have criminal records and ignore the old Congress moorings. An old Gandhian worker, Vikram's father, questions the mode of recruitment into political organization. During the Emergency he was arrested and kept in jail. While he is working over the Charkha in the jail, the camera moves for a while which signifies a political meaning. Charkha symbolizes many things for Gandhi and Indian people. It represents the independent path of development. The Indian state should create opportunity for providing work and employment for all. Work, employment and income are related. This helps a human being feel liberated. Indian state changed the track in the era of liberalization where small things do not look beautiful now. Here politics is a profession where serving wider humanity is not the main focus but self interest. To pursue it is like a business activity. There are other political groups such as Socialists led by Lohia and JP who are kept in jail with other opposition leaders. Indian politics which is vibrant before the Emergency gets changed in its contours. The Congress Party loses old political ideological moorings. The opposition gets attacked. Dissidence of any form gets threatened by the state. Indian democracy believes in argumentative basis of forming public policy. It should be a product of dialogue between people and elite. The Emergency brings an end to the deliberative basis of democracy. India as an idea representing plural culture and institutional democracy comes to a halt. This is shown in the film beautifully.

The story has a sub-text of communalism which has erupted in Meerut, a city nearer to Delhi. Communalism has brought various vested interests to play their game. People of India have a shared culture. This city is that its people, both Muslims and Hindus, have shared a common bond. During partition the city had not experienced any such riot; but in the early 1970s the city saw a large scale riot. This riot brought the various ruling groups to play their role; they got mischievously involved, with the communal forces to help them remain in power. Vikram is to come to Delhi University for study but his journey gets postponed because of the communal riot in Meerut. Here communalism helps the ruling class. As Gandhian workers and other concerned citizens started working for organizing peace march, the young entrepreneur son of Gandhian worker questions them that they are wasting time. The Congress Party is losing its secular credential while some of their leaders are alleged to be associated with the riot.

This film takes the women's question seriously. It is a bold film where the woman is the centre of activities. Indian films have a tradition of showing woman as the mother figure who is the site of virtue (Vasudevan, R : 2000). Gita is the central character where the male characters turn subordinates. She is not ideological in the beginning but once she is convinced of some thing she goes back to the working place which is a difficult one. "She is arrogant and opinionated one" (see the text of the film- author). She has her own opinion on every issue. She has taken a subordinated position neither with her first husband after marriage nor in live-in relations with Sidharth and Vikram. In the film, Gita and Vikram are going in a car on a lonely road where he asks about her opinion about her decision that she wants to break her marriage relationship. She is there with Vikram but she has taken a stand after serious thought that she wants to go back to Bhojpur to live with Sidharth. This is a situation depicted by T S Eliot in a poem about the modern man-woman relationship. Sudhir Mishra as a film director has a view of his own. He is influenced by 'Guide' where woman plays the central role as an independent human being taking initiative on her own. In an interview he says, "She played the role of a woman who chooses her own identity and her own expression of sexuality" (Delhi Times, 8 March, 2011). Here, the woman is expressing her sexuality on her own terms. She has abandoned her first husband who is an IAS officer because she did not enjoy his company; she even is going back to Bhojpur for doing her own work in social sphere rather than politics. She enjoys working as an independent woman different from her boyfriend who is in Naxalite politics. She has respect for his ideological persuasion but she is not convinced in the beginning. They have a live-in relation and have a child of their own. Once her boyfriend goes abroad with the child she has not changed her way of life. She has returned back to Bhojpur. She is living with another college friend who has abandoned his business and come back to her. This shows that her sexuality is not allowed to be exploited by neither her husband nor her boy friend. She has tremendous control over her own sexuality. The image of Vikram is shown as the man who has lost the memory of patriarchal values and becomes a friend of this girl. This represents that man-woman relation gets changed with every phase of radical politics. Somewhere political movement punctures the patriarchal relation and values and there is a struggle for equality of man and woman. The Naxalites seriously take the issue of patriarchal values exhibited by the high caste landlord over the women belonging to dalits. With the end of the movement, the women refuse to be exploited by these landlords. Here, the director tries to portray the heroine as the symbolic representative of revolution. Only those who fall in love make revolution. Moreover, only lovers are revolutionaries. Love and revolution need a romantic approach. Only romanticism shapes their consciousness as revolutionaries. Their experience as lovers helps them to have the excitement of the experience of revolution. This has happened in the case of Naxalites who have abandoned Delhi University where they have experimented with their love making more so to go to Bhojpur to experiment political revolution. In the end it is the heroine who is there in Bhojpur that means she represents here the revolution. But she also has a broad consciousness about social problems. She thinks that spread of literacy and health awareness can facilitate the growth of radical consciousness. Moreover, many Naxalites after returning from Bihar and other places have joined civil society activities. She has joined such activity but keeps in touch with the active Naxal leaders.

The camera is moving over the green patch of land in Bhojpur; this explains the social relationship there. It is not the patch of land with crops but with green grass. It explains symbolically that this patch is without agricultural productivity because of production relations. This is a part of Sone canal area which is an irrigated one but productivity is low because of production relations. If production relations are feudal and semi-feudal they restrict the productive forces to grow. The labour is in a semi-bondage stage which keeps them in a stage of low productivity. The feudal relations can be broken only with the radical mobilization of peasantry and working people. Here Naxalism has generated a new awareness against feudalism. That helps them to protest against feudalism. The symbolic attacks on persons belonging to the landlord represent attack on feudalism. Productivity will grow only if feudal relations are destroyed. Revolution believes in destruction and reconstruction simultaneously. Feudal relations will be destroyed and get replaced with capitalistic relations. This is a progressive relation which brings freedom for working class to sell their labour in a labour market.

Feudalism can be explained with the help of a binary model where feudal lords rule over a region, rural masses have consciousness to support them to rule over them. There is a case shown in the film that a brutal landlord who rapes a poor dalit woman is being opposed by the local masses. They threaten to kill him and direct their guns towards him. In the meantime he collapses due to a heart attack. They call for a doctor who is a dalit. His son does not allow the doctor to treat his father because of the doctor's low caste but people do not protest and support the landlord because of his heart problem. Feudal oppression has legitimacy in their collective consciousness. Feudal consciousness is so deep that it is difficult to attack without progressive cultural project. Culture has to be open and broadbased. There should be tolerance for innovation and dissidence in cultural world. In cultural world the party sympathizers can work and play very creative role in spreading democratic consciousness. It works in a binary manner that his oppression and high caste respectability get social support from the lower section of the society. To create democratic consciousness there is a requirement of cultural activities like folk theatre and songs but it is absent in Naxalite politics. Their mobilization is more political and economic rather than cultural. Cultural front was very strong among the Marxists during the national movement. They organized the Indian People's Theatre Association (IPTA) movement where a large number of artists, singers, film-makers were active and involved in the movement. Naxalites have a small cultural front that is working in the cities. They organized songs and plays in the university campus by singing popular songs of Bob Dylan who is a progressive singer. When a group of students in Delhi University decided to go to the field in Bihar, some of them withdrew because of their various other engagements but the Naxalites were very much intolerant towards them who were active in the cultural front.

There is a letter from London from Sidhartha to Gita who lives in Bhojpur that Naxalism has been able to destroy the feudal authority of high caste landlords. Now rape of dalit women or keeping labour in bondage stage are no more possible. A documented work by Kalyan Mukherji says, "The word Naxalite thereafter came to connote to many a person who would resist sexual oppression with his last drop of blood" (Mukherjee and Rajendra Singh, 1980 : 46). This letter indicates that the director has done some research work on the changing social relation in Bihar in particular and India in general where Naxalism has contributed a bit like other progressive movements led by the Marxists. This point needs to be probed here. Here it shows that historical facts are required to prove a theoretical point that social change has happened in Bihar. There is less attacks on dalits today. Now landlord class feel threatened to glance at the women of dalits. Moreover, there is class consciousness growing in rural Bihar cutting across the castes. Poor belonging to high castes, backward castes and dalits have joined hands in their common struggle. This has pushed the landlords to feel scared of them. They have fled away from their villages to the cities. It is interesting to note that the social trust among various castes has increased which has shaped their social capital in countryside. On a child's birthday in a poor dalit house the whole village people gathered in the district of Patna in 2000. These areas were influenced by Naxalism in 1970s where dalits actively got involved in politics. It is interesting to note that even the wage is higher here than in places where left politics has not mobilized the rural poor (Barik, R.K.: 2006).

Most of the Naxalites who worked with the rural poor in Bhojpur are targeted by the local police as the 'urban bastards' who are creating problems. There are fake encounters against them. It may be noted here that a Sub-Inspector in charge of the local police station created havoc but the administration was silent. The policing at the local level does not bother about the rules and regulations of administration of criminal justice system. They are involved in blatant human right violation against the Naxalites and also their friends. They keep the wounded Naxalites in a local hospital where hardly any medical facilities are available. They listen to local political leaders belonging to the ruling party and civil servants. Once an IAS officer comes and takes Gita without any problems whereas others suffer from humiliation there. The local political leaders come and try to help their friends and others. It is strange that the Indian state and its bureaucracy do not bother about the rule of law. Space in the Indian state is dominated by the bureaucrats and politicians backed by the corporate houses.

In reconstruction of the Indian Republic, the state has a role to play as it is supported by non-existent civil society. The society is based on a pyramidical social structure where Muslims and dalits are discriminated. Break of these social barriers are possible with the help of creative politics. Nehru's speech on Independence Day draws attention of Gandhians, Socialists, Communists who can help the evolution of a civil society, in which the Indian state would facilitate the developmental activities without violating human rights of ordinary citizens. But it is interesting to note here that common people living in rural hinterland suffer from humiliation and torture in the hands of the local administration. The local administration moves under the pressures of the corporate houses and the ruling party. There was commitment by the ruling Congress for implementing the Zamindari abolition; it was there in the election manifesto of the Congress Party for the 1946 election to the provincial assembly but it is ironical that the provincial administration in Bihar was at its worst on this front. The majority of the rural poor suffer in the hands of local landlords belonging to high caste. Caste oppression and class exploitation brought a section of the Communist Party to work for armed rebellion against these high caste landlords. The young people from Delhi University decided to join them in Bhojpur to mobilize the masses for structural changes. An impression has been created that they went from Delhi to create a new organization which is not correct (Mukherjee and Yadav : 1980).

Can it be called a political film? Indian film has got a parallel art film tradition which has a political meaning but not political film. This belongs to such a tradition but with a political text. An artist does not have to have political outlook to create such films. An artist as an autonomous actor in the creative world can create a film story with political message. This film does not create a political message not a melancholic feeling in the audience which is the purpose of a political film. Here Raghavendra's arguments are worth citing about 'Raajneeti' and 'Peepli Live' which are not political whereas 'Mother India' and 'Deewar' have political messages (Raghavendra, M. K., 2010, 13-15; 2011, 33-35). It is a beautiful art film done in an artistic manner (John Orr, 2000). In the era of globalization where corporate houses dominate the Hindi film world, there is a sharp decline in aesthetic standard of films in Bollywood (Rajadhyaksha, A., 2009). Sudhir Mishra's film (2003) is an exception.

A film has three languages which need to have unity to create a whole story. It has a literary text which tells a story. It uses romance of spoken words to tell the story. Secondly, the body language of actors signifies meanings through actions. Third, it has a cinematic language which is spoken with the help of movement of the camera. Intervention of technology has made it possible. This is the language of photography and symbolic meanings given to various metaphors. In this film all three languages have been blended together. The director of the film is trying to tell a human story with its various contours where a variety of emotions are playing together. Love, pathos and bravery are expressed in a symbolic manner. The story speaks about the human problem without unnecessary value judgment.

References :

Barik, R. K. (2006), *Land and Caste Politics in Bihar*, Shipra, New Delhi.

Eliot, T. S. 1980, 'The Love Song of J. Alfred Prufrock', in *New Golden Treasury of English Verse*, (ed) Macmillan Papermak, London.

John Orr (2000), *The Art and Politics of Film*, Edinburgh University Press, Edinburgh.

Mukherjee K. and Rajendra Singh Yadav (1980), *Bhojpur : Naxalism in the Plains of Bihar*, Radha Krishna, New Delhi.

Raghavendra, M. K. (2010), ''Peepli Live' and the Gesture of Concern' in *Economic and Political Weekly*, Vol VLV, No. 39.

— (2011), 'Renewal of Faith : 'Dabang' and Its Public' in *Economic and Political Weekly*, February 5, 2011 Vol XLVI No. 6.

Rajadhyaksha, Ashish (2009), *Indian Cinema in the Time of Celluloid : From Bollywood to the Emergency*, Tulika, New Delhi.

Vasudevan, R. (2000), 'Shifting Codes, Dissolving Identities' in Ravi Vasudevan (ed), *Making Meaning in Indian Cinema* (New Delhi : Oxford University Press).

The End is not Really the End : 'Sesh Sanghat' and the Media Obsession with Armed Resistance

Samata Biswas

The present paper is divided into three sections : the first is a somewhat detailed summary of the film, a summary that is deemed necessary for an analysis of it. Second is a critical engagement with the film that seeks to situate it in the socio-political context in which it was produced, and lays bare the techniques that the film utilizes to accommodate discourses of resistance into a narrative that nevertheless falls in line with the existing systems of domination. The third section tries to investigate the implications of such popular media engagement with people's movements.

I

The 2009 Bengali feature film 'Sesh Sanghat'[1] (to be roughly translated as the 'final confrontation') ought to be renamed following the 18th century English sentimental novel *Clarissa* : 'Raji - the Story of a Young Girl', both for the sentimentalism inherent in the film as well as the centrality of its female protagonist to the narrative and the action.

The title credits roll onto the screen at the beginning of the film with shots of faceless olive clad group of individuals rolling with hemp what looks like some kind of explosive, to be followed immediately with a landmine explosion in the middle of a road. With the end of the credits sequence the film moves on to something radically different - a village and its 'rural'ness : geese, pond, plants, and a baul.

The film begins with a baul singing and dancing to a song, clad in bright saffron, interspersed with establishing shots of children studying, kashphul, mud huts, and vessels of water being distributed to villagers by enterprising young girls. Several shots of him in the next half an hour or more, establish him to be an outsider, like the bauls would be, in a traditional village structure, but also an observer, through whose eyes we are first introduced to the young Raji (who would grow up to be Jayaprada), an active and pretty girl who also takes care of everyone and everything in the village. She catches the eye of the evil landlord - Ramanuj, who already has a wife and a mistress, and son born of the mistress but credited to be of the legal wife. This information becomes relevant later in the film. Both the wife and the mistress remonstrate with Ramanuj for his less than honourable intentions, but the girl is brought to his house by her parents who think that she is going to be a maid to the landlord's wife. Raji is raped in due course and becomes pregnant, an event that Ramanuj dislikes since that might get in the way of his electoral ambitions, he may have to forfeit his position as a leader of the lower castes - the tribes. Raji comes home to her parents, and after the child is born the entire village goes to confront Ramanuj who promises that Raji, along with the parents and the son will be taken to Kolkata where he has a house, and he will marry her eventually. Placated, the family starts on a journey to Kolkata, but they are attacked by Ramanuj's men who kill the parents, Raji becomes unconscious and the son is about to be killed. But a childless couple traveling along the same road rescues her, and Raji grows up, as the woman's sister. No one recognizes Raji while pulling water from the village well and discussing about the crimes against women that gets perpetrated at Ramanuj's home, Raji lashes out against them. But she also manages to attract the roving eye of Chhoto Sarkar (Ramanuj's son) as well as falling in love with her guardian's brother who has returned home after many years.

Parallel to this runs a narrative of the discovery of coal deposits in the land ruled by Ramanuj. He finds out that though the santhals of the area had leased out this land to his great grandfather for 999 years, under the new laws, tribal land can neither be bought, nor leased. He tries to find a way out, as the compensation for the coalmines to be dug up, he believes, ought rightfully to go to him, and not the tribes who now seem to be the owners of the land. Landmines also continue to explode, by 'adivasis' (distinguishable by their different dialects) who train in military fatigue, but fight with poisonous arrows. In a conversation, Pradip Basu points at the difference between the Maoist and the Naxalite movements, in terms of the modus operandi of the armed struggle. While the documents of Charu Majumdar advise the Naxalites to fight with the implements that they are most familiar with, so in the case of peasants, scythe and axes; the Maoists believe in the need to resist with the aid of modern arms and ammunitions. In 'Sesh Sanghat', the resistant forces are therefore the repositories of several signifying systems : termed "terrorists" by the authorities, by their own admission they are dispossessed adivasis; the visual and the narrative tropes of the film designate them as an iconic mix of popular and contemporary media references to the Naxalite and the Maoist movements.

Both the returned brother, Hemen and the baul help in linking together these two parallel narratives; they are both informers of the resistant group, as well as their leaders. They have knowledge of how to handle arms, and lead the group into successfully raiding Ramanuj's store of rice with the help of information delivered by a young boy who turns out to be Raji's son, rescued in the jungle by the baul, now referred as the Boss.

Chhoto Sarkar expresses the desire to marry Raji, in exchange of tax exemption for the entire village, and the village agrees. On their wedding night, Raji reveals to Chhoto Sarkar details of his bastard birth, and her relation with his father which puts her in the same position as his mother. He tries to kill her to prevent her from disclosing this to others, and in the ensuing scuffle, first blinds himself to a disembodied voice narrating the fate of Oedipus, and is killed.

Then things start to happen in rapid succession, Raji, having run away from the landlord's house, finds out the truth about the Boss and Hemen, and is captured in order to be burnt alive. She is helped to escape by Hemen, and when she and her son, on being pursued, asks the Boss to help them, he encourages them to help themselves. Raji finds herself in possession of unprecedented strength and defeats her captors. The Boss extols her by saying that throughout the ages people have believed that women depend on men for their well-being, but Raji, having proved them wrong, can now be the leader of the group. Through a session of training with both lathis and firearms, Raji emerges as a full-fledged member of the group. On the other hand, a new DIG of police is appointed to the region, which the audience is now told, lies in the Jharkhand border.

From Hemen's and Raji's speech to the people as well as to the DIG, the organization seems to have two demands. One, they seek reimbursement for the land that will be taken up for the coal mine (to which Ramanuj claims ownership) as following the 'new' laws, only the tribals are the rightful owners. Second, they do not want fertile land to be seized for industrial purposes, and predictably, like everything else in the film, Ramanuj is the force that seems to be driving the charge for industrialization as well. In her attempt to return the land deed to the tribals, Raji's son gets killed, and during a dialogue, so does Hemen.

Hemen's murder prompts Raji and the others to surrender to the DIG on the condition that their list of demands be met with. While congratulations start to pour in at his efficient handling of the 'extremists', the DIG is also promptly transferred so that Ramanuj can do away with the imprisoned. When he realizes that the corrupt politicians have no desire to honour his words, DIG, with a couple of other 'honest' police officers, free the prisoners, who are now being called "Naxalites". What ensues is fierce gun battle between the combined forces of Ramanuj, the military, the police on one side and the escaped members of the outfit with the DIG on the other. One by one most of resistant group die, including the Boss and their supporter, the DIG. Raji is one of the few survivors, beating and hanging Ramanuj from a tree, to be burnt alive by the villagers. Raji and the others are arrested by the police, and they are bid a tearful farewell by the village, the police van starts moving, with the words "Is this the end?" appearing on the centre of the screen.

II

This somewhat lengthy summary of the film is necessary in order to be able to better demonstrate some of the tropes that make this film interesting, and worthy of critical attention, in light of the impact of Naxalite and Maoist movements on cinema. Like much of mainstream Indian films, this one also draws on popular media discourses, images and understanding of these movements[2] , and on the relatively recent debates and movements surrounding land acquisition in Bengal[3]. So on one hand, a close examination of the film will reveal the narrative and cinematic strategies that the film uses and develops to deal with such contemporary incidents and discourses; while on the other hand, it serves as yet another reminder of how dominant discourses manage to accommodate resistance and dissent within overarching narratives that seek to maintain legitimacy for the systems of domination.

This can be best seen in the figure of Ramanuj. In Ramanuj is reinvented the conventional type of the evil landlord, with all the vices of nature concentrated in him. He is lascivious, lustful, malicious, corrupt and a murderer. The older structures of power enabled him to rule over and own all the surrounding land, tribal land. As in the real life situation, Ramanuj does not belong to the same castes or tribes that most of the villagers do. His caste is never mentioned, even though his upper-caste-ness is hinted at through the repeated assertion of the caste of the other, of Raji and her family, her surrogate family and her team members : they are Rajbangshi. The marker of this otherness is the different dialect that they speak in. However, it is extremely interesting to note that as soon as Raji and the others complete their training under the Boss and Hemen (both outsiders : the Boss as a baul does not have a specific location, and Hemen has just returned from the outside), who speak the same standardized Bengali that Ramanuj does, their (of the adivasis under training) dialects also assume the normative shape. More on this, later.

To return to Ramanuj : he adapts to new hierarchies after the abolition of Zamindari system, by becoming the MP for the area and effectively controlling the other MPs of the region. He wishes to collect compensation for the land which will be acquired by the government after coal deposits are found in the surrounding jungle. He also controls the local police and bureaucracy, and hoards food grains and ammunition. He also is the chief perpetrator of crimes against women.

Concentrating all kinds of criminal and violent tendencies in the person of Ramanuj, enables the film to construct him as an aberration, a perversion. Positing him as a perversion allows the film to depict the 'system', i.e. the legislative and judicial organs of the state, as fair and just. Since Ramanuj is an aberration, as are the corrupt bureaucrats and the police men, then the norm that they are an aberration to, must be the opposite of what they are, that is, must be fair. Even when the corrupt police and bureaucrats, who all seem to be Ramanuj's stooges, appear more numerous than the honest ones, both the resistant groups and the few honest ones maintain their faith in the rule of law.

The adivasis explain that they have taken up arms for two reasons. The first reason, and the one that has supporting evidence from the rest of the narrative is that after the government agencies find coal deposit in the forest inhabited by them, the adivasis become apprehensive that since they do not have the ownership deeds, Ramanuj would cheat them out of their legitimate compensation. They make claims of ownership to this land because according to the laws of post-independence India, "...tribal land can neither be sold, nor leased out". Nowhere is there a claim to be the rightful owner of this land because they are the "adivasis" - the original inhabitants. The rights discourse that informs their engagement with the state and its operatives, are also drawn from the state. They have rights over the land because the state has declared so; and the infringement of their rights is a result of the wrongdoings by some perverse elements like Ramanuj.

However, in a report regarding the Indian state's attitude towards the adivasi people, Stan Swamy (2010) writes, the crux of the way the state machinery functions is : "Dispossess them first, and [then] hunt them down as criminals". Writing about the situation of the adivasis in Jharkhand (and it has to be borne in mind that even the location of the film is supposed to be somewhere on the Jharkhand border), Swamy shows how a nexus of politicians, urbanites and bureaucrats, totaling only 23% of the population of the state place the burden of 'progress' and 'development' on the shoulder of the majority adivasis, usually forcing their displacement without any rehabilitation. The historic 'Samata Judgment' clearly stated that following the Forest Protection Act of 1980 - in the case of mining being prohibited in reserved areas, even the state had to adhere to the these prohibitions, as any other person (Krishnakumar 2004). What the very need for this judgment points to, is the injustice inherent in the logic of governmental practices, where the burden of development and progress is always to be borne by the already marginalized sections of the society.

In this film though, the logic of development or its impact upon the dispossessed is never questioned. Instead, as an aside, we are presented with the second reason for their resistance : land cannot be taken up for industrialization. While nowhere else in the film is there any mention of any proposed industry other than the coal mine, the rhetoric of the resistant group therefore contradicts itself. While they demand compensation for the coal mine to be built, as that compensation is their right, they oppose the imaginary industry. It is my contention that the film finds it necessary to include such contradiction within itself in order to safely place itself in a discourse of rights, guaranteed by the state. The logic of development that further alienates the already marginalized by not merely displacing them, but also taking away their livelihood and their existing way of life, is not something that the film opposes. Numerous reports have shown how Indian tribal land rights continue to be in jeopardy from coal mines, but by conveniently evading the question of whether the proposed mine will be a public or a private enterprise, the film shows that mere compensation for the land to be mined will safeguard tribal rights. The anti-industrialization rhetoric acts simply as a sop that refers back to the political situation in Bengal in the first decade of the 21st century. With the drive for development safely in place with the coal mine, the anti-industrialization speech by Raji and Hemen can simply be treated as an aside, since the charge of their action as well as that of the narrative falls well within the domain of development and rights, deemed to be guaranteed by the Indian state.

The figure of Ramanuj therefore allows the film to retain its faith in law and the Indian state (a faith shared by the resistant group as well). Therefore when the faith is broken, it is because some individuals chose to misuse their positions of power, like many of the bureaucrats and policemen do. On the other hand are honest police officers like the DIG, who seek to uphold the spirit of the constitutional guarantee of protection to all citizens. Being 'good' or being 'bad' therefore becomes a matter of choice, not something that is closely connected to structures of power. Inequality therefore is not structural, not inherent to the ways society and concepts of development etc. are organized, but are the result of some malpractitioners' willful corruption of the system.

In such a formation, resistance is also not a function of power; instead, it is also a matter of choice. All the adivasis in Ramanuj's jurisdiction are oppressed, but only some choose to resist - like Raji. In the scene where Raji fights to save herself and her son from Ramanuj's men, after almost being burnt alive, she is encouraged by the Boss to fight back, and that encouragement is all that she needs to find the strength to do so.

Interestingly, the charge for resistance comes from the outside. The baul who is found to be the Boss is not merely an outsider because of his position as a baul in the traditional village structure; also he is different from the people he leads through his diction, the syntax of his speech, his dialect. Ramanuj's nayeb and the DIG both address the Boss as an outsider; they charge him of inciting the people and making them rise up in revolt. It is the Boss who encourages Raji to take up arms and her as well as the other women's dialects changes with the training that they undergo, as they take on the Boss's dialect.

The women in question tell Raji how their lives, even without children or husbands, have changed for the better. And this conversation takes place in their newly acquired dialect, in the speech of the outsider. The way women are treated and viewed in this film also sheds light on the understanding of inequality within the context of the film. Towards the very beginning, while trying to caution Raji about Ramanuj's intentions, his legitimate wife mourns the lot of women. However, the rest of the film proceeds as if the repeated sexual violence directed against Raji by Ramanuj and his son, is a result of her being so attractive that she catches the eye of both the father and the son. When the camera views Raji from Ramanuj or the son's perspective, she is always shown to stand out among the group, either referring a wrestling match between boys, or bending over in a deserted courtyard, sweeping. Therefore, if sexual violence is perpetrated by sexually and otherwise perverse individuals, and perpetrated against exceptionally attractive/desirable women, then it is not engendered by the way patriarchal societies are structured, or the way sexual violence is used as a tool of control.

Hence injustice against the adivasis and that against women, are treated in a similar manner. Neither is inherent to the way societies, government or policies are structured, but are the result of individuals in positions of power exploiting the said societies, governments and policies, a fact which brings us to the point of this paper anyway, the impact of the Naxalite movement on films.

III

As mentioned earlier, the politics of nomenclature in the film raises interesting questions about the understanding of the Naxalite and Maoists movements in popular media, as well as their representation. While iconography of the resistance group in the film is clearly Maoist, with its uniformed fighters and the flag with scythe and hammer (especially prominent on the cover of the VCD), the film never calls the resistance by that name. They are terrorists to the police and Ramannuj, extremists to Amar Singh and the DIG, and Naxalites in one instance to a corrupt bureaucrat. This easy conflation of terrorism, extremism and Naxalism, with Maoist iconography points at the ease with which the plight of the dispossessed tribals has been solved in popular media rhetoric. They are simple and dispossessed, they have to be brought enlightenment and emancipation in two ways : one, through positive legislation and honest government agents who will implement that legislation, and second : through outside intellectual input like the Boss who will inform them of their dispossession and inspire them to be pro-active to end it. Women, when they are adivasis, are doubly dispossessed, but their dispossession can also be treated by breaking out of the family and being incorporated into a structure that replicates the familial space, including the space for desire. At the same time, it has to be noted that there is no space within the film for peaceful protests. It has been well-documented in various reports across India, that corporate and government attempts to acquire land for mines etc. have engendered peaceful protest among the indigenous population, protests that have been brutally cracked down either directly by state machinery or through state assisted vigilante groups[4].

The current protest against POSCO's acquisition of forest land in Orissa may be a case in point. In May 2010, armed police battalions attacked unarmed villagers who had been peacefully protesting against the acquisition, setting fire to shops, eateries and homes, firing upon unarmed villagers with rubber bullets at the dharna site. However, the movement again picked up momentum in 2011 when it successfully resisted armed forces trying to forcibly occupy their territory by thousands of people, with women and children at the forefront lying in thousands, upon hot sand dunes, showing their resolve and strength against corporate take-over of their land and livelihood. But it is very rarely that peaceful movements succeed, and even more rarely that they manage to capture popular media imagination. As the recent hullabaloo surrounding the anti-corruption protests show, the media houses and newspapers are driven by the interests of the people that are the consumers of the images that they produce : as a result the fast of Anna Hazare raises popular concern, and that of Irom Sharmila goes unnoticed for years.

The movement from peaceful protest to armed resistance is neither smooth nor uncomplicated, and armed resistances in all parts of India have their own specific histories and memories of oppression, histories that have been overlooked by 'Sesh Sanghat' in order to sensationalise its narrative and to cash in on the current media obsession with all things militant.

As the film works with positing a single repository of all things that merit resistance, it also puts forward a single mode of protest, and one single reason which makes it worth protesting. Ramanuj as the single signifier of all things evil and unjust[5] serves to accord legitimacy to the system from which he is an aberration. Similarly, the armed resistance that finally puts an end to Ramanuj (in this case through the extraordinary might of one woman) can only be used to annihilate such extraordinary and perverse injustice. But when the injustice is systemic, and perpetrated by the state (irrespective of the government in power) - the state that in universe of the film is the giver and protector of rights, then surely such means of protest will fail, as the surviving members of the group seem to realize at the end of the film, when they give in peacefully to the police. It is the film's inherent faith in the system that allows it to reach its resolution. The demon villain is defeated, and since it was through his corruption that the adivasis were denied their rights, after his death all wrongs must therefore be automatically righted. Hence, the need for the armed resistance is removed, and reconciliation with the state made possible.

The film self-consciously stops from naming the resistance movement of the adivasis, but at one instance its reluctance to name breaks down, and a corrupt bureaucrat calls them the "Naxals". Despite this one act of naming, and therefore framing the resistance, the film does not show any understanding of the Naxalite movement. It does not feel that "Inequitable government policies, absence of justice, land issues, a weak and corrupt administration, dearth of political actors who channelise people's concerns on the ground, forced displacement and insensitivity to non-violent movements have all contributed to creating space for an armed outfit that questions the legitimacy of the political system" (Jha 2009). But since the political system of the state is the legitimizing force in the film, the action of the resistance is confined to ousting Ramanuj, it does not raise any more questions, or demand further answers.

'Sesh Sanghat' therefore continues to be a narrative that seeks to reconcile contemporary popular and mass movements within the framework of existing structures : the system is deemed to be just and fair, all that is required is a few agents who will make it functional.

References :

Apoorv Anand (2010), "Violence and revolution" <http://kafila.org/2010/04/02/violence-and-revolution/> accessed on 23.04.2011.

Arati Choksi (2011), "POSCO and the People", <http://kafila.org/2011/09/08/posco-and-the-people-ayush-ranka-and-arati-choksi/> accessed on 09.09.2011.

Ashok Krishnakumar (2004), "The 'Samata Judgment" <http://www.hinduonnet.com/fline/fl2119/stories/20040924006001200.htm> accessed on 12.03.2011.

Deepankar Basu (2010), "Indepentdent People's Tribunal Reveal the Underbelly of Indian development" <http://sanhati.com/articles/2298/> accessed on 22.02.2011.

Partha Chatterjee (2011), "Against Corruption= Against Politics", <http://kafila.org/2011/08/28/against-corruption-against-politics-partha-chatterjee/> accessed on 29.08.2011.

Pradip Basu (Ed.) (2010), *Discourses on Naxalite Movement (1967- 2009)*, Kolkata : Setu Prakashani.

Prashant Jha (2009), "Complicating the 'Naxalite' Debate". <http://kafila.org/2009/10/22/complicating-the-naxalite-debate/> accessed on 25.04.2011.

Stan Swamy (2010), "Dispossess them first, and then hunt them down as criminals" <http://newswing.com/node/36> accessed on 12.03.2011.

"Indian tribal land rights in jeopardy from new coal mine" <http://www.minesandcommunities.org/article.php?a=1822> accessed on 14.03.2011.

Notes :

1. Directed by Ashok Viswanathan, produced by Jayaprada and Ramesh Gandhi. The lead role is played by Jayaprada, the erstwhile Hindi actress and now a Samajwadi Party MP. Important figures of the contemporary

Bengali film industry also feature in the film : Sabyasachi Chakrabarti as Hemen, Chiranjit as the Baul and Hindi actors like Ashish Vidyarthi and Jackie Shroff are also present. The Samamjwadi Party leader Amar Singh plays himself in a a cameo.

2. Examples of these discourses will be not merely newspaper reports, but also widespread paranoia fuelled speculations that lead to the blaming of the Maoists every time something blows up in Bengal (much like how in a pan-indian context terrorism has only an Islamic face), the suspicion of everything that calls itself radical left and the easy conflation of Naxalism and Maoism in such a manner that the two tags are often used interchangeably. This can be seen in the film in question as well.
3. Singur and Nandigram being the most visible cases in point.
4. The neo-liberal turn in the economic policies pursued by the Indian State since the mid-1980s has, in line with similar experiences in the rest of the world, spelt unmitigated disaster for the vast masses of the country. While a small section of the population has increased its income, wealth and social power at unimaginable speed and to preposterous levels, the majority of the population has continued to live in absolute poverty, marked by widespread hunger, malnutrition, and lack of access to even the most basic health and educational infrastructure necessary to guarantee a decent standard of living.... Not only has the neo-liberal economic paradigm meant increasing disparities, it has also meant dispossession and pauperization for already-vulnerable sections of the population, noted the interim observation of the people's jury. This is because a key component of the neo-liberal paradigm in India has been the attempt to foster unprecedented levels of State-assisted resource grab by big Indian and foreign capital. What a ministry of rural development report itself termed the biggest resource grab since the time of Columbus, has gradually encompassed arable (often extremely fertile and multi-cropped) land, forest land, mineral resources, and water and has resulted in forcibly cutting off access of the poor and marginalized sections to virtually all forms of common property resources. Coming on top of the five decade long "development disaster" of the Indian state, this forcible exclusion from access to common property resources has increased the economic vulnerability of the poor to unprecedented levels - Basu (2010).

5. Writing about the recent anti-corruption movement led by Anna Hazare, Partha Chatterjee (2011) shows how the anti-corruption rhetoric has managed to posit corruption as something that always "someone else does". He further shows how the conflation of corruption (in the current popular sense) with politics (as something that politicians do) has enabled the participants in the movement to dissociate the notion of corruption from their everyday lives. "The categorization of corruption as something that belongs to the domain of "the political" (in the popular sense, i.e., ministers, MPs, MLAs, bureaucrats) ensures that corruption can never touch "the people". It is something that only characterizes the enemy". In a similar manner, 'Sesh Sanghat' also manages to posit all the injustices in the person of the enemy, and from its statist point of view, manages to absolve the state of all responsibility.

'Hazaar Chaurasi ki Maa'

Shatarupa Sengupta

The Naxalite Movement of the 1960s and 1970s has been a constant source of inspiration for the literati resulting in numerous poems, novels, short stories and also movies. An entire generation which believed that it could bring a positive change in India's civil and political society marred by corruption, injustice, hunger and poverty fired the creative instincts of the Indian society's intellectuals who registered their protest through their writings or paintings or visual narrative. One such seminal work is Mahasweta Devi's Bengali novel *Hajar Churashir Ma* (Mother of 1084) which was later adapted as a Hindi movie, 'Hazaar Chaurasi Ki Maa' by Govind Nihalini of 'Aakrosh' and 'Ardh Satya' fame.

It is almost a cliché to say that one must never judge a book by its movie. Here we can turn this truism on its head and say that this movie cannot be judged by the novel. Though, an adaptation of the novel, the film 'Hazaar Chaurasi Ki Maa' has certain add-ons which display a completely different perspective. The novel ends in ambiguity which we will discuss later while the movie has a typical Hindi film style 'happy ending'. Perhaps the way this film ended enabled the Indian government to appropriate the memory of a movement which had died a violent death. This attempt at appropriation explains the National Award that it got in 1998 for best Regional Hindi Film. Also the film was made more than twenty five years after the movement had ceased to be a threat to the State. The novel was written sometime in 1973 or 1974 right after the movement had ceased to be active. Commenting on her novel Mahasweta Devi had once outlined her purpose,

> In the Seventies, in the Naxalite Movement, I saw exemplary integrity, selflessness and the guts to die for a cause. I thought I saw history in the making, and decided that as a writer it should be my mission to document it. As a writer, I feel a commitment to my times, to mankind and to myself. I did not consider the Naxalite Movement an isolated happening...In the Naxalite movement I saw only a further extension of the movements of the past, especially Tebhaga, Kakdwip and Telengana uprisings...In *[Hajar Churashir Ma]* I portrayed the Naxalite movement in its urban phase in 1971-74; and against that and a generation gap, I set an apolitical mother's quest to know her martyred Naxalite son, to know what he stood for; for she had not known the true Brati ever, as long as he had been alive. Death brings him closer to her through her quest[1].

The manner of Bratis and his comrades' killing reminds us of the Barasat killing in November 1970 when several young men were found murdered with their hands tied behind them and also the Baranagar killing of August 1971 which went largely un-reported, the space being taken up by jubilant reports of the Bangladesh Liberation War.

Sujata may have been apolitical but she yearns for an understanding of her son's death. As she begins her quest she is compelled to look at a society which had wasted into a state of fraudulence. Samik Bandopadhyay in his introduction in the translated version of *Hajar Churashir Ma* states that,

> In *Mother of 1084* even while Mahasweta evokes and re-creates the killings of the Naxalites, she concentrates on the later reactions - and lack of reaction - of a cross section of the survivors, both those who bear the scars and wounds - both literally and figuratively - of those horrible days and those who had lived through the days of violence in simulated insularity. The adoration of godmen, the euphoria over the Bangladesh war, the fashionable pretences of literary radicalism, and scandals, commercial and amorous, constituted for the latter a lifestyle that guaranteed their security. What stands out in Mahasweta's elaborate exposure of the Chatterjee family and its art of survival is their systematic denial of Brati and his defiance of the family....[2].

The cast of this film consists of Jaya Bhaduri as Sujata Chatterjee, Anupam Kher as her husband Dibyanath Chatterjee, Joy Sengupta as Brati Chatterjee, Nandita Das as Nandini Mitra, Milind Gunaji as Police Officer Saroj Pal, Seema Biswas as Somu's mother, Sandeep Kulkarni as Nitu, Yashpal Sharma as Laltu and others. While Jaya Bhaduri and Anupam Kher are mainstream Hindi film actors, Joy Sengupta and Nandita Das were fairly fresh faces. The dialogues are by Tripurari Sharma and the film was produced by Manmohan Shetty.

The movie is a mosaic of many features - it is a portrayal of decadent Bengal in the decades of the 60s and 70s, it satires the pretense of the Bengali affluent, the artists and self-styled intellectuals as is evident from the last scene, depicts the honest ideology of the Naxalites when Brati tells his father that he wishes for an egalitarian society, talks about the deviation that the movement went through when Brati and Nitu tell their comrades that individual acts of killing will not get them anywhere, shows the state-police-lumpen proletariat nexus when Brati, Somu, Partho and Bijit are killed by local goons, narrates the death of the movement and also its attempts to rise from its own ashes when Nandini tells Sujata that she will continue her fight against a repressive system and within so many varied themes it tells the story of Sujata Chatterjee, an upper-middle class working woman who receives a phone call one night asking her to come to the police morgue to identify the corpse of her youngest son Brati Chatterjee.

In the movie Sujata works in a commercial bank. We find out from the novel that she had to take on that job when Dibyanath had run into bad times and needed financial support. Thus Sujata's economic independence is not a matter of choice rather it is a decision taken out of need. Perhaps this explains her passivity in spite of her inherently independent nature which is revealed in the first scene itself. She has three older children either employed or married. She performs her duties as a wife and mother to perfection because that is what she has been taught since her girlhood days. It has almost become a habit.

Coming to the first scene what will perhaps strike the viewer is a much younger Sujata in a maternity clinic alone for the delivery of her youngest son Brati. She is not accompanied by her husband or family members as she struggles to climb the stairs of the clinic with her baggage. The novel reveals that Dibyanath never accompanied Sujata for childbirth. She has had four pregnancies and every time she takes care of her needs alone. Her husband keeps away lest the cries of the newborn disturb him.

We are struck by Sujata's self-sufficiency even in physical discomfort and mental anxiety. Her independence makes us question her subservience to her husband. She is not domesticated in the traditional sense where the woman occupies the personal space and has limited interaction with the public sphere, where she is protected by her father or husband or son. Sujata moves between the private and the public sphere and yet her economic independence has been subordinated to her duties at home as if her act of earning is merely an extension of her wifely and motherly duties. Her involvement at home is greater than her husband Dibyanath's and yet she is strangely alienated. Decisions are taken by her husband. She has no role in them. Her older children recognize their father's authority completely ignoring their mother. What does her subordination spring from? Or is it truly an act of subservience? Is it an attempt to maintain the fragile fabric of an imagined respectable bourgeois household where the husband indulges in adultery and ill-treatment and the older children turn a blind eye? Or is it Sujata's way to ignore a system which exploits her at every level? Is it her sense of pride and dignity which keeps her away from her husband and children? Her only true link with her family is her youngest son Brati whose death shatters her and impels her to rework her life.

Brati was a Naxalite, a fact Sujata discovers after his death. But what baffles her is the knowledge that she as a mother never came to know or understand her son's political beliefs. In a series of scenes moving between the present and the past she tries to reconstruct the last few days of her son as he spent with his Naxalite friends, his dreams, his ideologies and the frustration that the youth of his age felt over a rotting system. She finds a connection between her own oppression in the household to that of the poor and the downtrodden outside and finally decides to resist like her son.

To say that this movie is only about the Naxalite Movement would not be completely correct, though the director has captured the essence of the movement through Brati's conversations with his mother and comrades. It is more about an individual's interaction with society and the State and the conflict which emerges out of it. Sujata leaves the realm of her private space to find others like her, who belong to a different economic and social class like Somu's mother, a poor illiterate Bihari woman who had also lost her son the same night Brati was killed. In the novel Somu's family is depicted as the first generation partition refugees who had settled down in the slums of Calcutta. Perhaps the act of turning Somu's mother into an immigrant from Bihar is an attempt to evade a possible political controversy. The two women are united in their grief and provide Sujata a glimpse of life she had never seen or known before. She connects with Somu's mother the way she cannot connect with her other family members who are shown busy trying to hush up the news of Bratis' brutal death from people they know. Dibyanath and Jyoti are shown pulling the strings in the right circles to prevent the name of Brati appearing in the list of dead in the next day's newspapers. They refuse to go to 'Kantapukur', the police morgue to identify their son and brother. Sujata goes with Tuli her younger daughter.

Brati has been killed for being a Naxalite. He had aspired for an equal society where all human beings have access to equal rights and live a life of dignity and liberty. But the state does not recognize an individual's aspirations or dissatisfaction or anguish. It believes in greater good, in maintaining the status quo and in that process does not shirk away from sacrificing those who do not agree with it. It is a strict disciplinarian relentlessly striving to homogenize a plural society. It trespasses into the private sphere of an individual's grief and refuses Brati's mother the right to perform her son's last rites with dignity. It is a poignant moment when Sujata after identifying Brati in the morgue expresses her wish to take her "son" home and Saroj Pal, the Police Officer tells her that the "body" cannot be handed over to her. Brati, though dead is still alive in Sujata's memories, which makes her refer to him as her son while for the State he becomes body number 1084, a rebel who has been reduced to a body with a number, a nameless, lifeless body whose voice would not be heard again, who has ceased to be a threat to the state, who has received just punishment for being a "criminal" as Saroj Pal implied. A search of Brati's room after his death reveals a collection of his poems, some Marxist literature and a few harmless posters hailing the Naxalbari uprising. When Sujata asks for her son's collection of poems, Saroj Pal refuses by saying that it had to be confiscated as "criminal evidence" of Brati's subversive activities. He chastises Sujata's upbringing saying that it is her fault that her son had become a 'goonda' (criminal). He tells her that he belonged to a gang who called themselves Naxalites and it is every citizen's duty to help cull this gang. But Brati had committed no crime in the ordinary sense. He did not believe in the annihilation line of later Naxalite Movement as is evident from his conversation with his comrades Laltu, Nitu, Anindya and Nandini. In that scene he explicitly remarks on the mistake of killing petty police officials as that would alienate the populace from the movement. By attaching the tag 'criminal' to Brati and his comrades, the State is shown to use criminality as a way to shun resistance which could lead to a revolution.

Each character in this movie represents to perfection the various echelons of our society. Dibyanath Chatterjee, Sujata's husband and his three older children are a typical Bengali Bhadrolok family, immensely proud of their affluence, culture and education. They are ashamed of their association with Brati and work hard to keep the news of his death away from press for fear of retribution. They do not talk about him and neither do they allow Sujata the scope to grieve for her favorite child's death. For them life goes on as if nothing had happened, as if Brati as a living and thinking entity never existed.

The façade of Dibyanath's respectability is depicted sharply when slurring under the effect of alcohol, he tells Brati, "You are a national scholarship holder and belong to a respectable, cultured family. What else can you ask for?" It almost has a comical effect and is a rare moment in the movie where a viewer may smile. In another scene Brati's family members question each other's religious beliefs and Sujata intervenes by asking her daughter Tuli why she considers her belief correct and others' false? Tuli is a typical example of a class which refuses to look beyond its own understanding of the world we reside in. She is arrogant, self-contained and almost cruelly asks her mother to forget the dead and concentrate on the living.

Coming back to Somu's mother - she is a sharp contrast to Sujata as she belongs to the class of have-nots. Sujata meets her in her humble dwelling where Somu's mother breaks down on seeing someone who has also lost her child in the same incident. She is uninhibited in her display of grief over her son's loss. Unlike Sujata she is not impeded by her class status from expressing her mind and emotions. Her poverty and lack of "respectability" liberate her from the restrictions that Sujata is subjected to where she is hesitant about expressing her grief and cries under the cover of darkness. She addresses Sujata as 'didi'[3] which is an indication of her helplessness and deference. And yet Somu's mother's lot is hardest hit. While Sujata continues with her bank job, Somu's sister fails to find employment for being related to him. Somu's mother's illiteracy doesn't prevent her from understanding the basic class distinctions. She aptly sums up when she tells Sujata that her class ensures her immunity from social ostracism. She is also more aware about the movement and tells Sujata how hundreds of young people have lost their lives or homes to State repression. She scores a point over Sujata when she reveals her awareness about her son's participation in the Naxalite movement unlike Sujata who had no clue about Brati's political leanings. Somu's sister like Brati's siblings are angry and disgusted over her brother's political standing albeit the anger arises from a different source. While for Somu's sister it has become a daily struggle for survival, Brati's siblings find that it affects their status as scions of modern, rational, peaceful family to be associated with a Naxalite. Through the interaction of these two women belonging to two completely different classes, the director has movingly depicted how differently this movement affected the poor as well as the affluent. While Brati's family could buy their anonymity, Somu's family has to endure a constant threat.

Sujata's meeting with Nandini, Brati's comrade and also his love interest works as an eye opener for the former. Through a prolonged conversation with Sujata which at many times assumed the proportions of a monologue, Nandini brings alive Brati's revolutionary ideals as well as his inner contradictions. Through her Sujata comes to know that while he loved his mother immensely, he was disturbed over his father's behavior towards his mother. Perhaps Sujata's daily humiliation at the hands of Dibyanath forced Brati to re-think the social equations and question a society which believed in hiding infidelity, dishonesty, hypocrisy, immorality under the shroud of respectability. Perhaps his intense desire to see his mother free of this exploitation made him want to change the entire system. Nandini like Sujata is restrained but at the same time she is resolute to continue her struggle for her ideology. She believes in pure commitment to her cause and is not shaken by the verbal and physical torture she has been subjected to while doing her term in prison. Nonetheless, Nandini does not completely break the barrier of "socially imposed division of the sexes"[4]. During her interrogation at the hands of Saroj Pal we come to know that she acted as a messenger for Brati and his comrades, hid their arms and literature, attended meetings and was undergoing training in making pipe guns. She is the follower, providing support and inspiration when she reads out revolutionary poem to Brati in spite of the fact that she has thoroughly grasped the ideology of the movement. She is not an activist like Brati or Nitu or Laltu though at the end we see an older Nandini working among the tribals and also fighting a legal case against Saroj Pal for violating human rights. It is she who tells Sujata that they had made a mistake in deviating from the original line of organizing villages and tribal areas. It is she who identifies Anindya as the traitor and tells Brati several times that Anindya should not be trusted as his ideology is not consistent. In the movie Nandini tells Brati that he has left one 'group' to be in their 'group'[5] but in the novel the author is more lucid when Nandini says that they had not joined the party as dissidents whereas Anindya had broken away from the old party and had joined them with definite instructions. Nandini also tells Sujata that Brati was right about turning the Naxalbari uprising into a mass movement so as to make it successful. She tells Sujata that they will continue their fight, their resistance to an exploitative system.

Nandini acts as a catalyst for Sujata who begins questioning the system which exploits individuals at every level. She comes back home to make one last attempt to counter her family. In the novel she ticks off Tuli for laying a claim to Brati's share of family heirlooms, confronts Dibyanath and tells him that she has known all along about his infidelity and then dresses up as usual to play hostess to her guests for Tuli's engagement. In the movie we find her confronting Dibyanath and also expressing her reluctance to wear 'sindoor'[6] while dressing up for the ceremony. This denial is a clue to Sujata's new found independence where we find her trying to break free from the set pattern and also signals to the viewer that she may expect a transformation in Sujata in the epilogue.

The three women, Somu's mother, Sujata and Nandini though represent a hierarchy of self-assertion and independence[7] , are not water-tight compartments. There is a suggestion of movement between the rungs as is evident from Somu's mother's awareness about the movement or Sujata's increasing attempt at self-assertion.

The movie bursts out at the scene of Tuli's engagement ceremony on Brati's second death anniversary where a pseudo revolutionary poet Dhiman Roy is seen reciting pro-Naxalbari poems to a bored audience who ridicule him for plagiarism and cowardice. Roy, a typical representation of the bourgeois pseudo-intellectual, is shown writing about the Bangladesh Liberation War during the heat of the movement when most of the State-sponsored acts of terrorism took place. Once the movement ended he began writing about the thousands of young men languishing in the jails. This observation is generally true for other kinds of media as well. From April 1971, most of the newspapers in Bengal and also the national capital went quiet about the Naxalite movement and went into a frenzy reporting the East Pakistan and West Pakistan war in which India provided military, diplomatic and logistical support to the former. Especially worth noting is *Amrita Bazar Patrika* which carried page-long articles, pictures, editorials and op-eds. An enquiring mind today will search in vain to find out where the Naxalite movement in the first few years of the 1970s was heading if it relied on this newspaper[8].

We also see Dibyanath lauding the police for effectively handling the Naxalite situation and his friend stating that the movement would have any way died a natural death as revolutions do not achieve anything. We find the other guests criticizing Brati and his generation notwithstanding the fact that it was his second death anniversary and thus a sad day for his mother. Towards the end, Saroj Pal, the officer-in-charge of investigating and controlling the Naxalite uprising is shown attending the orgy. He refuses to get down from his jeep on pretext of duty[9]. He is a close friend of Tony, Tuli's fiancé and is thus a special invitee, notwithstanding the fact that he and the likes of him have been responsible for Brati and his friends' death. Again Sujata's reaction on seeing Pal is not clearly etched out in the movie. We can sense her anguish and also shock but we cannot gather what goes on in her mind. The novel tells us that Sujata wonders 'where is the unquiet? Where is the duty?' She realizes that Pal is out on his controlling and killing mission and before long another Brati will die.

The climax is reached when all the guests under the effect of alcohol sway to some lilting music. Their profligacy, pretense, snobbery and wealth disgust Sujata who cries out to Brati and asks him for what has he given up his life? Is it for a society that has died but continues to put up a veneer of living by denying thousands their fair share of life? She yells in pain and collapses, apparently from a burst appendix. The novel ends here. Mahasweta Devi has introduced a thin line of clue in the form of a recurring appendix pain throughout the novel. It is a signal which we begin to pick up towards the end of the story when we find Sujata relying increasingly on painkillers and lime juice to abate the shooting pain. Her last cry of pain is not only physical but 'spiritual'[10] as well.

Here the movie deviates from the novel. Sujata's collapse and

Dibyanath's exclamation indicate a new beginning when in the next scene Sujata is shown again in a maternity clinic with a newborn child. Whether it is a flashback about Brati's birth or whether this scene is a metaphor for Sujata's rebirth as a mother and a woman out on a journey of self-assertion is left to the viewer's imagination. The scene moves on to the Chatterjee household where a much older Sujata and Dibyanath are shown together. Dibyanath seems to have mellowed down. He also seems apologetic about his past behavior when he asks Sujata whether he can meet Nandini. He asks Sujata, "Do you think she will be annoyed to see me?" Nandini makes a comeback in their life when she calls up Sujata and expresses her desire to meet her. Sujata has taken up a new 'avatar'. She is now a Human Rights activist and helps run a documentation centre with Nitu, Brati's ex-comrade who we find out from the dialogues has become an academician. The four (Sujata, Dibyanath, Nandini and Nitu) meet at their documentation centre where we find out what each has been doing with his or her life.

In the last scene we find Nitu being shot dead in broad daylight in front of Sujata who manages to attach herself to one of the killers and impedes his escape long enough for the public to arrive and assist her. The movie ends with Sujata writing to Brati and telling him that another man has been killed, another act of cruelty has been committed but it has not gone un-resisted. She tells him that she has made his cause her own, not out of grief but out of a realization that resisting an act of cruelty or oppression is her cause as well and every time she does that she feels that she has given birth to Brati all over again and in that awareness she finds herself closer to him as a mother, friend and comrade. Thus for Sujata, Brati was no longer only a victim of State repression, he had become a symbol of resistance for his mother.

While the film ends on a note of hope, it also waters down the political content of the novel. Although a definite ending gives the film a neat look, it is also beset with a singular disadvantage - it does not linger in the mind of the viewer for long as once out of the theatre, she is ready to look for a new story. The sense of totality robs a depiction of its power to haunt the watcher for long. The viewer will no longer ponder on what the outcome may have been or what it should have been. It does not leave much to the interpretation of the audience. Ideally a political movie instead of making a statement should leave leads for critical thinking.

Nonetheless, as mentioned earlier in an attempt at appropriation it would have been dangerous to leave the ending ambiguous. An open end leaves a lot to the imagination of the viewer which may not be desirable. A relief must be provided to prevent the viewer from despairing or debating or rethinking the societal and political equations and also to make it acceptable to the powers that be.

Still we cannot deny the fact that 'Hazaar Chaurasi ki Maa' is definitely a political movie in more than one sense. If we compare it to another Hindi film made a few years later by Sudhir Mishra, ('Hazaaron Khwaishein Aisi' which roughly means 'A Thousand Such Desires'), it does not use the Naxalite motif simply to weave a story around the main characters. In that movie one of the characters is a Naxalite which offsets his difference from another character who was brought up in a household which believed in Gandhism. The political ideologies were not the central theme or even the sub-topic. The ideologies are just logos to demonstrate their distinction from one another. In that film the protagonists who is a Naxalite gives up the movement he had spearheaded in a poor province in North India to study medicine in England commenting that "perhaps the intricacies of human body would be less baffling than the human mind". This kind of stereotyping of brilliant men and women participating in the Naxalite movement and later giving up their politics to become a part of the mainstream as equally brilliant professionals has become common place. We find a part of that stereotype being repeated in this film as well when Brati, Somu and Nandini are depicted as brilliant students who have won scholarships throughout their student life or Nitu becoming an academician. This movement had participants from various rungs of society albeit mostly young men and women who were hardest hit by the crumbling economy and societal degeneration. Harping on only those who were brilliant is an act of negating those who made equal contributions to the movement.

Coming back to 'Hazaar Chaurasi ki Maa', the film has certain vague areas. The film is fuzzy about the Human Rights documentation centre. We do not know what exactly Sujata and Nitu do there. Neither does the director clarify how Sujata has been able to change her relation with Dibyanath. That one eruption of pain and burst appendix is insufficient to explain the transformation in Dibyanath's character who has throughout been shown as a typical chauvinist. The gap of twenty some years between Brati's death and Sujata's second meeting with Nandini cannot convincingly explain the new Sujata who is confident and serene. Time cannot overthrow the yokes of a repressive society or State. It needs conscious activism in the form of associations, institutions and movements to bring about a positive change. Sujata's observation that she took up this job after retirement is an indication that she had remained apolitical. Perhaps that is why she is shown as a Human Rights activist - an essentially apolitical area. Sujata unlike her son Brati is not de-classed. She ultimately remains a representative of her class by not leaving her personal space, her husband and her household which had been the centre of her exploitation.

References :

Banerjee, Sumanta, *In the Wake of Naxalbari*, Calcutta, Subarnarekha, 1980.

Basu, Pradip, *Towards Naxalbari*, Calcutta, Progressive Publishers, 2000.

Bose Sugata and Ayesha Jalal, *Nationalism, Democracy and Development*, New Delhi, OUP, 2011.

Chakravarti, Uma, *Gendering Class*, Calcutta, Stree, 2009.

Chatterjee, Partha, *The Partha Chatterjee Omnibus*, New Delhi, OUP, 2011.

Damas, Marius, *Approaching Naxalbari*, Calcutta, Radical Impression, 1991.

Devi Mahasweta, *Mother of 1084*, Translated by Samik Bnadopadhyay, Calcutta, Seagull Books, 2008.

V. Geetha, *Gender*, Calcutta, Stree, 2009.

--- *Patriarchy*, Calcutta, Stree, 2009.

Guha Ray, Siddhartha, *Human Rights, Democratic Rights and Popular*

Protests, Calcutta, Progressive Publishers, 2011.

Kumar, Radha, *The History of Doing*, New Delhi, Zubaan- an imprint for Kaali, 1993.

Notes :

1. Mahasweta Devi, *Mother of 1084*, trans Samik Bandopadhyay, Calcutta, Seagull, 2008. xi-xii.
2. Ibid, xiv.
3. Elder sister.
4. Rubin,Gayle, The Traffic in Women. 1975 Available at http://www.scribd.com/doc/52180831/Traffic-in-Women-by-Gayle-Rubin. Accessed on September 4, 2011.
5. The term group here is ambiguous. It is not made clear in the film what the director means by the word group. Whether he refers to a political group or just an organization is left to the imagination of the viewer who may come to faulty conclusions if not aware of the history of the Naxalite movement.
6. Vermillion powder worn by Indian Hindu women as a mark of being married.
7. Mahasweta Devi, *1084*, xvi.
8. For further reference one can check out the Newspaper Archive of National Library located at 5, Esplanade East, Calcutta.
9. Mahasweta Devi, *1084*, 125.
10. Samik Bandopadhyay has stated in his introduction to Mahasweta Devi's English Translation of *Hajar Churashir Ma* that he uses this word "in the absence of anything better to convey an inextricably intimate commingling of the rational and the emotional" (Mahasweta Devi, *1084*, viii-ix).

Celluloid Narrative of Power-Plunder-Protest Syndrome : An Avant-garde Study of Ray's 'Hirak Rajar Deshe'

Debasis Poddar

Introduction :

At the threshold of this initiative, its title deserves rationalization for contemplation of readership. In a way, this appears an avant-garde study as 'Hirak Rajar Deshe' ('Kingdom of Diamonds') is famous for its family entertainment potential rather than its political discourse. A minute study of the film, however, may decipher hyperlinked political underpinnings crafted with care and caution by its director.[1] Since assumption receives endorsement from Ray himself, whether and how far forthcoming study may deserve an adjective clubbed to the same in its title poses a moot point. A defense may be the methodology of this study being juridical in its essence.

The film, despite being in Bengali language, has transcended given linguistic barrier to be elevated to a celluloid epic of universal relevance vis-à-vis dissidence against evil law and governance irrespective of its regional geopolitical position in the world. A hallmark of its success lies in receiving the then state government as its producer in 1980- Left Front Government of West Bengal- against which message of this film would have been applicable in 2011 after three decades of virtual reign of terror with democratic veil. Thus allegorical algorithm of its anti-establishment message- though initially crafted against state of national emergency- hurt the then producer of the film at subsequent point of time with equal force to remove institutionalized Left Front from state power.[2] Besides power-plunder-protest syndrome underlying in this film, to be dealt with in forthcoming paragraphs, ultra left movement such as the Naxalite movement seems to have made a mark in its narrative as well, e.g. guerilla mode of struggle against state repression, revolutionary struggle from hinterland, student movement in support of working class, hide-n-seek with coercive force, intellectual leadership, statue being prime target as icon of state ideology, etc. Even Gupi and Bagha stand for bystander public patronage this movement received in and around the then Bengal.

State of Affairs in Affairs of State—Fact behind Fiction :

From plot summary of the film[3], gross cynicism and despair vis-à-vis state of affairs in affairs of state seems apparent. From the king's court scene, few points are clear : (i) there is face-off between the king and his subjects[4] (ii) members of working class are aggrieved with law and governance[5-6] (iii) even finance minister is not convinced of the legitimacy of law of taxation, but becomes eclipsed before the reign of terror[7] (iv) education minister initially seems not so comfortable with the legitimacy of order for closure of academic exercise, but later succumbs to royal edict[8] (v) other ministers in general, and defense minister in particular, are yes-men under tyranny of the king with no sense of their own[9] (vi) king's court astrologer is disappointed and, at times, caustic enough in his gesture to the throne.[10] Likewise, people are not allowed to raise their voice against king since the same will tantamount to waging war against state[11], which is a serious offence and deserves severe punishment since time immemorial. Such a legal position is in vogue in India till date[12]. No wonder that, in the absence of space for peaceful demonstration of public grievance and tolerant hearing offered to the same, it takes untoward turn to affect peace and tranquility in public life. Ultra left movement such as the Naxalite movement is a product of this political process.

Thus Ray identified genesis of extremist movement and the same seems applicable anywhere. Nowhere in the pages of world history, has anti-establishment movement become hostile in a liberal democratic society. The nature and feature of this ultra left movement here conveys a message that all is not well in Indian system of governance. Initiated by defacing the statue, a mass movement culminates in dismantling the same along with the throne. Likewise, an armed peasants' upheaval at Naxalbari, an unknown village of Siliguri subdivision in Darjeeling district of West Bengal during late sixties, its hostile flame is on its rise over large part of peninsular India and beyond to constitute a well known territory- red corridor- and offer sui generis line of control in practice between state force and militant force. This film is pregnant with prognostic message for "the State"[13], but its wisdom fell on deaf ears and the government, being producer of this film, got stuck to a trap of complacence on its part.

Vacuum in Good Governance—Non-State Actor on Its Rise :

A cursory view of such problematic state of affairs leaves the power-plunder-protest syndrome obvious though there are some variants in any sundry system of governance. With all its variants, however, basic structure of this conundrum remains the same- threshold limit of preponderance of power exceeding which may tend to topsy-turvy. This limit may vary from state to state and depends on permutation and combination of variants operative therein. Irrespective of their divergence, power-plunder-protest syndrome remains as commonality in all hitherto systems of governance and the same is the case in case of 'Kingdom of Diamonds' as well.

In given social order, intellectuals belong to most sensitive community and therefore receive and disseminate the feeler earlier than others. Thus a musician like Charandas and a teacher like Udayan become vulnerable in the wake of severe state repression to gross detriment of public interest[14-15]. Being a dated film, 'Kingdom of Diamonds' demonstrated state-sponsored expropriation what national capital experienced during national emergency. Had it been a contemporary one, state-sponsored expropriation to serve corporate interests in Narmada, Nandigram or Niyamgiri and pro-activist intellectuals like Medha Patkar, Binayak Sen etc. would have been accommodated. Interaction of Udayan with Gupi-Bagha (being foreign delegates to the kingdom) also demonstrates internationalization of national crisis which is a latest trend to formulate global public opinion against errant state for humanitarian intervention from abroad[16]. Thus Ray identified rights advocacy way back in late seventies.

Not without reason that, as anti-establishment intellectual, Udayan becomes headache of the king. People in power are left with no other option but to spend sleepless night for potential mischief to be perpetrated on his part in collusion of activist students[17]. Interestingly enough, members of working class themselves could not disturb the king while Udayan, struggling for their cause, did havoc to perpetrate nervous breakdown of the king. In a way or other, the king seems prudent in his prediction that Udayan is likely to create a trouble beyond his prediction[18].

On the contrary, despite not being involved in activism, ballad of Charandas seems no less instrumental as the same is inclined to a note of dissent and thereby indulges in genesis of protest with no agitation against errant state. People like Charandas are more vulnerable to state repression. While farmer, daily labour and teacher are sent to be treated by brain washing machine, Charandas receives death-in-exile sentence. He resembles conscience of his countrymen and his ballad evokes pro-people concern the way literary works raise upheaval in the history of revolution. In ultra left or Naxalite history, Charandas by and large resembles Gaddar (Vittal Rao).

A study of revolutionary upheaval in 'Kingdom of Diamonds' remains incomplete without contemplation on volatile character of the scientist- a profound character but left in complete isolation- who has screamed at least once out of his tragic position[19]. He is no yes-man to the throne. He dares to defy king's call to court and remains busy in his laboratory[20]. Later he appears before the king and surprises him with invention of brain washing machine. While he contributes to repression through his machine, the same man contributes to revolution with the same machine- a classic juxtaposition to identify science as a neutral substance which may at ease be applied for either side. Here also the king seems prudent in his understanding that scientific course of action falls beyond his understanding[21]. What he did is gross abuse of a scientific invention to perpetuate his regime to complete detriment of public interest. Indeed there are instances of aggression against people through scientific invention- state-sponsored intrusion into telephonic conversation through tapping as a matter of state practice to deal with dissidence is relevant in contemporary world- and Ray hereby condemns use of scientific invention with mala fide political motive. Thus vacuum in good governance may be filled in by wide variety of spatial politics, Naxalite politics being one of them, to provide operating space for non-state agents to the detriment of state as a political institution. Be the same Udayan or Charandas, none of them was by default active in politics but posited in the chessboard of power out of vacuum in good governance. They become by-products of such evil governance and political process involved therein. Role reversal of the machine as a boomerang against the king and his ministers illustrates spatial option available for the scientist to move crisscross in between divergent corridors of power.

Legality *Sans* Legitimacy of Governance—Subversion from within :
Besides potential threats from outside- e.g. non-state agents to topple the government, foreign elements (like Gupi-Bagha) in support of anti-establishment non-state agents- there are other threats well within a system of governance and operative from inside. Royal army is a crucial force not only in running a(ny) system of governance but also in removing the same. On the eve of structural change, there is a trend in royal army to change side under such circumstance. So far as range of change is concerned, from the French revolution to recent Arab spring, there are umpteen instances to this end. Due to want of integrity, the notorious king stands devoid of legitimacy, if not legality in technical sense of the term, and royal army lacks commitment to declining power of the king[22]. It is not out of time constraint for filmy representation of revolution that Ray preferred overnight topsy-turvy. In the pages of history, there is an instance of overnight topsy-turvy of power through the Bolshevik revolution in Russia. Even elected government may lack

legitimacy while being in power out of manipulation and the same seems no less vulnerable out of subversion from within the system. And here lies a potential threat of anti-establishment movement which is but end-product of evil governance. In terms of systemic subversion, royal army cannot stand alone. For instance, the king and his ministers are forced to undergo brainwashing operation under supervision of the scientist who is in royal service and well paid by the state[23]. Besides bribe, perhaps this is out of fear of retribution after structural change that some state-sponsored intellectuals may and do change side[24].

A sudden decline of such otherwise strong kingdom in this film reminds spectator of the century age-old wisdom of Green : 'Will, not force, is the basis of state'[25]. During transition period, therefore, there is resistance from no quarter and kingdom stands liberated by quiet and bloodless revolution. There may be a skepticism over viability of smooth transition beyond reel life though there is illustration in real life England of smooth transition through glorious revolution. Even in Bangladesh, self-motivated resignation of President Arshad ended a one-and-half decade long emergency to give way to workable democracy through free and fair election.

Positioning Surreal Dissidence in the Context of Real Dissidence :

The literary genre of underpinning profound message of life below covert expression is in vogue since time immemorial. In ancient world, there were instances in the text of literature to put such message behind a veil of something else, e.g. *Hitopodesh* (beneficial advice), *Kathasaritsagara* (ocean of the streams of stories), *Jataka Tales, Biblical Gospels, Aesop's Fables,* etc. An object of the genre was to reach people with its message, which may at times go against royal line of thought, without receiving royal wrath to the detriment of author. In this film, Udayan took resort to the same[26]. Indeed Ray himself did the same in course of filmmaking 'Kingdom of Diamonds', original inspiration being a typical allegorical narrative composed by Upendrakishore Raychoudhury (popular author for children and grandfather of Ray, the film director), in Bengali rhymes- 'Goopy Gyne Bagha Byne'- which Ray converted into film earlier. Here Ray remains faithful to rhyming dialogue of these characters (except of Udayan) partly to retain original flavor of his grandfather and partly to camouflage the state and its censor board and thereby escape ruthless scissor on its part to the detriment of this film. Dialogue of Udayan in prose has put forth a set of subtle statements : (i) his is a contemporary voice (ii) his voice transcends premature adolescent cacophony (iii) his dialogue is free from the rigour of rhyme and deserves better contemplation. Thus Ray posits his dramaturgy in specific context of this film.

Such juxtaposition is not meant to demean rhymed expression anyway. A lion's share of references in preceding paragraphs constitutes citation from those excellent rhymes as per subtitles of this film. What deserves attention of its spectator is Udayan's voice being one and only exception to this end and Ray thereby conveys a crystal clear note of dissent of his time and place. In given time and place of this filmmaking, perhaps late seventies since a(ny) filmmaking initiates with scriptwriting, ultra left/ Naxalite movement in the then national emergency remains as one and only derivative context upon which Ray might have conceptualized this film.

Last but not least, interpolation of comic-n-magic characters like Gupi-Bagha within an otherwise serious narrative is a masterstroke on his part to attain the cutting edge through which this film transcends either brand- innocent or seditious- by which censor board could have stamped to decide release of the same. Perhaps the producer being state government and the director being a man of international repute worked behind favourable decision on the part of censor board. Otherwise this seems indeed comic-n-magic decision by the then censor board to allow this film with all its songs, at least one of them being provocative enough[27], also there lies genesis of extremism against institutionalized establishment of state[28]. In this matter, Ray himself put forth no less wonder than the duo delegated to 'Kingdom of Diamonds'.

Their magical power apart, societal positioning of Gupi-Bagha deserves attention. Despite being connected to dissidence, albeit a top secret, they are but royal delegates at kingdom. The volatile fact refers to hyper-linkage between a fragment of top brass in given society and dissident force. Also the same refers to underlying vulnerability of state apparatus. Thus, with Gupi-Bagha being instrumental to political topsy-turvy of the kingdom, a message of Ray seems obvious- as mentioned earlier as well- that upheaval may not necessarily hurt from outside alone, but likely to hurt from within the system as well. In spite of its legality, which may be maintained by managing technical requirement, a government *sans* legitimacy is fragile in terms of sustenance and becomes vulnerable in front of well organized dissidence.

Their concluding chorus seems to have offered most profound message of this film each and every part of which is composed with care and caution[29]. In time of urgency, while people are in such trouble, bystanders will coordinate rescue operation though they may not be related to one another. People are required to send a message to them and thereafter all of them will come back again. Here two words- Shundi and again- carry covert implication, 'Palace of Shundi'. Where is this place? This may be placed nowhere and, at the same time, anywhere or everywhere; may be a place well within the corridor of power as well. A conscionable fragment from within (wo)men in power will come to rescue people from vagary of state-sponsored repression. Also they will come back 'again' and 'again', and not once by chance. In ancient Indian literature, veteran spectator may remember the text with an almost similar humane underpinning, albeit in an altogether divergent context[30]. Even in Marxist literature, by its own way anyway, same old eternal call for emancipation of proletarian people becomes evident with its modern class-consciousness[31].

Together these precedents fortify the premise Ray formulates to attain an assurance to offer on his part that present state of affairs in affairs of state is no destiny and we shall overcome someday- if the same may be quoted this way. Neither Lord Krishna nor Lenin entered into the nitty-gritty of prospective society. Likewise, Ray relieved Gupi-Bagha with throne of the kingdom overthrown.

There is but another side of the coin which requires equal contemplation. Surveillance on the part of rebel force is displayed by correspondence of Udayan with Bagha, and secret entry of Udayan to the kingdom for meeting Sugata, a student leader. Likewise state-sponsored surveillance is operative through which Udayan succumbs to arrest in his hide out- an incident which resembles arrest of Charu Majumdar, the topmost Naxalite leader, as high cost of his complacency. In course of secret operation, rebel leadership is so often than not oblivious of the counter-surveillance operation which may and do exceed efficiency of rebel force through best technological invention available to state force to ascertain omnipresence and consequent potential to perpetrate surprise assaults to an extent that the same becomes panoptic to the detriment of rebel force on one side and of people on the other[32]. This is a lacuna identified by Ray which becomes Achilles' heel for ultra left Naxalite leadership since the beginning of the movement.

Conclusion :

To sum up all these building blocks for construction of concerned discourse, none may defy the problematic perspective of power-plunder-protest syndrome prevalent in institutionalized state practice. Apart from authoritarianism, as is the case in case of 'Kingdom of Diamonds', even the political economy of a(ny) so called democracy (read mobocracy) may at ease be likewise; by courtesy massive manipulation power to vitiate electoral chessboard and the same seems not at all rare to scare the public in given system of governance. Thus the problematic syndrome may replicate itself in an otherwise democratic system of governance as well. Even without an emergency, catastrophic aftermath of the same perhaps prompted Ray to conceptualize this film. The syndrome may be experienced by people vulnerable in the wake of coercive state apparatus for umpteen reasons- be the same on occasion of anti-corruption agitation, forced land acquisition, police atrocity, and the like.

The history of all hitherto existing society is the history of class struggle- this axiom of Marx-Engels seems eternal since state is driven of, by and for the elite (sic) people- from Machiavellian politics to Keynesian economics- a keyword Lincoln skipped; whether unwittingly is a point apart. Good governance includes but never limits itself into politics and economics. What troubles the kingdom is lack of legitimacy in law of the land, e.g. law of taxation, labour law, laws vis-à-vis civil and political rights, socio-economic rights, etc. Indeed these are commands of the king and may therefore fulfill requirement of legality; but there seems no endorsement of his subjects behind these laws and therefore the same lack legitimacy.

In its essence, greatest potential of this classic film rests on an underlying tension between legality and legitimacy of state-sponsored law which has put the subjects and, in turn, their king and his court in perennial jeopardy. Any anti-establishment movement in the kingdom, as happens elsewhere, Naxalite movement being one of its militant variety, seems insignia of larger crisis and not a crisis in itself which culminates in a structural topsy-turvy. The more state may appreciate the same, the less will it suffer from setback out of subversion from within the system. Extraneous intervention, even if the same belongs to foreign policy of an errant state, cannot penetrate far unless and until foundation of governance becomes problematic. In this film, therefore, Ray cannot be posited as partisan filmmaker. What he offers is flip side of present system of governance and crises involved herein for contemplation of his spectator.

Notes :

1. Cineaste : Given the political climate in India, is the filmmaker's role one of passive observer or activist?

   Ray : Have you seen 'Hirak Rajar Deshe' ('Kingdom of Diamonds')? There is a scene of great clean-up where all the poor people are driven away. There is direct reflection of what happened in Delhi and other cities during Indira Gandhi's Emergency. In a fantasy like Kingdom of Diamonds, you can be forthright, but if you're dealing with contemporary characters, you can be articulate only up to a point, because of censorship. You simply cannot attack the party in power. It was tried in The Story of a Chair and the entire film was destroyed. What can you do? You are aware of the problems and you deal with them, but you also know the limit, the constraints beyond which you just cannot go.

Ray on Ray :Cineaste magazine interview with Ray, addressing its 14th question. Available at : http://www.satyajitray.org/about_ray/ ray_on_ray.htm retrieved on June 14, 2011.

2. The set of headlines of its trailer goes thus :

Once again Gupi-Bagha are back

To show there are lots of fun,

There are lots of beauties.

But there is also a dark side.

When outrage crosses its limit,

When freedom (is) in trouble,

A voice comes out

In "Hirak Rajar Deshe".

Available at : http://www.youtube.com/watch?v=FXEaGr6 Bido retrieved on June 15, 2011.

3. The musician duo of Goopi Gayin and Bagha Bayin make a comeback in this sequel, where they are invited to the court of the Hirak Raja (Diamond King), for their musical skills. They have to perform at the kingdom's Jubilee Celebrations. But coming to the kingdom, they use their natural goodness and curiosity to find out that all is not well in the kingdom. There is exploitation of poor farmers and diamond-miners. There are sycophant courtiers and ruthless armies. And there is a mad scientist with this Brain-washing machine. With the help of an upright school-master, Goopi and Bagha set out to correct the evils... with the help of their ghost-given skills, fast thinking and an impish sense of humour.

Plot summary for the 'Kingdom of Diamonds', prepared by

Diptakriti Chaudhuri. Available at : http://www.imdb.com/title/tt0080856/plotsummary retrieved on June 16, 2011.

4. Sentry : Your majesty, there are three visitors for you.

King : Who are they? What do they want?

Sentry : One is a farmer, one is a day labour, one is a singer.

King : How do they dare to come to me? What do they want?

Sentry : They say that they have some complaints.

King : Who? The farmer?

Sentry : The day labour too.

King : How dare they?

5. King : What do you want?

Fazl Mia : Your majesty, I only have two acres of land. I use them for farming. Last year there was famine. Harvest was not good. I have wife and children. I can't even feed them properly. Moreover I have to pay the interest of the money lender. I will die if I have to pay the revenue, o king.

King : Keeping revenue due is not a good thing to do.

Fazl Mia : But I will starve and die if I have to pay revenues.

King : Even if one does not have food, one should always pay the king.

6. King : What do you have to say?

Balaram : I work in the mine. It's tough job. I can't work for long time, my body aches, your majesty.

King : Don't you get your wages?

Balaram : That doesn't fill my stomach, your majesty. Moreover the soldiers whip us badly. That's unbearable, o king.

King : Those who say that whipping of soldiers is unbearable are wrong. Those who work in the mines, even the god of death is afraid of them.

Balaram : What is this, your majesty? This is not true. Workers of diamond mine don't have a long life. The air is poisonous inside the mine.

King : There is no repentance even we are empty stomach, eating stomach full makes people fat.

Balaram : This is not true, your majesty, this is not true.

7. King : Tell me, Finance Minister.

FM : Your majesty.

King : What is the news of the revenues?

FM : Your majesty, we have collected half of the revenues.

King : What are you saying? Still half left, what a state of lawlessness!

FM : The soldiers are collecting the rest of the revenues, your majesty. People are not willing to pay happily. I know collecting revenue this way is not fair, but we need money for the anniversary function.

King : Who said it's not fair? It's unfair when people don't want to pay the revenues. They won't be harmed if they pay revenues on time. Otherwise applying force is the only way. Right?

8. King : Education Minister.

EM : Your majesty.

King : The school should be shut down from today.

EM : Schools?

King : Are you deaf? The school should be shut down from today.

EM : As you say, your majesty.

King : And whatever books are there in the country, burn them all.

EM : Certainly, your majesty.

King : And whatever mythological books are there, all rubbish. Destroy them too. There is no harm in it.

9. King : Listen, Defense Minister.

DM : Yes, your majesty.

King : Tell the soldiers to wipe out all the signs of poverty from the side of the highway.

DM : They will definitely do that, your majesty. The soldiers will wipe out anything that looks bad.

King : Well. I don't want any guest to suspect anything.

10.Astrologer : Nothing is a problem to the king of Hirok. The night will become day. It's not that problem. Auspicious time will happen according to the king's will. Who cares what the calendar says.

King : And from the day of function, year of Hirak will commence. Do you understand court astrologer? The year of Hirak will commence from the day of the function.

Astrologer : As you say, your majesty, you are the lord.

King : No need to follow any other calculation. Wipe them all.

Astrologer : Do I have to wipe out any planet or star?

King : Shut up and do your work.

11. Udayan : (while trying to prevent destruction of books by royal force) Are you all mad?

EM : Beware. Don't try to stop the king's army.

12. Vide Chapter VI, with special reference to sections 121, read with 121A, Indian Penal Code, 1860.

13. Vide Article 12, read with 36, of the Constitution of India, 1950.

14. Charandas : The world is full of wonder, o my friend, the world is full of wonder.

Look good people are living in broken hut and bad people is sitting on a throne,

Those who harvest golden crops, don't have food for themselves,

The workers of diamond mine don't have a penny for themselves,

The world is full of wonder, o my friend, the world is full of wonder.

15. Udayan : If the king himself turns enemy of his subjects then it's an alarming situation. People fear the thunder but the anger of the king is more dangerous. Thunder strikes a particular place. But king's anger destroys the lives of so many people. ... If the subjects have to die, then, instead of obliging the king ...

16. Udayan : There is no one else more tyrant than the king of Hirok.

He never lets outsiders know about the truth,
He is mad … he has become crazy.
Poor people starve here,
Those who rebel are tamed by magic,
They keep on chanting the king's words,
He wanted to tame me too. But I escaped.
Now I hide in this hill.

17. King : I know that everything is his plan.
He had come and even convinced the school children.
How dare he …
He threw stone at the face of my statue in front of so many people.
He thought he'll snatch away my throne
… … …
God knows what problem he is going to create.

18. Udayan : Pull the rope and break the king into pieces …

19. Bagha : You are the king's man.
Scientist : I am alone, I am alone, I am alone.

20. King : Where is the scientist?
Sentry : He is in the laboratory, your majesty.
King : Why? What made him so busy? I called him, but still he didn't come. How dare he …
Call him. Ask him to come immediately or I won't spare him.

21. King : God knows what he does day and night in his laboratory. Gold, silver, iron, bronze, lead, frog, snake, vulture's leg, everything is there in that laboratory. He makes paste of metals in mortar and pestle. God knows what he burns in the oven all day and night, all that is a mystery.

22. Udayan : Now we have to bring the soldiers in our group.
Bagha : How?
Udayan :All royal servants take bribe in this country.

Gupi : We'll bribe them?

Udayan : Diamonds. No one can resist the temptation for diamonds.

23. King : He (the scientist) said he wants laboratory. From then on he is here. He has taken . seven lakhs coins. That day he was asking for diamonds. He wanted 2000 carat diamond.

... ...

King : Scientist, you like diamonds, don't you?

Scientist : Diamonds are alluring.

King : If your machine works, then you can take this (diamond necklace).

24. Udayan : King, if you do wrong, then you leave the throne,

Those who are the king's followers, their lives are also in danger.

It's a crime to torture the poor, king, you won't be spared,

The king of Hirak won't be spared, he is a devil.

25. For details, refer to Thomas Hill Green (1937), *Lectures on the Principles of Political Obligation,* London : Longmans, Green & Co.

26. EM : (to learners) What are you all learning today? What lesson? (after experiencing long silence from their side, to Udayan) Well teacher ...

Udayan :*Hitopodesh.*

27. Gupi : The king is cunning, the king is bad

The king is cunning, the king is treacherous

The king is mean, the king is cruel, the king is a robber

The king has crossed the limits of wrong deeds

He has snatched away food from poor people

And has invited misfortune to the country.

28. Gupi : The king has suppressed them; Of whom he is afraid of,

Whose wrath would have made his throne unstable.

Tell king, isn't it true, isn't it true,

The king should get tough punishment,

[translation deviated from given subtitle of the film]

29. We are Gupi and Bagha,

We are co brothers,

... ...

Give us a call,

Our address is the palace of Shundi.

Both of us will come,

We will come back again,

[translation deviated from given subtitle of the film]

30. Whenever and wherever there is decline in religious practice, O descendant of Bharata, and a predominant rise of irreligion- at that time, I descend myself.

A. C. Bhaktivedanta Swami (Online Ed.), (1971), *Bhagavadgita As It Is,* Sydney : Bhaktivedanta Book Trust.

31. We, however, shall break with the opportunists; and the entire class-conscious proletariat will be with us in the fight- not for a "shifting of the relation of force", but for the overthrow of the bourgeoisie, for the destruction of the bourgeois parliamentarianism, for a democratic republic of the commune type, or a republic of Soviets of Workers' and Soldiers' Deputies, for the revolutionary dictatorship of the proletariat.

V. I. Lenin (1917), 'The State and Revolution : the Marxist Theory of the State and the Tasks of the Proletariat in the Revolution', in V. I. Lenin, *Collected Works,* Vol. 25, Moscow : Progress Publishers.

32. Hence the major effect of the Panopticon : to induce in the inmate a state of conscious and permanent visibility that assures the automatic functioning of power. ... The Panopticon is a marvelous machine which, whatever use one may wish to put it to, produces homogeneous effects of power.

Alan Sheridan tr., Michel Foucault (1995), *Discipline and Punish : The Birth of the Prison,* 2nd ed., New York : Vintage Books.

Comparative

'Hazaar Chaurasi ki Maa' : A Faithful Document of the Turbulent Times on the Silver Screen

Ketaki Datta

Interesting it is to know that Mahasweta Devi's celebrated novel, *Mother of 1084,*[1] got translated into English by Samik Bandyopadhyay and it is more interesting to get the play-version of the same by Bandyopadhyay himself within the period of 2 to 3 years. *Mother of 1084* made its presence felt among the theatre-loving audience first, when, it got translated by Samik Bandyopadhyay in lucid English, with all turns of events and interactions among characters intact and vibrant [Cf. Bandyopadhyay, Samik tr. 'Mother of 1084' in G.P. Deshpande ed. *Modern Indian Drama : An Anthology,* Sahitya Akademi, New Delhi, 2000]. But, it reached a wider public when it had been filmed in 1998 as 'Hazaar Chaurasi ki Maa' by Govind Nihalani, who worked with Jaya Bachchan [Sujata] and Nandita Das [Nandini] as the major casts. Of course, a lot remains to be said about the film version of the play, as the screen has a different language, which can create a different ambience, disseminate added message to the cinema-goers than the theatre-frequenters. In the film, however, the blood-chilling, cannibalistic times of Naxalite Movement in the 'seventies gets a faithful and sympathetic representation, through the chiaroscuro of light and darkness, through the camera moving simultaneously on the trolley and in the hands of the cameraman. The director left a final touch of perfection through the uncertainty and the restlessness of Brati's mother, Sujata, and his fiancée, Nandini. A clash of realism and idealism also stirred the audience to the inmost depth, when people like Saroj Pal was seen to scrounge a reputation as an efficient cop, after trampling the most intellectual youths of the times who were running amuck to establish a utopian truth on the seedbed of a rotten society, which was not ready for that, as yet.

The film version of *Mother of 1084* ['Hazar Chaurasi ki Maa'] did successfully create the ambience, but, could hardly bring the audience to feel the dread and horrors of the '70s reeling under the trauma of loss of the Naxalite youths, as vividly, as the novel itself did. It was a decade of liberation, the novel declares in the selfsame tune and words. It was the turbulent period of bloodshed, faith, revolution, dream of a change for the better, and, lastly betrayal, a fiasco. History of the world has several instances, that, a revolution flares up, claims sundry lives and dies out, gets wiped off from the earth leaving a few pages dedicated to the perturbed times only. Naxalite movement, also, was no exception. It dreamt of ushering in liberty from all shackles, of faith, of living life, of thought,- in every sphere. But, too soon, too quickly, as though in a jiffy or at the batting of eyelids, the path of violence and militancy had been followed. Naturally, it had to die an untimely death, leaving just a few imprints on the pages of history,—painful, blood-chilling, tearful.

Before going straight into the analysis of the film, I would like to refer to the documents in print which talked about the turbulent times of the '70s in Bengal, which exploded in the form of revolution, with a promise of the birth of long-dreamt-of liberated era, though it died soon after it broke out, being powerless to be born. Mahasweta Devi believed in "the value of documentation", hence, she expressed in a powerful, yet touching way, how Sujata, Brati's mother, the mother of the corpse number 1084, lying at Kantapukur [the morgue] for identification, felt about her rebellious son's death, all alone, with none to share her feelings, not even her Chartered Accountant husband, Dibyanath, who had no qualms of conscience to remove all memoirs of his youngest son Brati, immediately after his death. He, even, hushed up the case of Brati's brutal death on the altar of political skullduggery. In fact, it was the cannibal times that mattered. It was time of butchery of all ideals, of all dreams, of all rebellious thoughts. In *In the Wake of Naxalbari,* Sumanta Banerjee writes intrepidly :

> With increasing help from the Centre and imported paramilitary and military forces, police retaliation against the CPI [M-L] urban guerillas began to gain momentum from the last quarter of 1970. No mercy was shown to any CPI [M-L] cadre or supporter if caught.... As the New Year 1971 began, the approach of another mid-term poll cast an ominous shadow over West Bengal. The old rivalry between the CPI [M] and CPI [M-L] cadres had already appeared in a much more virulent form. Leaders of both parties reared up their ranks on mutual suspicion and hostility ... Clashes between the ranks of the two parties increased ... Soon certain localities in Calcutta and its suburbs came to be demarcated by the two parties, each carving out its own sphere of influence. Trespass by any party man in areas dominated by the rival party was punished with death. A bloody cycle of interminable assaults and counter-assaults, murder and vendetta, was initiated. The ranks of both the CPI [M] and CPI [M-L] dissipated their militancy in mutual fightings leading to the elimination of a large number of their activists, and leaving the field open to the police and the hoodlums. It was a senseless orgy of murders, misplaced fury, sadistic tortures, acted out with the vicious norms of the underworld, and dictated by the decadent and cunning values of the petty bourgeois leaders... The lumpen proletariat were put to use in two ways. Some were used as agent-provocateurs, who precipitated some violent action and exposed the unwarned CPI [M-L] cadres in a locality to an unanticipated police raid. It was a sort of 'corpus delicti' which provided the police with an opportunity to pick up whom they wanted... In official parlance their actions came to be known as 'people's resistance to naxalite depredations...[2]

It is really surprising to note, that Sujata confessed at last, that she knew not her son, inside out. She was madly fond of her son, even though, the family with materialistic demands and aristocratic background was absolutely nonchalant to the presence of her youngest son in the cocoon of their household itself. Brati proved himself to be totally rebellious of the ideals of this family, by joining a group of young adults who felt deprived, outcast, who had only dreams galore in front of their eyes, like the surging tides of the sea. They dreamt of ushering liberation of thoughts, of ideals, of the political framework of the nation, of everything and all. It was the decade of Liberation, as the appellation ran. But, in reality, these rebellious youths were hounded out of this state, were butchered, and were stamped as anti-socials. Brati, just a day before his birthday, on the sixteenth of January that year, had gone to Somu's place, where in the dark of the night all these brats were called out by a group of boys who opposed their ideals and had been brutally hacked to death. Somu's father, running amuck, seeking justice from pillar to post, died immediately after, leaving the family in the lurch.

As the story ran, Sujata, a bank employee, went from one acquaintance of her dead son to the other, in search of sharing the inconsolable grief, in search of solace. But, at the end of the day, she came back home for her daughter's engagement, and, finding all pretences reaching their heights in the so-called elite social circle, she felt lonely, absolutely cooped up in her own world with the threadbare remembrances of her dead son, Brati, all around. The picture of the sham and pretensions has been faithfully etched by Mahasweta Devi, the novelist. Saroj Pal, who refused to hand the corpse of 1084 [of Brati] to Sujata, came to Tuli's engagement on invitation, though he dared not come upstairs to avoid a direct interaction with that Mother of 1084, to whom he had been rude and harsh. However, he never forgot to wish the newly-engaged couple a hearty congratulation. After all, he had been ON DUTY! Dibyanath, who loathed the ways of his son's life, kept pining for him, pretending as though they were the best son and father of the world, in front of all. Though he had to hush up his 'unruly' son's case, though he had to take all possible care to see that his son's name did not come up in the newspaper! All sorts of pretences, all sham! It was only Hem, the maid, who kept on weeping silently all day long, as it was the day Brati's existence had been ruthlessly wiped out from the face of the earth! It was only Sujata, who kept visiting the acquaintances and friends of Brati, sharing the memories of that very day his existence stood nullified, with those who suffered the same lot, losing the dearest of the dear ones, the breadwinner of their family. Sujata felt the presence of her dead son in their company, in Somu's room, in Nandini's place, where Brati seemed to whisper words of endearment in her ears. In her own house, in the midst of the merry-making, she was getting lost in the image of Brati, putting on the blue shirt, getting ready to leave, halting a while beneath the stairs, throwing a long look at her! Sujata fell on the ground, her appendix was suspected to get burst. It's not clear whether Sujata came home alive after the operation or succumbed to the long-nursed vermiform appendix that turned sore.

Such was the times, such was the crying urge for liberation, that drove many a family sonless, fatherless, breadwinner-less. Govind Nihalani strove hard to give a fullest expression to the turbulent times that rocked Bengal, sometime around the '70s. In fact, when in an issue of the Bengali journal *Prasad,* this novel by Mahasweta Devi got published it moved all and sundry to sympathy and tears. However, a few of the intelligentsia marked it as "sob stuff'. Whatever the case may be, the dialogues in Hindi on the lips of Sujata or Nandini, or Somu's mother could hardly serve the purpose as desired. It seemed as though, it would have been much widely accepted, if the characters could communicate with the audience in the language of the land, which was torn by the police, hounding the Naxalites from the pen and corner of the State, by tracking their hide-outs down.

Nihalani created an ambience by making the set somber and grave, to suit the temperament of the story. At the outset, Jaya Bachchan's shriek on uncovering the battered face of her son threw a chill down our spine. Right at that moment, the journey of the bereaved mother down the memory lane began and the audience stayed glued to the screen, with bated breath, tears welling up their eyes, every now and then. Jaya

Bachchan's dropping in at Nandini's house, Nandini's guttural voice, shabby surroundings, Somu's mother's wails in the dilapidated, ramshackle tenement, Somu's sister's hurt, angry looks-all kept the message of the original story intact. The only thing which appeared somewhat discordant was the peaceful atmosphere in the last scene, where Dibyanath and his children shared mirth in a family gathering. Sujata's musings ran on the screen in background, though her concern for the dead son seemed in no way lessened, rather went parallel to the din and bustle of the party, that was on.

Nihalani has tried to use the effect of chiaroscuro to make the atmosphere charged with the anxious concern as in the original writing. Nandini was too pensive to bring the character to life, quite credibly. However, the revolution and its aftermath ate up almost whole of the two-and-half hours of this 1998 film. Anyway, the film won good reviews and got forgotten soon after. But why? Was it because, the ideals were not clearly stated on the screen, was it because the director ladled out oodles of pain, or was it because the language was other than the people of Bengal talk in?

Now, let us really talk seriously about the pitfalls of the film. The film, as directed by the veteran director Govind Nihalani, held the audience back, only by the sheer documentation of a bygone era, which still assails us with a myriad of mind-boggling queries, and, by the deft use of light and darkness. Jaya Bachchan's serious, somber facial lines, her way of measured talking, halted speeches, her anxiety and Nandita Das's faithful representation of the only female revolutionary as drawn by Mahasweta Devi through a frustrated yet firm voice and countenance speak volumes for a good directorial effort. But, the streets of Calcutta in the '70s, the panic-stricken populace on the streets have not been such meticulously presented by the director. Rather, the director was busier in focusing the camera on the two families, in particular [Somu's and Brati's]. The scene in the morgue at Kantapukur, Jaya's heart-rending shriek, her frustrated, lonely cry throughout the film - all are faithfully brought on the silver screen. But, much remains to be desired by the audience as they want to get much elaborate version of a turbulent times on the screen. No doubt, Nihalani has done that faithfully by bits and snatches, but, a co-ordinated effect seems lacking, to some extent, of course, not wholly. Sometimes, long pause or stretches of silence speak volumes of the sad, anxious time that snatched many a son from their mothers' lap and devoured them. Cinematic technique, of course, helps drive the message home.

In fact,

> What is enigmatic about the aesthetic use of silence is its power to create a rhythm between itself and speech. Speech is overture; it has an ensconcing effect, a public meaning. It is a function of social organization, something that both creates and articulates meaning, in which the social structure is created. Silence is personal and in its actual impact, unnerving. It can express what is dialectically opposed to speech. It can reflect the sterility and inadequacies of the social system of human articulation. Silence, therefore, can have a deep metaphysical and poetic meaning. It can capture the more personal - and so the more oppressive - dialectic implicit in a confrontation between the individual and social system. But silence can be enunciated only within a pattern of sound....
>
> Film is both a spatial and a temporal record. It constructs space or rather reconstructs it. The film frame is a spatial frame and as Jean Mitry has pointed out, it produces a certain kind of tension. The space that is within the frame or the 'in-frame' space creates the feeling that if the camera were to move either to the left or to the right, it would reveal more of the space around"[3].

If we pick two most appealing scenes from the film, obviously one would be the morgue scene where Sujata gives vent to her emotion, and, the other is the touching conversation of Sujata with Nandini, especially where Nandini says that Sujata was yet to re-explore Brati from within. She knew only Brati, her son. But beyond that identity, Brati had several identities-Brati the rebel, Brati the idealist, Brati the lover, Brati the friend, so on, so forth. Nandini's grave voice added a new dimension to Sujata's search for her dead Brati in his friends and acquaintances, all day long. Save these two scenes, all the scenes get lost in the crowd of many more extraneous ones, run-of-the-mill mostly. When I take a look at my experience of watching the movie in '98 at Indira Movie House, Bhowanipore, Kolkata, I can vividly remember these two scenes only. When I asked my aunt who accompanied me that day, she shared the same opinion even. But why? It is because, while viewing the horrifying tale of the '70s on the screen, the audience shuddered at these two scenes only, as these might have been the picture of any other movement, leaving any mother shattered at the sight of her dead son's battered face, or, any other rebellious girl's reaction to a situation, she had been thrown into. Naturally, the scenes which transcended the barriers of Time and Place were only these two. People remember the scenes which can set time, place and action at naught and rise to the height of the Universal.

If we pit Govind Nihalani's 'Hazaar Chaurasi ki Maa' against two other films with the same motto, same theme, same sentiment, we will not find the ghastly echo of this film in the other two. Here, at the very outset, we find the mother is being rung up to come and have a look at his son, lying dead in Kantapukur [the morgue]. Her son has lost his identity, has been reduced to just a number : 1084. Somu, Bijit and Laltu-all had been hacked to death by the opponents, the foes of the rebellion. But, in Satarupa Sanyal-directed film 'Anu' [1999] save the rape to which Ananya [Indrani Haldar], the female rebel, the beloved of Sugato [Nirmalya Banerjee], a staunch Naxalite rebel, with a strong value-laden mindset, had been subject to, no other scene seemed so heartrending. In Amit Dutt's directorial venture 'Robibar Bikalbela' [2006], the focus is on a time which is " the tail end of the period when things began to settle down." And, the year he depicts on the screen is 1977, seven years after the peak hours of turbulence. Here, he tried to give the audience an idea of the effect of the quelled rebellion on the lives of the diehard rebels of the Naxalite Movement of the '70s. He etched the life of a revolutionary on the screen, who escaped abroad after murdering a foe of the revolution, and his mental agony on returning to the country being informed of his mother's death.

In 'Anu', the crushed sentiments of Ananya, the heroine of the film, could not dampen her rebellious spirits. Even after being raped by the hooligans who came to their house in search of Sugato, the fugitive rebel, she had not surrendered her faith to the so-called established notions of the society which curbed the freedom of women. Rather, she culled the courage to fight back alone. She took a job of a school teacher, and went some kilometers off Calcutta, to a safer nook. In the meanwhile, he kept in touch with Bharatda [Debesh Roy Chowdhury], a staunch rebel, who lost his one eye to the inhuman torture of the cops, in police custody. Anu used to feel for the damage of "Bharatda's eyes, hued with dreams and visions". Bharatda used to run a printing house after his eyesight went feeble. He joined Anu in her frantic search for Sugato who was being transferred from one jail to the other in Bengal. Anu got remembered of the fiery notions preached by her rebellious paramour, Sugato. Sugato believed in complete freedom of women. He never believed in the age-old rituals like putting vermilion in the parting of the hair of a married lady or putting on bangles and anklets. To him, these were the signs of keeping the womenfolk as slaves.

In the school also Ananya strove hard to establish her own ideals. She was loved by the students and colleagues alike. She tried to kindle the fire latent in each student's soul, who could register their protest against the age-old wrong conventions of the society, though, in many cases she failed. Ananya led a solitary life there, in a rented accommodation. She kept counting the days when Sugato would be set free to come and join her. The day, at last, dropped on her lap as a dream come true. Sugato came out of the jail, free to lead a life of his own. He was welcomed by Bharatda and Ananya. Ananya brought him straight to her own tenement and she dreamt of a happy married life.. After all, they shared the same views, in fact, she had been liberated mentally and ideologically by Sugato in the turbulent days of the '70s. She kept on sharing the past experiences with him. Even, she did not forget to relate the horrid incident of 'her chastity being outraged by the hooligans' who came baying for Sugato's blood, to their house. But, it came as a fire of trial for Sugato. The firebrand rebel who used to spew words of high ideals in his heyday, began to avoid the union with Anu's body, which had been ruthlessly torn and scratched by the opponents, who had a grand feast on her flesh. This abhorrence wrought a wide chasm in their conjugal tie. Without knowing the real reason, Anu was about to take him to a doctor, but, when in his absence it chanced upon her that it was because of his hatred for her being raped he could not accept her, she rebelled and asked him to walk out. He did so, immediately. Anu's wait for endless years began, till Sugato, the revolutionary, who taught her to be a liberated woman, both in mind and spirits returned....

The main point of contrast of 'Anu' with 'Hazaar Chaurasi ki Maa' is the former's protest against the 'loss of revolutionary ideals' which bound the two individuals together. In Mother of 1084, loss of ideals could not be a point at all, as Brati and his nearest pals had been no more. His beloved, Nandini, had been oppressed in the jail custody and had been debilitated in such a pathetic manner, that, she was no longer fit to come out of the cooped existence to start a life afresh, giving her dreams a proper shape. Sujata, after the loss of her son, was already a broken self, waiting for a final breakdown, which obviously happens at the close of the novel. Naturally, no betrayal of ideals or self is, beyond any scope, to result. 'Hazaar Chaurasi ki Maa' remains sacrosanct in its own domain, revolving round Sujata and Nandini who bore the brunt of the 'turbulent times', in the true sense of the term.

Again, so far as the cinematic excellence is concerned, 'Anu' has much more to offer as it deals with psychological interaction, aftermath of the rebellion, and, a harsh outcome by way of the clash of ideals or loss of ideals. The use of light and sound are much more lively, than in 'Hazaar Chaurasi ki Maa', though, that is quite obvious, as the latter deals with the sentiments of the mother of a dead son and his paramour, pitted against an insouciant society which cannot think in those self-effacing terms.

Now, another film, 'Robibar Bikalbela' [Sunday Afternoon] quite recently made [2006], is on the anvil for comparison and contrast with

'Hazaar Chaurasi ki Maa'. This film has been directed by Amit Dutt, and, it has a backdrop, which is far from giving any horrifying impression of the rebellion of the seventies. In fact, the protagonist, Shaon [Bhaswar Chattopadhyay], being inspired by the noble ideals of a Naxalite leader, joined the movement like two of his dear pals, and kills a foe of their rebellion, near the railway-station. "In order to establish our ideas of liberation, we have to kill quite a few who come in the way of it. Hold the pistol properly, aim at the foe and do not tremble to put an end to his life. It is for the noble cause of the revolution", so exhorted the leader [Arun Mukhopadhyay]. Hence, Shaon had no other option but to follow his words in verbatim. But, the reality bites. He had to flee the country, taking a job abroad. And, life had its own course to follow. But, again the past got raked up when he got the news of his mother's demise and decided to return home. Coming home, he found that the face of Calcutta had undergone a drastic change. His old pal, Palash [Abir Chattopadhyay], who had buried the old ideals of revolution and started living life anew, talked about the life which had nothing to do with the ideology of the 'decade of Liberation'. In Shaon's eyes, both Palash and himself, were dead souls. Only Biju who died on the altar of the noble cause survived as a living soul.

However, chance brought him to the house of that 'foe of the revolution', whom he killed before leaving the country. He was survived by his daughter [Sudipta Chakraborty] and his wife. On escorting the girl one evening to her house, as she failed to get a rickshaw to take her home, he came to see the portrait of that man hanging on the wall. He, however, got weak on the girl, who led a life of a prostitute, in Calcutta, on the sly. Her mother was under the impression that she worked in an office. He tried to disclose the fact of his father's murder to the girl, but failed. Lastly, he left for abroad, bidding adieux to his homeland, leaving revolutionary ideals behind. He left a note for the girl with the cook back home. Though, on a Sunday afternoon, the girl got it, while coming to meet him in person, it is not clear what was there in the small note, put in the envelope. However, the tears she kept wiping on reading the note suggest that, Shaon succeeded in relating the truth of his misdeed in the note. As she sat by a pond at the approach of the evening, the letter got blown by a sudden gush of wind and it floated down the water. The girl retraced her steps homeward, and, coming home, she was seen to close the lackluster, old windows, one after another. It seemed, as though, she was putting an end to all ties she could dream of. Lastly, of course, there is a 'nasty betrayal' of emotions, if not of ideals.

The message the film leaves is really hard to bear. It draws a pall over the corpse of the revolution that lighted fire in the young souls in the early seventies. Shaon finds the carcass of the revolution, lying supine on the streets of Calcutta. His bosom friend Palash is no longer a believer of the creed. Palash's sister is no longer a woman, who can make a home. Only Taranga mashi [aunt], the cook, has the same old affection for him. She only feels that the boy should come home to raise a family. The rest is carrion, bearing the stench of the crematorium. Shaon goes back abroad. Words in speck-less white pop up on the black screen as the scroll of 'cast' comes to a close :

Thousands of bright young people died in and around Calcutta because of the movement that went awry...

Many points of contrast and comparison may be drawn between this film and Nihalani's 'Hazaar Chaurasi ki Maa'. The first point of contrast is in theme. In 'Robibar Bikalbela', the whole film revolves round the agony and ecstasy of the revolution and more so round the fact of murder that demanded an outlet from Shaon's inmost within. In 'Hazaar Chaurasi ki Maa', there is no such burden of guilt. There is a sharing of common feelings, there is a quest to know the dead son better, inside out. That's all. But, in 'Robibar Bikalbela', the protagonist, on the one hand, believes the cause of the movement from the core of his heart, again, he tends to suffer from a feeling of guilt for murdering the 'enemy' of the revolution on instruction of their leader, as he finds the daughter of the killed man to be in a sorry plight, eking out her livelihood from an ignoble profession. Is it not sending a wrong signal to the audience? Don't the belief in an ideology and responsibility to the society, by and large, come at loggerheads then? The director loves to quote Nabanita Dev Sen's lines to support his viewpoint, "My exile in the jungle is over mother-now the jungle lives in me."

Cinematographically speaking, 'Robibar Bikalbela' [Sunday Afternoon] is more of a commercial film, with impeccable use of piano music and bright colour effect, avoiding the chiaroscuro one, or the shadows. He makes discreet use of piano by Till Martenes, Rob Blaikie, Wolfang Mit, Patrick J. Murphy, and guitar played by the musicians of Acoustic Guitar Workshop. In 'Hazaar Chaurasi…', silence, cries of people, wails of a bereaved mother form the acoustics, though in the party scene the clank of the glasses and wineglasses suffice as the background noise.

Among these three films, of course, 'Hazaar Chaurasi ki Maa', is closest to the ideals and perturbations of the times. In the other two films, the 'aftermath' has been dealt with to a considerable extent. In 'Hazaar Chaurasi ki Maa', Nandini, the female rebel stands a chance of being imprisoned once more. The kith and kin of the dead revolutionaries are afraid of keeping in touch with Brati's mother, as their families might stand threatened because of her frequent visits. Somu's sister throws an angry look at her as her chance of getting a job in near future may turn bleak, because of her presence in their ramshackle dwelling, where the bed they used to lie on before, has turned into a wooden plank supported by a pile of bricks. The morgue at Kantapukur, Sujata's aristocratic looks and exterior, her wails, her shriek, her torn, tormented within till her collapsing on the floor owing to a swollen appendix, in the end, certify the plight of the revolutionary's nearest one, who can bear the burden of the noble cause at all costs.

After all, "we see on the screen what the camera sees."[4]

All said and done, 'Hazaar Chaurasi ki Maa' is the most faithful document of the turbulent times of the early seventies.

References :

1. Devi, Mahasweta (tr. by Bandyopadhyay, Samik), *Mother of 1084*. Seagull Books, Kolkata, 1997.
2. Banerjee, Sumanta. *In the Wake of Naxalbari,* Subarnarekha, Calcutta, 1980.
3. Valicha, Dr. Kishore. *The Moving Image : A Study of Indian Cinema,* Orient Longman, 1988. pp. 103 & 115.
4. Mast, Gerald & Cohen, Marshall eds. *Film Theory and Criticism : Introductory Readings,* OUP, USA, 1974.

   VCDs and DVDs of the films 'Hazaar Chaurasi ki Maa' [dir. Govind Nihalani], 'Anu' [dir. Satarupa Sanyal], 'Robibar Bikalbela' [dir. Amit Dutt] have been consulted.

Films and Naxalism : The in-between

Sumana Sanyal

[Actually this writing has lost its established form. Maybe it's a one-act play or just some unarranged dialogues which didn't proceed in a fixed way like the Naxalite movement of 1970s, whatever it is .... I would like to leave the genre, the chronotope entirely to the readers. It's better that you'll decide how would you like to read this rhetoric.]

Now I'm going to engage myself to explore the in-between of Films and Naxalism.They possess a quite different shape from each other. I don't know what I shall get at the end...whether it'll be pain or satisfaction, wonder or disappointment...; however, I'll try to find out the relation or unrelation on the way to my critical engagement.

['I'm only twenty. I'm walking for last thousand years through Poverty, timidness and the Procession of dead bodies. I've gone through the history of last thousand years. History of Poverty, history of deceive, history of oppression']
('Kolkata 71' / Mrinal Sen's movie).

There are so many movies based on the Naxatite movement of 70s which become our centre of attraction today. What was the massive vibration that spurred these directors to make these? And the answer is simple. 'Time'. That blood-stained time. In Bengal,Charu Majumdar provided the ideological leadership to the Naxalbari movement and a large number of urban elites were attracted to this ideology, which spread through Majumdar's writing, particularly the 'Eight Historical

Documents' which formed the basis of the Naxalite movement (Bhattacherjee, 2009, 32-35).

Two Metaphorical Minds on Trial : A Film within Films :

'In his eyes you see no pride...yesterday's paper telling yesterday's news'(MacTell, 1969).

1st Scene

Once upon a time there was a home-sick Professor who used to walk alone with the sound of his crutch on the university corridor. One day, in a rainy evening, a lady, his former student and now a college teacher, Nandini, enters his living room. Nandini is a movie buff and rumors are roaming around the corridor about these fifty six and forty two.

She enters as an allegory to represent the heteroglossic relations of different voices ... To (re)present the love and war game.

Nandini : 'You've closed these windows again, don't you feel claustrophobic?'

Prof.: 'These windows won't open easily. But it's a real surprise to see you now. I was just thinking that the other name of rain is Nandini. Telepathy?'

Nandini : 'College will open on next Monday and I've got four days to stay here with you.'

Prof.: 'Another surprise! But it might be embarrassing for you and your family.'

Nandini : 'Leave it .... I've taken a decision.'

Prof.: 'What is that?'

Nandini : 'That I'll tell you later, but now I'm in a mood to show you some movies. You have to see these and think about yourself freshly.'

Prof.: 'I've nothing to think afresh.'

Nandini : 'I want from a former Naxalite to put his inner eye on some questions through these Films.'

Prof.: 'Okay. It's useless to argue with you. So, it's movie time now, is it?'

Nandini : 'And coffee time too, till then you please switch on the DVD player. Sometimes a movie is much more effective than a seminar.

Wait... I am coming...'

2nd Scene

The first movie that Nandini chooses is 'Kolkata 71' directed by Mrinal Sen.

The movie is a radiant documentation of that restless time of Kolkata. At the beginning, an announcement from the All India Radio breaks down the silence of the early morning -

'A bullet-pierced dead body of an unknown young man is discovered by the Police today in Maidan'.

'Kolkata 71' is a collection of stories depicting the 70s.The Naxalite activity, starvation of common people, social and political corruptions are shown" (Majumdar, 2004, 78-85).

Now the flashback starts - these are the histories of this unknown dead body.

1. The topsy-turvy family by the cyclone of 1933.

2. Shovona and her younger sister who had to choose prostitution to survive in the era of the Second World War.

3. The mother of 1953 who sent her son to the black market to smuggle rice. At the same time, in a dinner party the elites continued their conversation on the paintings of the hungry Bengal by Chittaprasad.

We can feel the hidden anger that insists Sen to make this movie. The director now plays with the expression and the film language like the technique of Godard with these images :

1963

Vote?

Election?

And the violent laughter of those industrialists in a party with the wine glasses, successfully acted by Ajitesh Bandyopadhyay and Rudraprasad Sengupta– A New India Is Being Born.

Here are some snapshots of the new born :

Politics

Bomb

Pistol
Pipe gun
Killing
Strike
Annihilation

These are the productions of the restless 70s. The aggressive Naxalite movement becomes the cause of the death of this Youngman. The dead voice awakes again - 'Don't worry. I'm dead. Today, in the early morning they chased me to the Maidan and then shot me from behind. I'm here to tell you that I know who the killers are. But I won't tell you their names. I want you to search them out by yourselves, and in this way of searching you'll suffer a lot. You'll feel the pain but I'm sure you won't be unperturbed.'

A youngman of 20 walks through history, poverty and death. He is 20 but has been killed so many times. Killed because he protested against the hegemony. He comes and goes between stories. Each story has its different backgrounds and characters but the focus is unchanged- 'poverty' and 'indignity'. At the end the young man appears again and provokes the viewers to react. This is the virtual reality and the director's response to the contemporary politics in Kolkata during the 70s, ignoring the traditional form of classical cinema inspired by the Brechtian agitprop method. This is such a political cinema that we can't judge typically, without creating any controversy. Avoiding this hole, Sen offers us a montage of some broken arrows…three stories in the form of a political metaphor on a common form- 'Poverty'.

In 'Kolkata 71' we can feel the wave of the 3rd cinema, "the Latin American film movement of 1960s-1970s which decries neocolonialism, the capitalist system and the Hollywood model of cinema as mere entertainment to money making" (Nicholas, 44-64).

The anger and restlessness are the products of the 70s' Kolkata and redefining the history Mrinal Sen shows us the flowing connection in this film as the 20-year old has lived this age for the last thousand year with morbidity (Sen, 2004).

The time was turbulent when Sen made this, but the movie somehow lacks in its emotional approach. Each story and the dead young man seem to be some kind of outsiders...as they are thrown within the plot on the way of re-exploring the history. We can remember the movie, 'Breathless' by Jean-Luc Godard, where the crook 'Michel' is killed by the cops in a very unattached way, saying a slang and we didn't feel any inner turmoil for him. Reason is the same- lack of emotion. So much speech can be monotonous some time and left us cold.

But 'Kolkata 71' with its Godardian mind and outlook becomes a vibrant and significant document of 70s' Kolkata.

Prof.: 'Then, what do you want to teach me from this? A new line of thinking?'

Nandini : 'I've nothing to teach but only to show you the wastage of life.'

Prof.: 'Wastage? Maybe ... But have you ever asked these questions, why did the cops behave like this in the film? Can any human being be such cruel that he will chase and shoot someone from behind in the name of freedom?

The house of ... the Congress MLA ... was turned into a torture chamber where Naxal students of Presidency College and Calcutta University were confined illegally by the Police and Congress cadres.'

Nandini : 'And what was the result? The dreams of revolution became only discolored bubbles.'

Prof.: 'Actually there was a huge public rejection of Charubabu's 'annihilation line'. A large section of Naxalites began to question Majumdar's leadership' (Rana, 1995, 112-117).

Nandini : 'Just like Sumit. He also questioned the policy of his Party line in 1971.'

Prof.: 'Sumit?'

Nandini : 'You've to see 'Padatik', another film of Mrinal Sen for knowing Sumit's Pain.'

Prof.: ''Padatik'? My memories act like a betrayer.'

Nandini : 'We'll see it tomorrow, but I won't allow you to close the middle door.'

Prof.: 'Go and sleep and please leave me alone.'

Day - 2

1st Scene

(They are watching 'Padatik' after lunch)

The film starts with these socio-political backgrounds :

Kerosene disappears

Death out of starvation

Factionalism inside political parties

Examination postponed

Government pledged to restore law and order

Parallel labor unions formed

Calcutta - a Problem city.

'Padatik' is in the chain of Mrinal Sen's Kolkata series. The last scene of 'Kolkata 71' re-appears here and a gloomy voice arises from the background- 'I find Calcutta an intimidating and even infernal city. Unredeemed and probably doomed.'

Though it's a story of the same old series but a new approach on the woman issue makes it different.

Film Summary :

As an underground activist Sumit (Dhritiman Chattopadhyaya) has to take shelter in an apartment of a working and divorcee woman Shila Mitra (Simi Garewall) with whom Sumit shares his loneliness getting tired by his recent lack of activities. The situation of outer Kolkata was turbulent by the murder of a Forward Block leader Hemanta Basu, mass killings of Baranagore and Kashipoor etc. One day, on the way of their conversation the other activist Biman enters the flat and suspects them of having an illicit relationship.

Sumit is suffering a lot with the contradiction which is now jumbling up his thought process; he is facing a dilemma of his choice. He thinks about the utterly wrong approach of his organization which seems to be a baseless one by the rejection of common people and he sends a letter to his group leader Nikhil saying that– 'history will not forgive us'.

And now, Sumit, like a betrayer to his comrades, has lost the support of his group and is ordered to vacate Shila's apartment.

Analysis :

Is it a bias of any ideology that it does not give anyone any right to question?

Sumit once said to Biman-'We are drowned in a large vacuum'...Now the question is whether this realization of Sumit is a product of his recent lack of activities because on the 1st half of the film his language was very aggressive when he argued with his father. If he didn't get enough idle time to think, if his mother was alive, if he was completely detached to the pain of his widower father, then what would be his feelings about this 'large vacuum'? And after all... a company of woman...some soft colors of life...snatches him away from a hardcore politics of abolishing the class enemies...can we take this matter in this way? Isn't it like the prodigal son who wants to return his home?

And the most important issue of this film is about women's liberation. A large section of this film is about Shila Mitra's working life in an advertising agency where she takes interviews of different women and they all are holding the same opinion that there can be no women's lib without economic independence.

Mao Tse-tung once said in his economic theory that woman is the source of the power of the people (Politt, 2008, 78-79). Mao considered women as a revolutionary power and a vital part of labor and production power and he wanted to erase the old conception about women by the cultural movement in the society; thus he gave the call to the women- 'Be united, take part into the political and productive activities' (Politt, 2008, 78-79).

But Mao could not achieve his goal for the negative social constraints, and the pictures remain unchanged. In 'Padatik' we see Shila's harassment by her husband. She is a working woman having the so-called economic independence. But then why should she suffer like this? Not only that, Biman and Nikhil also suspect Shila for an unhealthy relationship with Sumit. So, our question : is it the production of a great revolution, Naxalism, which considers a single woman just a commodity? Then, after how many movements this rotten society will respect a woman just the way she is? It is not just a mere issue of leaving a flat but perishing the likelihood of the (im)possible relation of a woman with the 'Other'...her exclusive 'Other'.

'And if you're offering me diamonds and rust...I've already paid'(Baez).

Nandini : 'Questions and questions ....'

Prof.: 'Charubabu gave sole importance to armed training but we didn't have mass level organization. I can remember throughout Calcutta, schools were shutdown. We found support among some of the educated elites and Delhi's prestigious St. Stephen's College became a hotbed of Naxalite activities.'

Nandini : 'Delhi ...St. Stephen's College .... Let's check it out .... Feel like taking a trip.'

Prof.: 'What do you mean? I know that you are whimsical to some extent, but .... Are you serious?'

Nandini : 'I'm only planning to see a film beyond Kolkata.'

Prof.: 'Would you please tell me how long you are going to continue your teaching phase?'

Nandini : 'Please have patience. This is a Sudhir Misra film, one of my favorite directors. 'Hazaaron Khwaishein Aisi' (thousand wishes like this). A Hindi film.

So, get ready to take off ....'

[1st viewer : 'All bogus. What are they doing?

This old ridiculous man and this middle-aged woman act like the first year students of coffee house. Even they are sleeping in two different rooms ... really monotonous!'

2nd viewer : 'Highly suspicious Felubabu! But I think we should concentrate on their dialogues and these movies.'

1st viewer : 'You are right. I think there is a deep relation between these Naxalite films and ...and ...love life... Both are un-arranged Laluda... anything can happen. As it is an adult subject so I sent Topshe to a distant shop for my Charminar.'***]

Day - 3

2nd Scene

'Where have all the young men gone, long time ago?...They're all in uniform'(Seeger).

'Hazaaron Khwaishein Aisi' - it's an epic tale of politics, love and ambition, directed by Sudhir Mishra. The film is critically acclaimed at 13 International Film Festivals.

Movie Summary :

The film is about the lives of three not-so-ordinary people in late 1960s and 70s when India was undergoing massive social and political changes. It was the turbulent time of Vietnam, the Emergency and the Naxalite movement in India.

The film opens in 1969 in Delhi's St. Stephen College with three students, Sidhdharth (Kay Kay Menon), Geeta (Chitrangada Singh) and Vikram (Shiney Ahuja) and the aspiration of these protagonists.

Sidhdharth is a driven revolutionary who dreams of bringing a revolution in the state of Bihar that will end the caste system and injustice there and change the society.

Vikram, son of a Gandhian politician who has grown up in less comfort than Sidhdharth and Geeta, wants to climb the social ladder at any cost.

Geeta is a London-returned South Indian girl and in love with Siddharth. But she is not sure to engage herself with Siddharth's Naxalite activities. Sidhdharth chooses his ideology over Geeta breaking her heart again and again.

In 1969 we hear the voice of Sidhdharth through his letter to Geeta in flashback- 'Calcutta was all inspiring'. And what was the actual situation of India and Kolkata? 'As per the AICCCR's February decision, a new party, CPIML was launched on the birth anniversary of Lenin. Charu Majumdar was elected the secretary of the central organizing committee (Pathak, 1995, 22).

Sidhdharth was moved by the Naxalite activities of Calcutta and mentioned the 'Eight Historical Documents' of Charu Majumdar. He leaves for Bihar to change the caste system and bring the revolution. Geeta leaves for Oxford and Vikram sets up an office in Delhi. The film evokes the spirit of 60s and 70s successfully and reminds us the quotation of William Faulkner- 'the past is not dead. It isn't even past' (Faulkner, 1929).

Sidhdharth is shown rushing to the barricades on the sides of the workers facing the torture by the police and we get a vivid picture of the role of the Naxalite students' organization. Sidhdharth believes that violence has a strong purpose- as a weapon to win the revolution. On a letter to Geeta he justifies his feelings- 'Violence is just, oppressor violence is unjust and to hell with the ethics'.

But at the same time this moment of the film raises a question : if it is the base of Marxian dialectics then which class is directing violence and against whom?

While Geeta has the charming and sharp image, Vikram's complexities and grayness makes him the most mysterious of them all.

Sidhdharth is swinging between the two ideas-idealism and realism. Gradually he loses his faith in his ideology. His weakness as a responsible man in a relationship is also exposed and he changes his path.

Sketches of the Main Characters :

The lead characters of the film unroll with its progress. As a college girl Geeta engaged herself fully in attempts to have the company of her love- Siddharth; even we see that the married Geeta still meets Sidhdharth cheating her husband. But this is not just a 'love in the time of cholera' syndrome but it makes her mature as she starts an adult literacy school for women and on the way of life she refuses to accompany Sidhdharth when he wants to leave, and behaves like a fugitive from the path of revolution.

From an idealist, Sidhdharth, as the movie ends, looks like a common, shattered individual whose dreams turned into despair. He voices his anguish in the last scene where he leaves Geeta and goes to London for studying medicine through a letter : 'I hope the mysteries of the human body will be less confusing.'

Sidhdharth, as a character, never gains any respect for many reasons. From the very beginning he was a fully whimsical person, sometimes opportunist, because in 1975, in Bhojpur, when he was shot by the police and admitted in a local hospital where Vikram was his companion, he acted like a selfish man. He left Vikram there during the night when the local Naxalites helped him to run away from the hospital despite knowing the fact that Vikram was there to release him.

Personally I don't feel that kind of a man can love anyone except himself. He did not show any responsibility towards Geeta also. Even we can't have anything serious or any deep thought from this pampered, Bob Dylan fan, lover-boy type guy of a rich family.

Vikram's character describes his inner mind through his letter to Geeta- 'While you people want to get out (of the system), I want to get in....' He is one of the power brokers on whom the Indian politics thrive.

The movie has its own moments to raise questions and instigate contradictions between the established and the revolutionary left.

In one of the scenes, Sidhdharth writes to Geeta that in spite of being oppressed for ages, the lower caste villagers worship their landlord. Has the left movement in India ever been able to reconcile the caste factor in this country? Sidhdharth realized that this is the limitation of the left parties in India.

The movie ends up with the handicapped Vikram's writing on the rock with brick : 'I love you Geeta' as he and Geeta both sit by a quiet lake and watch the sunset and the touchy last song of the movie becomes vibrant and effective : 'Baanwara Maan Dekhne Chala Ek Swapna'.

Day - 4

Nandini : 'So... today is my last day. The same old classroom, the same old faces from tomorrow but the mad mind is going to see a dream'.

Prof.: 'Dream?'

Nandini : 'That one day you'll write 'I love you Nandini' on the wall like Vikram. I'm going to see this dream tonight.'

Prof.: 'You are right. I've no such fortune like Vikram to write a note on a lakeside rock.'
Nandini : 'Again the same old complex. I'll take you to the Ooty Lake.'
Prof.: 'Ooty? What a dream .... The small fish of the bathtub goes to the big sea now. Shall I show the fishy goblin?'
Nandini : 'What?'
Prof. 'Heteroglossia Nandini .... Our destiny. Every dialogues are immanently sociological and the individual consciousness also a socio-ideological fact' (Bakhtin, 45).
Nandini : 'Individual consciousness!'
Prof.: 'I'm talking about the consciousness of Herbert. Herbert shouted at those rationalists. Nandini, after those blood-stained days, people said that there was no logic in our movement, only emotional blunder they saw in it. Though they are right to some extent, but the mass, the Government and the state don't know everything. Anything can happen anywhere. Nobody knows when the revolution will wake up. Everything is not like a pet dog of your reason.'
Nandini : 'Why are you talking like this?'
Prof.: 'Nandini, tomorrow you'll join your College - routine, syllabus, classes, students, no emotion - no argument, no illogicality. Before this, I would like to show you some kind of unreality ... a 'must see' film.'
Nandini : 'What a surprise! You have your own collection!'
Prof.: 'This is a gift for a movie buff. I bought it for you. You'll surely love this work of director Suman Mukhopadhyay. The movie 'Herbert' is based on the novel of Nabarun Bhattacharjee. Tonight we'll watch Herbert and celebrate the last night of your leisure.'

[And they enter the world of illogicality in the last night...in the irrational world of Herbert]

'Well, I'll be damned, here comes your ghost again' (Baez).

'Herbert' :

Herbert Sarkar, a product of a 'once upon a time aristocrat and rich' typical north Calcutta family, becomes a sensation of this doomed grimacing city, Kolkata, with the span of different decades. Herbert grows up on the charity of his relatives and is made out to be a good for nothing. Let's have a look at his eventful life : death of his wicked father and resourceless mother in his infancy, the hapless paralyzed condition of his whore-monger uncle, his powerless and loving aunt, the torturing crooked cousin 'Dhanna', flying kites on the terrace, sexual excitement for the first and last time with the next door girl 'Buki' in his puberty, a visualizing evidence of the 70s' Naxalite period of Kolkata to his turn into 'cosmic play business' like a godman.

Herbert moves back and forth in time like a pendulum assimilating the various shades of time, economy, sociology and politics...and in this way the movie becomes an album of 'Binu' 'Samir', 'Khoro-Robi' (Straw-Robi), the old and mossfull tank of 'Gangajal'with this moving city of different ideologies.

But here I'm going to explore the effect of Naxalism on movies, so there is no chance to discuss in detail about the other aspects of this film, e.g. the psychoanalytic sides of Herbert's dreams...the dreams of his dead relatives and friends, forgetting that dreaming is the only right one cannot forbid. Now it's time to talk about the Naxalite treatment in the movie. In flashback we see that the little Binu and the adolescent Herbert's play with the slogan-'Lenin Stalin Mao take our red salute' and 'pamphlet is a weapon of the revolution'- this is the line of thinking which Binu inherits from his hardcore communist father and takes it to the core of his heart. These are the sketches that play like the signifiers and give us a hint of the 70s' turbulent time.

When young Herbert goes for a movie with Binu's father (Herbert's cousin), then like a metaphor, the film turns out to be 'Battleship Potempkin'.

Binu (nephew of Herbert), now a bright student of the Presidency College, becomes an activist and a follower of Charu Majumdar and the agitated blood-stained Kolkata appears on the screen. Before going to the underground position Binu gives a book to Herbert-Marighella's 'urban guerilla warfare'. With the chain of sequences the days of 70s left its signs : Herbert's reading of Marighella and the killing scene of Samir (another comrade and Binu's friend), arrest of Binu with a prohibited pamphlet of Charu Majumdar and obviously the cruel interrogation scene in the hospital-

Police IG : 'Binay, you can survive with good treatment. I'll ask the doctors if you help me. I need some informations.You are a bright student. Why don't you cooperate? All you guys do this rant about Mao and Mao...that man knows nothing about Marxism. Political power comes up to the battle of the gun? You call it Marxism?'

Binu:-'Ridiculous'(and a blood clot comes out from his mouth).

Binu loved his 'Harbertkaka' and shared his thought with the school-dropped, ignored and unloved Herbert.

Binu was a dreamer and he didn't compromise with the police. In his last dialogue in the hospital he told Herbert- 'I can see that the old times are falling apart in tiny bits...a storm is brewing....'

After Binu's death Herbert returns to his world of unreality...planchette and dead souls and the cosmic play business- 'dialogues with the dead'. It means he doesn't have any sensibility about the Naxalite period except the killing of Binu by the state, by the system, by the police. The school-dropped is completely unaware about the Naxalite ideology, but most probably a strange feeling of a mystery and a latent anger took place in his mind from then.

One day a man, who lost his son, comes to Herbert for knowing the status of his dead son from Herbert and Herbert gives him a blank white paper. When the man amazingly asks him the reason, Herbert says- 'If the meaning is known, then mystery's over.' This is the mystery of 'emotion'. While most of the people say that the result of the Naxalite movement is totally negative or it was the wrong movement by some idiotic and deviated persons, then this is the answer for them. Why did those bright students sacrifice their careers and lives? What was the mystery? And the answer is- 'emotion'. Common people usually fail to understand and then it seems to be a great mystery for them.

But now his cosmic business is at a loss by the threat of the rationalists who trapped and jailed many cons like Herbert. From their conversations we can find the hidden anger in Herbert for Binu's death. He is not ready to accept the logic of science and care a damn about modernism, postmodernism etc. We hear him arguing with them-

Herbert : 'There will always be ghost. I saw Binu in my dreams. The police shot Binu dead. Whom have I cheated? (He brings some old books on planchette) Have you read this? You think it's a big fraud?'

At the end Herbert loses his battle like Binu. The state rejected Binu's 'Guerilla Warfare' and the ideology of Mao Ze-dong by saying it's a 'rant' and 'disturbance' and in the same way the logical and rational world rejects Herbert by branding him a 'bullshit'.

Like Binu, his 'Hertbertkaka' also doesn't cooperate with the hegemonic society and commits suicide.

This is not the end; the actual moment and starting point of the film is now on the screen...the body of the 'Immortal Martyr' Herbert enters the electric cremation oven...and after a few seconds there is a huge and dangerous sound of a blast. It's dynamite which in the Naxalite days of 70s, had been hidden within Herbert's mattress. This explosive-loaded mattress is the cause of this blast.

The state police can't understand anything and this 'dead human bomb' is a big mystery now. Some of them say- 'It's a mad man's work and all mad men are politicians'.

Some intellectual Police Officers began to converse on postmodernism and Foucault.

Whatever it is, it's a real mess now and at last the Police IG says- 'There is one moral of this story ... the government, the state, or the police will never exactly know from where and whom the explosion is coming.'

And in flashback we now see Binu and his friend talking about the high quality dynamite from Albania. Binu could not use it for his untimely death but Herbert, unknowingly, throws a warning to the state to be aware. Anything can happen at any moment. Thus the 'bullshit', illogical Herbert shakes the logical world as the unjustified movement of 70s.

Herbert proves himself true...there will always be ghosts. The ghosts of 70s wanted to crush the establishment. It's a resurrection of Binu, Samir and the other dead men of 70s.

In 'Herbert', the director applies the treatment of the 'Cinema Novo' movement in a very intelligent way : through the directorial pose of a film-maker of Herbert's dead father and his dead mother as an assistant director as we see them behind the camera on a trolley, taking shots of the whole movie. A flavor of the 'Neo-realism' and the direct cinema technique reminds us the Novo Cinema essence- 'a camera in the hand and an idea in the head' and it also reminds us the form of the Brechtian alienation (Bordwell and Thompson, 577).

Though 'Kolkata 71', 'Padatik', and 'Hazarron Khwaishein Aisi' become the bonafide documents of the Naxalite movement of 70s, I think these films mainly focus on the negative impact of an un-arranged movement of that time.

But 'Herbert' is the only movie in which we don't find any negation, and at last we salute the unreality and of course the fishy goblin, the (im)possible Herbert.

1st viewer : 'Test of failure Lalmohonbabu...first time Felu Mittir doesn't get any chance to capture them...I don't even know about the success or failure of the lady, what she wanted from that 'home film festival' session... if the gloomy, rigid man will finally come out of his darkness and accept her or not! I don't know if the desired actually happened or not. But one day, incidentally, I met the cook along with a travel agent of the locality of that professor. The cook informed me that after the film session, there was no sleeping pill on his table and the local travel agent was astonished and told me that the ridiculous professor booked two air tickets for the coming 'Puja' vacation like all those middleclass Bengalis.'

2nd viewer : 'Horrendous'***

References :

Bhattacherjee, Kamal, 'Basanter bajronirghosh :sei jhoro haoar dinguli', 2009, *Naxalbari Andoloner Dinguli,* edited by Arjun Goswami, pp.32-35, Knowledge Publishing House, Kolkata.

MacTell, Ralph, 'Streets of London', song, Westminster Music Ltd, 1969.

Majumdar,Pronob, 'Naxalbarir andolon,uttal sottor', *Manchitro,* little magazine, 2004, pp.78-85, Bardhoman.

Fernando Solanas and Octavio Getino , 'Towards a Third Cinema'in *Movies and Methods : An Anthology,* edited by Nicholas, Bill, Berkeley, pp.44-64, University of California Press, 1976, Kolkata.

Sen, Mrinal, 'Chitronatya', 2004, *Punashcho,* Kolkata.

Rana, Kumar,' Sottorer dinguli', *Godhuli,* little magazine, 1995, p.112-117, Baharampoor, Murshidabad.

Nari O Communism : Marx theke Mao, Translated by Manmath Sarkar, Edited by Politt, Harry, Jan, 2008, Radical Impression, Kolkata.

'Diamonds and Rust' (song) by Joan Baez, Sony Music Entertainment Inc. 1963.

'Where Have All The Flowers Gone'(song), Peter Seegar, Sony Music, 1962.

Pathak, Sudhir : 'Diary of a Spectator', translated by Kumar Rana, *Godhuli,* little Magazine, 1995, p.22.

Faulkner, William, 'The Sound and the Fury', 1929, Oxford University Press, *The Faulkner Reader : Selection from the Works of William Faulkner,* Random House, p.240, 1954, Random House.

Bakhtin, Mikhail, *Art and Answerability, Early Philosophical Essays,* trans V. Liapunov, University of Texas Press, Austin, Texas, 1990.

Bordwell, David and Thompson, Kristin edited, *Film History : An Introduction,* 2nd edition, McGraw Hill,2003,p.545.

Banerjee, Sumanta, *In the Wake of Naxalbari : A History of the Naxalite Movement in India,* 1980, Subarnarekha.

Dasgupta, Biplab, *The Naxalite Movement,* 1974, Allied Publishers.

Duyker, Edward, *Tribal Guerrillas : The Santals of West Bengal and the Naxalite Movement,* 1987, Oxford University Press.

Films :

'Kolkata71', Directed by Mrinal Sen, released in1972.

'Padatik' by Mrinal Sen, a 1973 film.

'Hazaaron Khwaishein Aisi', a Sudhir Mishra film, released in 2005.

'Herbert', Directed by Suman Mukhopadhyay, a 2005 film.

***(Feluda and Lalmohonbabu, detective Prodosh Chandra Mitra and his writer friend Lalmohon Ganguly, respectively are the two characters created by Satyajit Ray in his detective stories of Feluda).

On Cinematic Reconstruction of Blazing and Bleeding Hearts : A Naxalbari Follower's Appreciation of Two Bengali Films - 'Path' and 'Atmaja'

Saumen Guha

When 'Naxalbari' was born in 1967, I was twenty years old. Working as a supporter of the then CPI (M), I was searching for any pro-people culture, people's struggles against oppression and injustice. At that very moment, Naxalbari uprising came as a pathfinder to overthrow the fetters of exploiting machinery. Youths like me, had their dreams of revolutionary upheaval, for which they had their hearts blazing. I would like to use the term 'Naxalbari-follower', instead of 'Naxalite', to identify those who believed in the movements like Naxalbari in 1967.

Whether those Naxalbari-followers were right or wrong, that is another question. The dream of a revolution to eradicate exploitation and injustice, to protect the lives of the poor peasants, to uphold a lofty ideal of classless society, was very much valuable and appreciated in our society and families. But neither all youths were committed to follow this revolutionary 'Naxalbari' ideal and path, nor all the youths active as Naxalbari-followers had their lives dedicated to the same lofty and great ideals.

In this context, I look at the Bengali films 'Path' (The Road) and 'Atmaja' (Born Within). They were produced in 1990s. In an appreciation of how a psychological approach to the story can highlight the dynamics of emotional cinematic experience, our study presents a critical analysis of these two films 'Path' and 'Atmaja'. In the classical sociology of films, it is said : 'So far, film analysis has been left to the professional film reviewer who mainly reports only about his *personal* preferences. (Naturally there are exceptions : there are some film critics who do their best to analyse 'the meaning of film' in relation to its audience. But they are rather the exception than the rule)'[1].

The sociological and normative analysis of 'Path' and 'Atmaja' would need a larger space, which we cannot afford here. But its appreciation cannot be based solely on aesthetic analysis avoiding the social and normative context. Moreover, I personally find the 'meaning of film' here, while I associate some elements with my own experience. These are my '*personal* preferences'.

Influence of Pro-Naxalbari Ideals and Rebels :

In the shameful silence about the blazing and bleeding hearts, and the brutal police and gangster repression, I remember only a few but brilliant Bengali literatures of that time of late 1960s, like *Naxalbari* by Sudhanshu Ghosh, *Yenan theke Srikakulam* (From Yenan to Srikakulam) by Barun Sen etc., which were honestly reflecting the aspirations of youths and society agitated inwardly and outwardly. I also remember an eye-witness account of Baranagar and Kashipur massacre 1971, in a short story 'Bhor Holo' (Dawn Comes) by Sanjib Chattopadhyay published in the then *Amrita,* August 1971, and a cry of the bleeding heart of Bina Banerjee, mother of Kajal Banerjee, who was killed by the police, in her excellent literary piece in the form of a letter, 'Kajal Tumi Kothay' (Where are you, Kajal?), published in a least known little magazine. No fiction could ever reflect such a depth of bleeding heart.

Adherents of the dominant form of socio-cultural revolution prior to the suppression of pro-Naxalbari movements simply refused to consume the written and visual media of the mainstream. At this critical juncture, the name 'Naxalbari' was not a profit-making commodity. So far my knowledge goes, none ever tried to make films on the literatures *Naxalbari, Yenan theke Srikakulam* or 'Bhor Holo'.

In appreciation of the filmic presentation, we may divide the influence and reflections of pro-Naxalbari ideals and rebels in Bengali films mainly into three categories : firstly, the direct reconstruction of pro-Naxalbari activities in full or parts; secondly, the films depicting implicit or covert existence of pro-Naxalbari ideal or rebels; and thirdly, the films having the stories of struggles, ideals and rebels in facing the social evils and problems, which surfaced after Naxalbari uprising in 1967.

'Path' and 'Atmaja' belong to the second category of presentation. The films exhibit how the homogeneity of the committed social forces has always been a myth in 1990s, imposed from above.

For idealism, a conception of Bengali films as innately tied to place, space, and homeland is integral. To us, homeland means the country, society and habitat. Homeland becomes synonymous with the life. More specifically, the homeland is understood as the material trace denoting the linear history of invasion, conquest, and ultimately freedom, the historical mode of thought arising around the search of identity and recognition. The homeland is a reflection of the movement ranging from oppression to assertion of identity.

The existence of family is equally important. The family becomes powerful as the physical boundary of imagined identity, offering a rooted sense of place from which identity arises. This form of personal sentiments arose while attempting to claim the social identity.

Thus, the mother Sujata's life in 'Atmaja' outside her home and her occasional visit to Calcutta, express the rural and urban class divisions of moralities, sentiments and ideologies, which to some extent project the entity and role of homeland. At the end of the film, whenever Sujata went to Ajoy's lady-love Ratna, it is like a return to her native land which she cherished most.

However, our position of film appreciation is not one which relays the spectator through a hermeneutic play, the enigma of what is to come, but through existing paradigms of narrative knowledge, although these may be the subject to re-working.

It was a right time in 1972 to release Mrinal Sen's film 'Calcutta'71'. After 'Calcutta'71', unambiguously Ritwik Ghatak made his 'Jukti Takko O Gappo' (Logic Debate and Story) reflecting his concern about pro-Naxalbari activists. But both the film 'Calcutta'71' and 'Jukti Takko O Gappo' had no simple or plain story line. They amalgamated many cut-pieces, sometimes unrelated, together to point out something socio-political. Apparently, before that, there was a long gap between the filmic depiction and social realities, except Ritwik Ghatak's concerns about the lives of the refugee, victims of partition. In 1977, the documentaries like Anand Patwavardhan's 'Prisoners of Conscience', Utpalendu Chakraborty's 'Mukti Chai', raised the voice to free the pro-Naxalbari prisoners.

It is worthwhile to mention the Satyajit Ray's films 'Padatik' (Infantry) and 'Simabaddho' (Limited), which touched the middle class social issues in its own way. Though pro-Naxalbari ideology is not overtly expressed, the Bengali films of post-1977s unhesitatingly portrayed the corruption of police and political system, police-criminals-politicians nexus, exploitation of people by the state, etc. Gradually came the so-called 'new wave' films like Utpalendu Chakraborty's 'Moyna Tadanta' (Post Mortem), 'Chokh' (Eyes), commercially successful Anjan Choudhury's 'Shatru' (Enemy) etc., and Goutam Ghose's documentary 'Hungry Autumn', which had some contribution for thematic developments of the Bengali films.

Filmic Idioms and Political Ideology :

But Naxalbari is itself a genre, an idiom. In practical life, once the epithet 'Naxal' meant the 'Strong Protester'. In films, we find two things : too much analytical approach attached to pro-Naxalbari characters and plain rendering of sentiments and passion of pro-Naxalbari ideology. In 'Path and Atmaja' we feel that plain renderings of sentiments and passion.

Once Ritwik Ghatak said - "Cinema cannot but be engaged, committed, to be worthy of its mission. ....What is the mission of cinema?... I mean the awareness, the sense of reaction of a truthful artiste to small things of life."[2].

The blazing and bleeding hearts were burning reality in 1970s, and 'Path and Atmaja' expressed the awareness and sense of reaction with filmic idioms, however small things of life they were.

The rejection of popular culture as alien and debased in West Bengal can be understood historically as a gesture of resistance during the moment when identity building was occurring in the pro-Naxalbari movement toward establishing the People's Democracy.

About the movement, migration, and myths of Irish Cinema, researcher Dana C. Och analyzes the ways a collection of Irish films envision multiple 'other' Irelands that challenge the essentialist Ireland of the national imagination, frequently through the breakdown of boundaries between 'reality' and 'fantasy'[3].

In 'Path and Atmaja', the boundaries between 'reality' and 'fantasy' have been broken down. In 'Path', we find the defeat of the evils, and the victory of the positive forces in harmony with the rising sun. In 'Atmaja', at last Aju and Bidyut are born or reborn within Sujata in her dream! It is their resurrection. All these take us to a new land, place, identity and consciousness.

Bengali cinema cannot successfully adopt the closed nature of Latin American or African films, as the critical problems of Bengal cannot be isolated or contained within one historical moment. The inability to safely contain the past results in numerous temporal shifts that disorient the viewer inevitably, this loss of a clear temporal order within the film undermines any sense of the past's 'separateness' and reinforces the strong connections between the past and the subsequent eras that the film is concerned to make.

It seems that ethnographic studies of pro-Naxalbari are guaranteed to fail because the historians are systematically dehumanized. The lie of the history is actually the failure of ethnography, which attempts to find the movement's cultural tradition, consisting of pure national origins and exclusionary boundaries, rather than seeing their human dynamics as most important and inclusive.

The purpose of one modern study of 'Political Reelism' is to view and discuss how political campaigns and politicians have been depicted in films, and how the movies function rhetorically and appeal to core values.

In genres such as the political film, the narrative process assumes audience knowledge of the narrative totality it refers to, so that a fragmentary, episodic structure can be deployed. In a discussion of political contents of two Indian films, it is observed that - "One film ('Earth') shuns the conventions of Bollywood cinema while the other ('Lagaan') embraces them; one promotes an openly left-wing political agenda and interpretation of history while the other oscillates between Marxist overtones and a very conservative image of society; one targets an elite high-brow Indian and international audience while the other tries to court India's masses"[4].

'Path' is extrovert and has an unambiguous political overtone, whereas 'Atmaja' is introvert and only renders the inner worlds of bleeding hearts. But both of them are searching for a new life and society.

Two central characters Animesh and Sujata in 'Path and Atmaja' observe the struggle for ideological existence and identity, and the narratives of two films are made around them. The cognitive migration that is exhibited through the reconstructed characters extends in the films 'Path and Atmaja' to a consideration of the ways that Bengali traditional positive characters are equally erased from the imagination of the mainstream.

In no way, 'Path and Atmaja' are nonfiction films. Because - "The nonfiction film dramatizes fact instead of fiction. The nonfiction film maker focuses his personal vision and his camera on actual situations - persons, processes, events - and attempts to render a creative interpretation of them"[5].

But the political contents of the films are undoubtedly explicit. In 1995, Ravi S. Vasudevan in discussing 'the political culture of address in a transitional cinema and Indian popular cinema', summed up :

> In terms of narrative form, the popular imperative engages in a series of transactions, both with methods and idioms marked as traditional or culturally distinctive as well as those defined as modern. Here, I would like to consider the location of the spectator's position around three issues : (i) how is the ideology

> of the traditional constituted in cinematic narration; (ii) what are the functions of cinematic techniques of subjectivity in the construction of narrative space; (iii) how does the overall attraction based, presentational rather than re-presentational field of the popular film system address the spectator"[6].

Here the spectators are not expected to be the witnesses of the depicted social realities, but both 'Path and Atmaja' uphold the idealist political views of social struggles, sometimes loud but sublime. They disclosed some naked truths and pursued positive goals.

In its narrative, 'Path' vividly portrays the betrayal of the leaders of revolutionary movements, like Jagada or Jagannath Mitra and Paban Sarkar, the ideology of self-sacrifice and dedication of Suchetadi for the people, personal love metamorphosed to hope, and the struggles of the people and by the people.

'Atmaja' does not try to narrate any such story. Instead, Sujata shows deep silent respect for Ajoy and Bidyut's lives, ideology and struggles. Sujata discovers Aju in Bidyut.

Features of 'Path and Atmaja' :

I reject in general the complicated criteria by which many critics identify a film as typical Bengali. Even within these limits the films 'Path and Atmaja' should be considered Bengali. The directors are Bengali, the source material is a Bengali story, and the film was made in Bengal.

'Path' (The Road) is directed by Pintu Chatterjee with a story and script by Ranajit Gupta, and participated by Victor Banerjee, Rituparna Sengupta, Indrajit Chakravarty, Mamata Shankar, Rajatabha Dutta as actors in the main roles.

'Atmaja' (Born Within)'s script, dialogues and direction are done by Nabyendu Chatterjee, and based on a story by Sebabrata Chowdhuri, and the film is participated by Gauri Ghosh, Arjun Chakravorty, Mahasweta Bandopadhyaya, Shyamal Ghoshal as actors in the main roles. Both the films are in colour.

These two films are less known to film buffs, and much ignored by mainstream film critics, though 'Atmaja' fetched National Award Silver Lotus as the Best Bengali Film in 1990.

At no place, in both the films, the name 'Naxalbari' or 'CPI (ML) is overtly or explicitly pronounced. But we can guess unambiguously the ideal presence of Naxalbari from the context and ambience of the stories of the two films. This phenomenon made these two films more sensitive and touching. One has to feel the facts with one's own experience and cognition.

In 'Path', we identify the presence of pro-Naxalbari ideology in various slogans and dialogues explaining the context of the struggles against exploitation and injustice. Once a graffiti, 'China's Chairman is our Chairman', appearing after other two graffiti of parliamentary parties Indira Congress and CPI (M), tells the affinity of the central theme of the film. All three slogans of three political parties are only seen in the 1970s, like 'People's Democratic Revolution' of CPI (M). Thus the graffiti seemed to tell the 'time-frame' of 'Path' to be 1970s.

No such 'time-frame' can be assumed in 'Atmaja' from the available scenes. But Paritosh's underground life, his death in 'police encounter', and the police station remind us of the ambience of 1970s.

Recently 'Political Reelism' prevails, where it is seen - "By interpreting real life, political films entertain us, perhaps satirically poking fun at familiar people and events. However, the filmmakers complete this form of entertainment through the careful integration of American values or through the absence of, or attack on those values. In some cases, film mirrors our commitment to values, and in other cases film mock the values Americans usually cherish"[7].

In our experience, the literary cinema framework helps to defend the late development of indigenous political film, in effect ignoring the decades' long fight for justice and humanity. Furthermore, the rhetoric attempts to delineate a strong position for Bengali cinema as a political cinema.

Prologues of Two Stories :

'Path' begins with the scene where some hooligans were drinking and condemning the revolutionary ideals and activities.

Animesh was a young man ignorant of any political activities. He was preoccupied with his studies and living outside his home. He was coming back to his home and witnessing a political murder. This was first time Animesh saw a bloody act. He came back home with a tremendous mental shock.

At this time he asked his family members about his elder brother Paritosh. Paritosh used to be involved in some political activities for which he left home and was working underground. Animesh came to know from his family the name of Jagannath or Jagada, who was the leader or mentor of the political group which Paritosh belonged to.

Animesh met one Paban Sarkar at first to be brought to the leader Jagada. From Jagada he got the permission for meeting Paritosh. Animesh secretly met his elder brother Paritosh at a riverside, and requested Paritosh for coming back home. Paritosh unhesitatingly refused Animesh upholding his own fighting spirit and ideal.

Animesh and Paritosh walked together crossing the graffiti of Indira Congress, CPI (M) and pro-Naxalbari CPI (ML), as if they were determining their own path or road to make a society free from exploitation and injustice. They departed, but Paritosh was violently attacked by some gangsters, who hated his 'revolutionary' ideals.

Animesh saw the killing of Paritosh. He was bound to conceal it from his family. He was to live with a suppressed bleeding heart.

His lady-love Rimi was living happily with her dear father. Rimi met Animesh at his home and broke his painful silence. She came to know the death of Paritosh. Afterwards the family of Animesh also came to know the shocking death of Paritosh. His mother fainted and became mentally deranged.

Incidentally, once Animesh found one of the killers of Paritosh and rushed to attack him. He could not kill the gangster due to the extreme opposition by Rimi and others. This was the first outburst of a silent bleeding heart metamorphosed into a blazing heart.

'Atmaja' began with the train journey of middle aged widow Sujata, the mother of Ajoy and Bijoy. The first part of the story was gradually unfolded through flash back. Several pieces of earlier incidents were intercut with the solitary journey of Sujata with a bleeding heart.

Sujata asked Bijoy or Biju about her elder son Ajoy or Aju -- "What kind of people is he hobnobbing with? Is he with some political party? . . . I am just an ordinary mother. I want to know what my son is doing."

Finally, Aju was absconding. The police came in search for Aju, and Sujata had to face the police interrogation. Even at the police station, she was facing the question - "Do you know the whereabouts of your son?" Her strongest answer was - "If I had known, I could have told you, I know, but I won't tell!"

That fateful day came to Sujata, when she was taken to the police station for identifying the blood-stained clothes of Ajoy. That punjabi Aju liked most and he was filled with joy when Sujata presented it to him. We are shocked to hear Sujata crying at the top of her voice - "Aju!" Now on, Sujata's heart was bleeding.

'Atmaja' shows the incidents onwards full of feelings for the bleeding hearts of the mother Sujata and Aju's lady-love Ratna. Biju is established and wealthy. Sujata visits their house, and meets his wife and daughter. But she felt lonely, in the affluent culture of Biju's family.

Sujata met Bidyut during her morning walk. She visited his family in a slum. But Bidyut died at a workers' agitation. Sujata returned to Biju's house with her clothes stained with Bidyut's blood.

Recalling Realities :

'Path and Atmaja' strike the chords which cause resonance of some realities I know.

I recall the murder of my friend and comrade Naxalbari-follower Shakti Roy on 9 August 1970, in the hands of some political hooligans in the broad daylight on a street of Howrah. The murder of Paritosh reminds that incident in real life. Mother of Shakti was mentally deranged, as in 'Path'.

In 1971, Ashok Dutta of Taltala was killed by the police and his body was thrown to the Ganges. Since then his mother was mentally deranged. 'Path and Atmaja' reflect that shock.

After the murders of many Naxalbari-followers, like Shakti, hearts of some young men were blazing. These blazing hearts committed to uphold the revolutionary ideals of the murdered souls, like Animesh in 'Path'.

Ajoy used to meet Ratna secretly, and Ratna brought some food for him. Their love affair did not go farther. But in her new conjugal life, Ratna recalled her heart dedicated to Aju. She invited Sujata to her home. Two bleeding hearts felt each other.

But it is very common feature of any revolutionary movements to create some opportunist leaders and traitors, like Jagada and Paban Sarkar. It is also common that the uterine brothers and sisters of revolutionary activist become greedy and opportunist, like Bijoy.

To know the whereabouts of Animesh, the police officer Gagan Roy brutally tortured and molested Rimi in presence of her father in the police station. Rimi's father committed suicide. This sequence reminds us the torturer-police in 1970s, like Runu Guha Neogy, in real life.

The leader like Jagada and Paban Sarkar usually instruct the honest activists to take arms for revolution and revenge, and afterwards they stab at the back of those activists and activities fulfilling their vested interests. We can identify the staircase and environs of the Writers' Buildings in 'Path', where Jagada is a minister. In practice, any kind of People's Democratic Revolution or working class movement tends to bear the venomous teeth of the Parliamentary elections.

Structural Paradigm :

We cannot begin creativity in Bengali films in a pre-planned way. As the Soviet cinema showed - "The new creative school in the Soviet cinema emerged spontaneously. The new school was started... as a spontaneous reaction against social realism, and subsequently developed into a movement which consciously tries to avoid contemporary subjects and strives towards complete individuality"[8].

The sublime linearity and traditional characterizations of the film narratives of 'Path and Atmaja' conflict with the tortuous, and sometimes contradictory, unfolding of real history. In several instances, sociopolitical and aesthetic considerations explain deliberate misrepresentations, omissions, or selective emphases in the two films, specially in 'Atmaja', that are designed to convey an openly political interpretation of the past-or to fit in what directors and producers believe their audiences would wish to see.

By highlighting some characters' alienation from mainstream culture, the definition of the revolutionary as rendered in these two films, through ideology and the construction of an ideal human being, as a reflection of the difference from the mainstream and the habitual living of the people, is revealed as equally important.

'Naxalbari' may be taken as an abstraction in filmic idioms, and to the present spectators it is a kind of 'defamiliarisation' as it is said - "In fact, one could describe 'abstraction' itself as a threshold word, a border post between the two categories central to Kickasola's thesis : a formal abstraction that can be (and often is) discussed in the same breath as Antonioni and might be called 'defamiliarisation', and an abstraction open to the transcendent or metaphysical"[9].

In 'Path and Atmaja', 'Naxalbari' has its invisible presence. And the ideological differences between the different forms of structural paradigms and their concomitant imagination of the revolutionary life and system crystallize in short scenes and intercuts in 'Atmaja'.

The inclusion of the memories becomes a device through which notions of the authenticity of self and other can be established, as they are a dynamic structural paradigm within the filmic idioms that remain outside the dominant definition of pure political identity.

But too much abstraction may lead to absurdity, which we cannot avoid, and - "In the Theatre of the Absurd, the spectator is confronted with the madness of the human condition, is enabled to see his situation in all its grimness and despair. Stripped of illusions and vaguely felt fears and anxieties, he can face this situation consciously, rather than feeling it vaguely below the surface of euphemisms and optimistic illusions"[10]. Anything absurd in 'Path and Atmaja' is like the images of the spectators' subconscious mind happening yesterday.

The amalgamation of the urban and the rural, the two imaginations of Bengal, disrupts the notion of an irreducible real, as also does Sujata's tendency to switch direction from urban to rural without much complex motivation.

Some Bengali poems have cinematic expressions[11]. Inversely, we can say that some films may have poetic expressions. That we find in 'Atmaja'.

The soul of this genre of films demands increasing thought, even if thought begins by undoing the system of actions, perceptions and affections on which these films have fed up to that point. As this stage of cultural parameters was adopted by the mainstream mass, its exclusions and prejudices are often naturalized and projected on the older social parameters.

Instead, the use of authentic locations, which are ideologically positioned as falsely constructed traditional environs, serves as entry into a critical mode that complicates notions of authenticity and reality by revealing their constructed natures.

The song 'Shesh Kothay Pather' (Where is the end of this road) of Rabindranath displays this function of 'frontal' address across genres, reaching over and beyond the space of the scenes of 'Path', locking the spectator into a direct auditory relay.

Thus, one central representational strategy of the political films is the reproduction of literary flavours, artefacts, and landscapes which already have a privileged status within the accepted definition of the filmic idioms.

The uncomfortable relationship between the mainstream mass and the committed revolutionaries serves as the basis for why the pro-revolutionary activists were so active in the movement for classless society and the development of early stages of new cultural identities.

The film 'Path' extends beyond the actions to include various human characters, defrocked opportunists, and women who live beyond the pale of the moral order through, for example, disorderly life outside and inside the family, all positions that literally subvert regularity and tradition.

Melodrama and Anti-Drama :

'Path' ends with a melodramatic sequence, begins with the now minister Jagada's plan for killing Animesh. Police officer Gagan Roy was given a chance to kill his old enemy Animesh. Rimi was told that she could call Animesh to meet her. Animesh was overwhelmed by Rimi's voice and agreed to meet Rimi. Rimi was taken by Jagada's car, where Gagan was hiding.

Sucheta talked to Jagada, and understood the conspiracy to kill Animesh. Her own worker also told the fate of Animesh. She rushed to the spot.

Gagan hurled bombs, and Jagada came from another side with huge force of gangsters. Rimi and Animesh survived the bomb blast, and took a side. Animesh was attacked by the gangsters at the instruction of Jagada. There was a long fight, and Animesh was finally attacked by notorious police Gagan. In return, Gagan was killed by Animesh.

Finally, the mass of people with their house-hold tools came to beat the gangsters. Jagada tried to escape by his own car, where Sucheta was sitting. Sucheta killed Jagada to take revenge. Rimi and Animesh united at the end of the film.

To me, this over-simplified melodrama does not match the main serious thread of events in 'Path', but not unexpected. After all, it gives the viewer an imaginary relief from the negative elements like notorious Jagada, Gagan and their associates. If there is any conclusion or message at the end, that is the inevitable defeat of wrong-doers in the hands of right-doers.

Removing the traditional realism from the films 'Path and Atmaja' will result in the complete loss of context, particularly in relation to which the films are attempting, whether successfully or unsuccessfully, to override through manipulations the dominant genre and conventions. In many post-1970s Bengali films, this over-simplified melodrama of the defeat of bad elements in the hands of the heroic good characters is common.

Symbolically, in the last scene of 'Path', Rimi drew attention of Ani to the red rising sun. This typical hope and optimism prevail beyond the end of the film 'Path'.

But in 'Atmaja', we do not find any melodramatic end. On the contrary, 'Atmaja' ends in an anti-drama with a message. To make end, last two consecutive sequences are strongly amalgamated in 'Atmaja'. The depicted characters seem to condemn the popular version of history that defends police state's actions as a political necessity.

Sujata's most valuable collection was the clothes stained with blood of Ajoy and Bidyut! In the last sequence, Sujata was dreaming her labour. In a vast space she delivered a baby. She was rocking the baby on the cradle. The baby was transformed in Ajoy, then Bidyut, born within Sajata, smiling. Sujata's dream was broken at the call of Ratna and Bijoy. Sujata departed from Bijoy's house, carrying her invaluable blood-stained clothes with Ratna, leaving behind the new clothes given by Bijoy.

Socio-Political Authenticity and Documentation :

The humanscapes in both 'Path and Atmaja' refuse to remain autonomous. Their different spaces of the classes of opportunists and activists constantly intersect, attesting to the impossibility of the separateness of the classes and people in the supposed hierarchy of socio-political struggles.

The pains in 'Path and Atmaja' make the films both humanistic and purposeful. In Iranian cinema -- 'Dabashi is unambiguous about his strong objections to aesthetic judgments framed solely in terms of humanism : "Iranian aesthetics are entirely purposeful and have emerged from the pain of the suffering we have as a people endured. Do not let a saccharine and generic "humanism" assimilate the specificity of your cinema - the blood and bone of its reality..."[12].

The difference between mainstream and revolutionary ideals perceivable in the films is that dominant notions, in particular concerning the invisibility of the pro-Naxalbari struggles in the blazing stage, are complicated rather than reaffirmed.

Now, how we conclude our appreciation? In Bengali film semiology, roughly from the 1970s to the end of the 1990s, one of the boldest proposals was the idea that understanding rests upon the rule-governed relations between a material thing, like an image and a concept. My common-sense may not be 'our' common-sense. Here I am singular, a Naxalbari-follower of the past. So that, Paritosh, Animesh, Ajoy, Bidyut, the violence, sufferings, the bleeding and blazing hearts, cannot remain in filmic frames to me. The films 'Path and Atmaja' recall the days ablaze when I was young.

References :

1. J. P. Mayer (1946), *Sociology of Film : Studies and Documents,* London: Faber and Faber.
2. Ritwik Ghatak (1965), 'Bengali Cinema Literary Influence', reprinted *Chitrabikshan,* January-April, 1976, 99-101.
3. Dana C. Och (2006), 'The World Goes One Way and We Go Another': *Movement, Migration, and Myths of Irish Cinema* (Doctor of Philosophy Dissertation, University of Pittsburgh).
4. Giacomo Lichtner and Sekhar Bandyopadhyay (2008), 'Indian Cinema and the Presentist Use of History : Conceptions of "Nationhood" in Earth and Lagaan', *Asian Survey,* Vol. 48, Issue 3, pp. 431-452.
5. Rechard Meram Barsam (1974), *Nonfiction Film : A Critical History,* London : George Allen & Unwin.
6. Parts of his analyses were originally published in Ravi S. Vasudevan (1995), 'Addressing the Spectator of a "Third-world" National Cinema: the Bombay Social Film of the 1940s and 1950s', *Screen 36* (4) 1995.
7. Jennifer Lee Walton (2006), *Political Reelism : a Rhetorical Criticism of Reflection and Interpretation of Political Films,* Doctor of Philosophy Dissertation, Bowling Green State University.
8. Jeanne Vronskaya (1972), *Young Soviet Film Makers,* London : George Allen & Unwin.
9. Paul Coates (2005), 'From the Immediate to the Transcendent', *Film Studies,* 6, Summer 2005, 97-98.
10. Martin Esslin (1974), *The Theatre of the Absurd, Middlesex :* Penguin Books.
11. Nishith Kumar Mukhopadhyay (1986), *Bangla Sahitya o Bangla Chalachchitra* (in Bengali), Calcutta : Anandadhara.
12. Farouk Mitha (2009), 'Review of 'Masters and Masterpieces of Iranian Cinema by Hamid Dabashi", *Arab Media & Society,* January, 2009, p.2.

From 'Hazaar Chaurasi ki Maa' to 'Hazaaron Khwaishen Aisi'—A Million Dreams : A Study of Naxalism in Hindi Cinema

Devapriya Sanyal

(I)

Thomas Elsaesser in his article discusses at length the idea of history, representation and cinema. I would prefer to quote him at length,

> History, when it is not just what's past but what is being passed on, seems to have entered a twilight zone, not least because it has become a past that cinema and television can 'master' for us by digitally remastering archival material...what of the memory of the events which live in the culture because of the images they have left etched on our retinas, too painful too disturbing not to remember? No longer is storytelling the culture's meaning-making response; an activity closer to therapeutic practice has taken over, which acts of re-telling, re-membering and repeating all pointing in the direction of obsession, fantasy, trauma"[1].

While there were many cultural and intellectual responses to the Naxalbari movement immediately after its inception and progress through to the mid 1970s, as the movement went past its prime, the responses became muted. However, the interest never died down completely since the movement did not completely peter out. In the mid 80s, there was a resurgence of interest through the publishing of books and making of films as the movement seemed to revive itself.

It is not surprising therefore that during the last twenty years or so a number of significant works dealing with the theme of Naxalism have been published in various Indian languages and also a number of film directors have focused their cinematic creativity on the theme of Naxalism. More prominent among them are Mahasweta Devi's *Hajaar Churashir Maa,* Nabarun Bhattacharyya's *Herbert* and films like Mrinal Sen's 'Padatik', 'Kolkata 71', 'Interview', Satyajit Ray's 'Pratidwandi' and more recently films like Sudhir Mishra's 'Hazaaron Khwaishen Aisi', Mani Ratnam's 'Raavan', Govind Nihalani's 'Hazaar Chaurasi Ki Maa' and regional Bengali films like 'Herbert' and 'Kalbela'.

It is generally believed that when cultural workers, writers, theatre persons, other performers and film-makers turn to an event or a movement of the past, there is always a contemporaneous reason for it. Today India is at a crossroad where a national debate has begun on major questions surrounding development, particularly the models of development. The major focus of this debate is the question of land - something which was at the core of the Naxalbari movement as well. Land is being acquired by both the state and private developers under various garbs ranging from developing the infrastructure to setting up of schools, hospitals and public facilities. But instead it is being diverted for non-public, non-infrastructure purposes. In fact, farmers across the country are up in arms, challenging such acquisitions for which they were short changed primarily by the state. They are challenging it both legally and politically[2].

The situation is no better in the tribal areas and areas notified as forest land both of which are a no-no as far as land acquisition is concerned. And yet the land mafia along with the mineral mafia is milking these areas dry thereby threatening the livelihoods -- at times the very lives -- of the tribals. It is this that has once again given a new impetus to the Naxal movement and also to the response by cultural workers.

Together with this, the most recent national focus on mega corruption, particularly by the state has also forced a national debate on the state-sponsored models of development pursued during the last sixty five years of independence.

(2)

A noticeable turn in aesthetics in Bollywood was noticed with the kind of films made and showcased after Mrinal sen's 'Bhuvan Shome' was released in 1969. A change was noticed vis-a- vis the diversity displayed both in terms of form, theme, techniques as well as political positions. A few of such films were Basu Chatterji's 'Sara Akash', Kantilal Rathod's 'Kanku', Shivendra Sinha's 'Phir Bhi', Mani Kaul's 'Uski Roti', Kumar Shahani's 'Maya Darpan', Avtar Kaul's '27 Down', Basu Bhattacharyya's 'Anubhav', Chidananada Dasgupta's 'Bilet Pherat', Pattabhi Rama Reddy's 'Samskara', Satyadev Dubey's 'Shannata, Court Chalu Ahe', Mrinal Sen's 'Interview', 'Calcutta 71', 'Chorus' and Adoor Gopalakrishnan's 'Swayamvaram' to name just a few (Prasad 1998 : 188). It is with this, Madhava Prasad, in his remarkable work, notes that "the travails of the urban middle class, questions of women's agency and sexuality, social satire, agit prop, critiques of feudal power structures, conflicts of modernity and tradition ...were being explored (Prasad 1998 : 188-89)[3].

Govind Nihalani's 1998 adoption and representation of the Naxalite movement in his film 'Hazaar Chaurasi Ki Maa' therefore comes as no surprise, for along with Shyam Benegal, Govind Nihalani has always been one of the most prominent faces of parallel cinema in India. It is based on a seminal novel by the prominent Bengali writer, Mahasweta Devi. It is scripted carefully throughout, keeping in mind the idealism and truth of the Naxalbari movement, a not so distant troubled and painful chapter etched in the history of Bengal.

During the tenure of the CPI-M's coalition government in the late 1960s, the movement spread rapidly, finally reaching the cities especially Calcutta and infecting the urban youth with its idealism and the promises of a better world.

The Calcutta of the 1960s and 70s is captured brilliantly on celluloid. The city alive with revolutionary fervour in which most of the educated and intellectually gifted Bengali youth reacted with anger against hypocrisies, injustices, betrayals and counter-violence measures practised by the state. In the film, Brati, the young intellectual Naxalite sums it up aptly at a critical point in the film, "Maine ekh sapna dekha hai Ma, koi chhota sa nehi bahut badah, kranti ka sapna, sab kuch ulat pulat kar dene ka sapna, kuch badal dalne ka sapna...." (I have seen a dream mother, not a small one but a big one, a dream of revolution to come - that will turn everything upside down, change everything).

During this period the city was in the grip of a Marxist-Leninist-Maoist movement which professed working for the downtrodden, the farmers and liberating them from the oppression and atrocities inflicted on them by upper class landlords. Thousands of young men were arrested and many were shot in what came to signify the horrifying ordeal of "encounter". A special force, organized by the government to tackle these young revolutionaries, was given the authority to use brute force to handle the situation.

The film begins with a phone call, asking Sujata Chatterjee to come to Kantapukur - a police morgue to identify her son's corpse. The body has now been reduced to a mere numerical - 1084. Her 22 year old son Brati Chatterjee, the scion of an educated, cultured upper class bhadralok family is identified as "a criminal", a "goonda"[4] and killed. Dibyanath Chatterjee, Brati's father and other family members disown Brati to hush up what according to them is a death, the news of which will bring nothing but shame and disgrace to the family. We get to know Brati as his mother embarks on a journey to investigate the cause of her son's death as well as those of his friends and comrades.

In this odyssey of discovering his militant revolutionary commitment and in trying to understand his struggles against the exploitative system that is feudalism, Sujata begins to realize that she herself is alienated as a woman, a wife and a mother thanks to the typical bourgeois social values prevalent in the upper and middle class social circles of Calcutta of those times.

Sujata, the mother in an attempt to regain a sense of self from the intense psychological and emotional trauma of losing her favourite child gains some insights through her interaction with various other women characters in the film. While Somu's mother is a lower class illiterate woman from Bihar whose son has also been killed during the same clash with neighbourhood goons in the pay of CPI-M in which Brati was murdered, she seems much more aware of the ongoing movement and especially of her son's beliefs and leanings. As she narrates the events of that fateful night, she is suddenly struck dumb by the enormity of the question which strikes her as she watches a sedate and composed Sujata, Brati's mother, piecing the puzzle that was her son. While it was understandable that Somu belonging to the group of have-nots would raise his voice in protest against the injustices and inequality meted out to them, why was it that Brati, considerably privileged become a Naxalite? That was something difficult for Sujata to understand initially.

Sujata is left speechless and wondering until she discovers the answer at her daughter's engagement party. In a 'voice-over', we come to know that she has at last come to understand Brati's disgust, withdrawal from the family and subsequent identification with the Naxalite philosophy of changing the world. She has also come to identifying herself completely with Brati's beliefs and dreams. For her, the engagement party is now nothing but a charade of social pretension and hypocrisy.

However, it is Brati's lover, Nandini, an idealist, and ardent believer of all that Naxalism stood for, who provides Sujata with the key to doing something meaningful with her life. Nandini helps her reconnect to Brati by recalling his words, his ideals and his beliefs. Being a revolutionary, she goes beyond her personal grief to becoming an uncompromising fighter against the atrocities committed by the police against her and other party members.

Brati, listed as 1084 - Hazaar Chaurasi - in the Police and State records simply ceases to exist to the world except in the memories of Sujata, Somu's mother and Nandini's. The story is much an unraveling of Brati's character and ideology as it is a journey of self discovery for Sujata albeit through Brati's immolation.

Brati's death comes to symbolize the early and painful death of the promising movement that had inspired young hearts and minds to dream anew, to envisage a better world not given to corruption, greed and injustice. While Mahasweta Devi's text ends with a Sujata rendered unconscious by a burst appendix, Nihalini goes a step further in providing a much needed postscript to the novel. It is a woman, Sujata, the mother, who provides an alternate philosophy as it were, to her son's. While she does not for once protest against the doctrine of violence practised by his party, she builds on her son's world by running a Human Rights Documentation Centre after her retirement from the bank, a move that would help people in a constructive way and by protesting against Nitu's murder when she witnesses it.

The film ends on a note of hope - perhaps of a better tomorrow that Brati and scores of other young men had dreamed of. When Sujata writes (voice-over),

> Brati, aur ekh hatya hui aaj, raha chalte, khule aam, sab ke samne, Nitu tumhara sathi jo pichle kai saalon se mera bhi saathi tha, usse do hatyaaraon ne goliya daag kar mar dala. Woh silsala hatyaon o ka jiski tum, Partho, Somu, Bijit gariya ho, ruka nehi, chal raha hai, tamam koshishon ke bawajoot. Par koshish bhi thaki nehi, Nandini aur Nitu ke saath mein bhi ismeh shamil hu. Ek gam ko seeneh se laga kar nehi arman ko apna banaye huye.Tumhe apna beta nehi manti ab, tumhare sapne ki sajidar hu mein, ek sathi, comrade, dost. Jitna ageh badti hu utna hi tumhare paas tak ati hu, aur tum mere. Zindagi se lamba ekh dhaaga hai jo hum dono ko bandta hai, jortah hai. Beinsafi ke khilaf jab jab kuch dekhti hu, samajhti hu, karti hu, tab tab tumhara hi koi nayi pehlum nazar aneh laghta hai mein phir phir tumhe janam deti hu aur har baar naya patih hu. Sau sau baar tumhe naya aur apna...

(Brati, there was another killing today, in the open. Nitu, your companion who for many years have been mine as well was gunned down by two assailants. That series of murders whose witnesses you all - Partho, Somu and Bijit are, hasn't despite many efforts stopped as yet and goes on. But our efforts haven't exhausted themselves. Together with Nandini and Nitu, I too am in it, not drowning myself in sorrow but surviving on a far dream. Now I don't think of you merely as my son -

I share your dreams, I'm your companion, a comrade, a friend. The more I evolve, the distance between us gets ever shorter and we draw closer - you and I. A chord larger than life, joins us, binds us together. Whenever I see any instances of protest against injustice, whenever I protest, it is then that I come to discover some new aspect of your being. It is at those times that I give birth to you again and again and find you anew. A hundred times afresh and just mine...), we come to realize that the ghastly tormenting memories have at last been laid to rest and Sujata and Brati's dreams have coalesced into one, largely through her efforts in trying to make a positive contribution to society and trying to better the lot of human kind.

(3)

Bihar, which forms the backdrop of Sudhir Mishra's film 'Hazaaron Khwaishen Aisi' was in the grip of the Naxalite movement about the same time as the movement gained momentum in West Bengal as well as other states. Sumanta Banerjee notes,

> In early October 1970, the police launched an operation in the Ranchi district of Bihar...soon after this, on 4 November that year, about 400 military police launched an operation in the Monghyer district of Bihar. Large scale arrests followed throughput the state. By January 1971, the police had thrown about 1500 alleged CPI (M-L) activists and sympathizers behind bars (Sumanta Banerjee 1984 : 219).

The film opens at Delhi University, in Hindu College, revolving around three students - Siddharth Tyabji (Kay Kay Menon), Geeta Rao (Chitrangada Singh) and Vikram Malhotra (Shiney Ahuja). It follows their lives over the next couple of years after they leave college heading towards their respective goals.

Siddharth, the son of a retired judge, born and raised in luxury and privilege is attracted by the Communist movement, especially the Naxalite movement in Bengal. He ponders on the social inequalities around him and is convinced that a revolution is the key to cleansing the world.

Siddharth with his political activism and involvement in the struggle for a Naxalite revolution is a typical example of one among many students in universities across the country becoming increasingly supportive of peasants and the oppressed who were unable to change and overturn an archaic and hegemonic social order. He is a driven revolutionary who dreams of bringing about changes in caste-ridden Bihar and changing the society for the better.

Geeta is portrayed as a London-returned South Indian in love with the firebrand Siddharth. She has led a very sheltered life thus far and is yet to explore the rugged terrain of the Indian socio-political landscape. While she finds the Naxalism-spewing Siddharth attractive, she doesn't quite find herself warming up to it. She leaves for Oxford when Siddharth decides to leave for Bihar.

After a lapse of some years, we now see Geeta married to a promising IAS officer who as Geeta tells Vikram, "has it all". Vikram is now a fixer in the power corridors of the government while Siddharth is still trying to foment a revolution. But Geeta still meets him on the sly, cheating on her husband.

She decides to divorce her husband, even though she does not want to hurt his feelings. Geeta joins Siddharth in the village where she starts teaching the children while the police repeatedly try to hunt down her now - husband, Siddharth. She bears a child to Siddharth but eventually sends him away to her parents in London.

Eventually the police rounds up the entire village, capturing both Siddharth and Geeta on charges of intent to cause unrest. While Siddharth is brutally beaten up, Geeta appears to have been mercilessly raped. Geeta is soon bailed out by her now influential ex-husband. Siddharth escapes from prison but is shot by the police, admitted to a local hospital and placed under arrest. Later, local Naxalite leaders break into the crude makeshift hospital and free Siddharth. Soon Siddhartha and Geeta are reunited once again, but while Siddharth seeks escape to London, Geeta refuses to accompany him. We only hear him through a letter (a 'voice-over') which he has written to Geeta, explaining his anguish and disillusionment with the idea of revolution. He writes, "I hope the mysteries of the human body will be less confusing". He has given up on his revolution while Geeta goes back to continuing work in the village and taking care of the handicapped Vikram.

Mishra succeeds in portraying the futility of fighting against the governing structure without a definite direction to the cause. Perhaps, it is because he believes that women are stronger than men which is why he portrays the woman so positively[5]. From mere hero-worship, Geeta moves onto living with Siddharth in the midst of danger and squalor and finally taking up the cudgels even when Siddharth has escaped to London lead a safe life.

While we see Siddharth no more (we merely hear him through a voice-over), we see Geeta till the very end as she walks amidst green fields in a rural village to a school as the credits start rolling. What strikes me as important is the persistence Geeta shows in continuing to think for the marginalized and the downtrodden. She has imbibed her lover's thoughts, realized the essence of his philosophy and bettered the cause by deciding to educate the children, who will be enpowered to think on their own and fend for themselves.

A telling moment occurs early in the film when Geeta and Siddharth are listening to a speech given by a Naxalite to a group of semi-literate villagers. In the speech, Hitler is referred to quite explicitly but as Geeta points out angrily such intellectual and historical references fail to make an impact on a group of people who are hardly literate. What Mishra hopes to highlight is the fact that any kind of political and ideological education was pointless without the propagation of some kind of effective literacy programme in the villages. Geeta's intelligent observation and foresight underlines that the failure to initiate widespread revolution is an inevitability that Siddharth will painfully have to come to terms with many years later. It is Geeta who goes back to Bhojpur to realize this very goal.

The historical context is articulated through the narrative but it is done subtly and does not dissolve into preachy political moments. In a recent interview, Mishra talks about how his film documents the Naxal movement in rural Bihar, "Back in the '60s and early '70s, a lot of young people from upper-class backgrounds like my hero Siddharth were drawn to the Naxal movement because of the total violence and obscenity evident in the oppression of people in rural India at the time. Radicals like him tried to change the world for the better, and failed"[6].

(4)

Before looking at the two films and talking about their respective worldviews I thought it pertinent to discuss and look at the models of development which I had referred to earlier in the paper. The model of development generally followed by the State Post-Independence, has been that of industrialization. Copied from the West, this model primarily meant setting up more industries and making major investments in the field of industrial production with the hope that this would bring in more jobs which in turn would lead to economic betterment of people's lives. However, this has led to what may be called skewed development since industrialization has expanded at the cost of agricultural development. More and more agriculturally fertile lands were taken away for setting up industries, as a result of which marginal farmers and farm labourers, who were pushed out of their land have become labourers in industries and factories where not only they lost their lifestyles related to land, but they actually came down in terms of their standards of living.

As for the tribals, the same thing happened in their land, whether it were areas notified as tribal areas or the jungles or places they inhabited which provided not only their livelihoods but also acted as a support to their way of life. Felling of trees and vast areas of forest land, illegal mining and rampant industrialization disrupted their lives and their cultures in a huge way.

This had led to the beginning of the peasants' and farmers' movement and the movement by tribals whose aftermath was the Naxalbari Movement in the mid '60s. The mid '80s saw a revival of the movement and renewed a debate against the above mentioned model of industrialization which now as the data shows did not result in the improvement, particularly economic, of the people affected by such industrialization. As a result, this not only revived the Naxal movement, spreading it fast into new areas but a very acrimonious debate has begun suggesting alternative models of sustainable development. It is in this context that films like 'Hazaar Chaurasi ki Maa' and 'Hazaaron Khwaishen Aisi' came to be made.

Even though the two films deal with the theme of Naxalism - they vary in the representation of the ideology, as well as in their treatment. Nihalani's film is not antithetical to the cause, on the other hand, it seems to celebrate the ideology of Naxalism. In this regard, Nandini almost acts as his mouthpiece. It is a more honest and sympathetic presentation, at the same time not dissolving into either melodrama or needless sentimentalism as is rampant in Hindi cinema. It seems Nihalani has made a serious study of the movement, absorbed the essence of the philosophy and presented his understanding of the same through his screenplay. This is demonstrated to the hilt especially in the scene in which Nandini interacts with Sujata at length. In a voice full of suppressed emotion Nandini tells Sujata that Naxalism as a philosophy has always been understood as one that spewed hatred and advocated violence but it was not so, some day, she hoped, people would understand that it was instead a philosophy of love, how else did the party workers give up everything they cared for or believed in to fight for a nameless and faceless mass of the downtrodden and the marginalised? This I believe is a unique way in which Nihalani presents the Naxalite philosophy. Through this sequence we also come to know about the sad plight of the Bengali middle class - we now know that an entire generation aged between 16-40 had been sacrificed for the cause during those times. Banerjee says, "In May 1967, there was a peasant uprising at Naxalbari - an area in the north-eastern tip of India, bordering Nepal on the west, Sikkim and Bhutan on the north, and East Pakistan on the south. It was led by armed Communist revolutionaries who until then had been members of the Communist Party of India

(Marxist) (CPI-M), but they were later to break away and form a separate party - the Communist Party of India (Marxist- Leninist) (CPI-M-L). The uprising was crushed by the police within a few months. But from then on nothing could ever be quite the same in the Indian countryside" (Banerjee 1984 : Introduction, i). In the light of Nandini's declaration of the deaths of so many young people, I believe nothing would ever be the same anywhere - not just the Indian countryside - even after this movement was crushed. It changed the way people viewed the world around, raising their level of political consciousness. For years to come it was also going to influence the Government policy-making -- they were to become more people oriented. Scores of lives were to change for the better or for the worse. While some found their voices and discovered their humanity through it (in this regard I would like to mention Geeta of 'Hazaaron Khwaishen Aisi') there were also people like Brati's mother who lost their only means of sustenance (a reading of the novel as well as the film makes it very clear that it was only Brati who was of some comfort to his mother and loved her in his own unselfish way).

Mishra's film however is a downplaying of the same. By making his hero Siddharth run away from the scene of action instead of fighting it out (here we must recall that Brati, Nihalani's Naxalite hero, had perished for his beliefs), it only goes to show that Mishra did not believe this ideology to be a practical one.

However, in spite of the two different representations of the ideology of Naxalism by the two film directors, one notices that women occupy a very important position in both the narratives. After all, as I have stated before, 'Hazaar Chaurasi Ki Maa' is all about Sujata discovering herself albeit helped on by her son's untimely and unfortunate death. And it goes without saying the central and most important character in 'Hazaaron Khwaishen Aisi' is Chitrangada Singh's Geeta. It is her innate idealism that draws her to revolutionary ideas (in the guise of her lover, Siddharth in the beginning) but it is this very thing that influences the final choice that she makes as she leaves behind all material comforts, her hunger for a family, even love, to take up the position of a teacher in remote Bhojpur. She is the most human of all the characters in the film. It is her inner strength and resolve that sees her through even as Siddharth's fails. In this context it is important to remember that the ongoing peasants' and farmers' movements as well as those of the tribals often had women playing a major role in taking the movement forward. Some tribal societies were often matriarchal in nature in which women were at par with the men and were given equal powers of decision-making. Perhaps a study of all these influenced the directors as the story unfolded in their respective minds and the way they chose to portray them.

At the heart of Sudhir Mishra's political chronicle of the India of the 1970s revolving around the lives of the three protagonists, there is an inherent appeal which cries out for reforms valid not only for those turbulent times but even now. As the title of Mishra's film goes onto suggest, it is indeed about a thousand such dreams that have been left unrealised or lost in the India of those times. What Mishra does is to adapt the cinematic language to tell us an allegory of the State as he found it. Vikram's story of unrequited love and the state he is reduced to, is an allegory of all that we have been left with. Siddharth's subsequent disillusionment with the ideology only goes onto symbolize the failure of the Naxalite movement as does Brati's death. But in spite of all this, Geeta finds her voice. She matures as her character experiences significant upheavals in terms of love, hope, and disappointment to finally the dawning of comprehension.

Marx's famous statement, "Men make their own history, but they do not make it just as they please", seems apt when applied to characters like Siddharth and Brati. While one seeks escapism to quell his disillusionment, the other dies needlessly. But in their wake, they bring in redeeming realization and leave them indelibly changed.

Notes :

1. I found Thomas Elsaesser's article, 'Subject Positions, Speaking Positions: From Holocaust, Our Hitler, and Heimat to Shoah and Schindler's List' to be particularly relevant in this regard as he discusses the role Cinema

plays in representing History." It is important in as much as it helps me in trying to understand the need to return again and again to this painful but relevant bit of Indian Political History. Perhaps it may be "mourning work" by the intellectuals and cultural workers on behalf of the State.

2. Particularly important are the uprisings in recent times by farmers in the states of West Bengal, Maharashtra, Uttar Pradesh.
3. The emphasis is mine. This heralds a major change in the trend in the way Bollywood now chose to make films.
4. The police officer in the film, Swaraj Paul referred to Brati and his comrades in these terms. This is the way the Police and the State continued to view the movement.
5. Sudhir Mishra's interview, "I get inspired by women" by Sumit Jha, TNN, available on http://articles.timesofindia.indiatimes.com/2011-07-14/new-interviews. Accessed on 27th May, 2011.
6. Sudhir Mishra's interview, "Follow your dream" available on http://www.musicondiaonline.com/ar/i/movie-name. Accessed on 3rd June, 2011.

References :

Banerjee, Sumanta, 1984. *India's Simmering Revolution,* London : Zed Books.

Basu, Pradip, 2010. *Discourses on Naxalite Movement, 1967-2009 : Insights into Radical Left Politics,* Calcutta : Setu Prakasani.

Marx, Karl, 1852. 'The Eighteenth Brumaire of Louis Bonaparte' in *Collected Works,* Moscow : Progress Publishers.

Prasad, Madhava, 1998. *Ideology of the Hindi Film,* New Delhi : OUP.

Sen, Asit, 1980. *An Approach to Naxalbari,* Calcutta : Institute of Scientific Thoughts.

Vasudevan, Ravi, 2000. *Making Meaning in Indian Cinema,* New Delhi : OUP.

The Naxalite Movement, the Trilogy of Satyajit Ray and Beyond

Ananda Das Gupta

The Prelude :

'Naxal' - the name of the movement that is run by revolutionary communists born out of a split in the Indian communist movement started as a proletarian movement in Naxalbari, a small village in West Bengal, where 49-year old Charu Mazumdar and Kanu Sanyal of Communist Party of India (Marxist) led a militant peasant uprising in 1967 (for details, see Banerjee 1980, 1984). Their aim was to promote and build a "revolutionary opposition" in order to establish "revolutionary rule" in India. Largely influenced by Mao Ze-dong (Mao Tse-tung) - father of the modern republic of China, Charu Mazumdar advocated that the peasants and lower classes must overthrow the government and upper class (for details, see Dasgupta 1974; also see Banerjee 1980, 1984).

The popularity of Naxalbari movement and growing strength of Naxal groups alarmed the government of India to set up a committee for looking into the matter. The committee, in its report revealed that the basic cause of unrest was the defective implementation of laws enacted to protect the interests of the poor farmers and tribals (for details on tribal participation in the Naxalite movement, see Duyker 1987).. But, instead of taking measures to safeguard the rights of farmers and tribals and make them believe the democratic system of governance, government, worried over the law and order situation in the areas of Naxal influence, took reactionary steps by raising strong police action against the Naxalites. Through this, the government succeeded in weakening the Naxalite rebellion to some extent. Charu Mazumdar was captured from a Calcutta hideout in July 1972 who died in police custody 12 days after his arrest. This incident raised suspicion about the treatment meted out to him by the police in the custody and the allegation of the ill-treatment meted to the detainees was made by intellectuals across the country, left wing politicians and scholars. However, these developments had a great role in carrying the Naxal message to people at the grassroot level of Indian society (for details, see Ghosh 1975, Banerjee 1980, 1984).

Films of Satyajit Ray, which talk about unemployment, crippling education system, corrupt business class and aloof, selfish elites are mostly ignored in these three films - 'Pratidwandi' (The Adversary), 'Jana Aranya' (The Middleman) and 'Seemabaddha' (The Limited Company), which form the Calcutta trilogy. The protagonist in 'Pratidwandi' is a man in early 20s struggling to get a job. He is not radical enough to join the Naxal movement like his younger brother. At the same time, he is not ready to shed his ideas about equality and revolution, which make it just too difficult for him to clear any interview. The protagonist in 'Jana Aranya' is a hard working bright student, who can not get a high score in his graduation. This leads to disillusionment with the middle class way of life. He happens to meet a middleman who explains him the nuances of his business.

This is the where he breaks the boundaries of sanitized middle class world and it finally ends with him having to arrange a girl for his client, who turns out to be his friend's sister. While there is no transition in the character in 'Pratidwandi', there is a clear change in the attitude of the lead in 'Jana Aranya'. He may be sad for fixing up his friend's sister but he does it nonetheless. The protagonist of 'Seemabaddha' changes his way of life in the first few minutes of the film itself. He was a teacher but opts for a more lucrative job in a company. Here onwards, there is a steep decline in his morals and value system. This ends with him orchestrating a strike in his own company's factory in connivance with his boss. This results in death of one worker. These three characters can very well be three stages in life of one character only.

The three films do not simply digress in their content from his earlier films but they are also different in his approach towards film-making. Most of his films prior to Calcutta trilogy were based on literature written in Bengal in the late 19th or the early 20th century. That was when the way of life in India was very slow especially in comparison to the western part of the world. Ray kept this thing in mind and therefore those films were really slow. However, Calcutta trilogy is shot in almost the same manner the way European masters like Ingmar Bergman and Federico Fellini used to shoot their films. For instance, there is constant interplay between the real happenings and subconscious mind in 'Pratidwandi'. The protagonist's sister wants to become a model and his brother is involved in Naxal uprising. There is a scene in the film when the protagonist imagines his sister posing for photos wearing a bikini (that was a lot to do in India then) and his brother being chased and hunted down by police. The photography especially in 'Pratidwandi' is really sharp so that it hits the audience. This was unlike his earlier films, when subtlety was the norm.

The Adversary :

Siddhartha is forced to discontinue his medical studies due to unexpected and brutal death of his father. He has to now find a job in stead. In one job interview, he is asked to name the most significant world event in the last ten years. His reply is 'the plain human courage is being shown by the people of Vietnam', instead of the expected - man landing on moon. The interviewer asks is he is a communist. It is needles to say that he does not get the job..He reaches a coffee shop where he is offered to work for the communist party. When he does not show any interest the party leader tells him about an opening for a medical representative. To escape from the heat and have a snooze, he goes in to a cinema. As a government propaganda newsreel is being shown before the feature, a bomb explodes in the cinema hall. In the stampede that follows, Siddhartha breaks his watch. He goes to a watchmaker but he cannot afford the repairs.

Waiting to cross the road, he notices a sexy girl. He drifts back to his days as a medical student in a flashback. The professor is explaining anatomy of female breast. Many flashbacks and dreams occur to Siddhartha through the film. On his way to hostel, he has an encounter with some hippies. Along with an ex-classmate, he goes out to see a porn film but to their disappointment, the film turns out to be not-so-pornographic.

'Pratidwandi' literally means Adversary, Opponent or Competitor in Bengali. It's a 1970 Indian Bengali Film directed by Satyajit Ray based on the novel by Sunil Gangopadhyay. It is the first part of the Calcutta Trilogy by Ray, second being 'Seemabaddha' (Company Limited, 1971) and 'Jana Aranya' (The Middleman, 1975). Set during the Naxalite movement in Bengal, 'Pratidwandi' tells the story of Siddhartha, an educated middle class man caught within the turmoils of social unrest. Corruption and unemployment is rampant, and Siddhartha cannot align himself with either his revolutionary activist brother, or career-oriented sister.

The historical background of the film 'Pratidwandi' is set on the decade of a wide range of political turmoil in India. The huge influx of refugees during the partition of India and loss of economic activity in the hinterland of Kolkata resulted in the stagnation of the economy of Kolkata. The Naxalbari movement under Charu Majumdar saw splitting in the Communist party and an uprise in Naxalite movement inspired by the Maoist doctrine (for details, see Dasgupta 1974; also see Banerjee 1980, 1984). Kolkata saw the most amount of activities of the Maoist revolutionary group who constantly preached the local students and intellectuals. The main character Siddhartha's brother is an example of one such. The film is stylistically unusual for Ray; featuring techniques inspired by the French New Wave, such as jump-cuts, edgy framing, dream sequences, and sexual metaphors. Some of the experimental techniques which the film pioneered include photo-negative flashbacks and X-ray digressions.

The seventies were a difficult period for India and West Bengal. The corruption was rampant; the Naxalite movement had created havoc in Calcutta. In fact, they had turned parts of Calcutta into 'liberated zones' (for details, see Banerjee 1980, 1984). By the time the Naxalite movement died down, in 1975, Mrs. Indira Gandhi (then, Prime Minister of India) suppressed the fundamental rights and declared "Emergency" for her own political survival. Her son, Sanjay Gandhi became a dictator of sorts without any official designation. The opposition leaders were thrown into prisons. This powerful psychological drama follows a young executive's climb up the corporate ladder and his slow immersion into corruption, seen through the eyes of his young sister-in-law.

Company Limited :

Shyamal (Barun Chanda) is an ambitious Marketing Manager in a British firm in Calcutta, manufacturing fans. He's married to Dolan, and lives in a company flat. He aspires to become the company director. For this he has to compete with a colleague who has a relative in the board of directors.

His sister-in-law Tutul arrives from Patna to spend a few days with them. She has been a great admirer of the ideologist Shyamal and was envious of her sister's marriage with him. Tutul is Shyamal's conscience. Shyamal shows her the delights of city life - the cocktail parties, the clubs and horse racing. Life goes on smoothly for Shyamal until he learns that a consignment of fans meant for exports is defective. There is not much time to rectify the fans. It could result in cancellation of the export contract and an end to his dream of becoming a director. Hopeless, Shyamal takes Tutul in confidence though not his wife. Late at night, he hatches a plan with the labor officer to provoke a strike at the factory. A factory watchman is badly injured and a lockout is declared. The export contract is saved. Shyamal becomes a director but he has fallen low both in the eyes of Tutul and his own.

This is the second film of the Calcutta Trilogy.. All the three films study the effect the big city of Calcutta has on the educated youth and the price it extracts from them. With an effortless conviction, Ray builds up the narrative, and characters including the minor ones. The film has a poetic and understated ending. As triumphant Shyamal returns home after being named a director, the elevator is out of order. A joyous Shyamal begins to climb the stairs. As he ascends his steps become slower. When he reaches the top, both physically and metaphorically, his joy has vanished. Tutul who has witnessed fall of her hero, sits beside him, they exchange glances. Without making a sound Tutul removes the watch that he had gifted her. She places it on the table. We see Shyamal from above a ceiling fan, with his head bowed in his hand and Tutul fading away (http://cliched-monologues.blogspot.com/2011/02/'Seemabaddha'-company-limited-1971.html).

The Middleman :

The film begins with blatant cheating in the examination hall. Somnath, an honest student, finds himself doing badly in the exams due to an overworked examiner, without his glasses who is unable to read his small handwriting. As he is in no position to marry, his girlfriend gets married to someone else due to pressure from her family. A bright and idealistic young man, Somnath begins search of a job along with his more realistic friend Sukumar. With the job market flooded with thousands of hopefuls, Somnath faces some absurd interviews. He gives up his search after an interview in which he asked, 'What is the weight of the moon?' Later, he encounters an older man, the street-smart businessman, Bisuda. On Bisuda's advise, Somnath becomes a middleman, an order supplier paid on commission. His father, an upright middle-class man considers this business to be disgraceful to the family reputation.

Somnath, soon, finds himself earning through petty deals but he is ambitious and wants to grow his enterprise. His friend Sukumar, however, has not had much luck and now works as a taxi driver. There is chance of Somnath landing up with a big order but the client seems to be in no hurry to sign the deal. An acquaintance, Mr. Mitter, advises him to supply the client with a prostitute to clinch the deal. After much hesitation, he agrees. They go in search of a prostitute. After visiting two brothels, they finally find a girl. She turns out to be his friend Sukumar's sister. Somnath asks her to take the money and leave, but she is a professional and would not take money with out earning it. Somnath agrees and delivers her to his client's room in a hotel. He gets the contract but it does not bring him any happiness. Finally, as he enters his family house through a dark door, he is no longer an innocent boy but a corrupt man who has discovered the advantages of corruption. This is the final film of trilogy known as the Calcutta Trilogy. All the three films study the effect the big city of Calcutta has on the educated youth and the price it extracts from them. The film is about corruption of a young man; from an idealistic individual to a corrupt businessman who ends up offering his best friend's sister to a client for a business favour.

Satyajit Ray painted a dark and searing examination of urban life in his masterful Calcutta Trilogy; 'Seemabaddha' was the second installment of the trilogy. While 'Pratidwandi' examined the left-wing affiliations of the city's educated youth, and 'Jana Aranya' portrayed the dark underbelly of the city, in 'Seemabaddha' Ray focused on the corporate side of 1970s Calcutta. The protagonist here is Shyamalendu Chatterjee, a smart, intelligent, ambitious and upwardly mobile young man, who is just a step away from a grand promotion. Around the same time he gets an extended visit by Sudarsana (Tutul), his pretty sister-in-law, he discovers a problem with what ought to have been the company's latest shipment, which in turn could seriously jeopardize his corporate ambitions. Based on a cue that Tutul gave in jest, he hatches a secret, sinister plan to set things right. The film, straightforward narrative-wise, is in essence a subtle and fascinating character study, as also a probing look into the socio-political commentary. Barun Chanda, as the likeable Sales Manager in a big British firm, is excellent, but the cake is taken by Sharmila Tagore as the enigmatic young lady, whose penetrative mind manages to see beyond the artificiality of Shyamal's existence. The expertly photographed, marvelously written and crisply paced film, with a terrific finale, leaves its viewers with uncomfortable questions rather than just easy answers.

The Interlude :

In contrast to Ray, his contemporary Mrinal Sen and others set out to expose the dark underside of India's lower middle-class and unemployed. Here are some of the expositions :

'Calcutta 71' :

Mrinal Sen made 'Calcutta-71' when Calcutta was passing through a terrible time. People were getting killed every day. The most militant faction of the Communist Party-the Naxalites-had rejected all forms of parliamentary politics. At the same time they had a host of differences with the other two Communist Party factions. These, in turn, led to many inter party clashes. Invariably all of the factions ignored the main issue of mobilizing forces against the vested interests-the establishment (for details, see Banerjee 1980, 1984).

'Herbert' :

Based on Nabarun Bhattacharya's (son of the strongest anti-establishment voice Mahashweta Devi) eponymous Sahitya Academy award-winning novel (1997), 'Herbert' comes as a crucial intervention when the city's future looks drastically different from its past. And what one gets out of this richly layered text is a complicated tapestry of images that constantly challenge and tease our rational notions of known and unknown worlds. Herbert, an orphaned member of a crumbling household, becomes a metaphor of the collapsing city, with the narrative spanning several decades. Herbert, who grows up on the charity of his relatives, is made out to be a good-for-nothing dimwit, thereby denied a normal life.

His life holds in it a range of experiences from being bullied by his crooked cousin, to running errands for all and sundry, flying kites and feeding crows on the terrace as his favourite pastime, a chance landing in the Naxalite movement of the '70s to finally declaring that he can "dialogue with the dead" in the globalised economy of the '90s.

Herbert, who finds himself as someone who talks to the dead, is accused as charlatan by the Rationalists' Society, and the harmless do-gooder commits suicide. The body in the incinerator causes an explosion, recalling the bomb that his cousin, in the thick of the students' movement of the '70s, had hidden in his bed. In an article, 'Meeting the Challenge', the writer ironically observes how the ghosts of the '70s Naxalite movement, quashed to annihilation by the Establishment, get resurrected from the dead with this episode.

In this highly stylistic film, Suman Mukhopadhyay uses some brilliant techniques which gel amazingly well with the narrative. For instance, the shift from a sepia tone past to a technicolour present is also the movement from the period of individual faith to one which is totally governed by market forces. This comes so convincingly in the scene where Herbert flying kites and feeding pigeons on his terrace is juxtaposed with the dish antenna staking its claim over what was once Herbert's private space.

'Kalbela' :

Based on a 1980s novel by Samaresh Majumdar, the film sets itself up, quite self-consciously, within a certain tradition of films, namely radical political Bengali cinema of the 1970s and 1980s. It thus establishes an intertextuality and a certain connection with them. By situating itself and the story it has to tell, within this matrix of the 1970s radical Bengali cinema, Ghose anchors the film squarely within that time. The mood and the events certainly, but even the way black and white shots are used, underlines a somewhat documentary - and thus temporally limited - way these sequences are put to use.

Animesh Mitra is simpleton who arrives at Calcutta from Jalpaiguri, during hostile times (1967), to study at the Scottish Church College. He is scheduled to take refuge at the residence of his father's friend Mr. Debabrata, but he accidentally gets shot in the limb and ends up at the Calcutta Medical College. Eventually things move on and Animesh develops a deep friendship with Debabrata's daughter Neela. He takes admission in the M.A classes of Scottish Church College on Bengali Literature and ultimately becomes intertwined with the unresting times of the youth intellect.

He turns to become a Communist under the mentorship of Ramen and Subash Sen, but after a year he feels that their organisation (B.P.S.F) has been deviating from the ideals of building up an egalitarian society. With the idealistic ideas of Subhash Sen and others Animesh rediscover himself as a hardcore Naxalite, rampaging the interiors of northern West Bengal. In the meantime Animesh gets ripped up between his ideals and his love (Madhabilata). Madhabilata gets pregnant out of wedlock while Animesh abandons her for greater idealism. Animesh's roommate, the unquenchable poet Tridip, accompanies him with a dreamy vision of a noncompartmentalized nation. But outrageous planning leads the Naxalite movement to be a tragic demise (for details see, Dasgupta 1974; also see, Banerjee 1980, 1984).

Subash Sen and other leaders get slaughtered by the brutal Congressian Police. Tridip is shot dead in front of Animesh and Animesh is tortured by the state to such an extent that he becomes crippled. His nervous systems (below and from the hips) breaks down completely, making him a man who can sit and stagger. Madhabilata gives birth to a baby boy (Arka). Neela stands beside Madhabilata like a wall and delivers immense support. Finally in 1977, the Left Front Government decides to release every political prisoner; a devastated Animesh comes out from jail custody after meeting minister Sudip (his compatriot during his days at the Scottish). The film ends with silver lining when Animesh unites with his estranged family in a slum (wife and son) with nothing to vie for but with a spark of hope against aghast capitalism and return back to mainstream with a new theology.

'Hazaar Chaurasi ki Maa' :

HCKM is Nihalani's adaptation of Mahasweta Devi's novel Hazaar Churashir Ma (originally written in Bengali). Set in Calcutta in the early 70?s HCKM is an emotional story of a mother's awakening to her son's beliefs after his death. This is a well-told tale, but seems like it wants to say more, and can't get the words across. Poignant, yes. Mind-blowing, no.

Sujata Chatterjee is an upperclass Bengali woman, a bank-officer, with 4 adult children out of whom the youngest, Brati (Sengupta) is her favorite. She no longer sees eye-to-eye with her philandering husband (Kher) of many years, and their relationship now is one of aloofness and discord. She wakes up one morning from normal life to get news of Brati's death. His body is in the police morgue, corpse number 1084. Brati was involved in the Naxalite movement and was killed in a skirmish with anti-Naxalites/policemen. His family is now called to the morgue to identify the body.

While Brati's father (Kher) and his brother hasten to cover up Brati's connection to the Naxal movement and prevent his name from being published in the paper, to avoid "dishonor" to the family, Sujata is plagued by pangs of guilt at not having known her son well enough, or sensed his thoughts and concerns. She tries to find out more about Brati's beliefs and his need to join the movement. In this quest, she meets his friends, and girlfriend (Nandita Das) who is also a Naxalite. She also meets the mother (Biswas) of Somu, one of his friends and comes to know of the incidents which lead to Brati and Somu and their friend's deaths. In this process, she becomes aware of the world around her, and senses it's hypocrisy. Gradually she steps out of her traditional boundaries, and questions the mores and customs which culture and society force on her.

One of her dialogues which caught in my mind, runs like this (don't remember the exact words) : "Why would I not do what was expected of me ? That was what I was taught, that was how I was brought up. (They said) a woman must serve, her family, her parents, her children, always someone."

Although the film does not offer any moments of epiphany, it beautiful depicts the love between a mother and her son, and gives voice to some strong truths. Jaya Bachchan is an immaculate actress, and she is supported ably by Kher, Sengupta and the rest of the stellar cast. Direction is good, but the script and the narrative spine could have been tighter.

'Hazaaron Khwaishein Aisi' :

The film revolves around three characters primarily : Siddharth [Kay Kay], Geeta [Chitrangada] and Vikram [Shiny Ahuja]. It is a love story against a backdrop of a politically decaying India, from the late 1960s to the 1970s. Geeta is in love with Siddharth, but politics is Siddharth's first love. Vikram too is in love with Geeta, but she treats him as a mere friend. Geeta gets married to a bureaucrat in Britain. Vikram becomes a fixer in the corridors of power in Delhi, whilst Siddharth decides to join the Naxal movement in Bihar. 'Hazaaron Khwaishein Aisi' is a realistic film handled by Sudhir Mishra. The start of the film itself gives you the jitters! Scripted by Mishra, Ruchi Narain and Shiv Kumar Subramaniam, the film has several interesting moments. But the execution of the subject is such, it caters more to the intelligentsia or the discerning viewer. Cinematography captures the mood of the film with precision. The background score is appropriate.

'Hazaaron Khwaishein Aisi' digs into a section of this crazy chapter of history through its three protagonists - Siddharth (Kaykay Menon), Geeta (Chitrangada Singh and Vikram The three study in a prestigious Delhi college and come from different strata of society. In the beginning, the three friends are carefree and desultory. But as they get out in the real world, they learn the ropes of survival.

Siddharth dreams of revolution. He becomes part of the Naxal movement in the villages of Bihar. His emotional attachment to Geeta doesn't stop him from his political pursuits. Post-college, Geeta is married to an IAS officer but she continues to see Siddharth on the sly.

Vikram too has always nursed unconditional love in his heart for Geeta. But that's all there is to his soft side. A small town boy once, Vikram climbs the social ladder by networking in the big league unabashedly. Geeta ends her marriage and starts living in the village with Siddharth. This is the time in the film when Geeta's character evolves. From a London-bred girl to teaching village women, or having a child out of wedlock or asking favours from Vikram in hours of need to a lot of other gruesome realities, Geeta discovers herself.

Siddharth is the most real. In the beginning, he appears to be a rebel for effect. Gradually, his seriousness about his cause unveils. Later, his aggravation at the futility of it all unfolds. His weaknesses as the man in a relationship aren't hidden either. Eventually, he changes the course of his journey. The fire of his conviction still smoulders, but the flame is missing. The actors do complete justice to their brilliantly etched out characters. Kay Kay moves you with his intensity. And Shiny is a startling improvement from the lacklustre cop he played in 'Karam'. But Chitrangada Singh, whose face draws inevitable comparisons to Smita Patil, is definitely someone to watch out for. She is a complete natural who zaps the camera with a passionate performance.

The protagonists act like metaphors for the maddening 1970s. The rush of youth is long gone. The restrain of experience has sunk in. The whiff of a bittersweet memory lingers. But that's all it is – a memory – a chapter of history that has closed.

'Padatik' :

Acclaimed director Mrinal Sen cast the beautiful Bollywood heroine Simi Garewal with the sharp and intelligent Dhritiman Chattejee in the 1973 Bengali movie 'Padatik'. 'Padatik' is the final film in Mrinal Sen's Calcutta Trilogy, 'Interview' (1970) and 'Calcutta '71' (1972) being the other two, films which are deeply rooted in the social, cultural and political milieu of the city of Calcutta, which the film's prologue describes as "an intimidating and infernal city, unredeemed and probably doomed", during the period. Employing innovative and often daring cinematic compositions Sen in these films attempts to chronicle and analyse those turbulent times within a broad Marxist ideological framework. These films also established Sen's reputation as one of the most politically conscious and stylistically avant-garde filmmakers of the Indian New Cinema movement."

'Padatik' is a clinical study of isolation and in the sequences that depict Sumit's stay in Shilpi's apartment before she returns from her sojourn in New Delhi wonderfully capture the sense of boredom and fear that overwhelm his every moment. The film is able to convey the sense of fear that every ring of the doorbell or the telephone that is created in the mind of fugitive Sumit. The sense of boredom is best captured in the manner in which Sumit chain-smokes packets of Charminar cigarette and his desultory reading of the works of Lenin which ironically theorize about choosing the true friends of the revolution. And in one of the films finest moments which also demonstrates the director's immense control over the medium of cinema, Sumit plays the role of the docile servant and ceremoniously serves bed-tea with one and half teaspoons of sugar to himself in the role of the master! But, despite these phases of wit and sarcastic humour, the film remains shorn of dramatic emotions and is deliberately constructed as an essay on the mental state of the political activist and thus Sumit's trials and tribulations fail to raise any empathy.

Concluding Observation - The Epilogue :

Film-makers always want to pick up a contentious issue as that enables them to add high voltage drama to the film. Naxalism is a burning issue now so it gives them ample scope to bring in elements like clashes, violence and conflicts that attract the masses to cinema halls. There are those who believe that cinema that deals with burning social issues immediately strikes a chord with the audience. Movies are a vehicle of social message everywhere in the world. The art cinema movement in India has raised important issues in our society. But the demands of making a masala movie can often make directors compromise on reality.

References :

The Naxalite Movement, Biplab Dasgupta, Allied Publishers, New Delhi, 1974.

The Naxalite Movement : A Maoist Experiment, Sankar Ghosh, Firma K. L. Mukhopadhyay, 1975. ISBN 0883865688.

The Naxalite Movement in India : Origin and Failure of the Maoist Revolutionary Strategy in West Bengal, 1967-1971, Sohail Jawaid, Associated Pub. House, 1979.

In the Wake of Naxalbari : A History of the Naxalite Movement in India, Sumanta Banerjee, Subarnarekha, 1980.

India's Simmering Revolution : The Naxalite Uprising, Sumanta Banerjee, Zed Books, 1984. ISBN 0862320372.

Tribal Guerrillas : The Santals of West Bengal and the Naxalite Movement, Edward Duyker, Oxford University Press, 1987.

http://hubpages.com/hub/Films-and-Books accessed on 21/09/2011.

http://www.satyajitray.org/ accessed on 18/09/2011.

http://cliched-monologues.blogspot.com/2011/02/'Seemabaddha'-company-limited-1971.html accessed on 23/09/2011.

http://www.telegraphindia.com/1100711/jsp/7days/story_12670028.jsp accessed on 30/10/2011.

Editor

Pradip Basu : Faculty in Political Science, Scottish Church College [Calcutta University (CU)]; Guest Faculty, Political Science, CU; Guest Faculty, Philosophy, CU; Chief Editor, *Journal of Humanities and Social Sciences;* Ph.D. (CU, supervisor : Partha Chatterjee, topic : pre-Naxalbari inner-party struggle); was active in Naxalite politics (1974-1981); supervises Ph.D. research (CU) on Charu Majumder; ex-Research Scholar, CSSSC; Ex-Doctoral Fellow, ICSSR; MRP, UGC on 'Politics of Derrida's Deconstruction'; authored & edited books : *Naxalbari-r Purbakshan; Towards Naxalbari; Uttar Adhunik Rajniti o Marxbad; Postmodernism, Marxism, Postcolonialism; Discourses on Naxalite Movement; Uttar Adhunik Rajniti; Avenel Companion to Modern Social Theorists; Colonial Modernity; [Monone Srijone Naxalbari; Naxalbari theke Lalgarh : Ekti Bohumatrik Critique; Modern Social Thinkers; India Today*– all in press]; *Oxford Reader on Naxalism* [forthcoming]. Email<pradipbasu2@gmail.com>

Contributors

Amitava Nag : Editor of the Kolkata-based cinema magazine *Silhouette;* writes extensively on cinema; also writes poems and short fictions in English and Bengali, his topics mostly veering on the sub-alterns; works in a software company to earn his daily rice and dreams of making his own film one day.

Ananda Das Gupta : Ph.D.; Faculty, Organizational Development, etc., Indian Institute of Plantation Management, Bangalore; Adjunct Faculty, Indian Institute of Management, Kozhikode; Life Fellow, Indian Academy of Social Sciences; Member, Indian Society of Labour Economics; edited Special Issue on India of *International Journal of Social Economics,* England; Guest Editor, *Social Responsibility Journal,* England; books : *Human Values in Management,* Ashgate; *Ethics in Business,* Rawat; *Corporate Citizenship,* Cambridge Scholars.

Arya Aiyappan : a former Faculty in English, Christ University, Bangalore; her Ph.D. (University of Kerala, Thiruvananthapuram) research was on the construction of gender identities in contemporary Middle cinema in Hindi; interests : film studies, cultural studies, representation theories and middle cinema; now doing independent research; published articles in books and journals.

Bernd Zywietz : M.A., Ph.D.; student and lecturer, Film Studies, Johannes Gutenberg University Mainz, Germany; Dissertation topic : terrorism in international cinema; film critic, journalist, author and editor; Member of the Society of Media Studies and chairman of the German based Network Terrorism Studies; delivered Conference lectures in London and at the German Military Academy in Munich.

Binayak Bhattacharya : pursuing Ph.D. on 'Left Politics and Cinema in India' (Film Studies, English and Foreign Languages University, Hyderabad); M. A. dissertation, 'Issues of Political Films in the Bangla Film Industry', looks at the tradition of political films in Bengal; writes on cultural politics for journals, books, newspapers; was Visiting Faculty, English, Osmania University, Hyderabad.

Darshana Sreedhar.M : pursuing Ph.D. in Cinema Studies (Jawaharlal Nehru University, Delhi); M.A. in English (University of Delhi); M.Phil. in Social Sciences (Center for Studies in Social Sciences, Calcutta); working on soft porn in Malayalam Cinema; interests : gender, sexuality, visual culture, film studies, caste, identity politics, social-political history of Kerala; presentations at conferences; publications in journals.

Debasis Poddar : Faculty, National University of Study and Research in Law, Ranchi; areas of interest : interdisciplinary areas of other social sciences appurtenant to juridical science; as a specialist in public law, he explores contemporary issues vis-à-vis law and governance, policy matter, human rights, etc.; published articles in books and journals.

Devapriya Sanyal : pursuing Ph.D. at the Centre for English Studies, Jawaharlal Nehru University, New Delhi on Satyajit Ray's films; earlier worked on 'Schindler's List' for her M.Phil. Dissertation; holds a Master's degree in English from Jawaharlal Nehru University, New Delhi; published articles in books and journals.

Dibyakusum Ray : pursuing Ph.D. (topic : 'The Emergence of Liminality in Postcolonial Theory') at the Department of Commonwealth Studies, The English and Foreign Languages University (EFLU), Hyderabad; M.A., M.Phil. (distinction) from EFLU; visited 'Comparative Caribbeans : An Interdisciplinary Conference', Emory University, USA; published essays/articles in books, magazines and webzines; active in theatre and classical music.

Indrani Bhattacharya : pursuing Ph.D. at the Comparative Literature Department, Jadavpur University, Kolkata on 'Changing Mode of Leftist Slogan : A Socio-linguistic Survey in West Bengal'; did her M.A. in Linguistics from Calcutta University; formerly Language Instructor, American Institute of Indian Studies, Kolkata; published articles in books and journals.

Indranil Mitra : Faculty in English and Communication, Meghnad Saha Institute of Technology, Kolkata; writing his M.Phil. dissertation at the Department of English, Jadavpur University; M.A. in English from Jadavpur University, Kolkata; research interests include psychoanalysis, gender and critical theory; published articles in books and journals.

Kanchan Sarker : Faculty in Sociology, University of British Columbia, Okanagan, Canada; he was with Sociological Research Unit of Indian Statistical Institute, Kolkata; taught at universities in Canada, USA since 2000; Ph.D. on Trade Union Movements in Tea Plantation (North Bengal University); MBA in International Business (Cleveland State University, USA, 2003); Vice-President, Society for Socialist Studies, Canada.

Ketaki Datta : Faculty in English, Acharya Brojendra Nath Seal College, Coochbehar, West Bengal; articles and translations in *Indian Literature, Harvest, Pratibha India, The Statesman;* edited *Indo-Anglian Literature...;* translated novel *The Voyage;* attended IFTR conference at University of Lisbon; translated novel *The Last Tribute* being published (Sahitya Akademi); novel *A Bird Alone;* edited volume *New Literatures in English...;* contributor to Festival Number of *The Statesman;* 'Professional Woman of the Year 2005' [by American Biographical Institute, North Carolina]. <ketaki.datta@gmail.com>.

Ketaki Dwivedi : pursuing Ph.D. at Centre for the Study of Social Systems, Jawaharlal Nehru University, New Delhi; topic : 'Corporate Social Responsibility in India : A Sociological Study of Two Automobile Industries'; her areas of interest include Sociological Theories, issues related to Social Security and Corporate Social Responsibility; contributed in national and international publications.

Manoj Kumar : Faculty in Political Science and International Relations, Wollega University, Ethiopia; former Guest Faculty in the University of Mumbai; former Visiting Faculty in Guru Nanak College (Mumbai); former Research Associate in TISS (Mumbai); Ph.D. (Arts—Politics), University of Mumbai; areas of interests : socio-political movements, international politics, and African and gender issues.

MK Raghavendra : Film scholar and critic; received Swarna Kamal Award for Best Film Critic in 1997; awarded Homi Bhabha Fellowship in 2000-01; books : *Seduced by the Familiar : Narration and Meaning in Indian Popular Cinema* (Oxford, 2009), *50 Indian Film Classics* (HarperCollins, 2009) and *Bipolar Identity : Region, Nation and the Kannada Language Film* (Oxford, 2011).

Monalisa Basu : Faculty in Political Science, Scottish Church College (Calcutta University); pursuing Ph.D. from Calcutta University on

'Role of Individual in History - Charu Majumdar in Naxal Movement : A Case Study'; published articles on various aspects of the Naxalite movement in different books and journals.

Praskanva Sinharay : student of M. Phil. in Social Sciences at the Center for Studies in Social Sciences, Calcutta (CSSSC); did his M.A. in International Relations from Jadavpur University, Kolkata; member, Jadavpur Association of International Relations [JAIR] (tied up with M.E.A., Government of India); published articles in books and journals.

Radhakanta Barik : Faculty in Public Administration, Indian Institute of Public Administration, New Delhi; his Ph.D. research was on the peasant movements in Bihar (Delhi University); books: *Politics of JP Movement; Land and Caste in Bihar Politics; Saffron Regime, Ideology, Liberal Intelligentsia and Fear;* contributed fifty research papers on politics, culture and history in journals and books.

Saikat Maitra : pursuing Ph.D. in Social Anthropology at the University of Texas at Austin, USA; his doctoral dissertation focuses on different issues of urban development, spaces of consumption as well as labour in contemporary Kolkata; published articles in books and journals; <saikatmaitra@yahoo.co.in>.

Samata Biswas : Faculty in English, Haldia Government College, West Bengal; pursuing her Ph.D. at The English and Foreign Languages University (EFLU), Hyderabad; started on a Minor Research Project of the University Grants Commission (Government of India) on fitness discourses in contemporary Bengal; interested in popular culture, feminism and the body.

Samrat Sengupta : Faculty in English at Kharagpur College, West Bengal and also a Ph.D. scholar in the Centre for Studies in Social Sciences, Calcutta; area of research : ethics and politics of postcolonial resistances in Bengal; co-edited an anthology of critical essays on postcolonialism and neocolonialism titled *Anxieties, Influences and After.* <samrat19802003@yahoo.co.in>.

Sananda Sen : M.A. in Philosophy and M.Phil. in Women's Studies from Jadavpur University, Kolkata; M.Phil. in Social Work with specialization in NGO Management from Global Open University; writes on gender studies and critical theory; plans to pursue doctoral work on nineteenth century Bengal; published articles in books and journals.

Saumen Guha : activist in Naxalbari politics, imprisoned (1974-1977), began 'Archana Guha Case' against police torture, counsel for prosecution, won after 19 years in 1996; authored and edited books : *Battle of 'Archana Guha Case'; Notes on Human and Civil Right; Swarnakumari Devi's 'The Fatal Garland'; Na Hiroshima Nagasaki Chai Na; Eisenstein;* pioneer of anti-Nuclear Movement in West Bengal; Independent Filmmaking in 1980s; paintings on Life and Humanity; thirty years' research on History of Torture in India; memoir of 37 years of 'Archana Guha Case' forthcoming.

Shatarupa Sen Gupta : submitted doctoral dissertation on 'Politics of Representation : Naxalite Movement and Print Media in Bengal (1967-1972)', supervisor : Kunal Chattopadhyay (History, Jadavpur University, Kolkata); written for Immanuel Ness edited *International Encyclopedia on Protest and Revolution* and for Pradip Basu edited *Discourses on the Naxalite Movement;* article in *Jadavpur University Journal of History.*

Shoma A. Chatterji : Ph.D.; Fellow, Indian Council of Social Science Research (ICSSR), Delhi; freelance journalist, film scholar; won National Award as Best Film Critic (1991) and for Best Book on Cinema (2003); won BFJA Award and Lifetime Achievement Award from UNFPA-'LAADLY'(NGO); authored 17 books which include *Subject Cinema : Object Woman; Parama and Other Outsiders; P. C. Barua; Gender and Conflict.*

Sukanta Acharya : Ph.D. (Jawaharlal Nehru University, New Delhi); Faculty in Political Science at Asutosh College (University of Calcutta); writes for international journals on American neoconservatism, security, human rights, humour, jokes, gender, communication, etc; book on language of global communication is forthcoming; reviews papers submitted for publication in *Political Studies* and *Journal of Communication Inquiry.*

Sumana Sanyal : Faculty in Bengali, Sonamukhi College, Bankura, West Bengal; pursuing Ph.D. on 'Psychoanalysis in Tagore's Poetry' (University of Burdwan, West Bengal); papers on 'Tagore Songs and Poetry', Fellow in Tagore Studies, Asiatic Society (2003-2004); interests : psychoanalysis, literary theories, film, music; articles in *Ebong Mushayera, Ei Sahasrodhara, Nandan, Charitartho Jibaner Bani* (Aruna); book : *Abibaho Lekha Chhilo* (Bengali poetry), (Ananda).

Torsa Ghosal : M.A., Ph.D. student in English (postmodern narratology, digital media), Ohio State University, USA; M.A. (Jadavpur University); recipient of National Balshree Honour in Creative Writing from President of India; papers at international conferences; won Debabrata Mukherjee Memorial Award 2011 from Jadavpur University; runner up for CD Narasimhaiah prize at annual conference of Indian Association for Commonwealth Literature and Language Studies 2011.